A Taxonomy for Learning, Teaching, and Assessing

4.1 THE KNOWLEDGE DIMENSION

MAJOR TYPES AND SUBTYPES	EXAMPLES
A. FACTUAL KNOWLEDGE—The basic elements students must know to be acquainted with a discipline or solve problems in it	
Aa. Knowledge of terminology	Technical vocabulary, music symbols
Ab. Knowledge of specific details and elements	Major natural resources, reliable sources of information
B. CONCEPTUAL KNOWLEDGE—The interrelationships among the basic elements within a larger structure that enable them to function together	
Ba. Knowledge of classifications and categories	Periods of geological time, forms of business ownership
Bb. Knowledge of principles and generalizations	Pythagorean theorem, law of supply and demand
Bc. Knowledge of theories, models, and structures	Theory of evolution, structure of Congress
C. PROCEDURAL KNOWLEDGE—How to do something, methods of inquiry, and criteria for using skills, algorithms, techniques, and methods	
Ca. Knowledge of subject-specific skills and algorithms	Skills used in painting with water colors, whole-number division algorithm
Cb. Knowledge of subject-specific techniques and methods	Interviewing techniques, scientific method
Cc. Knowledge of criteria for determining when to use appropriate procedures	Criteria used to determine when to apply a procedure involving Newton's second law, criteria used to judge the feasibility of using a particular method to estimate business costs
D. METACOGNITIVE KNOWLEDGE—Knowledge of cognition in general as well as awareness and knowledge of one's own cognition	
Da. Strategic knowledge	Knowledge of outlining as a means of capturing the structure of a unit of subject matter in a text book, knowledge of the use of heuristics
Db. Knowledge about cognitive tasks, including appropriate contextual and conditional knowledge	Knowledge of the types of tests particular teachers administer, knowledge of the cognitive demands of different tasks
Dc. Self-knowledge	Knowledge that critiquing essays is a personal strength, whereas writing essays is a personal weakness; awareness of one's own knowledge level

A Taxonomy for Learning, Teaching, and Assessing

A Revision of Bloom's Taxonomy of Educational Objectives

ABRIDGED EDITION

EDITORS

LORIN W. ANDERSON
DAVID R. KRATHWOHL
PETER W. AIRASIAN
KATHLEEN A. CRUIKSHANK
RICHARD E. MAYER
PAUL R. PINTRICH
JAMES RATHS
MERLIN C. WITTROCK

Longman

New York   San Francisco   Boston
London   Toronto   Sydney   Tokyo   Singapore   Madrid
Mexico City   Munich   Paris   Cape Town   Hong Kong   Montreal

Series Editor: Arnis E. Burvikovs
Acquisitions Editor: Aurora Martinez-Ramos
Marketing Managers: Brad Parkins, Kathleen Morgan
Production Manager: Donna DeBenedictis
Project Coordination, Text Design, and Electronic Page Makeup: Pre-Press Company, Inc.
Cover Design Manager: Linda Knowles
Manufacturing Buyer: Megan Cochran

For permission to use copyrighted material, grateful acknowledgment is made to the copyright holders on pp. 287, which are hereby made part of this copyright page.

Library of Congress Cataloging-in-Publication Data

A taxonomy for learning, teaching, and assessing : a revision of Bloom's taxonomy of educational objectives / editors, Lorin W. Anderson, David R. Krathwohl ; with Peter W. Airasian ... [et al.].
     p. cm.
   Includes bibliographical references.
   ISBN 0-321-08405-5 (hardcover : alk. paper) -- ISBN 0-8013-1903-X (softcover : alk. paper)
     1. Bloom, Benjamin Samuel, 1913- Taxonomy of educational objectives. 2.
   Education--Aims and objectives. I. Anderson, Lorin W. II. Krathwohl, David R. III.
   Bloom, Benjamin Samuel, 1913- Taxonomy of educational objectives.

LB17 .T29 2001
370'.1--dc21   00-063423

This book is a revision of *The Taxonomy of Educational Objectives, The Classification of Educational Goals, Handbook I: Cognitive Domain*, Benjamin S. Bloom (Ed.), Max D. Englehart, Edward J. Furst, Walker H. Hill, and David R. Krathwohl, published by David McKay Company, Inc., New York, 1956.

Please visit our website at http://www.ablongman.com

ISBN 0-8013-1903-X (softcover)

25 24   13 14

*This volume is dedicated to
those teachers who advance
the learning and development
of their students every day;
we hope they find it helpful.*

Brief Contents

Detailed Contents   xi
List of Tables and Figures   xix
Preface   xxi
Foreword   xxvii

SECTION I The Taxonomy: Educational Objectives and Student Learning   1

    CHAPTER 1 *Introduction*   3

    CHAPTER 2 *The Structure, Specificity, and Problems of Objectives*   12

SECTION II The Revised Taxonomy Structure   25

    CHAPTER 3 *The Taxonomy Table*   27

    CHAPTER 4 *The Knowledge Dimension*   38

    CHAPTER 5 *The Cognitive Process Dimension*   63

SECTION III The Taxonomy in Use   93

    CHAPTER 6 *Using the Taxonomy Table*   95

    CHAPTER 7 *Introduction to the Vignettes*   110

    CHAPTER 8 *Nutrition Vignette*   119

    CHAPTER 9 *Macbeth Vignette*   136

    CHAPTER 10 *Addition Facts Vignette*   158

    CHAPTER 11 *Parliamentary Acts Vignette*   171

    CHAPTER 12 *Volcanoes? Here? Vignette*   190

    CHAPTER 13 *Report Writing Vignette*   210

    CHAPTER 14 *Addressing Long-standing Problems in Classroom Instruction*   232

Appendixes   261

*Appendix A: Summary of the Changes from
          the Original Framework   263*

*Appendix B: Condensed Version of the Original Taxonomy
          of Educational Objectives: Cognitive Domain   271*

References   279

Credits   287

Index   289

Detailed Contents

List of Tables and Figures   xix
Preface   xxi
Foreword   xxvii

SECTION I **The Taxonomy: Educational Objectives
and Student Learning   1**

CHAPTER 1 *Introduction   3*
The Need for a Taxonomy   3
Using Our Increased Understanding   6
  The Taxonomy Table, Objectives, and Instructional Time   6
  The Taxonomy Table and Instruction   7
  The Taxonomy Table and Assessment   8
  The Concept of Alignment   10
Teachers as Curriculum Makers Versus Teachers as Curriculum
  Implementers: A Closing Comment   10

CHAPTER 2 *The Structure, Specificity, and Problems of Objectives   12*
The Structure of Objectives   12
  Content Versus Knowledge   12
  Behavior Versus Cognitive Processes   13
Specificity of Objectives   15
  Global Objectives   15
  Educational Objectives   15
  Instructional Objectives   16
  Summary of Levels of Objectives   16
What Objectives Are Not   17

A Changing Vocabulary of Objectives   18

Problems with Objectives   20

Specificity and Inclusiveness   20

The Lock-Step Nature of Objectives   21

What Does an Objective Represent—Learning
or Performance?   21

The Restricted Use of Objectives   22

Concluding Comment   23

SECTION II   The Revised Taxonomy Structure   25

CHAPTER 3   *The Taxonomy Table*   27

Categories of the Knowledge Dimension   27

Categories of the Cognitive Process Dimension   30

The Taxonomy Table and Objectives: A Diagrammatic
Summary   30

Why Categorize Objectives?   34

Our Use of Multiple Forms of Definition   36

Verbal Descriptions   36

Sample Objectives   37

Sample Assessment Tasks   37

Sample Instructional Activities   37

Closing Comment: A Look Ahead   37

CHAPTER 4   *The Knowledge Dimension*   38

A Distinction Between Knowledge and Subject Matter Content:
A Tale of Four Teachers   39

Different Types of Knowledge   40

A Distinction Between Factual and Conceptual
Knowledge   41

A Rationale for Metacognitive Knowledge   43

Categories of the Knowledge Dimension   45

Factual Knowledge   45

Knowledge of Terminology   45

Knowledge of Specific Details and Elements   47

Conceptual Knowledge   48

Knowledge of Classifications and Categories   49

Knowledge of Principles and Generalizations   51

Knowledge of Theories, Models, and Structures   51

Procedural Knowledge   52

   Knowledge of Subject-Specific Skills and Algorithms   53

   Knowledge of Subject-Specific Techniques and Methods   54

   Knowledge of Criteria for Determining when to Use
      Appropriate Procedures   54

Metacognitive Knowledge   55

   Strategic Knowledge   56

   Knowledge About Cognitive Tasks Including Contextual and
      Conditional Knowledge   57

   Self-Knowledge   59

Assessing Objectives Involving Metacognitive Knowledge   60

Conclusion   62

CHAPTER 5   *The Cognitive Process Dimension*   63

A Tale of Three Learning Outcomes   64

   No Learning   64

   Rote Learning   64

   Meaningful Learning   64

Meaningful Learning as Constructing Knowledge
   Frameworks   65

Cognitive Processes for Retention and Transfer   65

The Categories of the Cognitive Process Dimension   66

Remember   66

   Recognizing   69

   Recalling   69

Understand   70

   Interpreting   70

   Exemplifying   71

   Classifying   72

   Summarizing   73

   Inferring   73

   Comparing   75

   Explaining   75

Apply   77

   Executing   77

   Implementing   78

Analyze   79

   Differentiating   80

Organizing   81

Attributing   82

Evaluate   83

Checking   83

Critiquing   84

Create   84

Generating   86

Planning   87

Producing   87

Decontextualized and Contextualized Cognitive Processes   88

An Example of Educational Objectives in Context   89

Remembering What Was Learned   90

Making Sense of and Using What Was Learned   90

Conclusion   91

SECTION III | **The Taxonomy in Use   93**

CHAPTER 6   *Using the Taxonomy Table   95*

Using the Taxonomy Table in Analyzing Your Own Work   95

Using the Taxonomy Table in Analyzing the Work of Others   96

The Taxonomy Table Revisited   97

The Learning Question   97

The Instruction Question   99

The Assessment Question   101

The Alignment Question   102

Problems in Classifying Objectives   105

The Level of Specificity Problem   105

The Prior Learning Problem   105

Differentiating Objectives from Activities   106

Some Helpful Hints   107

Consider the Verb-Noun Combination   107

Relate Type of Knowledge to Process   107

Make Sure You Have the Right Noun   108

Rely on Multiple Sources   109

CHAPTER 7   *Introduction to the Vignettes   110*

Characterization of the Vignettes   110

The Curriculum Unit   111

Central Components of the Vignette Descriptions   112

Using the Taxonomy Table to Analyze the
Vignettes   114

The Analytic Process: A Summary   117

Organization and Structure of the Vignette
Chapters   117

A Closing Comment   118

CHAPTER 8   *Nutrition Vignette*   **119**

Section I: Objectives   119

Section II: Instructional Activities   120

Section III: Assessment   127

Section IV: Closing Commentary   128

The Learning Question   128

The Instruction Question   128

The Assessment Question   130

The Alignment Question   130

Section V: Closing Questions   131

Attachments   133

CHAPTER 9   Macbeth *Vignette*   **136**

Part I: Objectives   137

Part II: Instructional Activities   137

Part III: Assessment   143

Part IV: Closing Commentary   146

The Learning Question   146

The Instruction Question   146

The Assessment Question   148

The Alignment Question   148

Part V: Closing Questions   149

Attachments   151

CHAPTER 10   *Addition Facts Vignette*   **158**

Part I: Objectives   158

Part II: Instructional Activities   159

Part III: Assessment   165

Part IV: Closing Commentary   168

The Learning Question   168

The Instruction Question   168

The Assessment Question   169
The Alignment Question   169
Part V: Closing Questions   169

CHAPTER 11   *Parliamentary Acts Vignette*   171
Part I: Objectives   171
Part II: Instructional Activities   173
Part III: Assessment   180
Part IV: Closing Commentary   182
The Learning Question   182
The Instruction Question   184
The Assessment Question   184
The Alignment Question   184
Part V: Closing Questions   184
Attachments   186

CHAPTER 12   *Volcanoes? Here? Vignette*   190
Part I: Objectives   190
Part II: Instructional Activities   191
Part III: Assessment   201
Part IV: Closing Commentary   205
The Learning Question   205
The Instruction Question   205
The Assessment Question   205
The Alignment Question   205
Part V: Closing Questions   206
Attachments   208

CHAPTER 13   *Report Writing Vignette*   210
Part I: Objectives   210
Part II: Instructional Activities   213
Part III: Assessment   220
Part IV: Closing Commentary   223
The Learning Question   223
The Instruction Question   223

The Assessment Question   225

The Alignment Question   225

Part V: Closing Questions   226

Attachments   228

CHAPTER 14   *Addressing Long-Standing Problems in Classroom Instruction*   232

Generalizations Related to the Learning Question   234

Using Complex Processes to Facilitate Mastery of Simpler Objectives   234

Choosing Varieties of Knowledge   236

Generalizations Related to the Instruction Question   239

Recognizing Links Between Knowledge Types and Cognitive Processes   239

Differentiating Instructional Activities from Objectives   242

Generalizations Related to the Assessment Question   245

Using Summative and Formative Assessments   245

Dealing with External Assessments   248

Generalizations Related to the Alignment Question   250

Aligning Assessments with Objectives   250

Aligning Instructional Activities with Assessments   253

Aligning Instructional Activities with Objectives   255

A Final Comment   256

Unsolved Problems   257

The Time Demands of Analysis   257

The Linkage of Objectives and Instruction   257

Lack of Progress in Multiple-Choice Item Formats   258

Relationship to a Theory of Learning and Cognition   258

Relationships Among the Domains   258

In Closing   259

Appendixes

Appendix A: Summary of the Changes from the Original Framework   263

Four Changes in Emphasis   263

Four Changes in Terminology   265

Four Changes in Structure   266

The Inclusion of Understanding and the Omission of Problem
  Solving and Critical Thinking   269

*Appendix B: Condensed Version of the Original Taxonomy of Educational
  Objectives: Cognitive Domain*   271

References   279

Credits   287

Index   289

List of Tables and Figures

TABLE 2.1   *Relationship of Global, Educational, and Instructional Objectives*   17

TABLE 3.1   *The Taxonomy Table*   28

TABLE 3.2   *The Major Types and Subtypes of the Knowledge Dimension*   29

TABLE 3.3   *The Six Categories of the Cognitive Process Dimension and Related Cognitive Processes*   31

FIGURE 3.1   *How an Objective Is Classified in the Taxonomy Table*   32

TABLE 4.1   *The Knowledge Dimension*   46

TABLE 5.1   *The Cognitive Process Dimension*   67

TABLE 5.2   *Completed Taxonomy Table for Hypothetical Ohm's Law Unit*   92

TABLE 6.1   *Placement of the Objective in the Taxonomy Table*   98

TABLE 6.2   *Placement of the Objective and Instructional Activities in the Taxonomy Table*   100

TABLE 6.3   *Placement of the Objective, Instructional Activities, and Assessment in the Taxonomy Table*   103

TABLE 7.1   *Our Collection of Vignettes*   111

TABLE 7.2   *Elements Relevant to Taxonomic Analysis of the Vignettes*   115

TABLE 8.1   *Analysis of the Nutrition Vignette in Terms of the Taxonomy Table Based on Stated Objectives*   121

TABLE 8.2   *Analysis of the Nutrition Vignette in Terms of the Taxonomy Table Based on Instructional Activities*   124

TABLE 8.3   *Analysis of the Nutrition Vignette in Terms of the Taxonomy Table Based on Assessments*   129

TABLE 9.1   *Analysis of the Macbeth Vignette in Terms of the Taxonomy Table Based on Stated Objectives*   138

TABLE 9.2   *Analysis of the Macbeth Vignette in Terms of the Taxonomy Table Based on Instructional Activities*   144

TABLE 9.3   *Analysis of the Macbeth Vignette in Terms of the Taxonomy Table Based on Assessments*   147

TABLE 10.1   *Analysis of the Addition Facts Vignette in Terms of the Taxonomy Table Based on Stated Objectives*   160

TABLE 10.2   *Analysis of the Addition Facts Vignette in Terms of the Taxonomy Table Based on Instructional Activities*   165

TABLE 10.3   *Analysis of the Addition Facts Vignette in Terms of the Taxonomy Table Based on Assessments*   167

TABLE 11.1   *Analysis of the Parliamentary Acts Vignette in Terms of the Taxonomy Table Based on Stated Objectives*   174

TABLE 11.2   *Analysis of the Parliamentary Acts Vignette in Terms of the Taxonomy Table Based on Instructional Activities*   179

TABLE 11.3   *Analysis of the Parliamentary Acts Vignette in Terms of the Taxonomy Table Based on Assessments*   183

TABLE 12.1   *Analysis of the Volcanoes Vignette in Terms of the Taxonomy Table Based on Stated Objectives*   192

TABLE 12.2   *Analysis of the Volcanoes Vignette in Terms of the Taxonomy Table Based on Instructional Activities*   202

TABLE 12.3   *Analysis of the Volcanoes Vignette in Terms of the Taxonomy Table Based on Assessments*   204

TABLE 13.1   *Analysis of the Report Writing Vignette in Terms of the Taxonomy Table Based on Stated Objectives*   213

TABLE 13.2   *Analysis of the Report Writing Vignette in Terms of the Taxonomy Table Based on Instructional Activities*   221

TABLE 13.3   *Analysis of the Report Writing Vignette in Terms of the Taxonomy Table Based on Assessments*   224

FIGURE A.1   *Summary of the Structural Changes from the Original Framework to the Revision*   268

Preface

In 1956 a framework for categorizing educational objectives was published by B. S. Bloom (editor), M. D. Engelhart, E. J. Furst, W. H. Hill, and D. R. Krathwohl as *The Taxonomy of Educational Objectives, The Classification of Educational Goals, Handbook I: Cognitive Domain*.[1] Since its publication over 40 years ago, the *Handbook* has been translated into more than twenty languages (Krathwohl, 1994) and has provided a basis for test design and curriculum development not only in the United States but throughout the world (Chung, 1994; Lewy and Bathory, 1994; Postlethwaite, 1994). Shane (1981) conducted a survey on the significant writings that influenced curriculum in the first three-quarters of the twentieth century, and the *Handbook* was one of four that tied for eighth through eleventh place. More recently, a national panel was asked by the Museum of Education at the University of South Carolina to "identify the education books that 'had a significant influence, consequence or resonance' on American education during the 20th century" (Kridel, 2000, p. 5). Their list included both the *Handbook* and the affective domain taxonomy (Krathwohl, Bloom, and Masia, 1964) (Kridel, 2000, pp. 72–73). References to and examples from the *Handbook* have appeared in numerous measurement, curriculum, and teacher education textbooks. Its impact nationally and internationally was the subject of a National Society for the Study of Education yearbook (Anderson and Sosniak, 1994). This book is a revision of the *Handbook*.

WHY A REVISION?

Given the *Handbook*'s longevity and importance, one may reasonably ask Why would anybody tinker with a publication that has such a record? Why is a revision necessary? We have two reasons. First, there is a need to refocus educators' attention on the value of the original *Handbook*, not only as a historical document but also as one that in many respects was "ahead of its time" (Rohwer and Sloane, 1994). We believe that many of the ideas in the *Handbook* are valuable to today's educators as they struggle with problems associated

---

[1] Throughout this volume, Taxonomy refers to the classification system, and *Handbook* refers to the publication in which the classification system appears.

with the design and implementation of accountability programs, standards-based curriculums, and authentic assessments.

Second, there is a need to incorporate new knowledge and thought into the framework. Numerous changes in American society since 1956 have influenced the way we think about and practice education. Now we know more about how children develop and learn and how teachers plan for, teach, and assess their students. These increases in knowledge support the need for a revision.

After you have had a chance to consider our changes, you may decide that we should have left well enough alone. However, we hope you will withhold final judgment until you have read this book and have attempted to use our framework to inform your practice.

INTENDED AUDIENCES

We hope to reach several audiences, and teachers are one of the most important. There is ample evidence that teachers determine what takes place in their classrooms through the curriculum they actually deliver to their students and the way in which they deliver it. Consequently, if our revision of the Taxonomy is to have an impact on the quality of education, it must dramatically influence the way teachers think and act. Toward this end, we have tried to make this revision much more practical and useful for teachers.

Curriculums are currently expected to be standards based (Glatthorn, 1998), and the majority of states have passed accountability legislation (Frymier, 1996; Gandal, 1996; Rebarber, 1991). Proponents of these approaches seek to improve substantially the quality of teachers' teaching and students' learning. Such approaches become classroom realities, however, only if they are embraced, understood, and acted upon by classroom teachers.

What can bring about this change? We suggest that teachers need a framework to help them make sense of objectives and organize them so that they are clearly understood and fairly easy to implement. This framework may help teachers plan and deliver appropriate instruction, design valid assessment tasks and strategies, and ensure that instruction and assessment are aligned with the objectives. The authors of the original *Handbook* believed their Taxonomy might be such a framework. In our revision, we have sought to (1) revise and extend their approach, (2) use common language, (3) be consistent with current psychological and educational thinking, and (4) provide realistic examples of the use of the framework.

For instance, in both Chapters 1 and 2 we explore the relationship between standards and objectives. The whole of Section III is devoted to demonstrating the application of our framework to the classroom. Chapters 8–13 consist of vignettes written by teachers describing units they have developed and taught, together with our analyses of how our framework might help teachers understand and ultimately improve the units. Chapter 14 gathers together some of the wisdom revealed by the vignette analyses for classroom practice. Our hope, then, is that many teachers will read this volume and find it of value.

Teachers are so busy teaching that they often get their information "second hand." In this regard, Bloom said the original *Handbook* was "one of the most widely cited yet least read books in American education" (Anderson and Sosniak, 1994, p. 9). Therefore, among our audiences we hope to include several groups that interact with and attempt to influence both practicing and prospective teachers. To more efficiently meet the needs of these groups, this book is published in two editions, one an abridged and the other a complete. The abridged edition includes in its 14 chapters the content that we believe to be of greatest interest, value, and immediate practical use to teachers. The complete edition includes three additional chapters and one additional appendix. One of these chapters describes alternative frameworks for categorizing objectives, one summarizes empirical studies of the structure of the original Taxonomy, and a final one discusses still unsolved problems (an abridged version appears as the final section of Chapter 14 of the abridged edition). We believe the complete edition will be of greater interest to those persons who are most familiar with the original *Handbook,* as well as university professors, educational researchers, and scholars who wish to learn more about this and other frameworks.

Our intended audiences include groups of people who influence teachers both directly and indirectly. Among those who interact with and have a direct effect on classroom teachers are teacher educators who plan and deliver preservice teacher education programs. For them, the abridged edition should provide important adjunct or supplementary reading for their primary textbooks. It follows that the authors of the textbooks used in teacher education courses, as they cite the Taxonomy and build upon it, provide another avenue for bringing the framework to teachers' attention. We anticipate that these educators will adapt their current coverage of the Taxonomy to the revision.

Curriculum coordinators and educational consultants who are involved in ongoing professional development activities and help teachers in their classrooms also have the potential to influence teachers directly. In designing programs, they may find it profitable to use our vignettes as case studies of how the framework relates to practice.

Several audiences that indirectly affect teachers may also find this revision of value. Test designers and test publishers have used the *Handbook* extensively as a basis for organizing the objectives their achievement tests are intended to measure. Our revised framework should be at least as useful and perhaps even more so.

Although the *Handbook* did not address policy makers (e.g., school boards and state legislators) and the media, these audiences are increasingly important. Our framework can offer policy makers perspectives on where the standards to be met by schools and graduates fall in the panorama of possible goals and whether their intentions are met. Similarly, the framework may enable journalists to raise questions about what achievement scores really represent.

Our final audience is the authors and publishers of the textbooks that elementary and secondary teachers use to teach their students. These authors and publishers have the greatest potential for influencing both teachers and students if, as many have in the past, they incorporate our framework in their texts and show how it can be used to help teachers analyze their objectives, instruction, and assessments and determine the alignment of the three.

THIS BOOK'S ORGANIZATION

Following this Preface is a Foreword describing the development of both the original *Handbook* and our revision. The remainder of the book is divided into four sections. Section I consists of two chapters. The first describes the need for taxonomies and the ways in which educators can use our Taxonomy. The second chapter discusses the nature of objectives, their relationship to standards, and their role in education.

The three chapters in Section II describe the structure of our revised Taxonomy. The two-dimensional table known as the Taxonomy Table is presented in Chapter 3. The next two chapters describe the structure of our revised framework and provide greater detail on the table's two dimensions: the knowledge dimension (Chapter 4) and the cognitive process dimension (Chapter 5). Each dimension consists of a set of categories that are defined and illustrated.

The nine chapters in Section III demonstrate the uses and usefulness of the Taxonomy Table. Chapter 6 describes how the Taxonomy Table can be used to develop learning objectives, plan instruction, design assessments, and align these three activities. Chapter 7 presents an overview of the vignettes, including how they can be analyzed and how they may be useful to teachers. Chapters 8–13 contain the vignettes themselves, which are descriptions of actual course units written by the teachers who developed and/or taught them. Each vignette is analyzed in terms of its objectives, instruction, assessment, and alignment using the Taxonomy Table. Finally, Chapter 14 discusses a series of generalizations derived from our analyses of the vignettes.

Section IV, which is available only in the complete version, examines the Taxonomy in perspective. In Chapter 15 we compare and contrast 19 alternative frameworks that have appeared since the publication of the original *Handbook*; we examine them in the context of the framework and our revision of it. In Chapter 16 we summarize and review the empirical data that bear on the assumed cumulative hierarchy of the original Taxonomy, and we discuss the implication of these data for our revision. Finally, in Chapter 17 we look ahead to some problems that remain to be solved by authors of future revisions. Both the abridged and complete editions contain two appendixes: one summarizes the changes the revision made in the original framework, and the other presents the framework of the original edition. A third appendix, which appears only in the complete edition, displays the data on which the meta-analysis in Chapter 16 is based.

AUTHORS

A work of this duration and magnitude required numerous revisions of every chapter. The vast majority of the chapters retained primary authors throughout; several chapters had multiple "contributing" authors. The chapter authors are listed here:

Peter W. Airasian, Boston College—primary author, Chapter 2; contributing author, Chapter 1; vignette commentary, Chapters 10 and 11.

Lorin W. Anderson, University of South Carolina—primary author, Chapters 1, 6, and 14; contributing author, Chapters 3 and 7; vignette commentary, Chapters 8, 9, 10, 11, and 12.

Kathleen A. Cruikshank, Indiana University—contributing author, Chapter 1; vignette commentary, Chapters 9 and 12.

David R. Krathwohl, Syracuse University—primary author, Chapters 3, 15, 16, and 17; contributing author, Chapter 6.

Richard E. Mayer, University of California, Santa Barbara—primary author, Chapter 5; contributing author, Chapters 3 and 4.

Paul R. Pintrich, University of Michigan—primary author, Chapter 4; contributing author, Chapters 3 and 5.

James Raths, University of Delaware—contributing author, Chapters 1 and 7; vignette commentary, Chapter 13.

Merlin Wittrock, University of California, Berkeley—contributing author, Chapters 3, 4, and 5.

ACKNOWLEDGMENTS

We are especially grateful to these teachers, who wrote the descriptions of their teaching that are the "heart" of the vignettes in Chapters 8–13:

Chapter 8: Nancy C. Nagengast, Maple Lane Elementary School, Wilmington, Delaware.

Chapter 9: Margaret Jackson, A. C. Flora High School, Columbia, South Carolina.

Chapter 10: Jeanna Hoffman, Satchel Ford Elementary School, Columbia, South Carolina.

Chapter 11: Gwendolyn K. Airasian, Wilson Middle School, Natick, Massachusetts.

Chapter 12: Michael J. Smith, American Geographical Institute, Alexandria, Virginia.[2]

Chapter 13: Christine Evans, Brandywine (Delaware) School District, and Deanne McCredie, Cape Henlopen (Delaware) School District.

The authors of the vignettes were given the opportunity to see a late draft of the manuscript and were requested to send comments to the publisher on the draft in general and especially on the presentation and analysis of their own vignette. The authors of Chapter 13, which was added later, also had the opportunity to review their own vignette as it was presented and analyzed. The authors' comments and suggestions were used in preparing the final draft.

Copies of this manuscript in several stages of preparation were sent to various scholars, teachers, and educators. Many of these people returned

---

[2] Dr. Smith observed the teaching of the unit as part of a National Science Foundation project. An experienced teacher taught the unit.

comments that were extremely valuable to the authors in preparing this final version. We are grateful to all those who saw early drafts, including: Gwen Airasian, Wilson Middle School, Natick, MA; Patricia Alexander, University of Maryland; James Applefield, University of North Carolina, Wilmington; Richard Arends, Central Connecticut State; Hilda Borko, University of Colorado; Jere Brophy, Michigan State University; Robert Calfee, Stanford University; Nathaniel Gage, Stanford University; Robert Glaser, University of Pittsburgh; Thomas L. Good, University of Arizona; Jeanna Hoffman, Satchel Ford Elementary School, Columbia, SC; Margaret Jackson, A. C. Flora High School, Columbia, SC; James Johnson, Departments of Education and Labor, Washington, D.C.; Greta Morine-Dershimer, University of Virginia; Nancy Nagengast, Maple Lane Elementary School, Wilmington, DE; Melody Shank, Indiana Essential Schools Network; Wayne H. Slater, University of Maryland; Michael Smith, American Geographic Institute, Alexandria, VA; Susan Stodolsky, University of Chicago; and Anitia Woolfolk, Ohio State University.

We are most grateful to Dr. Virginia (Ginny) Blanford, formerly Education Acquisitions Editor of Addison Wesley Longman, for her strong support of the project from the beginning to the end. She was instrumental in getting funds from Longman for the first meeting of the editors and authors. Succeeding meetings over the years and in-between expenses were funded out of the royalties from the first edition.

Any revision inevitably treads the same ground as the original edition, and this book is no exception. We not only used ideas expressed in the first edition without continuously attributing them, which would get annoying, but in some instances used the original phrasing as well. As a group, we have been ever mindful of the debt we owe those on whose work this new effort has been based, and we are most grateful that they did the foundation work.

Finally, as editors, we are especially indebted to those who labored with us in this effort. It has been a special joy to work with them. We have had many spirited discussions and changed the manuscript so many times it has been hard to keep track of what went where. But through it all we've looked forward to our semiannual meetings and thoroughly enjoyed one another's contributions and company. One of the editors (DRK) especially thanks everyone for holding all the meetings in Syracuse when a family situation made it difficult for him to travel.

We are extremely sorry that Benjamin Bloom, who originated the idea of the Taxonomy, edited the original *Handbook*, and served as mentor to some of us, developed Alzheimer's disease and could not participate in our revision. Ben passed away shortly before this book was published. Most who worked on the original *Handbook* predeceased this revision's publication; the others are retired. One of the original authors, however, Dr. Edward Furst, supplied us with some useful materials and suggestions. Comments also came from Dr. Christine McGuire, a member of the original group. You'll also note that another member, Dr. Nathaniel Gage, was one of our helpful reviewers. We hope that all of them will consider this revision the improvement we intend it to be.

Lorin W. Anderson
David R. Krathwohl

Foreword

Although this Taxonomy, indeed the very idea of a taxonomy, may be new to many of our readers, it is a revision of a framework that has been in use for almost a half-century. For those unfamiliar with the *Handbook*, this Foreword provides some background on its original development and on the process of this revision.

In 1948 an informal meeting held in Boston was attended by a group of college and university examiners who believed that a common framework for classifying intended student learning outcomes could promote the exchange of test items, testing procedures, and ideas about testing. As examiners, these individuals were responsible for preparing, administering, scoring, and reporting the results of comprehensive examinations for undergraduate courses taught at their respective institutions.

Since developing good multiple-choice questions is time-consuming, the examiners hoped to create significant labor savings by facilitating the exchange of items. They proposed to establish a standard vocabulary for indicating what an item was intended to measure. Such regularized meanings were to result from a set of carefully defined categories and subcategories into which any educational objective and, therefore, any test item could be classified. Initially the framework would be limited to the mainstays of all instruction, cognitive objectives.

The original group always considered the framework a work in progress, neither finished nor final. Indeed, only the cognitive domain was developed initially. The affective domain was developed later (Krathwohl, Bloom, and Masia, 1964), and although both Simpson (1966) and Harrow (1972) provided frameworks for the psychomotor domain, the original group never did.

Furthermore, there was a great deal of concern among the members of the original group that the Taxonomy would freeze thought, stifling the development of new frameworks. That this did not occur is evident from the large number of alternative frameworks that have been advanced since the *Handbook* was published. A compilation of 19 of these frameworks appears in Chapter 15 of the complete version of this book.

In a memorandum circa 1971 Bloom stated: "Ideally each major field should have its own taxonomy of objectives in its own language—more detailed, closer to the special language and thinking of its experts, reflecting its own appropriate sub-divisions and levels of education, with possible new categories, combinations of categories and omitting categories as appropriate." [In his handwriting, a note refers the reader to Bloom, Hastings, and Madaus (1971), which showed how the Taxonomy could be so adapted.] There has always been and remains to this day an expectation that the Taxonomy would be adapted as educators in different fields used it, as education changed, and as new knowledge provided a basis for change. Our revision, then, is both overdue and expected.

REVISION OF THE *HANDBOOK*

The idea of revising the Taxonomy and the entire *Handbook* began with a series of discussions between David Krathwohl, one of the authors of the original *Handbook*, and Dr. Virginia Blanford, Senior Education Editor of Addison Wesley Longman, Inc. Since Longman owned the rights to the original *Handbook*, Dr. Blanford was aware of the need for a revision and was interested in marketing it. A group met to discuss revision and laid some plans, but little progress was made until the publication of *Bloom's Taxonomy: A Forty-Year Retrospective* (Anderson and Sosniak, 1994). Following its publication, David Krathwohl and Lorin Anderson began planning for an initial meeting of a new group of interested parties to discuss the desirability and feasibility of revising the Taxonomy and the *Handbook*.

As the plans for the meeting progressed, attention turned to who should participate. A decision was made to choose representatives of three groups: cognitive psychologists, curriculum theorists and instructional researchers, and testing and assessment specialists. An initial meeting, held in Syracuse, New York, in November 1995, was attended by these eight people (arranged by group):

> *Cognitive psychologists:* Richard Mayer, Paul Pintrich, and William Rohwer. Merlin Wittrock was invited but could not attend.
>
> *Curriculum theorists and instructional researchers:* Lorin Anderson and Kathleen Cruikshank. Jean Clandinin, Michael Connelly, and James Raths were invited but could not attend. Clandinin and Connelly later withdrew from the project.
>
> *Testing and assessment specialists:* Peter Airasian, Linda Crocker, and David Krathwohl.

The meeting resulted in a draft table of contents for the revision and writing assignments. Like the original *Handbook*, the revision was a group effort. Drafts of various documents were prepared during the remainder of 1996 and first distributed to all group members in late 1996 and early 1997. The group then met twice yearly in the spring and fall to review drafts; discuss strengths, weaknesses, omissions, and redundancies; and determine appropriate next steps. A draft of the framework was presented for public comment at a symposium at the American Educational Research Association in April 1998; it was generally well received. The reaction suggested the revision might be ready for more detailed review.

At a June 1998 meeting in Syracuse, plans were laid to prepare a draft for external review. Addison Wesley Longman was generous in lining up a large number of blind reviews, and a draft manuscript was distributed in November 1998. Based on the reviews, revisions were made during the summer of 1999. A revised draft manuscript was the focus of discussion at a final Syracuse meeting held in October 1999.

The revision during the summer of 1999 removed many references to the original *Handbook* that we had included not only because we gratefully give credit to the original group but also because we wished, at appropriate points, to show how our revision builds on the original framework. However, the reviewers reminded us that many of our readers would be totally unfamiliar with the original *Handbook*. Consequently, such references would likely convey little meaning, get in the way, and unduly complicate the text. Therefore, for the most part, this volume has been written as though the reader were coming to the topic fresh.

Some readers will nevertheless be curious to know how the revision differs from the original, especially those who are familiar with the original and have used it. For these readers, we have summarized in Appendix A 12 of the major changes that we made. In addition, we have included a condensed version of the original Taxonomy in Appendix B. We hope that we have conveyed the tremendous debt we owe the framers of the original Taxonomy.

A Taxonomy for Learning, Teaching, and Assessing

The Taxonomy:
Educational Objectives
and Student Learning

CHAPTER 1

Introduction

In life, objectives help us to focus our attention and our efforts; they indicate what we want to accomplish. In education, objectives indicate what we want students to learn; they are "explicit formulations of the ways in which students are expected to be changed by the educative process" (*Handbook*, 1956, p. 26). Objectives are especially important in teaching because teaching is an *intentional* and *reasoned* act. Teaching is intentional because we always teach for some purpose, primarily to facilitate student learning. Teaching is reasoned because what teachers teach their students is judged by them to be worthwhile.

The reasoned aspect of teaching relates to *what* objectives teachers select for their students. The intentional aspect of teaching concerns *how* teachers help students achieve the teachers' objectives, that is, the learning environments the teachers create and the activities and experiences they provide. The learning environments, activities, and experiences should be aligned with, or be consistent with, the selected objectives.

Teachers' objectives may be explicit or implicit, clearly or fuzzily conceived, easily measurable or not. They may be called something other than objectives. In the past they were called aims, purposes, goals, and guiding outcomes (Bobbitt, 1918; Rugg, 1926a and b). Today they are more likely to be referred to as content standards or curriculum standards (Kendall and Marzano, 1996; Glatthorn, 1998). Regardless of how they are stated and what they are called, objectives are present in virtually all teaching. Stated simply, when we teach, we want our students to learn. What we want them to learn as a result of our teaching are our objectives.[1]

THE NEED FOR A TAXONOMY

Consider a recent lament from a middle school teacher: "When I first heard about the possibility of statewide standards, I was intrigued. I thought that it

---

[1] Throughout this volume we use the term *objectives* to refer to intended student learning outcomes. Thus, *objectives, curriculum standards,* and *learning goals* all refer to intended student learning.

might be nice to have a clear idea of what students were expected to know and be able to do in each subject at each grade level. But when I saw the drafts of the standards, I was appalled. There were so many. There were 85 standards in sixth-grade English language arts (my specialty area); there were more than 100 in sixth-grade mathematics. And they were so vague. I remember one in particular. 'Describe connections between historical and cultural influences and literacy selections.' What connections? What influences? What selections? And what do they mean by describe? I asked myself, 'How can these things possibly help me teach better and my students learn better?'"

What can teachers do when confronted with what they believe to be an exceedingly large number of vague objectives? To deal with the vast number of objectives, they need to organize them in some way. To deal with the problem of vagueness, they need to make the objectives more precise. In a nutshell, then, these teachers need an organizing framework that increases precision and, most important, promotes understanding.

How can a framework help teachers make sense of such statements of objectives? A framework consists of a set of categories related to a single phenomenon (e.g., minerals, fiction). The categories are a collection of "bins" into which objects, experiences, and ideas can be placed. Objects, experiences, and ideas that share common characteristics are placed in the same "bin." The criteria that are relevant in the sorting process are determined by a set of organizing principles—principles that are used to differentiate among the categories. Once classified, the characteristics of each category as well as the characteristics of the other categories in the framework help teachers to better understand what is placed in the category.

Consider the phylogenetic framework (with categories of mammals, birds, arthropods, and so on). The organizing principles (or "sorting criteria") include body characteristics (e.g., presence and/or location of skeleton, warm-blooded vs. cold-blooded) and birth and care of young (e.g., eggs vs. live birth; absent vs. nurturing). To use the framework to enhance our understanding, we learn the defining features of each category. For example, what makes a mammal a mammal? We learn that mammals are air-breathing, are warm-blooded, nurse their young, provide more protection and training of their young than do other animals, and have a larger, more well-developed brain than do other animals. If we hear that a hyrax is a mammal, then we understand something about the hyrax by virtue of its placement in the framework. If we are then told that a giraffe is a mammal, we know that hyraxes and giraffes share some common characteristics because they are placed in the same category of the framework.

A taxonomy is a special kind of framework. In a taxonomy the categories lie along a continuum. The continuum (e.g., the wave frequencies underlying color, the atomic structure underlying the periodic table of the elements) becomes one of the major organizing principles of the framework. In our Taxonomy we are classifying objectives. A statement of an objective contains a verb and a noun. The verb generally describes the intended cognitive process. The noun generally describes the knowledge students are expected to acquire or construct. Consider the following example: "The student will learn to distinguish (the cognitive process) among confederal, federal, and unitary systems of government (the knowledge)."

In contrast with the single dimension of the original Taxonomy, the revised framework is two-dimensional. As suggested in the preceding paragraph, the two dimensions are cognitive process and knowledge. We refer to their interrelationships as the Taxonomy Table (see the inside front cover). The cognitive process dimension (i.e., the columns of the table) contains six categories: *Remember, Understand, Apply, Analyze, Evaluate,* and *Create.* The continuum underlying the cognitive process dimension is assumed to be cognitive complexity; that is, *Understand* is believed to be more cognitively complex than *Remember, Apply* is believed to be more cognitively complex than *Understand,* and so on.

The knowledge dimension (i.e., the rows of the table) contains four categories: *Factual, Conceptual, Procedural,* and *Metacognitive.* These categories are assumed to lie along a continuum from concrete (*Factual*) to abstract (*Metacognitive*). The *Conceptual* and *Procedural* categories overlap in terms of abstractness, with some procedural knowledge being more concrete than the most abstract conceptual knowledge.

To begin to see how the Taxonomy Table helps us understand objectives, consider the aforementioned objective regarding systems of government. The verb—"distinguish"—provides clues to the desired cognitive process. As will be seen in Chapter 5, "distinguish" is associated with the cognitive process category *Analyze.* The noun phrase—"confederal, federal, and unitary systems of government"—gives clues to the desired type of knowledge. As will be seen in Chapter 4, "systems" signify *Conceptual knowledge.* In terms of the Taxonomy Table, then, the objective involves *Analyze* and *Conceptual knowledge.*

Consider a second example, this one from mathematics: "The student will learn to differentiate between rational numbers and irrational numbers." Differentiating, like distinguishing, is a subcategory in the process category *Analyze.* The nouns, rational and irrational numbers, are numerical categories. Categories are concepts, and concepts lie at the heart of *Conceptual knowledge.* In terms of the Taxonomy Table, this second objective also involves *Analyze* and *Conceptual knowledge.*

In the Taxonomy Table, both objectives are placed in the cell where the row labeled *Conceptual knowledge* intersects the column labeled *Analyze.* Despite their different subject matter, then, these two objectives about social studies and mathematics are classified in the same cell of the Taxonomy Table. Both are grounded in *Conceptual knowledge;* both require students to engage in the process *Analyze.* Once we understand the meaning of *Conceptual knowledge* and the meaning of *Analyze,* we know a great deal about both of these objectives. Just as placing an animal into the phylogenetic framework helps us better understand the animal, placing an objective into our framework increases our understanding of that objective.

USING OUR INCREASED UNDERSTANDING

Although we may gain a better understanding of an objective using the Taxonomy Table, how does this increased understanding help us? Teachers traditionally have struggled with issues and concerns pertaining to education, teaching, and learning. Here are four of the most important organizing questions:

1. What is important for students to learn in the limited school and classroom time available?   (the learning question)

2. How does one plan and deliver instruction that will result in high levels of learning for large numbers of students?   (the instruction question)

3. How does one select or design assessment instruments and procedures that provide accurate information about how well students are learning? (the assessment question)

4. How does one ensure that objectives, instruction, and assessment are consistent with one another?   (the alignment question)

These four organizing questions reappear throughout the book and provide a basis for showing how the Taxonomy framework can be used. We describe them in greater detail in the next four sections of this chapter.

THE TAXONOMY TABLE, OBJECTIVES, AND INSTRUCTIONAL TIME

One of the most common and long-standing curriculum questions is What is worth learning? This is the first of the organizing questions. At an abstract level, the answer defines what it means to be an educated person. At a more concrete level, the answer defines the meaning of the subject matter being taught. Is mathematics, for example, a discrete body of knowledge to be memorized or an organized, coherent, conceptual system to be understood? Does reading consist of remembering a set of sound-symbol relationships or gaining meaning from the words on a printed page? Similar questions can be asked of science, history, art, music, and other fields.

Today's emphasis on state-level standards is intended to provide at least a partial answer to the learning question. But as our middle school teacher's comments suggest, simply having standards does not necessarily provide a sound, defensible answer. "Grocery lists" of standards may be more confusing and frustrating than enlightening and useful. Teachers must still answer the question What is worth learning? They answer it, in large part, by the way they allocate time in the classroom and by the emphasis they convey to their students about what is *really* important.

Over the past century, the number of possible answers to this fundamental curriculum question has increased as our collective knowledge and the amount of information available to us have increased. We continue to operate educationally, however, within virtually the same length of school year that we used a hundred years ago. If the difficult decisions are not made about what is worth learning, then teachers are likely to simply run out of time. When teachers operate within a textbook-based curriculum, for example, they complete as many chapters as time permits.

Looking through the lens of the Taxonomy Table, teachers can see more clearly the array of possible objectives as well as the relationships among them. Thus, when we analyze all or part of a curriculum in terms of the Taxonomy Table, we can gain a more complete understanding of the curriculum. Rows, columns, and cells that have numerous entries become evident, as do those that have no entries at all. An entire row or column that has no entries can alert us to the possibility of including objectives that heretofore had not been considered.

In sum, the Taxonomy framework obviously can't directly tell teachers what is worth learning. But by helping teachers translate standards into a common language for comparison with what they personally hope to achieve, and by presenting the variety of possibilities for consideration, the Taxonomy may provide some perspective to guide curriculum decisions.

THE TAXONOMY TABLE AND INSTRUCTION

Once an objective has been placed into a particular cell of the Taxonomy Table, we can begin systematically to attack the problem of helping students achieve that objective. Thus, the second organizing question involves instruction. We have used two objectives as examples:

- The student will learn to distinguish among confederal, federal, and unitary systems of government.
- The student will learn to differentiate between rational numbers and irrational numbers.

We placed both of these objectives in the cell that corresponds to the intersection of *Analyze* and *Conceptual knowledge*; that is, both are of the form *analyze conceptual knowledge*. How does this placement help us plan our instruction?

Categories and classifications form the basis of *Conceptual knowledge*. Thus, instruction related to these objectives must help students form the categories and classifications inherent in the objective: confederal, federal, and unitary systems of government, on the one hand, and rational and irrational numbers, on the other. From a variety of research studies we know that examples help students form categories and classifications (Tennyson, 1995). Thus, examples should be incorporated into instructional plans for objectives that involve *Conceptual knowledge*.

Looking back at the two objectives, we see that distinguishing and differentiating are both cognitive processes associated with *Analyze*. In fact, differentiating involves distinguishing the parts of a whole structure in terms of their relevance or importance. In the first objective the whole structure is "systems of government." The parts are confederal, federal, and unitary, and they differ in many respects. The question is What are the most relevant or important differences? Similarly, in the second objective the whole structure is the "real number system." The parts are rational and irrational numbers. Again, the question is What are the most relevant or important differences among the "parts" in the context of the "whole"?

Regardless of the specific objective, then, when instruction is directed at objectives classified as *Analyze Conceptual knowledge*, one might expect activities that:

- focus students' attention on categories and classifications;
- use examples and nonexamples to help students form the proper categories;
- help students see specific categories in relation to a larger classification system; and
- emphasize the relevant and important differences among the categories within the context of the larger system. (Tennyson, 1995)

Now consider a third objective: "Students will learn the names of the major works of American and British novelists." In our framework, "learn the names of" indicates *Remember,* and "names of the major works of American and British novelists" suggests *Factual knowledge.* Thus, this objective is of the form *remember factual knowledge.* Instruction designed for this objective is different from instruction designed for the first two objectives. Instructional plans for objectives classified as *Remember Factual knowledge* might lead one to expect the teacher to:

- periodically remind students of the specific details to be remembered (e.g., names, not plot or characters);
- give students strategies (e.g., rehearsal) and techniques (e.g., mnemonic devices) for helping them memorize the relevant knowledge; and
- provide opportunities for students to practice these strategies and techniques. (Pressley and Van Meter, 1995)

Two points should be made here. First, different types of objectives require different instructional approaches, that is, different learning activities, different curricular materials, and different teacher and student roles. Second, similar types of objectives—regardless of differences in the topic or subject matter—may require similar instructional approaches (Joyce and Weil, 1996). Given particular kinds of instructional goals, Romizowski (1981), for example, lists a variety of instructional characteristics that facilitate their achievement. Classifying a particular objective within our framework, then, helps teachers systematically plan a way of effectively facilitating students' learning of that objective.

THE TAXONOMY TABLE AND ASSESSMENT

The two points made in the preceding paragraph apply to assessment as well, which brings us to the third organizing question. Different types of objectives (that is, objectives in different cells of the table) require different approaches to assessment. Similar types of objectives (that is, objectives in the same cells of the table) likely involve similar approaches to assessment. To illustrate these points, we continue with our three sample objectives.

To assess students' learning with respect to the systems of government objective, we could provide each student with a description of the system of government of an imaginary country and ask the student to answer questions about the government. An imaginary country is used to ensure that the student has not encountered it in the past and thus cannot answer the questions based on memory alone. Three example questions follow:

- What system of government is this (federal, confederal, or unitary)?
- How do you know that it is the type of government remember system you say it is?
- What changes would need to be made to transform the country's system into the other two systems? That is, if it is a federal system, what changes would make it a confederal system or a unitary system?

To assess students' learning with respect to the number systems objective, we could provide each student with a list of, say, six numbers, all of which are either rational or irrational numbers, and ask the student to answer questions about the list of numbers. The numbers selected should be as different as possible from the numbers in the textbook or discussed during class. Three example questions follow:

- To what number system, rational or irrational, do all of these numbers belong?
- How do you know that it is the type of number system you say it is?
- How could you change each number so it is an example of the other number system? That is, if it is an irrational number, change it to a rational number, and if it is a rational number, change it to an irrational number.

Note the parallelism in these two sets of questions. Both begin with an example or a set of examples in one of the categories. In both cases, the example or set of examples is different from examples included in the text or mentioned in class. This condition is needed to ensure that understanding, rather than remembering, is being assessed. The three questions are essentially the same: To what category does the example or examples belong? How do you know that? How can you change the example or examples so they belong to the other category or categories? This blueprint, then, can be used for designing assessments for many objectives of the form *analyze conceptual knowledge*.

The third sample objective was to learn the names of the major works of American and British novelists. Here, we want all of the works and novelists included in the assessment instrument to be those contained in the text or discussed in class. The emphasis is on remembering, not understanding. A frequently used assessment format for such objectives is matching. The names of the novels are listed in, say, column A, and the names of the American and British novelists are listed in column B. Students are asked to locate the novelist in column B who wrote each of the novels in column A. Notice that this format is appropriate for many objectives of the form *remember factual knowledge*.

THE CONCEPT OF ALIGNMENT

Alignment refers to the degree of correspondence among the objectives, instruction, and assessment; it is the topic of the fourth and last organizing question. In the systems of government example, the objective is of the form *analyze conceptual knowledge*. Instruction that focuses students' attention on the three specific categories, that uses examples to help students form the proper categories, that helps students see the three specific categories in relation to a larger system, and that emphasizes the relevant and important differences among the categories within the larger system is well aligned with the objective. Similarly, assessment tasks that provide students with information about an unfamiliar government and ask them to classify the government into one of the three types, defend the classification made, and describe the changes necessary to modify the government into the other two types are well aligned with the objective.

Severe misalignment can cause problems. If, for example, instruction is not aligned with assessments, then even high-quality instruction will not likely influence student performance on those assessments. Similarly, if assessments are not aligned with objectives, then the results of the assessments will not reflect achievement of those objectives.

Typically, the degree of alignment is determined by comparing objectives with assessment, objectives with instruction, and instruction with assessment. This comparison often results in a surface-level analysis, however. The Taxonomy Table offers an important alternative to facilitate comparisons. The table is a kind of touchstone; its carefully defined terms and organization provide precision across all three comparisons. Thus, a special Taxonomy Table can be prepared using different notations for objectives, for instruction, and for assessments as each is classified in the cells of the table. By determining whether notations for all three—objectives, instructional activities, and assessments—appear together in the individual cells of the table (strong alignment), or some cells contain only two of them (weaker alignment), or many cells contain only one of them (weakest alignment), we gain a deeper-level examination of alignment. The examination emphasizes consistency in terms of intended student learning. This approach is illustrated in the vignettes in Chapters 8–13 of this volume.

TEACHERS AS CURRICULUM MAKERS VERSUS TEACHERS AS CURRICULUM IMPLEMENTERS: A CLOSING COMMENT

In the span of a hundred years, much of the control over what is taught has shifted from the schoolhouse to the statehouse—an often turbulent transition made reluctantly and grudgingly. State leaders, more than ever, are at the helm, still trying to fulfill the hope and promise for public education their counterparts were striving for a century ago. (Manzo, 1999, p. 21)

It should be clear from the introduction to this chapter that we expect our work to be used in the context of "teachers as curriculum implementers"; that is, teachers are given sets of objectives (e.g., in textbooks or increasingly state- or district-mandated standards) and are expected to deliver instruction that enables a large proportion of students to achieve those standards. The Taxonomy Table should help teachers do this and do it reasonably well.

At the same time, however, we recognize that some curriculum theorists, teacher educators, and teachers themselves believe teachers should be "curriculum makers" (see, for example, Clandinin and Connelly, 1992). Is our framework useful in this context as well? We believe it is. For these teachers, however, the framework is more likely to function as a heuristic than as a guide. For instance, the Taxonomy may suggest the range and types of cognitive objectives to consider. As further evidence for the framework's usefulness, we recommend examining the analyses of the vignettes to see how they facilitate curriculum development. These vignettes were prepared by teachers functioning as curriculum makers. Some of the teachers were quite free to design their units as they saw fit. Others were constrained to a greater or lesser degree by legislative regulations, state standards, district guidelines, textbook adoptions, and the like. Regardless of the degree of freedom available to the teachers, our framework provided us with a level of understanding of their teaching practices that was hitherto not evident. Strengths and areas in need of improvement were both apparent.

It is our hope that, whether the curriculum was given to the teachers or designed by them, this revision of the Taxonomy will help teachers make sense of the curriculum, plan instruction, and design assessments that are aligned with the objectives inherent in the curriculum and ultimately improve their teaching quality. Furthermore, our framework should provide a common way of thinking about and a common vocabulary for talking about teaching that enhances communication among teachers themselves and among teachers, teacher educators, curriculum coordinators, assessment specialists, and school administrators.

CHAPTER 2

The Structure, Specificity, and Problems of Objectives

Given the importance of objectives in education, in this chapter we address the structure, specificity, and criticisms of objectives. We recognize that objectives exist in many forms, ranging from highly specific to global and from explicit to implicit. We also recognize that there is debate over the merits and liabilities of objectives in their varied forms. We concentrate mainly on those objectives that we believe are most useful for identifying the intended cognitive outcomes of schooling, for guiding the selection of effective instructional activities, and for selecting or designing appropriate assessments. We understand that other types and forms of objectives may be useful in different ways.

THE STRUCTURE OF OBJECTIVES

The most commonly used model of educational objectives is based on the work of Ralph Tyler (1949). Tyler suggested that "the most useful form for stating objectives is to express them in terms which identify both the kind of *behavior* to be developed in the student and the *content* . . . in which this behavior is to operate" (p. 30) (emphasis ours). In Chapter 1 we indicated that a statement of an objective contains a verb and a noun. We went on to say that the verb generally describes the intended *cognitive process*, and the noun generally describes the *knowledge* students are expected to acquire or construct. In our formulation, then, we used "cognitive process" in place of "behavior" and "knowledge" in place of "content." Because these substitutions were intentional, let us consider them in greater detail.

CONTENT VERSUS KNOWLEDGE

In the educational literature, content is often discussed but rarely defined. We read of content domains and disciplinary content (Doyle, 1992), content knowledge and pedagogical content knowledge (Shulman, 1987). The *Merriam-Webster Dictionary* (online at *www.m-w.com/home*) contains several definitions of *content*. The one most pertinent to our discussion is "matter dealt with in a field of study." This definition suggests that content is equivalent to what has traditionally been referred to as "subject matter" (that is, a content domain).

The dictionary lists as a synonym, "substance." When applied to a particular subject matter, then, content is its substance.

Who determines the substance of a given subject matter? Traditionally, this task has fallen to scholars who have spent their lives studying and working in a field: mathematicians, scientists, historians, and the like. Over time they reach a consensus on what might be termed the "historically shared knowledge" that defines the subject matter of their academic discipline. This "historically shared knowledge" is not static; changes are made as new ideas and evidence are accepted by the scholarly community. In this context, then, content is "historically shared knowledge." Accordingly, we use the term *knowledge* to reflect our belief that disciplines are constantly changing and evolving in terms of the knowledge that shares a consensus of acceptance within the discipline.

"Knowledge" and "subject matter content" are also related in another way, however. Confusion often arises between subject matter as the knowledge in an academic discipline and subject matter as the materials used to convey the knowledge to students. For educational purposes, subject matter content must be "packaged" in some way. Examples of packaging include textbooks, grade levels, courses, and, increasingly, multimedia "packages." Packaging involves selecting and organizing content so it can be presented in "forms that are pedagogically powerful and yet adaptive to the variations in ability and background presented by the students" (Shulman, 1987, p. 15). This confusion between subject matter as the content of a discipline and "packaged subject matter" designed to promote learning is largely eliminated by referring to the former as knowledge and the latter as curricular materials, instructional materials, or simply materials.

In summary, then, we have two reasons for substituting "knowledge" for "content." The first is to emphasize the fact that subject matter content is "historically shared knowledge" that is arrived at through a currently shared consensus within a discipline and is subject to change over time. The second reason is to differentiate the subject matter content of an academic discipline from the materials in which the content is embedded.

BEHAVIOR VERSUS COGNITIVE PROCESSES

In retrospect, Tyler's choice of the word *behavior* was unfortunate for at least two reasons. First, because behaviorism was the predominant theory of psychology at the time, many people incorrectly equated Tyler's use of the term *behavior* with behaviorism. From Tyler's perspective, a change in behavior was the intended result of instruction. Specifying student behavior was intended to make general and abstract learning goals more specific and concrete, thus enabling teachers to guide instruction and provide evidence of learning. If the teacher could describe the behavior to be attained, it could be recognized easily when learning occurred.

Behaviorism, in contrast, was a means by which desired ends could be achieved. Principles of instruction, within the context of behaviorism, included instrumental conditioning and the formation of stimulus-response associations. It was not surprising then that critics who confused behaviors with behaviorism suggested that Tyler's objectives were oriented mainly toward teaching through manipulation and control.

Second, aided by the popularity of management-by-objectives, task analysis, and programmed instruction in the 1950s and 1960s, *behavior* became an adjective modifying objectives. The level of specificity and detail of these new "behavioral objectives" went well beyond Tyler's original concept of objectives to include the conditions under which students were to demonstrate their learning and the standards of performance that would indicate that successful learning had taken place. Consider this typical behavioral objective of the 1950s and 1960s: "**Given a map or chart**, the student will correctly define *six of the eight* representational devices and symbols on it." The bold print indicates the conditions; the italicized material indicates the standard of performance. It is understandable that critics who equated Tyler's more generally stated objectives with behavioral objectives saw them as narrow and inadequate.

In part to eliminate confusion, we have replaced "behavior" with the term "cognitive process." This change reflects the fact that cognitive psychology and cognitive science have become the dominant perspectives in psychology and education. We can make better sense of the verbs in objectives by using the knowledge gained from cognitive research. To illustrate this point, consider the following set of verbs: *list, write, state, classify, explain,* and *attribute.*

The first three verbs—*list, write,* and *state*—are staples of traditional behavioral objectives (e.g., "The students will be able to list three reasons for the rise of communism in Eastern Europe"). However, these verbs are vague in terms of their underlying cognitive processes. How, for example, did the students arrive at their lists? Did they remember a list provided by the teacher or encountered in a textbook? Or, did they analyze material contained in several books to develop their lists? In this case, a single verb—*list*—can be associated with two very different Taxonomy categories—*Remember* and *Analyze.*

In contrast, the second set of three verbs—*classify, explain,* and *attribute*—have specific meanings within our framework. *Classify* means to determine whether something belongs to a particular category. *Explain* means to construct a cause-and-effect model of a system. *Attribute* means to determine the point of view, bias, values, or intent underlying presented material. This increased specificity helps us focus on what we want students to learn (e.g., "classify") rather than on how we expect them to demonstrate their learning (e.g., "list"). Our use of the term "cognitive process" in place of "behavior" thus not only eliminates the confusion with behaviorism but also reflects our effort to incorporate cognitive psychological research findings into our revision of the framework.

Accordingly the two main dimensions of the Taxonomy Table are the four types of knowledge and the six major cognitive process categories.

SPECIFICITY OF OBJECTIVES

The general domain of objectives is best represented as a continuum ranging from quite general to very specific. Along this continuum, Krathwohl and Payne (1971) identified three levels of specificity called global, educational, and instructional guidance objectives, with the latter now more commonly referred to as instructional objectives. As we discuss these three levels, you should bear in mind that they represent three positions on a continuum of specificity, so that classifying any objective involves a judgment about the level in which it best fits.

GLOBAL OBJECTIVES

Global objectives are complex, multifaceted learning outcomes that require substantial time and instruction to accomplish. They are broadly stated and encompass a large number of more specific objectives. Here are three examples of global objectives:

- All students will start school ready to learn.
- All students will leave Grades 4, 8, and 12 having demonstrated competency over challenging subject matter.
- All students will learn to use their mind well, so they will be prepared for responsible citizenship, further learning, and productive employment in our nation's economy.

These global objectives are taken from *Goals 2000*, a set of goals for U.S. education to be achieved by the year 2000 (U.S. Department of Education, 1994).

The function of global objectives, or goals, is to provide a vision of the future and a rallying cry for policy makers, curriculum developers, teachers, and the public at large. The goals indicate in a broad-brush way what is deemed relevant in a good education. Thus, a global objective is "something presently out of reach; it is something to strive for, to move toward, or to become. It is an aim or purpose so stated that it excites the imagination and gives people something they want to work for" (Kappel, 1960, p. 38).

EDUCATIONAL OBJECTIVES

For teachers to use global objectives in their planning and teaching, the objectives must be broken down into a more focused, delimited form. The very generality of global objectives that is necessary to "excite the imagination" makes them difficult to use to plan classroom activities, define suitable assessment procedures, and evaluate student performances in a meaningful way. More specific objectives are necessary for those tasks.

One of the main aims of the original *Handbook* was to focus attention on objectives somewhat more specific than global objectives. These were called educational objectives. The following objectives, taken from the *Handbook*, illustrate the nature and increased specificity of educational objectives:

- "The ability to read musical scores" (p. 92)
- "The ability to interpret various types of social data" (p. 94)
- "Skill in distinguishing facts from hypotheses" (p. 146)

Consistent with Tyler's description of educational objectives, each of these objectives describes a student behavior (e.g., to read, to interpret, to distinguish) and some content topic (e.g., musical scores, various types of social data, facts and hypotheses) on which the behavior will be performed.

Educational objectives occupy the middle range on the objective continuum. As such, they are more specific than global objectives but more general than the objectives needed to guide the day-to-day classroom instruction that teachers provide.

INSTRUCTIONAL OBJECTIVES

Subsequent to publication of the *Handbook*, educational trends created a need for even more specific objectives (Airasian, 1994; Sosniak, 1994). The purpose of these instructional objectives was to focus teaching and testing on narrow, day-to-day slices of learning in fairly specific content areas. Examples of instructional objectives follow:

- The student is able to differentiate among four common punctuation marks.
- The student learns to add two one-digit numbers.
- The student is able to cite three causes of the Civil War.
- The student is able to classify objectives as global, educational, or instructional.

Instructional objectives have substantially greater specificity than educational objectives.

SUMMARY OF LEVELS OF OBJECTIVES

Table 2.1 compares the scope, time dimension, function, and use of the three levels of objectives. In terms of scope, global objectives are "broad," whereas instructional objectives are "narrow"; that is, global objectives do not deal with specifics, and instructional objectives deal only with specifics. Global objectives may require one or even many years to learn, whereas instructional objectives can be mastered in a few days. Global objectives provide vision that quite often becomes the basis for support for educational programs. At the other end of the spectrum, instructional objectives are useful for planning daily lessons.

In the middle of the continuum lie educational objectives. They are moderate in scope and provide the basis for planning units containing objectives that

TABLE 2.1 Relationship of Global, Educational, and Instructional Objectives

	LEVEL OF OBJECTIVE		
	GLOBAL	EDUCATIONAL	INSTRUCTIONAL
SCOPE	Broad	Moderate	Narrow
TIME NEEDED TO LEARN	One or more years (often many)	Weeks or months	Hours or days
PURPOSE OR FUNCTION	Provide vision	Design curriculum	Prepare lesson plans
EXAMPLE OF USE	Plan a multiyear curriculum (e.g., elementary reading)	Plan units of instruction	Plan daily activities, experiences, and exercises

require weeks or months to learn. Our framework is designed to facilitate working with educational objectives.

WHAT OBJECTIVES ARE NOT

To this point we have discussed what objectives are. We now discuss what objectives are *not*. Some educators have a tendency to confuse means and ends. Objectives describe ends—intended results, intended outcomes, intended changes. Instructional activities, such as reading the textbook, listening to the teacher, conducting an experiment, and going on a field trip, are all means by which objectives are achieved. Stated simply, instructional activities, if chosen wisely and used properly, lead to the achievement of stated objectives. To emphasize the difference between means and ends—between instructional activities and objectives—the phrases "be able to" or "learn to" are either included or implied in our statements of objectives. Thus, for example, "Students will learn to apply the criteria for writing coherent paragraphs" is a statement of an objective. The act of writing paragraphs is an activity that may or may not lead to the objective. Similarly, "Students will learn the algorithm for solving simultaneous equations in two unknowns" is an objective. The act of working on simultaneous equations is an activity. Once again, students may or may not learn to solve simultaneous equations by working on them.

When objectives are not stated explicitly, they are often implicit in the instructional activity. For example, an activity might be for students to "read *The Sun Also Rises*." To determine the objective associated with this activity, we can ask the teacher, "What do you want your students to learn by reading *The Sun Also Rises*?" The answer to this question is the objective (e.g., "I want my students to understand Hemingway's skill as a writer"). If multiple answers are given, there are likely to be multiple objectives.

Just as instructional activities are not objectives, neither are tests or other forms of assessment. For example, "Students should be able to pass the statewide high school proficiency test" is not an educational objective. To determine the educational objective, we must seek out the knowledge and cognitive processes students must learn or possess to pass the test.

In summary, it is important not to confuse objectives with instructional activities or assessments. Although each of these can be used to help identify and clarify intended student learning outcomes, it is only after an activity or assessment is articulated in terms of intended student learning that the objective becomes evident.

A CHANGING VOCABULARY OF OBJECTIVES

As mentioned in Chapter 1, *objective* is not the only term used to describe an intended student learning outcome. The vocabulary of intended student learning is ever-changing. Today's terminology is driven by the current emphasis on school improvement through standards-based education. At the heart of the standards-based movement is the state-level specification of intended student learning outcomes in different subject matters at each grade level. Generally, statewide assessment programs linked to the standards are intended to monitor the extent to which individual students and entire schools have achieved them.

Despite the recent changes in vocabulary, the various terms used in conjunction with state standards fit nicely into the three levels of objectives: global, educational, and instructional. The following two standards are taken from South Carolina's primary grades mathematics curriculum. In primary mathematics, students will:

- Establish a strong sense of number by exploring concepts such as counting, grouping, place value, and estimating; and
- Develop the concepts of fractions, mixed numbers, and decimals and use models to relate fractions to decimals and to find equivalent fractions.

Though not quite as general as earlier examples of global objectives, these standards are best considered global objectives because they include broad topics (e.g., sense of number) or multiple topics (e.g., fractions, mixed numbers, decimals) and rather vague processes (e.g., establish, explore, and develop).

To assess the attainment of these standards, teachers in South Carolina are provided with more specific objectives called "indicators" for each standard. For the first standard above, sample indicators include:

- Students will be able to write whole numbers in standard form, expanded form, and words; and
- Students will learn to estimate the number of objects in a variety of collections.

For the second standard, sample indicators include:

- Students will understand the meaning of fractions, mixed numbers, and decimals; and

- Students will interpret concrete or pictorial models that represent fractions, mixed numbers, decimals, and their relationships.

These indicators most closely resemble educational objectives, insofar as they narrow the specificity of the global standards to the unit level but not to the lesson level.

Objectives are used not only in standards-based curriculums but also in statewide and district-wide accountability programs designed to determine, among other things, whether a student will be placed in a remedial class, awarded a high school diploma, or promoted to the next grade. When the results of testing are consequential for students or teachers, litigation becomes a possible threat. An accountability program that is linked to clear, publicly stated objectives and standards provides some legal protection.

Objectives, in the form of subject matter standards, have been produced by a variety of professional organizations and associations (e.g., American Association for the Advancement of Science, 1993; National Council for the Social Studies, 1994; National Council of Teachers of English and International Reading Association, 1996; National Research Council, 1996). The National Council of Teachers of Mathematics (NCTM) (1989) was the first association to recommend what were called content standards. One of the NCTM standards states: "In grades 5–8, the mathematics curriculum should include explorations of algebraic concepts and processes." Note that this "standard" describes what the curriculum should include (i.e., the content), not what students are to learn from it (i.e., the objective). Thus, this content standard does not meet our criteria for objectives. However, this content standard can quite easily be translated into an educational objective. Examples include: "The student should understand the concepts of variable, expression, and equation"; "The student should learn to analyze tables and graphs to identify properties and relationships"; and "The student should be able to apply algebraic methods to solve a variety of real-world and mathematical problems."

As mentioned earlier, most standards-based curriculums include both global objectives (i.e., standards) to provide general expectations and educational objectives (i.e., indicators) to guide the design of curriculum units. Since it is difficult to make statewide or national pronouncements regarding the specifics of classroom teaching, standards-based approaches leave the development of instructional objectives to classroom teachers. To develop instructional objectives from indicators, a teacher continues to narrow the cognitive process and content knowledge. Consider, for example, the following educational objective/indicator: "Students will understand the meaning of fractions, mixed numbers, and decimals." Associated instructional objectives might include: "Students will learn to write decimals as fractions and fractions as decimals"; "Students will be able to write equivalent fractions"; and "Students will learn to write mixed numbers as improper fractions and decimals."

When there are no specific instructional objectives, teachers often turn to the assessment instruments to clarify the meaning and instructional focus of global and educational objectives. In these situations, assessment tasks *de facto* become the educational or instructional objectives. Although this is a time-honored practice, it often leads to concerns about teaching to the test.

PROBLEMS WITH OBJECTIVES

Despite the many and widespread uses of objectives in education, authors have raised concerns about their adequacy and consequences (Furst, 1981; De-Landsheere, 1977; Dunne, 1988). In this section we explore some of these concerns, addressing particular issues related to the specificity of objectives, their relationship to teaching, and their claimed value-free status vis-à-vis educational philosophy and curriculum.

SPECIFICITY AND INCLUSIVENESS

Even before the publication of the *Handbook* in 1956, a debate was ongoing about how specific objectives should be. Because global objectives are too general to be of practical use in guiding instruction and assessment, the main debate has focused on educational and instructional objectives.

Like global objectives, educational objectives are criticized as being too general to guide teaching and assessment. They do not provide teachers the specific direction they need to plan, facilitate, and assess student learning (Mager, 1962; Popham, 1969). This argument has some truth. As noted earlier, however, it is also true that educational objectives convey a more open, richer sense of intended student learning than that conveyed by narrower instructional objectives. The authors of the *Handbook* recognized this point and consciously rejected overly narrow objectives, seeking instead objectives that had "a level of generality where the loss by fragmentation would not be too great" (p. 6). Educational objectives were to provide a path to more specific instructional objectives, but the authors aimed to identify the forest before proceeding to the trees.

Moreover, educational objectives allow for classroom teachers to interpret and select the aspects of the educational objective that fit their particular students' needs and readiness. This benefit is consistent with the current emphasis on teacher judgment and empowerment. Many who criticize objectives for being overly specific, constraining, and "behavioral" may not adequately differentiate educational objectives from instructional objectives.

Although the specificity of instructional objectives provides a focus for instruction and assessment, such specificity can lead to large numbers of atomistic, narrow objectives. The question then becomes whether these specific objectives will coalesce into broader, integrated understandings that are more than the sum of the individual objectives (Broudy, 1970; Dunne, 1988; Hirst, 1974).

On a related matter, critics have argued that not all important learning outcomes can be made explicit or operational (Dunne, 1988; Armstrong, 1989; Marsh, 1992) and that the role of tacit understanding and open-ended situations was underrepresented in the *Handbook*. There is, for example, a difference between learning experiences that are expected to lead to common learning out-comes and those that are intended to lead to idiosyncratic learning. Objectives are meant to describe the former. Although learning does result from the latter experiences, it is virtually impossible to specify the nature of that learning in advance.

The lesson from discussions about intended versus unintended learning outcomes is that not all important learning outcomes can, should, or must be stated as a priori objectives. This assertion, however, should not deter efforts to articulate important intended student learning outcomes, even though these may not be the only outcomes that result from classroom instruction.

THE LOCK-STEP NATURE OF OBJECTIVES

A variation on the theme above is the criticism of the lock-step nature of objectives that prescribe the same intended learning outcomes for all students. Eisner (1979) pointed out that not all objectives need to produce the same student learning. In fact, Eisner identifies "expressive outcomes," which he defines as "the consequences of curriculum activities that are intentionally planned to provide a fertile field for personal purposing and experience" (p. 103). An expressive outcome may derive from an experience or activity such as visiting a museum, seeing a play, or listening to classical music. Expressive outcomes result from activities that have no a priori intended learning outcome except that each student will be uniquely changed in some way from exposure to the experience or activity. Such outcomes are evocative, not prescriptive, in the sense that purpose does not precede the activity but rather uniquely grows from it.

Expressive outcome activities result in learning, but what students are expected to learn from participating in these activities cannot be stated in advance. Furthermore, what is learned will likely differ from one student to another. Note that expressive objectives may be more applicable to certain subject areas than others and to more complex forms of cognition than less complex ones. They provide a *direction* for learning but not a particular *destination*.

To some extent, all objectives are expressive, in that not all students learn the same things from the same instruction even when the intended objective is the same. Ancillary learning is always going on. The current emphasis on performance assessment or authentic assessment encourages the use of assessment procedures that allow students to produce a variety of acceptable responses to the same assessment task or set of tasks. Although these newer forms of assessment do not quite mirror the nature of expressive objectives, they are clearly intended to do so. We merely point out that these forms of assessment are more likely to be appropriate for educational objectives than for global and instructional objectives.

WHAT DOES AN OBJECTIVE REPRESENT—LEARNING OR PERFORMANCE?

At the heart of many criticisms of objectives is the question of what an objective really represents (Hirst, 1974; Ginther, 1972). For example, the more specific an objective is, the easier it is to assess, but also the more likely we are to blur the distinction between the intended meaning of the objective and its assessment. Stated simply, the assessed performance is used to make inferences about intended student learning as it is described in the objectives. So-called performance objectives to the contrary, performance is not the objective per se.

Furthermore, with few exceptions, the tasks (e.g., questions, test items, problems) used to assess an objective are only a sample of the possible tasks that could be used. Consider the following instructional objective: "The student will learn to add three two-digit numbers with regrouping." This objective can be assessed by many items because of the many possible two-digit combinations from which to select (e.g., 25 + 12 + 65; 15 + 23 + 42; 89 + 96 + 65). Inevitably, teachers select a sample of the possible tasks and use students' performance on that sample to infer how they would do on other similar, but unassessed, tasks. The more general an objective, the larger the universe of possible assessment tasks.

Now compare the relatively narrow range of evidence needed to assess the two-digit addition objective with the broader range of evidence needed to assess learning of the following educational objective: "The student will learn to apply various economic theories." The specificity of the first objective permits inferences to be made about student learning from relatively few assessment tasks. In contrast, the second objective is much broader, thereby allowing for an almost unlimited set of assessment tasks. Because any single assessment can sample only a small portion of the assessment tasks, the more general an objective, the less confident one is about how adequately a student's performance validly represents his or her learning across its full breadth. Again, this concern is particularly salient when objectives emphasize more general knowledge categories or more complex cognitive processes.

THE RESTRICTED USE OF OBJECTIVES

Critics have pointed out that the ease of stating objectives differs greatly from one subject matter to another (Stenhouse, 1970–71; Seddon, 1978; Kelly, 1989). Stating objectives in creative writing, poetry, and art interpretation, for example, may be difficult. When required to formulate objectives, teachers in these areas may select lower-level objectives that are easy to state but do not really represent what they believe to be important for their students to learn. Alternatively, objectives that appear to call for complex student learning may not actually do so in light of how the objectives are taught and/or assessed. Correctly classifying an objective requires either knowing or inferring how the objective was taught by the teacher and learned by the student.

In some subject areas, it may be easy to state objectives but difficult to obtain broad community endorsement for the objectives. Especially in subjects such as social studies, sex education, and religion, differences in values and political views lead to difficulties in reaching a consensus about the appropriateness of stated objectives. In these cases it is usually easier to obtain agreement on global objectives (e.g., good citizenship) than on more specific educational and instructional ones.

Difficulty is inherent in stating objectives in some areas and in obtaining consensus on objectives in others. In fact, these are the two reasons that objectives in some subject areas are limited, if they are stated at all. Given the importance of objectives, however, these problems are to be overcome, not avoided.

CONCLUDING COMMENT

Our framework is a tool to help educators clarify and communicate what they intend students to learn as a result of instruction. We call these intentions "objectives." To facilitate communication, we have adopted a standard format for stating objectives: "The student will be able to, or learn to, _verb_ _noun_," where the verb indicates the cognitive process and the noun generally indicates the knowledge. Furthermore, although objectives can range from very broad to highly specific, we prefer and advocate the use of the midrange, that is, educational objectives.

Our focus on objectives does not encompass all possible and important student learning outcomes, in part because we focus exclusively on cognitive outcomes. In addition, we do not deny that incidental learning takes place in every school and classroom. Where learning cannot be anticipated, however, it lies beyond the scope of our work. Similarly, expressive experiences produce a myriad of unanticipated reactions and responses that depend largely on the students themselves. Our omission of incidental learning and expressive experiences does not mean they are not important or useful in many situations.

In sum, our emphasis is on student-oriented, learning-based, explicit, and assessable statements of intended cognitive outcomes. By adopting this emphasis, we are following the lead of the authors of the original _Handbook_. We have, like them, endeavored to produce a framework that we anticipate will be used in many but not all ways, by many but not all educators.

The Revised Taxonomy Structure

CHAPTER 3

The Taxonomy Table

As we mentioned in Chapter 1, our framework can be represented in a two-dimensional table that we call the Taxonomy Table (see Table 3.1. For convenient reference, it is also reproduced on the inside front cover). The rows and columns of the table contain carefully delineated and defined categories of knowledge and cognitive processes, respectively. The cells of the table are where the knowledge and cognitive process dimensions intersect. Objectives, either explicitly or implicitly, include both knowledge and cognitive processes that can be classified in the Taxonomy framework. Therefore, objectives can be placed in the cells of the table. It should be possible to place any educational objective that has a cognitive emphasis in one or more cells of the table.

CATEGORIES OF THE KNOWLEDGE DIMENSION

After considering the various designations of knowledge types, especially developments in cognitive psychology that have taken place since the original framework's creation, we settled on four general types of knowledge: *Factual, Conceptual, Procedural,* and *Metacognitive.* Table 3.2 summarizes these four major types of knowledge and their associated subtypes.

Factual knowledge is knowledge of discrete, isolated content elements—"bits of information" (p. 45). It includes knowledge of terminology and knowledge of specific details and elements. In contrast, *Conceptual knowledge* is knowledge of "more complex, organized knowledge forms" (p. 48). It includes knowledge of classifications and categories, principles and generalizations, and theories, models, and structures.

Procedural knowledge is "knowledge of how to do something" (p. 52). It includes knowledge of skills and algorithms, techniques and methods, as well as knowledge of the criteria used to determine and/or justify "when to do what" within specific domains and disciplines. Finally, *Metacognitive knowledge* is "knowledge about cognition in general as well as awareness of and knowledge about one's own cognition" (p. 55). It encompasses strategic knowledge; knowledge about cognitive tasks, including contextual and conditional knowledge; and self-knowledge. Of course, certain aspects of metacognitive knowledge are

3.1 THE TAXONOMY TABLE

THE KNOWLEDGE DIMENSION	THE COGNITIVE PROCESS DIMENSION					
	1. REMEMBER	2. UNDERSTAND	3. APPLY	4. ANALYZE	5. EVALUATE	6. CREATE
A. FACTUAL KNOWLEDGE						
B. CONCEPTUAL KNOWLEDGE						
C. PROCEDURAL KNOWLEDGE						
D. META-COGNITIVE KNOWLEDGE						

3.2 THE MAJOR TYPES AND SUBTYPES OF THE KNOWLEDGE DIMENSION*

MAJOR TYPES AND SUBTYPES	EXAMPLES
A. FACTUAL KNOWLEDGE—The basic elements students must know to be acquainted with a discipline or solve problems in it	
AA. Knowledge of terminology	Technical vocabulary, musical symbols
AB. Knowledge of specific details and elements	Major natural resources, reliable sources of information
B. CONCEPTUAL KNOWLEDGE—The interrelationships among the basic elements within a larger structure that enable them to function together	
BA. Knowledge of classifications and categories	Periods of geological time, forms of business ownership
BB. Knowledge of principles and generalizations	Pythagorean theorem, law of supply and demand
BC. Knowledge of theories, models, and structures	Theory of evolution, structure of Congress
C. PROCEDURAL KNOWLEDGE—How to do something, methods of inquiry, and criteria for using skills, algorithms, techniques, and methods	
CA. Knowledge of subject-specific skills and algorithms	Skills used in painting with watercolors, whole-number division algorithm
CB. Knowledge of subject-specific techniques and methods	Interviewing techniques, scientific method
CC. Knowledge of criteria for determining when to use appropriate procedures	Criteria used to determine when to apply a procedure involving Newton's second law, criteria used to judge the feasibility of using a particular method to estimate business costs
D. METACOGNITIVE KNOWLEDGE—Knowledge of cognition in general as well as awareness and knowledge of one's own cognition	
DA. Strategic knowledge	Knowledge of outlining as a means of capturing the structure of a unit of subject matter in a textbook, knowledge of the use of heuristics
DB. Knowledge about cognitive tasks, including appropriate contextual and conditional knowledge	Knowledge of the types of tests particular teachers administer, knowledge of the cognitive demands of different tasks
DC. Self-knowledge	Knowledge that critiquing essays is a personal strength, whereas writing essays is a personal weakness; awareness of one's own knowledge level

not the same as knowledge that is defined consensually by experts. This issue is discussed in more detail in Chapter 4.

CATEGORIES OF THE COGNITIVE PROCESS DIMENSION

The categories of the cognitive process dimension are intended to provide a comprehensive set of classifications for those student cognitive processes that are included in objectives. As shown in Table 3.1, the categories range from the cognitive processes most commonly found in objectives, those associated with *Remember,* through *Understand* and *Apply,* to those less frequently found, *Analyze, Evaluate,* and *Create. Remember* means to retrieve relevant knowledge from long-term memory. *Understand* is defined as constructing the meaning of instructional messages, including oral, written, and graphic communication. *Apply* means carrying out or using a procedure in a given situation. *Analyze* is breaking material into its constituent parts and determining how the parts are related to one another as well as to an overall structure or purpose. *Evaluate* means making judgments based on criteria and/or standards. Finally, *Create* is putting elements together to form a novel, coherent whole or to make an original product.

Each of the six major categories is associated with two or more specific cognitive processes, 19 in all, also described by verb forms (see Table 3.3). To differentiate the specific cognitive processes from the six categories, the specific cognitive processes take the form of gerunds, ending in "ing." Thus, *recognizing* and *recalling* are associated with *Remember; interpreting, exemplifying, classifying, summarizing, inferring, comparing,* and *explaining* are associated with *Understand; executing* and *implementing* with *Apply;* and so on.

THE TAXONOMY TABLE AND OBJECTIVES: A DIAGRAMMATIC SUMMARY

Figure 3.1 depicts the analytic journey from the statement of an objective to its placement in the Taxonomy Table. The journey begins by locating the verb and noun in the objective. The verb is examined in the context of the six categories of the cognitive process dimension: *Remember, Understand, Apply, Analyze, Evaluate,* and *Create.* Placing the verb into the appropriate category is usually facilitated by focusing initially on the 19 specific cognitive processes, rather than on the larger categories. Likewise, the noun is examined in the context of the four types in the knowledge dimension: *Factual, Conceptual, Procedural,* and *Metacognitive.* Again, focusing initially on the subtypes within the knowledge categories typically aids in the proper placement. One can classify the objective as initially stated, as it was taught, and as it was assessed, and ask whether these classifications are aligned. This latter process is illustrated in the vignettes in Chapters 8–13.

Consider the rather straightforward example shown in Figure 3.1: "The student will learn to apply the reduce-reuse-recycle approach to conservation."

3.3 THE SIX CATEGORIES OF THE COGNITIVE PROCESS DIMENSION AND RELATED COGNITIVE PROCESSES*

PROCESS CATEGORIES	COGNITIVE PROCESSES AND EXAMPLES
1. REMEMBER—Retrieve relevant knowledge from long-term memory.	
1.1 RECOGNIZING	(e.g., Recognize the dates of important events in U.S. history)
1.2 RECALLING	(e.g., Recall the dates of important events in U.S. history)
2. UNDERSTAND—Construct meaning from instructional messages, including oral, written, and graphic communication.	
2.1 INTERPRETING	(e.g., Paraphrase important speeches and documents)
2.2 EXEMPLIFYING	(e.g., Give examples of various artistic painting styles)
2.3 CLASSIFYING	(e.g., Classify observed or described cases of mental disorders)
2.4 SUMMARIZING	(e.g., Write a short summary of the events portrayed on videotapes)
2.5 INFERRING	(e.g., In learning a foreign language, infer grammatical principles from examples)
2.6 COMPARING	(e.g., Compare historical events to contemporary situations)
2.7 EXPLAINING	(e.g., Explain the causes of important eighteenth-century events in France)
3. APPLY—Carry out or use a procedure in a given situation.	
3.1 EXECUTING	(e.g., Divide one whole number by another whole number, both with multiple digits)
3.2 IMPLEMENTING	(e.g., Determine in which situations Newton's second law is appropriate)
4. ANALYZE—Break material into constituent parts and determine how parts relate to one another and to an overall structure or purpose.	
4.1 DIFFERENTIATING	(e.g., Distinguish between relevant and irrelevant numbers in a mathematical word problem)
4.2 ORGANIZING	(e.g., Structure evidence in a historical description into evidence for and against a particular historical explanation)
4.3 ATTRIBUTING	(e.g., Determine the point of view of the author of an essay in terms of his or her political perspective)
5. EVALUATE—Make judgments based on criteria and standards.	
5.1 CHECKING	(e.g., Determine whether a scientist's conclusions follow from observed data)
5.2 CRITIQUING	(e.g., Judge which of two methods is the best way to solve a given problem)
6. CREATE—Put elements together to form a coherent or functional whole; reorganize elements into a new pattern or structure.	
6.1 GENERATING	(e.g., Generate hypotheses to acount for an observed phenomenon)
6.2 PLANNING	(e.g., Plan a research paper on a given historical topic)
6.3 PRODUCING	(e.g., Build habitats for certain species for certain purposes)

FIGURE 3.1   HOW AN OBJECTIVE (THE STUDENT WILL LEARN TO APPLY THE REDUCE-REUSE-RECYCLE APPROACH TO CONSERVATION) IS CLASSIFIED IN THE TAXONOMY TABLE

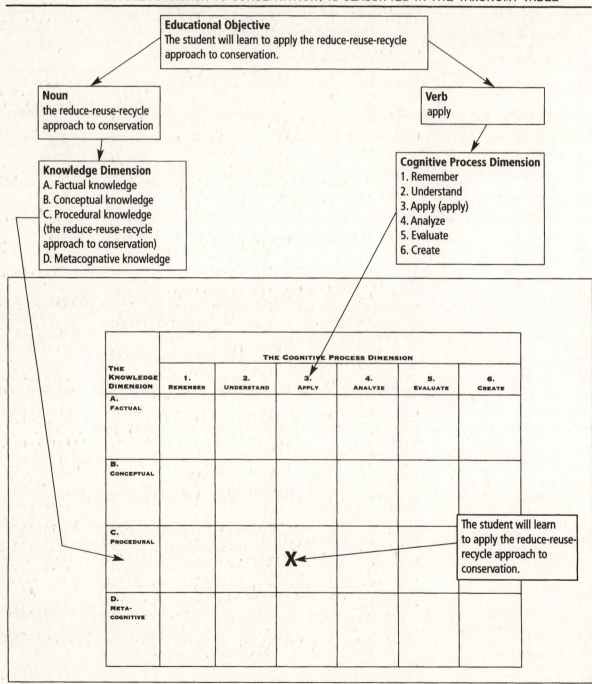

The verb is "apply." Since *Apply* is one of the six cognitive process categories, we have to look no further than the six categories in this example. The noun phrase is "the reduce-reuse-recycle approach to conservation." An approach is a method or technique, and in Table 3.2 methods and techniques are associated with *Procedural knowledge*. Thus, this objective is placed in the cell corresponding to the intersection of *Apply* and *Procedural knowledge*.

Unfortunately, classifying objectives is often more difficult than this example suggests. There are two reasons for this difficulty. The first is that statements of objectives may contain more than verbs and nouns. In the objective "The student will be able to give examples of the law of supply and demand in the local community," for example, the phrase "in the local community" is extraneous for our classification. The verb is "exemplify" (i.e., "to give examples") and the noun phrase is "the law of supply and demand." The phrase "in the local community" establishes the conditions within which the examples must be selected.

Consider a third objective: "The student will be able to produce original works that meet the criteria of appropriate oral and written forms." The verb is "produce" and the noun is "criteria." The phrase "of appropriate oral and written forms" simply clarifies the meaning of "criteria." So, modifying phrases or clauses should be ignored in classifying the objective; they may cause confusion when one is attempting to identify relevant parts for categorizing.

The second reason for the difficulty in classifying objectives is that the verb may be ambiguous in terms of the intended cognitive process or the noun may be ambiguous in its intended knowledge. Consider the following objective: "The student will learn to describe changes in matter and the causes of those changes." "Describe" can mean many things. Students can describe what they have recalled, interpreted, explained, or generated. *Recalling, interpreting, explaining,* and *generating* are quite different processes. One would have to infer which process the teacher intended in order to classify the objective.

Similarly, in some statements of objectives, the noun tells us little if anything about the relevant knowledge. This is a particular problem with objectives that address more complex cognitive processes. Consider the following objective: "The student will be able to evaluate editorials in newspapers and news magazines." The verb is "evaluate," and the noun phrase is "editorials in newspapers and news magazines." As we discussed in Chapter 2, editorials are curricular or instructional materials, not knowledge. In this case, the knowledge is implicit—namely, the criteria students should use to evaluate the editorials (e.g., presence or absence of bias, clarity of point of view, logic of the argument). So, the objective should be classified as *Evaluate* and *Conceptual knowledge*.

It should now be evident that the people who are classifying objectives must make inferences. Consider the following two objectives; the first is rather straightforward, and the second requires more inference.

The first objective is "The student should be able to plan a unit of instruction for a particular teaching situation" (*Handbook,* p. 171). This objective combines the unit plan (the noun) with the act of planning (the verb). Where does this objective fit in the Taxonomy Table? Plans are *models* that guide future actions. Referring back to Table 3.2, we see that "models" appears in the third subtype of *Conceptual knowledge*, the second row of the Taxonomy Table (i.e., row B). Referring to Table 3.3, we see that "planning" is the second cognitive process within *Create*, the sixth column of the Taxonomy Table (i.e., column 6). Our analysis suggests that the objective falls into the cell corresponding to the intersection of row B, *Conceptual knowledge*, and column 6, *Create*. This objective, then, has to do with students *creating conceptual knowledge.*

The second objective is "The student should be able to recognize the point of view or bias of a writer of a historical account" (*Handbook,* p. 148). In this case, the noun is "historical account." Like textbooks and essays, a historical account is best considered curricular or instructional material. The question remains, then, what type of knowledge is involved. We suggest two possibilities: *Factual knowledge* or *Conceptual knowledge.* Which type it is depends on (1) the structure of the account, (2) the way the account is "introduced" to the students, or most likely (3) some combination of these. The verb phrase is "recognize the point of view or bias." The verb is *not* "recognize." If it were "recognize," we would place it in the category *Remember.* However, the act of recognizing (i.e., determining) a point of view or bias defines the cognitive process *attributing* (see Table 3.3). *Attributing* is associated with *Analyze,* a category at a much higher level of complexity. So we place the objective somewhere in the fourth column, *Analyze.* Since the knowledge could be either of two types, *Factual knowledge* or *Conceptual knowledge,* we place the objective in two cells, one corresponding to the intersection of *Analyze* and *Factual knowledge* (cell A4) and the other to the intersection of *Analyze* and *Conceptual knowledge* (cell B4).

To confuse matters even further, the teacher could teach students **how to** recognize points of view or biases, and this would be *Procedural knowledge.* Since students would be expected to **use** the *Procedural knowledge* (as taught to them) with the historical account, the cognitive process category would likely shift from *Analyze* to *Apply.* Now the objective would be placed in cell C3.

In summary, then, the Taxonomy Table can be used to categorize objectives, provided that the person or persons doing the categorization make correct inferences. Because inference is involved and because each person may have access to different information, individuals may disagree about the correct classification of an objective. As seen throughout this chapter, the most obvious source of information is the objective as stated, but the stated objective and the objective as taught and assessed may differ. So, other sources of information to be considered are observations of classrooms, examinations of test items and other assessment tasks, and discussions with or among teachers. From our experience, using multiple sources of information is likely to result in the most valid, defensible classification of objectives.

WHY CATEGORIZE OBJECTIVES?

Why would anyone want to categorize objectives? What is the point of using our framework to guide the classification? We offer six answers to these questions. The first is that *categorization within our framework permits educators to examine objectives from the student's point of view.* What is it that students must know and be able to do in order to achieve a particular objective? Will a "grocery list" of discrete facts suffice (*Factual knowledge*), or do students need some cohesive structure that holds these facts together (*Conceptual knowledge*)? Do students need to be able to classify (*Understand*), to differentiate (*Analyze*), or to do both? We typically ask these questions as we work with objectives within our framework in an attempt to answer the "learning question" (see Chapter 1).

Our second answer is that *categorization within our framework helps educators consider the panorama of possibilities in education.* This was one of the primary values of the original *Handbook,* raising the possibility of teaching for so-called higher-order objectives. Our revision adds the possibility and desirability of objectives that emphasize *Metacognitive knowledge.* Metacognitive knowledge is empowering to students and is an important basis for "learning how to learn" (Bransford, Brown, and Cocking, 1999). Classifying objectives for this purpose once again helps us address the "learning question."

The third answer is that *categorization within our framework helps educators see the integral relationship between knowledge and cognitive processes inherent in objectives.* Can students realistically be expected to *apply factual knowledge,* or is it easier for them if they are helped to *understand procedural knowledge* before they attempt to apply it? Can students learn to *understand conceptual knowledge* by having them *analyze factual knowledge*? These are the types of questions we ask as we struggle to answer the "instruction question."

Our fourth answer to the question of why anyone would want to categorize objectives is consistent with the original *Handbook: It makes life easier!* With the Taxonomy in place, examiners do not have to approach every objective as a unique entity. Rather, they can say to themselves, "Oh, this is an analysis objective. I know how to write examination items for analysis objectives." They can pull out their "templates" (the sample test items in the *Handbook*) and, with modifications dictated by differences in subject matters, write several items in a fairly short time. Thus, by classifying objectives we are more able to deal with the "assessment question."

Likewise, we expect those who use the Taxonomy Table to come to a common realization: "Oh, this is an objective that emphasizes *understanding conceptual knowledge.* I know how to teach for *Conceptual knowledge* objectives. I could focus on critical attributes of the concept. For many kinds of *Conceptual knowledge,* I could include examples and nonexamples. I may want to embed a particular concept within a larger conceptual framework and discuss similarities and differences within the framework." Similar statements can be made for assessment: "I could design assessment tasks that require students to *exemplify* and *classify.* I need to ensure that the assessment tasks are not identical to those in the textbook or those I used during class." So, once again, classifying objectives helps us deal with the "instruction and assessment questions."

Our fifth answer is that *categorization makes more readily apparent the consistency, or lack of it, among the stated objectives for a unit, the way it was taught, and how learning was assessed.* Comparisons of the categorizations based on stated objectives, instructional activities, and assessment tasks show whether these phases of the educational experience are congruent with one another both in their nature and in their relative emphasis. An important caveat was suggested, however, by a teacher, Melody Shank, who reviewed an earlier draft of our revision (personal communication, 1998):

> I can imagine teachers fretting over whether they placed their objectives, activities, and assessments in the proper cell . . . instead of thoughtfully examining their implicit and explicit objectives, planned activities, and assessments. Becoming aware of whether their planned activities are aligned with their intended (stated or intuited) objectives and how they might adjust those activities is the important activity, not whether they have each component instructional part in the proper cell. . . . I would want teachers to have thoughtful, productive discussion throughout the analysis, rather than arguments about the proper placement of the items in the table.

This comment states well the emphasis that we place on the use of the Taxonomy Table and that will be exemplified in the later analysis of the vignettes. So, classifying objectives helps educators deal with the "alignment question."

The sixth and final answer is that *categorization within our framework helps educators make better sense of the wide variety of terms that are used in education.* Our 19 cognitive processes have very specific meanings. *Inferring* requires that students recognize some pattern in the information given, whereas *explaining* requires a search for causality in that pattern. *Implementing* requires adjusting a process to a new situation; *executing* does not. *Generating* requires divergent thinking, whereas *organizing* requires convergence. *Checking* concerns internal consistency; *critiquing,* consistency with external criteria. To the extent that we can associate other words and terms with our framework, then, we increase their level of precision. With increased precision comes the likelihood for better communication.

OUR USE OF MULTIPLE FORMS OF DEFINITION

To be useful, the definitions of the knowledge types and subtypes and the process categories and specific cognitive processes must be understood clearly and precisely. Since multiple kinds of definition tend to contribute to greater understanding, we present four definitional forms in the chapters that follow: verbal descriptions, sample objectives, sample assessment tasks, and sample instructional activities.

VERBAL DESCRIPTIONS

Verbal descriptions are similar to good dictionary definitions. Furthermore, "the exact phrasing of these definitions has been the subject of much debate among us and while the present definitions are far from ideal, every effort has been made to describe the major aspects of each category as carefully as possible" (*Handbook*, p. 44). That statement made by the original group applies to this volume as well. The verbal descriptions are given in Chapters 4 and 5.

SAMPLE OBJECTIVES

Sample objectives provide a second means of understanding the categories. The sources of the sample objectives are attributed where they appear. Some were taken from publicly available statements, like those of *Goals 2000* and of the National Council of Teachers of Mathematics, because they typify objectives of interest and concern to many teachers at present. Teachers' editions of textbooks, test publishers' manuals, and vignettes prepared by teachers (see Section III) were additional sources.

SAMPLE ASSESSMENT TASKS

The sample assessment tasks in Chapter 5 and the assessments in the vignettes provide yet another means of understanding the categories in our framework. The tasks were chosen to illustrate some ways of assessing combinations of knowledge and cognitive processes. Some people consider the means used to assess learning as the "real" goals of instruction because, regardless of fancy statements, the concrete representation of objectives in tests and other assessments often determines what students study as well as how they study it.

SAMPLE INSTRUCTIONAL ACTIVITIES

The illustrative instructional activities in the vignettes offer our fourth and final way of understanding the categories of the framework. These vignettes provide additional examples of both knowledge and cognitive processes and, perhaps more important, their interplay. In addition to aiding in the understanding of the categories, the vignettes are designed to make the Taxonomy Table more useful and usable for teachers, teacher educators, curriculum developers, assessment specialists, and educational administrators.

CLOSING COMMENT: A LOOK AHEAD

Having examined the classification of objectives in the Taxonomy Table, we now turn to a detailed examination of the two dimensions that make up the table: knowledge and cognitive process. The four types of knowledge together with their subtypes are described in Chapter 4. The six major cognitive process categories and the 19 cognitive processes that help define them are described in Chapter 5.

CHAPTER 4

The Knowledge Dimension

Current conceptions of learning focus on the active, cognitive, and constructive processes involved in meaningful learning. Learners are assumed to be active agents in their own learning; they select the information to which they will attend and construct their own meaning from this selected information. Learners are not passive recipients, nor are they simple recorders of information provided to them by parents, teachers, textbooks, or media. This move away from passive views of learning toward more cognitive and constructivist perspectives emphasizes what learners **know** (knowledge) and **how they think** (cognitive processes) about what they know as they actively engage in meaningful learning.

In instructional settings, learners are assumed to construct their own meaning based on their prior knowledge, their current cognitive and metacognitive activity, and the opportunities and constraints they are afforded in the setting, including the information that is available to them. Learners come into any instructional setting with a broad array of knowledge, their own goals, and prior experiences in that setting, and they use all of these to "make sense" of the information they encounter. This constructivist process of "making sense" involves the activation of prior knowledge as well as various cognitive processes that operate on that knowledge.

It is important to keep in mind that students can and often do use the information available to them to construct meanings that do not coincide with authentic aspects of reality or with well-accepted, normative conceptions of the information. In fact, much of the literature on conceptual change and student learning is concerned with how students come to construct conceptions of everyday phenomena, such as heat, temperature, and gravity, that **do not** match the commonly accepted scientific knowledge and models of these phenomena. Of course, there are different stances to take on these "personal" conceptions, "naive" conceptions, or "misconceptions." In our opinion, educators should guide students toward the authentic and normative conceptions that reflect the most commonly accepted and best current knowledge and thinking in the academic disciplines and subject matter areas.

Accordingly, we are fully aware that students and teachers construct their own meanings from instructional activities and classroom events and that their own constructions of the subject matter content may differ from authentic or normative conceptions. Nevertheless, adopting this cognitive and constructivist perspective does not imply that there is no knowledge worth learning or that all knowledge is of equal worth. Teachers can, do, and should make decisions about what is worth teaching in their classrooms. As we pointed out in Chapters 1 and 2, a key question concerns what students should learn in school. Educational objectives offer teachers some guidance as they try to determine what to teach.

The four types of knowledge described in this chapter can help educators distinguish what to teach. They are designed to reflect the intermediate level of specificity associated with educational objectives. As such, their level of generality allows them to be applied to all grade levels and subject matters. Of course, some grade levels or subject matters may be more likely to have a greater number of objectives that can be classified as, say, *Conceptual knowledge*. This is most likely a function of the content of the subject matter, beliefs about students and the way they learn, the way in which the subject matter is viewed by the teacher, or some combination of these factors. Nonetheless, we argue that the four types of knowledge included in our framework are useful for thinking about teaching in a wide variety of subject matters as well as at different grade levels.

A DISTINCTION BETWEEN KNOWLEDGE AND SUBJECT MATTER CONTENT: A TALE OF FOUR TEACHERS

We begin by illustrating the important distinction between knowledge and content made on pages 12–13. The example involves four teachers—Mrs. Patterson, Ms. Chang, Mr. Jefferson, and Mrs. Weinberg—and their educational objectives for a unit on *Macbeth*. Each has a different perspective on what students should learn during the unit. Of course, all four teachers have multiple educational objectives, but the example highlights how these teachers focus on objectives that reflect different types of knowledge.

Mrs. Patterson believes that her students should know the names of the characters in the play and the readily apparent relationships among them (e.g., Macbeth and MacDuff were enemies). Students should know the details of the plot, and they should know which characters said what, even to the point that they can recite certain important passages from memory. Because Mrs. Patterson focuses on the specific details and elements of *Macbeth*, in the language of the Taxonomy Table she seems to be concerned with *Factual knowledge*.

Ms. Chang believes that *Macbeth* enables students to learn about important concepts such as ambition, tragic hero, and irony. She also is interested in having her students know how these ideas are related to one another. For example, what role does ambition play in the development of a tragic hero? Ms. Chang believes that a focus on these ideas and their relationships makes *Macbeth* come alive to her students by allowing them to make connections between the actual play and these different concepts that can be applied to understanding the human condition. In terms of the Taxonomy Table, she is concerned with *Conceptual knowledge*.

Mr. Jefferson believes that *Macbeth* is but one of many plays that could be included in the English literature curriculum. His goal is to use *Macbeth* as a vehicle for teaching students how to think about plays in general. Toward this end, he has developed a general approach that he wants students to use as they read a play. The approach begins by having the class discuss the plot, then examine the relationships among the characters, then discern the messages being conveyed by the playwright, and finally consider the way the play was written and its cultural context. Given that these four general steps make up a procedure that can be applied to all plays, not just *Macbeth*, Mr. Jefferson seems to be focused on applying *Procedural knowledge*, in the language of the Taxonomy Table.

Like Mr. Jefferson, Mrs. Weinberg sees *Macbeth* as one of many plays that students will encounter in high school as well as beyond. She also wants her students to learn a set of general procedures or "tools" they can use to study, understand, analyze, and appreciate other plays. However, Mrs. Weinberg is also concerned that students do not just apply or use these tools in a rote or mechanical fashion. She wants her students to "think about what they are doing as they do it," to be self-reflective and metacognitive about how they are using these tools. For example, she wants them to note any problems they have in using the procedures (e.g., confusing plot with character development) and learn from these problems. Finally, she hopes that students will learn something about themselves, perhaps their own ambitions or their own strengths and weaknesses, by identifying with the characters in the play. In the language of the Taxonomy Table, Mrs. Weinberg is concerned with *Metacognitive knowledge*.

In all four examples the content of the play is the same. However, the four teachers use this content in different ways to focus on varied objectives that emphasize different types of knowledge. All subject matters are composed of specific content, but how this content is structured by teachers in terms of their objectives and instructional activities results in different types of knowledge being emphasized in the unit. Accordingly, how teachers set their educational objectives, organize their instruction to meet these objectives, and even assess student learning of the objectives results in different outcomes, even when the content is ostensibly the same.

DIFFERENT TYPES OF KNOWLEDGE

The problem of how to characterize knowledge and how individuals represent knowledge is a classic and enduring question in philosophy and psychology. It is well beyond the scope of this chapter to survey all the different philosophical positions and psychological theories and models of knowledge. Our general perspective is informed by current perspectives in cognitive science and cognitive psychology on knowledge representation. We do not adhere to a simple behaviorist view that knowledge is best represented as an accumulation of associations between stimuli and responses (although some surely is) or merely a quantitative increase in bits of information (a hallmark of the empiricist tradition—see Case, 1998; Keil, 1998). Rather, our perspective reflects the idea that knowledge is organized and structured by the learner in line with a rationalist-constructivist tradition. Reflecting recent cognitive and developmental psychological research (e.g., Case, 1998), however, we also do not adhere to the idea that knowledge is organized in "stages" or in system-wide logical structures as in traditional developmental stage models of thinking (e.g., Piagetian models).

Based on cognitive science research on the development of expertise, expert thinking, and problem solving, our perspective is that knowledge is domain specific and contextualized. Our understanding of knowledge should reflect this domain specificity and the role that social experiences and context play in the construction and development of knowledge (Bereiter and Scardamalia, 1998; Bransford, Brown, and Cocking, 1999; Case, 1998; Keil, 1998; Mandler, 1998; Wellman and Gelman, 1998).

There are many different types of knowledge and seemingly even more terms used to describe them. In alphabetical order, some of the terms are: conceptual knowledge, conditional knowledge, content knowledge, declarative knowledge, disciplinary knowledge, discourse knowledge, domain knowledge, episodic knowledge, explicit knowledge, factual knowledge, metacognitive knowledge, prior knowledge, procedural knowledge, semantic knowledge, situational knowledge, sociocultural knowledge, strategic knowledge, and tacit knowledge (see, for example, Alexander, Schallert, and Hare, 1991; deJong and Ferguson-Hessler, 1996; Dochy and Alexander, 1995; Ryle, 1949).

Some of the different terms signify important differences among the varieties of knowledge, whereas others are apparently just different labels for the same knowledge category. Later in this chapter we point out that the distinction between "important differences" and "different labels" is central to the different types and subtypes of knowledge in the revised Taxonomy. Given the many different terms and the lack of agreement about the many aspects of the knowledge dimension, it is a difficult task to develop a taxonomy of knowledge that captures the complexity and comprehensiveness of our knowledge base while being relatively simple, practical, and easy to use, as well as maintaining some parsimony in the number of categories. In considering these multiple constraints, we arrived at our four general types of knowledge: (1) *Factual Knowledge*, (2) *Conceptual Knowledge*, (3) *Procedural Knowledge*, and (4) *Metacognitive Knowledge*.

In the next major section of this chapter we define all four types of knowledge along with their associated subtypes. First, however, we give our reasons for including both factual and conceptual knowledge and for including metacognitive knowledge.

A DISTINCTION BETWEEN FACTUAL AND CONCEPTUAL KNOWLEDGE

In cognitive psychology, declarative knowledge is usually defined in terms of "knowing that": *knowing that* Bogota is the capital of Colombia, or *knowing that* a square is a two-dimensional figure with four perpendicular sides of equal length. This knowledge can be (1) specific content elements such as terms and facts or (2) more general concepts, principles, models, or theories (Alexander, Schallert, and Hare, 1991; Anderson, 1983; deJong and Ferguson-Hessler, 1996; Dochy and Alexander, 1995). In the revised Taxonomy, we wanted to distinguish knowledge of discrete, isolated content elements (i.e., terms and facts) from knowledge of larger, more organized bodies of knowledge (i.e., concepts, principles, models, or theories).

This differentiation parallels a general distinction in cognitive psychology between the knowledge of "bits of information" and more general "mental models," "schemas," or "theories" (implicit or explicit) that individuals may use to help them organize a body of information in an interconnected, non-arbitrary, and systematic manner. Accordingly, we have reserved the term *Factual Knowledge* for the knowledge of discrete, isolated "bits of information" and the term *Conceptual Knowledge* for more complex, organized knowledge forms. We think this is an important distinction for teachers and other educators to make.

Moreover, research has shown that many students do not make the important connections between and among the facts they learn in classrooms and the larger system of ideas reflected in an expert's knowledge of a discipline. Although developing expertise in an academic discipline and disciplinary ways of thinking is certainly an important goal of education, students often do not even learn to transfer or apply the facts and ideas they learn in classrooms to understanding their experiences in the everyday world. This is often labeled the problem of "inert" knowledge; that is, students often seem to acquire a great deal of factual knowledge, but they do not understand it at a deeper level or integrate or systematically organize it in disciplinary or useful ways (Bereiter and Scardamalia, 1998; Bransford, Brown, and Cocking, 1999).

One of the hallmarks of experts is that not only do they know a lot about their discipline, but also their knowledge is organized and reflects a deep understanding of the subject matter. In combination, *Conceptual knowledge* and deep understanding can help individuals as they attempt to transfer what they have learned to new situations, thereby overcoming some of the problems of inert knowledge (Bransford, Brown, and Cocking, 1999).

Accordingly, on both empirical and practical grounds, we distinguish between *Factual knowledge* and *Conceptual knowledge*. The distinction may not be appropriate in terms of formal psychological models of knowledge representation (e.g., propositional network models or connectionist models), but we do think it has meaning for classroom instruction and assessment. Educational objectives can focus both the teacher and students on acquiring small bits and pieces of knowledge without concern for how they "fit" within a larger disciplinary or more systematic perspective. By separating *Factual knowledge* from *Conceptual knowledge*, we highlight the need for educators to teach for deep understanding of *Conceptual knowledge*, not just for remembering isolated and small bits of *Factual knowledge*.

A RATIONALE FOR METACOGNITIVE KNOWLEDGE

Our inclusion of *Metacognitive knowledge* reflects recent research on how students' **knowledge** about their own cognition and **control** of their own cognition play an important role in learning (Bransford, Brown, and Cocking, 1999; Sternberg, 1985; Zimmerman and Schunk, 1998). Although behaviorist psychology models generally excluded ideas such as consciousness, awareness, self-reflection, self-regulation, and thinking about and controlling one's own thinking and learning, current cognitive and social constructivist models of learning emphasize the importance of these activities. Because these activities focus on cognition itself, the prefix *meta* is added to reflect the idea that metacognition is about or "above" or "transcends" cognition. Social constructivist models also stress self-reflective activity as an important aspect of learning. In this case, both cognitive and social constructivist models agree about the importance of facilitating students' thinking about their own thinking. Accordingly, we have added this new category to the Taxonomy to reflect current research and theory on the importance of metacognitive knowledge in learning.

The term *metacognition* has been used in many different ways, but an important general distinction concerns two aspects of metacognition: (1) **knowledge about cognition** and (2) **control, monitoring, and regulation of cognitive processes**. The latter is also called metacognitive control and regulation as well as more generally, self-regulation (Boekaerts, Pintrich, and Zeidner, 2000; Bransford, Brown, and Cocking, 1999; Brown, Bransford, Ferrara, and Campione, 1983; Pintrich, Wolters, and Baxter, in press; Zimmerman and Schunk, 1998). This basic distinction between metacognitive knowledge and metacognitive control or self-regulation parallels the two dimensions in our Taxonomy Table. Accordingly, we have limited *Metacognitive knowledge* to knowledge about cognition. The aspect of metacognition that involves metacognitive control and self-regulation reflects different types of cognitive processes and therefore fits into the cognitive process dimension, which is discussed in Chapter 5.

Metacognitive knowledge includes knowledge of general strategies that may be used for different tasks, the conditions under which these strategies may be used, the extent to which the strategies are effective, and self-knowledge (Bransford, Brown, and Cocking, 1999; Flavell, 1979; Pintrich, Wolters, and Baxter, in press; Schneider and Pressley, 1997). For example, learners can know about different strategies for reading a chapter in a textbook and also about strategies to monitor and check their comprehension as they read. Learners also activate relevant knowledge about their own strengths and weaknesses on the reading assignment as well as their motivation for completing the assignment. For example, students may realize that they already know a fair amount about the topic of the chapter in the textbook and that they are interested in the topic. This *Metacognitive knowledge* could lead them to change their approach to the task by adjusting their speed or using an entirely different approach.

Learners also can activate the relevant situational, conditional, or cultural knowledge for solving a problem in a certain context (e.g., in this classroom, on this type of test, in this type of situation, in this subculture). For example, they may know that the teacher uses only multiple-choice tests. Furthermore, they know that multiple-choice tests require only recognition of the correct answers, not actual recall of the information as in essay tests. This *Metacognitive knowledge* might influence how they prepare for the test.

During the meetings that led to the preparation of this revised Taxonomy, we discussed frequently and in great detail both the inclusion and proper placement of *Metacognitive knowledge*. Our inclusion of *Metacognitive knowledge* is predicated on our belief that it is extremely important in understanding and facilitating learning, a belief that is consistent with the basic precepts of cognitive psychology and supported by empirical research (Bransford, Brown, and Cocking, 1999). Just as the original Taxonomy raised the possibility of teaching for "higher-order" objectives, our revised framework points to the possibility of teaching for *Metacognitive knowledge* as well as self-regulation.

In terms of proper placement, we debated several issues. Should *Metacognitive knowledge* be a separate dimension, thus producing a three-dimensional figure? Should the focus of *Metacognitive knowledge* be on metacognitive processes and self-regulation rather than knowledge and, if so, wouldn't it be better placed along the Cognitive Process dimension of the Taxonomy Table? Doesn't *Metacognitive knowledge* overlap with *Factual*, *Conceptual*, and *Procedural knowledge* and, if so, isn't it redundant? These are legitimate questions we grappled with for a long time.

We chose to place *Metacognitive knowledge* as a fourth knowledge category for two primary reasons. First, metacognitive control and self-regulation require the use of the cognitive processes included on the other dimension of the Taxonomy Table. Metacognitive control and self-regulation involve processes such as *Remember, Understand, Apply, Analyze, Evaluate,* and *Create*. Thus, adding metacognitive control and self-regulation processes to the cognitive process dimension was seen as redundant. Second, *Factual, Conceptual,* and *Procedural knowledge* as conceived in the original Taxonomy pertain to subject matter content. In contrast, *Metacognitive knowledge* is knowledge of cognition and about oneself in relation to various subject matters, either individually or collectively (e.g., all sciences, academic subjects in general).

Of course, *Metacognitive knowledge* does not have the same status as the other three types of knowledge. We noted earlier that these types of knowledge were developed through consensus within a scientific or disciplinary community. This is clearly not the case with *self-knowledge* (Dc), which is based on an individual's own self-awareness and knowledge base. *Strategic knowledge* (Da) and *knowledge about cognitive tasks* (Db) have been developed within different communities. For example, cognitive psychology has developed a wealth of information on the usefulness of different cognitive strategies for memory, learning, thinking, and problem solving. When students come to know and understand metacognitive knowledge about strategies that is based on scientific research, they may be better prepared than when they rely on their own idiosyncratic strategies for learning.

CATEGORIES OF THE KNOWLEDGE DIMENSION

Four types of knowledge are listed in Table 4.1. The first three categories of our revised framework include all the knowledge categories from the original Taxonomy (see Appendix B). Some of the labels are different, however, and some of the original subtypes are collapsed into more general categories. Moreover, reflecting the prescient nature of the original *Handbook*, much of the text and many of the examples in the sections that follow are taken from the original *Handbook*. Finally, as we mentioned earlier, the fourth category, *Metacognitive knowledge*, and its subtypes are all new.

A. FACTUAL KNOWLEDGE

Factual knowledge encompasses the basic elements that experts use in communicating about their academic discipline, understanding it, and organizing it systematically. These elements are usually serviceable to people who work in the discipline in the very form in which they are presented; they need little or no alteration from one use or application to another. *Factual knowledge* contains the basic elements students must know if they are to be acquainted with the discipline or to solve any of the problems in it. The elements are usually symbols associated with some concrete referents, or "strings of symbols" that convey important information. For the most part, *Factual knowledge* exists at a relatively low level of abstraction.

Because there is a tremendous wealth of these basic elements, it is almost inconceivable that a student could learn all of them relevant to a particular subject matter. As our knowledge increases in the social sciences, sciences, and humanities, even experts in these fields have difficulty keeping up with all the new elements. Consequently, some selection for educational purposes is almost always required. For classification purposes, *Factual knowledge* may be distinguished from *Conceptual knowledge* by virtue of its very specificity; that is, *Factual knowledge* can be isolated as elements or bits of information that are believed to have some value in and of themselves. The two subtypes of *Factual knowledge* are *knowledge of terminology* (Aa) and *knowledge of specific details and elements* (Ab).

AA. KNOWLEDGE OF TERMINOLOGY

Knowledge of terminology includes knowledge of specific verbal and nonverbal labels and symbols (e.g., words, numerals, signs, pictures). Each subject matter contains a large number of labels and symbols, both verbal and nonverbal, that have particular referents. They are the basic language of the discipline—the shorthand used by experts to express what they know. In any attempt by experts to communicate with others about phenomena within their discipline, they find it necessary to use the special labels and symbols they have devised. In many cases it is impossible for experts to discuss problems in their discipline without making use of essential terms. Quite literally, they are unable to even think about many of the phenomena in the discipline unless they use these labels and symbols.

4.1 THE KNOWLEDGE DIMENSION

MAJOR TYPES AND SUBTYPES	EXAMPLES
A. FACTUAL KNOWLEDGE—The basic elements students must know to be acquainted with a discipline or solve problems in it	
AA. Knowledge of terminology	Technical vocabulary, musical symbols
AB. Knowledge of specific details and elements	Major natural resources, reliable sources of information
B. CONCEPTUAL KNOWLEDGE—The interrelationships among the basic elements within a larger structure that enable them to function together	
BA. Knowledge of classifications and categories	Periods of geological time, forms of business ownership
BB. Knowledge of principles and generalizations	Pythagorean theorem, law of supply and demand
BC. Knowledge of theories, models, and structures	Theory of evolution, structure of Congress
C. PROCEDURAL KNOWLEDGE—How to do something, methods of inquiry, and criteria for using skills, algorithms, techniques, and methods	
CA. Knowledge of subject-specific skills and algorithms	Skills used in painting with watercolors, whole-number division algorithm
CB. Knowledge of subject-specific techniques and methods	Interviewing techniques, scientific method
CC. Knowledge of criteria for determining when to use appropriate procedures	Criteria used to determine when to apply a procedure involving Newton's second law, criteria used to judge the feasibility of using a particular method to estimate business costs
D. METACOGNITIVE KNOWLEDGE—Knowledge of cognition in general as well as awareness and knowledge of one's own cognition	
DA. Strategic knowledge	Knowledge of outlining as a means of capturing the structure of a unit of subject matter in a textbook, knowledge of the use of heuristics
DB. Knowledge about cognitive tasks, including appropriate contextual and conditional knowledge	Knowledge of the types of tests particular teachers administer, knowledge of the cognitive demands of different tasks
DC. Self-knowledge	Knowledge that critiquing essays is a personal strength, whereas writing essays is a personal weakness; awareness of one's own knowledge level

The novice learner must be cognizant of these labels and symbols and learn the generally accepted referents that are attached to them. As the expert must communicate with these terms, so must those learning the discipline have a knowledge of the terms and their referents as they attempt to comprehend or think about the phenomena of the discipline.

Here, to a greater extent than in any other category of knowledge, experts find their own labels and symbols so useful and precise that they are likely to want the learner to know more than the learner really needs to know or can learn. This may be especially true in the sciences, where attempts are made to use labels and symbols with great precision. Scientists find it difficult to express ideas or discuss particular phenomena with the use of other symbols or with "popular" or "folk knowledge" terms more familiar to a lay population.

Examples of Knowledge of Terminology

- Knowledge of the alphabet
- Knowledge of scientific terms (e.g., labels for parts of a cell, names for subatomic particles)
- Knowledge of the vocabulary of painting
- Knowledge of important accounting terms
- Knowledge of the standard representational symbols on maps and charts
- Knowledge of the symbols used to indicate the correct pronunciation of words

Ab. Knowledge of Specific Details and Elements

Knowledge of specific details and elements refers to knowledge of events, locations, people, dates, sources of information, and the like. It may include very precise and specific information, such as the exact date of an event or the exact magnitude of a phenomenon. It may also include approximate information, such as a time period in which an event occurred or the general order of magnitude of a phenomenon. Specific facts are those that can be isolated as separate, discrete elements in contrast to those that can be known only in a larger context.

Every subject matter contains some events, locations, people, dates, and other details that experts know and believe to represent important knowledge about the field. Such specific facts are basic information that experts use in describing their field and in thinking about specific problems or topics in the field. These facts can be distinguished from terminology, in that terminology generally represents the conventions or agreements within a field (i.e., a common language), whereas facts represent findings arrived at by means other than consensual agreements made for purposes of communication. Subtype Ab also includes knowledge about particular books, writings, and other sources of information on specific topics and problems. Thus, knowledge of a specific fact and knowledge of the sources of the fact are classified in this subtype.

Again, the tremendous number of specific facts forces educators (e.g., curriculum specialists, textbook authors, teachers) to make choices about what is basic and what is of secondary importance or of importance primarily to the expert. Educators must also consider the level of precision with which different facts must be known. Frequently educators may be content to have a student learn only the approximate magnitude of the phenomenon rather than its precise quantity or to learn an approximate time period rather than the precise date or time of a specific event. Educators have considerable difficulty determining whether many of the specific facts are such that students should learn them as part of an educational unit or course, or they can be left to be acquired whenever they really need them.

EXAMPLES OF KNOWLEDGE OF SPECIFIC DETAILS AND ELEMENTS

- Knowledge of major facts about particular cultures and societies
- Knowledge of practical facts important to health, citizenship, and other human needs and concerns
- Knowledge of the more significant names, places, and events in the news
- Knowledge of the reputation of a given author for presenting and interpreting facts on governmental problems
- Knowledge of major products and exports of countries
- Knowledge of reliable sources of information for wise purchasing

B. CONCEPTUAL KNOWLEDGE

Conceptual knowledge includes knowledge of categories and classifications and the relationships between and among them—more complex, organized knowledge forms. *Conceptual knowledge* includes schemas, mental models, or implicit or explicit theories in different cognitive psychological models. These schemas, models, and theories represent the knowledge an individual has about how a particular subject matter is organized and structured, how the different parts or bits of information are interconnected and interrelated in a more systematic manner, and how these parts function together. For example, a mental model for why the seasons occur may include ideas about the earth, the sun, the rotation of the earth around the sun, and the tilt of the earth toward the sun at different times during the year. These are not just simple, isolated facts about the earth and sun but rather ideas about the relationships between them and how they are linked to the seasonal changes. This type of conceptual knowledge might be one aspect of what is termed "disciplinary knowledge," or the way experts in the discipline think about a phenomenon—in this case the scientific explanation for the occurrence of the seasons.

Conceptual knowledge includes three subtypes: *knowledge of classifications and categories* (Ba), *knowledge of principles and generalizations* (Bb), and *knowledge of theories, models, and structures* (Bc). Classifications and categories form the basis for principles and generalizations. These, in turn, form the basis for theories, models, and structures. The three subtypes should capture a great deal of the knowledge that is generated within all the different disciplines.

BA. KNOWLEDGE OF CLASSIFICATIONS AND CATEGORIES

Subtype Ba includes the specific categories, classes, divisions, and arrangements that are used in different subject matters. As a subject matter develops, individuals who work on it find it advantageous to develop classifications and categories that they can use to structure and systematize the phenomena. This type of knowledge is somewhat more general and often more abstract than the knowledge of terminology and specific facts. Each subject matter has a set of categories that are used to discover new elements as well as to deal with them once they are discovered. Classifications and categories differ from terminology and facts in that they form the connecting links between and among specific elements.

When one is writing or analyzing a story, for example, the major categories include plot, character, and setting. Note that plot **as a category** is substantially different from the plot **of this story**. When the concern is plot as a category, the key question is What makes a plot a plot? The category "plot" is defined by what all specific plots have in common. In contrast, when the concern is the plot of a particular story, the key question is What is the plot of this story?—*knowledge of specific details and elements* (Ab).

Sometimes it is difficult to distinguish *knowledge of classifications and categories* (Ba) from *Factual knowledge* (A). To complicate matters further, basic classifications and categories can be placed into larger, more comprehensive classifications and categories. In mathematics, for example, whole numbers, integers, and fractions can be placed into the category rational numbers. Each larger category moves us away from the concrete specifics and into the realm of the abstract.

For the purposes of our Taxonomy, several characteristics are useful in distinguishing the subtypes of knowledge. Classifications and categories are largely the result of agreement and convenience, whereas knowledge of specific details stems more directly from observation, experimentation, and discovery. *Knowledge of classifications and categories* is commonly a reflection of how experts in the field think and attack problems, whereas knowledge of which specific details become important is derived from the results of such thought and problem solving.

Knowledge of classifications and categories is an important aspect of developing expertise in an academic discipline. Proper classification of information and experience into appropriate categories is a classic sign of learning and development. Moreover, recent cognitive research on conceptual change and understanding suggests that student learning can be constrained by misclassification of information into inappropriate categories. For example, Chi and her colleagues (see Chi, 1992; Chi, Slotta, and deLeeuw, 1994; Slotta, Chi, and Joram, 1995) suggest that students may have difficulty understanding basic science concepts such as heat, light, force, and electricity when they classify these concepts as material substances rather than as processes. Once concepts are classified as substances or objects, students invoke a whole range of characteristics and properties of "objects." As a result, students try to apply these object-like characteristics to what are better described in scientific terms as processes. The naive categorization of these concepts as substances does not match the more scientifically accurate categorization of them as processes.

The categorization of heat, light, force, and electricity as substances becomes the basis for an implicit theory of how these processes are supposed to operate and leads to systematic misconceptions about the nature of the processes. This implicit theory, in turn, makes it difficult for students to develop the appropriate scientific understanding. Accordingly, learning the appropriate classification and category system can reflect a "conceptual change" and result in a more appropriate understanding of the concepts than just learning their definitions (as would be the case in the *Factual knowledge* category).

For several reasons, it seems likely that students will have greater difficulty learning *knowledge of classifications and categories* than *Factual knowledge*. First, many of the classifications and categories students encounter represent relatively arbitrary and even artificial forms of knowledge that are meaningful only to experts who recognize their value as tools and techniques in their work. Second, students may be able to operate in their daily life without knowing the appropriate subject matter classifications and categories to the level of precision expected by experts in the field. Third, *knowledge of classifications and categories* requires that students make connections among specific content elements (i.e., terminology and facts). Finally, as classifications and categories are combined to form larger classifications and categories, learning becomes more abstract. Nevertheless, the student is expected to know these classifications and categories and to know when they are appropriate or useful in dealing with subject matter content. As the student begins to work with a subject matter within an academic discipline and learns how to use the tools, the value of these classifications and categories becomes apparent.

EXAMPLES OF KNOWLEDGE OF CLASSIFICATIONS AND CATEGORIES

- Knowledge of the variety of types of literature
- Knowledge of the various forms of business ownership
- Knowledge of the parts of sentences (e.g., nouns, verbs, adjectives)
- Knowledge of different kinds of psychological problems
- Knowledge of the different periods of geologic time

Bb. Knowledge of Principles and Generalizations

As mentioned earlier, principles and generalizations are composed of classifications and categories. Principles and generalizations tend to dominate an academic discipline and are used to study phenomena or solve problems in the discipline. One of the hallmarks of a subject matter expert is the ability to recognize meaningful patterns (e.g., generalizations) and activate the relevant knowledge of these patterns with little cognitive effort (Bransford, Brown, and Cocking, 1999).

Subtype Bb includes knowledge of particular abstractions that summarize observations of phenomena. These abstractions have the greatest value in describing, predicting, explaining, or determining the most appropriate and relevant action or direction to be taken. Principles and generalizations bring together large numbers of specific facts and events, describe the processes and interrelationships among these specific details (thus forming classifications and categories), and, furthermore, describe the processes and interrelationships among the classifications and categories. In this way, they enable the expert to begin to organize the whole in a parsimonious and coherent manner.

Principles and generalizations tend to be broad ideas that may be difficult for students to understand because students may not be thoroughly acquainted with the phenomena they are intended to summarize and organize. If students do get to know the principles and generalizations, however, they have a means for relating and organizing a great deal of subject matter. As a result, they should have more insight into the subject matter as well as better memory of it.

Examples of Knowledge of Principles and Generalizations

- Knowledge of major generalizations about particular cultures
- Knowledge of the fundamental laws of physics
- Knowledge of the principles of chemistry that are relevant to life processes and health
- Knowledge of the implications of American foreign trade policies for the international economy and international good will
- Knowledge of the major principles involved in learning
- Knowledge of the principles of federalism
- Knowledge of the principles that govern rudimentary arithmetic operations (e.g., the commutative principle, the associative principle)

Bc. Knowledge of Theories, Models, and Structures

Subtype Bc includes knowledge of principles and generalizations together with their interrelationships that present a clear, rounded, and systemic view of a complex phenomenon, problem, or subject matter. These are the most abstract formulations. They can show the interrelationships and organization of a great range of specific details, classifications and categories, and principles and generalizations. This subtype, Bc, differs from Bb in its emphasis on a set of principles and generalizations related in some way to form a theory, model, or structure. The principles and generalizations in subtype Bb do not need to be related in any meaningful way.

Subtype Bc includes knowledge of the different paradigms, epistemologies, theories, and models that different disciplines use to describe, understand, explain, and predict phenomena. Disciplines have different paradigms and epistemologies for structuring inquiry, and students should come to know these different ways of conceptualizing and organizing subject matter and areas of research within the subject matter. In biology, for example, knowledge of the theory of evolution and how to think in evolutionary terms to explain different biological phenomena is an important aspect of this subtype of *Conceptual knowledge*. Similarly, behavioral, cognitive, and social constructivist theories in psychology make different epistemological assumptions and reflect different perspectives on human behavior. An expert in a discipline knows not only the different disciplinary theories, models, and structures but also their relative strengths and weaknesses and can think "within" one of them as well as "outside" any of them.

EXAMPLES OF KNOWLEDGE OF THEORIES, MODELS, AND STRUCTURES

- Knowledge of the interrelationships among chemical principles as the basis for chemical theories
- Knowledge of the overall structure of Congress (i.e., organization, functions)
- Knowledge of the basic structural organization of the local city government
- Knowledge of a relatively complete formulation of the theory of evolution
- Knowledge of the theory of plate tectonics
- Knowledge of genetic models (e.g., DNA)

C. PROCEDURAL KNOWLEDGE

Procedural knowledge is the "knowledge of how" to do something. The "something" might range from completing fairly routine exercises to solving novel problems. *Procedural knowledge* often takes the form of a series or sequence of steps to be followed. It includes knowledge of skills, algorithms, techniques, and methods, collectively known as procedures (Alexander, Schallert, and Hare, 1991; Anderson, 1983; deJong and Ferguson-Hessler, 1996; Dochy and Alexander, 1995). *Procedural knowledge* also includes knowledge of the criteria used to determine when to use various procedures. In fact, as Bransford, Brown, and Cocking (1999) noted, not only do experts have a great deal of knowledge about their subject matter, but their knowledge is "conditionalized" so that they know when and where to use it.

Whereas *Factual knowledge* and *Conceptual knowledge* represent the "what" of knowledge, procedural knowledge concerns the "how." In other words, *Procedural knowledge* reflects knowledge of different "processes," whereas *Factual knowledge* and *Conceptual knowledge* deal with what might be termed "products." It is important to note that *Procedural knowledge* represents only the knowledge of these procedures; their actual use is discussed in Chapter 5.

In contrast to *Metacognitive knowledge* (which includes knowledge of more general strategies that cut across subject matters or academic disciplines), *Procedural knowledge* is specific or germane to particular subject matters or academic disciplines. Accordingly, we reserve the term *Procedural knowledge* for the knowledge of skills, algorithms, techniques, and methods that are subject specific or discipline specific. In mathematics, for example, there are algorithms for performing long division, solving quadratic equations, and establishing the congruence of triangles. In science, there are general methods for designing and performing experiments. In social studies, there are procedures for reading maps, estimating the age of physical artifacts, and collecting historical data. In language arts, there are procedures for spelling words in English and for generating grammatically correct sentences. Because of the subject-specific nature of these procedures, knowledge of them also reflects specific disciplinary knowledge or specific disciplinary ways of thinking in contrast to general strategies for problem solving that can be applied across many disciplines.

CA. KNOWLEDGE OF SUBJECT-SPECIFIC SKILLS AND ALGORITHMS

As we mentioned, *Procedural knowledge* can be expressed as a series or sequence of steps, collectively known as a procedure. Sometimes the steps are followed in a fixed order; at other times decisions must be made about which step to perform next. Similarly, sometimes the end result is fixed (e.g., there is a single prespecified answer); in other cases it is not. Although the process may be either fixed or more open, the end result is generally considered fixed in this subtype of knowledge. A common example is knowledge of algorithms used with mathematics exercises. The procedure for multiplying fractions in arithmetic, when applied, generally results in a fixed answer (barring computational mistakes, of course).

Although the concern here is with *Procedural knowledge*, the result of using *Procedural knowledge* is often *Factual knowledge* or *Conceptual knowledge*. For example, the algorithm for the addition of whole numbers that we use to add 2 and 2 is *Procedural knowledge*; the answer 4 is simply *Factual knowledge*. Once again, the emphasis here is on the student's knowledge of the procedure rather than on his or her ability to use it.

EXAMPLES OF KNOWLEDGE OF SUBJECT-SPECIFIC SKILLS AND ALGORITHMS

- Knowledge of the skills used in painting with watercolors
- Knowledge of the skills used to determine word meaning based on structural analysis
- Knowledge of the various algorithms for solving quadratic equations
- Knowledge of the skills involved in performing the high jump

Cb. Knowledge of Subject-Specific Techniques and Methods

In contrast with specific skills and algorithms that usually end in a fixed result, some procedures do not lead to a single predetermined answer or solution. We can follow the general scientific method in a somewhat sequential manner to design a study, for example, but the resulting experimental design can vary greatly depending on a host of factors. In this subtype, Cb, of *Procedural knowledge*, then, the result is more open and not fixed, in contrast to subtype Ca, *Knowledge of skills and algorithms*.

Knowledge of subject-specific techniques and methods includes knowledge that is largely the result of consensus, agreement, or disciplinary norms rather than knowledge that is more directly an outcome of observation, experimentation, or discovery. This subtype of knowledge generally reflects how experts in the field or discipline think and attack problems rather than the results of such thought or problem solving. For example, knowledge of the general scientific method and how to apply it to different situations, including social situations and policy problems, reflects a "scientific" way of thinking. Another example is the "mathematization" of problems not originally presented as mathematics problems. For example, the simple problem of choosing a checkout line in a grocery store can be made into a mathematical problem that draws on mathematical knowledge and procedures (e.g., number of people in each line, number of items per person).

Examples of Knowledge of Subject-Specific Techniques and Methods

- Knowledge of research methods relevant to the social sciences
- Knowledge of the techniques used by scientists in seeking solutions to problems
- Knowledge of the methods for evaluating health concepts
- Knowledge of various methods of literary criticism

Cc. Knowledge of Criteria for Determining When to Use Appropriate Procedures

In addition to knowing subject-specific procedures, students are expected to know *when* to use them, which often involves knowing the ways they have been used in the past. Such knowledge is nearly always of a historical or encyclopedic type. Though simpler and perhaps less functional than the ability to actually use the procedures, knowledge of when to use appropriate procedures is an important prelude to their proper use. Thus, before engaging in an inquiry, students may be expected to know the methods and techniques that have been used in similar inquiries. At a later stage in the inquiry, they may be expected to show relationships between the methods and techniques they actually employed and the methods employed by others.

Here again is a systematization that is used by subject matter experts as they attack problems in their field. Experts know when and where to apply their knowledge. They have criteria that help them make decisions about when and where to use different types of subject-specific procedural knowledge; that is, their knowledge is "conditionalized," in that they know the conditions under which the procedures are to be applied (Chi, Feltovich, and Glaser, 1981). For example, in solving a physics problem, an expert can recognize the type of physics problem and apply the appropriate procedure (e.g., a problem that involves Newton's second law, $F = ma$). Students therefore may be expected to make use of the criteria as well as have knowledge of them.

The ways in which the criteria are used in actual problem situations is discussed in Chapter 5. Here, we refer only to *knowledge of criteria for determining when to use appropriate procedures*. The criteria vary markedly from subject matter to subject matter. Initially, they are likely to appear complex and abstract to students; they acquire meaning as they are related to concrete situations and problems.

EXAMPLES OF KNOWLEDGE OF CRITERIA FOR DETERMINING WHEN TO USE APPROPRIATE PROCEDURES

- Knowledge of the criteria for determining which of several types of essays to write (e.g., expository, persuasive)

- Knowledge of the criteria for determining which method to use in solving algebraic equations

- Knowledge of the criteria for determining which statistical procedure to use with data collected in a particular experiment

- Knowledge of the criteria for determining which technique to apply to create a desired effect in a particular watercolor painting

D. METACOGNITIVE KNOWLEDGE

Metacognitive knowledge is knowledge about cognition in general as well as awareness of and knowledge about one's own cognition. One of the hallmarks of theory and research on learning since the publication of the original *Handbook* is the emphasis on making students more aware of and responsible for their own knowledge and thought. This change cuts across different theoretical approaches to learning and development from neo-Piagetian models, to cognitive and information processing models, to Vygotskian and cultural or situated learning models. Regardless of their theoretical perspective, researchers generally agree that with development students will become more aware of their own thinking as well as more knowledgeable about cognition in general, and as they act on this awareness they will tend to learn better (Bransford, Brown, and Cocking, 1999). The labels for this general developmental trend vary from theory to theory but include metacognitive knowledge, metacognitive awareness, self-awareness, self-reflection, and self-regulation.

As we mentioned earlier, an important distinction in the field is between **knowledge of cognition** and the **monitoring, control, and regulation of cognition** (e.g., Bransford, Brown, and Cocking, 1999; Brown, Bransford, Ferrara, and Campione, 1983; Flavell, 1979; Paris and Winograd, 1990; Pintrich, Wolters, and Baxter, in press; Schneider and Pressley, 1997; Zimmerman and Schunk, 1998). Recognizing this distinction, in this chapter we describe only students' knowledge of various aspects of cognition, not the actual monitoring, control, and regulation of their cognition. In the way that the other types of knowledge described in this chapter are acted upon in some way by the cognitive processes described in Chapter 5, the same is true of *Metacognitive knowledge*.

In Flavell's (1979) classic article on metacognition, he suggested that metacognition included knowledge of strategy, task, and person variables. We have represented this general framework in our categories by including students' knowledge of general strategies for learning and thinking (*strategic knowledge*) and their knowledge of cognitive tasks as well as when and why to use these different strategies (*knowledge about cognitive tasks*). Finally, we include knowledge about the self (the person variable) in relation to both cognitive and motivational components of performance (*self-knowledge*).

DA. STRATEGIC KNOWLEDGE

Strategic knowledge is knowledge of the general strategies for learning, thinking, and problem solving. The strategies in this subtype can be used across many different tasks and subject matters, rather than being most useful for one particular type of task in one specific subject area (e.g., solving a quadratic equation or applying Ohm's law).

This subtype, Da, includes knowledge of the variety of strategies that students might use to memorize material, extract meaning from text, or comprehend what they hear in classrooms or read in books and other course materials. The large number of different learning strategies can be grouped into three general categories: rehearsal, elaboration, and organizational (Weinstein and Mayer, 1986). Rehearsal strategies involve repeating words or terms to be recalled over and over to oneself; they are generally not the most effective strategies for deeper levels of learning and comprehension. In contrast, elaboration strategies include the use of various mnemonics for memory tasks as well as techniques such as summarizing, paraphrasing, and selecting the main idea from texts. Elaboration strategies foster deeper processing of the material to be learned and result in better comprehension and learning than do rehearsal strategies. Organizational strategies include various forms of outlining, drawing "cognitive maps" or concept mapping, and note taking; students transform the material from one form to another. Organizational strategies usually result in better comprehension and learning than do rehearsal strategies.

In addition to these general learning strategies, students can have knowledge of various metacognitive strategies that are useful in planning, monitoring, and regulating their cognition. Students can eventually use these strategies to plan their cognition (e.g., set subgoals), monitor their cognition (e.g., ask themselves questions as they read a piece of text, check their answer to a math problem), and regulate their cognition (e.g., re-read something they don't understand, go back and "repair" their calculating mistake in a math problem).

Again, in this category we refer to students' knowledge of these various strategies, not their actual use.

Finally, this subtype, Da, includes general strategies for problem solving and thinking (Baron, 1994; Nickerson, Perkins, and Smith, 1985; Sternberg, 1985). These strategies represent the various general heuristics students can use to solve problems, particularly ill-defined problems that have no definitive solution method. Examples of heuristics are means-ends analysis and working backward from the desired goal state. In addition to problem-solving strategies, there are general strategies for deductive and inductive thinking, including evaluating the validity of different logical statements, avoiding circularity in arguments, making appropriate inferences from different sources of data, and drawing on appropriate samples to make inferences (i.e., avoiding the availability heuristic—making decisions from convenient instead of representative symbols).

EXAMPLES OF STRATEGIC KNOWLEDGE

- Knowledge that rehearsal of information is one way to retain the information
- Knowledge of various mnemonic strategies for memory (e.g., the use of acronyms such as Roy G Biv for the colors of the spectrum.)
- Knowledge of various elaboration strategies such as paraphrasing and summarizing
- Knowledge of various organizational strategies such as outlining or diagramming
- Knowledge of planning strategies such as setting goals for reading
- Knowledge of comprehension-monitoring strategies such as self-testing or self-questioning
- Knowledge of means-ends analysis as a heuristic for solving an ill-defined problem
- Knowledge of the availability heuristic and the problems of failing to sample in an unbiased manner

DB. KNOWLEDGE ABOUT COGNITIVE TASKS, INCLUDING CONTEXTUAL AND CONDITIONAL KNOWLEDGE

In addition to knowledge about various strategies, individuals accumulate knowledge about cognitive tasks. In his traditional division of *Metacognitive knowledge*, Flavell (1979) included knowledge that different cognitive tasks can be more or less difficult, may make differential demands on the cognitive system, and may require different cognitive strategies. For example, a recall task is more difficult than a recognition task. The recall task requires the person to search memory actively and retrieve the relevant information, whereas the recognition task requires only that the person discriminate among alternatives and select the correct or most appropriate answer.

As students develop knowledge of different learning and thinking strategies, this knowledge reflects both what general strategies to use and how to use them. As with *Procedural knowledge,* however, this knowledge may not be sufficient for expertise in learning. Students also need to develop the conditional knowledge for these general cognitive strategies; in other words, they need to develop some knowledge about the when and why of using these strategies appropriately (Paris, Lipson, and Wixson, 1983). All these different strategies may not be appropriate for all situations, and the learner must develop some knowledge of the different conditions and tasks for which the different strategies are most appropriate. Conditional knowledge refers to knowledge of the situations in which students may use *Metacognitive knowledge.* In contrast, *Procedural knowledge* refers to knowledge of the situations in which students may use subject-specific skills, algorithms, techniques, and methods.

If one thinks of strategies as cognitive "tools" that help students construct understanding, then different cognitive tasks require different tools, just as a carpenter uses different tools for performing all the tasks that go into building a house. Of course, one tool, such as a hammer, can be used in many different ways for different tasks, but this is not necessarily the most adaptive use of a hammer, particularly if other tools are better suited to some of the tasks. In the same way, certain general learning and thinking strategies are better suited to different tasks. For example, if one confronts a novel problem that is ill defined, then general problem-solving heuristics may be useful. In contrast, if one confronts a physics problem about the second law of thermodynamics, then more specific *Procedural knowledge* is more useful and adaptive. An important aspect of learning about strategies is the conditional knowledge of when and why to use them appropriately.

Another important aspect of conditional knowledge is the local situational and general social, conventional, and cultural norms for using different strategies. For example, a teacher may encourage the use of a certain strategy for monitoring reading comprehension. A student who knows that strategy is better able to meet the demands of this teacher's classroom. In the same manner, different cultures and subcultures may have norms for the use of different strategies and ways of thinking about problems. Again, knowing these norms can help students adapt to the demands of the culture in terms of solving the problem. For example, the strategies used in a classroom learning situation may not be the most appropriate ones to use in a work setting. Knowledge of the different situations and the cultural norms regarding the use of different strategies within those situations is an important aspect of *Metacognitive knowledge.*

EXAMPLES OF KNOWLEDGE ABOUT COGNITIVE TASKS, INCLUDING CONTEXTUAL AND CONDITIONAL KNOWLEDGE

- Knowledge that recall tasks (i.e., short-answer items) generally make more demands on the individual's memory system than recognition tasks (i.e., multiple-choice items)

- Knowledge that a primary source book may be more difficult to understand than a general textbook or popular book

- Knowledge that a simple memorization task (e.g., remembering a phone number) may require only rehearsal
- Knowledge that elaboration strategies like summarizing and paraphrasing can result in deeper levels of comprehension
- Knowledge that general problem-solving heuristics may be most useful when the individual lacks relevant subject- or task-specific knowledge or in the absence of specific *Procedural knowledge*
- Knowledge of the local and general social, conventional, and cultural norms for how, when, and why to use different strategies

Dc. Self-knowledge

Along with knowledge of different strategies and cognitive tasks, Flavell (1979) proposed that *self-knowledge* was an important component of metacognition. In his model self-knowledge includes knowledge of one's strengths and weaknesses in relation to cognition and learning. For example, students who know they generally do better on multiple-choice tests than on essay tests have some self-knowledge about their test-taking skills. This knowledge may be useful to students as they study for the two different types of tests. In addition, one hallmark of experts is that they know when they do not know something and they then have some general strategies for finding the needed and appropriate information. Self-awareness of the breadth and depth of one's own knowledge base is an important aspect of self-knowledge. Finally, students need to be aware of the different types of general strategies they are likely to rely on in different situations. An awareness that one tends to overrely on a particular strategy, when there may be other more adaptive strategies for the task, could lead to a change in strategy use.

In addition to knowledge of one's general cognition, individuals have beliefs about their motivation. Motivation is a complicated and confusing area, with many models and theories available. Although motivational beliefs are usually not considered in cognitive models, a fairly substantial body of literature is emerging that shows important links between students' motivational beliefs and their cognition and learning (Snow, Corno, and Jackson, 1996; Pintrich and Schrauben, 1992; Pintrich and Schunk, 1996).

A consensus has emerged, however, around general social cognitive models of motivation that propose three sets of motivational beliefs (Pintrich and Schunk, 1996). Because these beliefs are social cognitive in nature, they fit into a taxonomy of knowledge. The first set consists of self-efficacy beliefs, that is, students' judgments of their capability to accomplish a specific task. The second set includes beliefs about the goals or reasons students have for pursuing a specific task (e.g., learning vs. getting a good grade). The third set contains value and interest beliefs, which represent students' perceptions of their personal interest (liking) for a task as well as their judgments of how important and useful the task is to them. Just as students need to develop self-knowledge and awareness about their own knowledge and cognition, they also need to develop self-knowledge and awareness about their own motivation. Again, awareness of these different motivational beliefs may enable learners to monitor and regulate their behavior in learning situations in a more adaptive manner.

Self-knowledge is an important aspect of *Metacognitive knowledge*, but the accuracy of *self-knowledge* seems to be most crucial for learning. We are not advocating that teachers try to boost students' "self-esteem" (a completely different construct from *self-knowledge*) by providing students with positive but false, inaccurate, and misleading feedback about their academic strengths and weaknesses. It is much more important for students to have accurate perceptions and judgments of their knowledge base and expertise than to have inflated and inaccurate *self-knowledge* (Pintrich and Schunk, 1996). If students are not aware they do not know some aspect of *Factual knowledge* or *Conceptual knowledge* or that they don't know how to do something (*Procedural knowledge*), it is unlikely they will make any effort to learn the new material. A hallmark of experts is that they know what they know and what they do not know, and they do not have inflated or false impressions of their actual knowledge and abilities. Accordingly, we emphasize the need for teachers to help students make accurate assessments of their *self-knowledge* and not attempt to inflate students' academic self-esteem.

EXAMPLES OF SELF-KNOWLEDGE

- Knowledge that one is knowledgeable in some areas but not in others
- Knowledge that one tends to rely on one type of "cognitive tool" (strategy) in certain situations
- Knowledge of one's capabilities to perform a particular task that are accurate, not inflated (e.g., overconfident)
- Knowledge of one's goals for performing a task
- Knowledge of one's personal interest in a task
- Knowledge of one's judgments about the relative utility value of a task

ASSESSING OBJECTIVES INVOLVING METACOGNITIVE KNOWLEDGE

The assessment of objectives for *Factual knowledge*, *Conceptual knowledge*, and *Procedural knowledge* is discussed in the next chapter because all objectives are some combination of the Knowledge and Cognitive Process dimensions. Accordingly, it makes no sense to discuss assessment of the knowledge categories without also considering how the knowledge is to be used with the different cognitive processes. Because *Metacognitive knowledge* is not discussed in much detail in the next chapter, however, a word about the assessment of *Metacognitive knowledge* is warranted here.

The assessment of objectives that relate to *Metacognitive knowledge* is unique because the objectives require a different perspective on what constitutes a "correct" answer. Unless the verb in the objective is associated with the cognitive process *Create*, most assessment tasks for objectives that relate to *Factual knowledge*, *Conceptual knowledge*, and *Procedural knowledge* have a "correct" answer. Moreover, this answer is the same for all students. For example, for an objective that involves *remembering factual knowledge*, the date on which Lincoln delivered the Gettysburg Address is the same for all students. For objectives that involve *Metacognitive knowledge*, in contrast, there may be important individual differences and perspectives on the "correct" answer. Further, each of the three subtypes of *Metacognitive knowledge* may require a different perspective on the "correct" answer.

For the first subtype, *strategic knowledge*, some knowledge about general strategies may be "correct." For example, if students are asked to simply recall some information about general strategies for memory (e.g., the use of acronyms), then there is in fact a correct answer. On the other hand, if students are asked to apply this knowledge to a new situation, then there may be many possible ways for them to use acronyms to help them remember the important information.

The other two subtypes of *Metacognitive knowledge* provide even more possibilities for individual differences to emerge in assessment. The subtype pertaining to cognitive tasks does include some knowledge that calls for a correct answer. For example, it is a truism that recognition tasks are easier than recall tasks, so a question about this relationship does have a correct answer. On the other hand, there are many different conditions, situations, contexts, and cultures that change the way general cognitive strategies can be applied. It is difficult to specify a correct answer to an assessment task without some knowledge of these different conditions and contexts.

Finally, assessing *self-knowledge* presents even more possibilities for individual differences. Within this subtype it is assumed that individual students vary in their knowledge and motivation. Moreover, how does one determine "correct" answers for self-knowledge? Self-knowledge may even be faulty (e.g., a student believes that he does best on tests if he eats pepperoni pizza the night before), and there should be occasions to correct these faulty and superstitious beliefs. Perhaps the best way of assessing self-knowledge, however, is by helping students become more aware and conscious of their own beliefs, helping them determine the feasibility of these beliefs in light of what currently is known about learning, and helping them learn how to monitor and evaluate these beliefs.

It is difficult to assess *Metacognitive knowledge* using simple paper-and-pencil measures (Pintrich, Wolter, and Baxter, in press). Consequently, objectives that relate to *Metacognitive knowledge* may be best assessed in the context of classroom activities and discussions of various strategies. Certainly, courses designed to teach students general strategies for learning and thinking (e.g., classes on learning strategies, thinking skills, study skills) engage students in learning about all three aspects of *Metacognitive knowledge*. Students can learn about general strategies as well as how other students use strategies. They then can compare their own strategies with those used by other students. Moreover, class discussions in any course, not just strategy courses, that focus on the issues of learning and thinking can help students become aware of their own *Metacognitive knowledge*. As teachers listen to students talk about their strategies in these discussions, have conversations with students individually, or review student journals about their own learning, teachers may gain some understanding of their students' *Metacognitive knowledge*. We have much to learn about the best ways to assess *Metacognitive knowledge*, but given its importance in learning, it seems timely to continue our efforts in this area.

CONCLUSION

In this chapter we identified and described four types of knowledge: *Factual, Conceptual, Procedural,* and *Metacognitive. Factual knowledge* and *Conceptual knowledge* are most similar in that they involve the knowledge of "what," although *Conceptual knowledge* is a deeper, more organized, integrated, and systemic knowledge than just knowledge of terminology and isolated facts. *Procedural knowledge* is the knowledge of "how" to do something. These three categories were all represented in the original Taxonomy. Reflecting recent cognitive science and cognitive psychological research on the importance of metacognition, we have added a fourth category: *Metacognitive knowledge*. In simplest terms, *Metacognitive knowledge* is knowledge about cognition.

Although the importance of differentiating among these four types of knowledge may be apparent after reading this chapter, the next chapter reinforces this view. In Chapter 5 we show how different types of knowledge tend to be associated with certain types of cognitive processes. The differentiation of these knowledge types is further explicated in the discussion of the vignettes and their analysis in Chapters 8–13.

CHAPTER 5

The Cognitive Process Dimension

In Chapter 4 we described each of the four types of knowledge in detail. Although much of schooling focuses on *Factual knowledge*, we suggested that this limited focus can be expanded by placing greater emphasis on a broader range of knowledge types, including *Conceptual knowledge*, *Procedural knowledge*, and *Metacognitive knowledge*. Similarly, in this chapter we suggest that although instruction and assessment commonly emphasize one kind of cognitive processing—*Remembering*—schooling can be expanded to include a broader range of cognitive processes. In fact, the predominant use of the original framework has been in the analysis of curricula and examinations to demonstrate their overemphasis on remembering and their lack of emphasis on the more complex process categories (Anderson and Sosniak, 1994). The purpose of this chapter is to describe the full range of processes in more detail.

Two of the most important educational goals are to promote retention and to promote transfer (which, when it occurs, indicates meaningful learning). Retention is the ability to remember material at some later time in much the same way as it was presented during instruction. Transfer is the ability to use what was learned to solve new problems, to answer new questions, or to facilitate learning new subject matter (Mayer and Wittrock, 1996). In short, retention requires that students **remember** what they have learned, whereas transfer requires students not only to remember but also to **make sense of** and **be able to use** what they have learned (Bransford, Brown, and Cocking, 1999; Detterman and Sternberg, 1993; McKeough, Lupart, and Marini, 1995; Mayer, 1995; Phye, 1997). Stated somewhat differently, retention focuses on the **past**, whereas transfer emphasizes the **future**. After students read a textbook lesson on Ohm's law, for example, a retention test might ask them to write the formula for Ohm's law. In contrast, a transfer test might ask students to rearrange an electrical circuit to maximize the rate of electron flow or to use Ohm's law to explain a complex electric circuit.

Although educational objectives for promoting retention are fairly easy to construct, educators may have more difficulty in formulating, teaching, and assessing objectives aimed at promoting transfer (Baxter, Elder, and Glaser, 1996; Phye, 1997). Our revised framework is intended to help broaden the typical set of educational objectives to include those aimed at promoting transfer. We begin this chapter by introducing retention and transfer. Next, we describe our six cognitive process categories (one that emphasizes retention and five that, although they may facilitate retention, emphasize transfer). We end the chapter with an example of how this discussion can be applied to teaching, learning, and assessing a lesson on Ohm's law.

A TALE OF THREE LEARNING OUTCOMES

As an introduction, we briefly consider three learning scenarios. The first exemplifies no learning (that is, no intended learning), the second rote learning, and the third meaningful learning.

NO LEARNING

Amy reads a chapter on electrical circuits in her science textbook. She skims the material, sure that the test will be a breeze. When she is asked to recall part of the lesson (as a retention test), she is able to remember very few of the key terms and facts. For example, she cannot list the major components in an electrical circuit even though they were described in the chapter. When she is asked to use the information to solve problems (as part of a transfer test), she cannot. For example, she cannot answer an essay question that asks her to diagnose a problem in an electrical circuit. In this worst-case scenario, Amy neither possesses nor is able to use the relevant knowledge. Amy has neither sufficiently attended to nor encoded the material during learning. The resulting outcome can be characterized as essentially **no learning**.

ROTE LEARNING

Becky reads the same chapter on electrical circuits. She reads carefully, making sure she reads every word. She goes over the material and memorizes the key facts. When she is asked to recall the material, she can remember almost all of the important terms and facts in the lesson. Unlike Amy, she is able to list the major components in an electrical circuit. When she is asked to use the information to solve problems, however, she cannot. Like Amy, she cannot answer the essay question about the diagnosis of a problem in an electrical circuit. In this scenario, Becky possesses relevant knowledge but cannot use that knowledge to solve problems. She cannot transfer this knowledge to a new situation. Becky has attended to relevant information, but she has not understood it and therefore cannot use it. The resulting learning outcome can be called **rote learning**.

MEANINGFUL LEARNING

Carla reads the same textbook chapter on electrical circuits. She reads carefully, trying to make sense out of it. When she is asked to recall the material, she, like Becky, can remember almost all of the important terms and facts in the lesson. Furthermore, when she is asked to use the information to solve problems, she generates many possible solutions. In this scenario, not only does Carla possess relevant knowledge, but she also can use that knowledge to solve problems and to understand new concepts. She can transfer her knowledge to new problems and new learning situations. Carla has attended to relevant information and has understood it. The resulting learning outcome can be called **meaningful learning**.

Meaningful learning provides students with the knowledge and cognitive processes they need for successful problem solving. Problem solving occurs when a student devises a way of achieving a goal that he or she has never previously achieved, that is, of figuring out how to change a situation from its given state into a goal state (Duncker, 1945; Mayer, 1992). Two major components in problem solving are problem representation—in which a student builds a mental representation of the problem—and problem solution—in which a student devises and carries out a plan for solving the problem (Mayer, 1992). Consistent with recent research (Gick and Holyoak, 1980, 1983; Vosniadou and Ortony, 1989), the authors of the original *Handbook* recognized that students often solve problems by analogy. That is, they reformulate the problem in a more familiar form, recognize that it is similar to a familiar problem type, abstract the solution method for that familiar problem type, and then apply the method to the to-be-solved problem.

MEANINGFUL LEARNING AS CONSTRUCTING KNOWLEDGE FRAMEWORKS

A focus on meaningful learning is consistent with the view of learning as knowledge construction, in which students seek to make sense of their experiences. In constructivist learning, as mentioned on page 38, students engage in active cognitive processing, such as paying attention to relevant incoming information, mentally organizing incoming information into a coherent representation, and mentally integrating incoming information with existing knowledge (Mayer, 1999). In contrast, a focus on rote learning is consistent with the view of learning as knowledge acquisition, in which students seek to add new information to their memories (Mayer, 1999).

Constructivist learning (i.e., meaningful learning) is recognized as an important educational goal. It requires that instruction go beyond the simple presentation of factual knowledge and that assessment tasks require more of students than simply recall or recognition of factual knowledge (Bransford, Brown, and Cocking, 1999; Lambert and McCombs, 1998; Marshall, 1996; Steffe and Gale, 1995). The cognitive processes summarized in this chapter provide a means of describing the range of students' cognitive activities in constructivist learning; that is, these processes are ways in which students can actively engage in the process of constructing meaning.

COGNITIVE PROCESSES FOR RETENTION AND TRANSFER

If we were interested mainly in teaching and assessing the degree to which students learned some subject matter content and retained it over some period of time, we would focus primarily on one class of cognitive processes—namely, those associated with *Remember*. In contrast, if we wish to expand our focus by examining ways to foster and assess meaningful learning, we need to examine processes that go beyond remembering.

What cognitive processes are used for retention and transfer? As we discussed, our revised framework includes six categories of processes—one most closely related to retention (*Remember*) and the other five increasingly related to transfer (*Understand, Apply, Analyze, Evaluate,* and *Create*). Based on a review of the illustrative objectives listed in the original *Handbook* and an examination of other classification systems (e.g., DeLandsheere, 1977; Metfessel, Michael, and Kirsner, 1969; Mosenthal, 1998; Royer, Ciscero, and Carlo, 1993; Sternberg, 1998), we have selected 19 cognitive processes that fit within these six categories. Table 5.1 provides a brief definition and example of each cognitive process, lists their alternative names, and indicates the category to which it belongs. These 19 specific cognitive processes are intended to be mutually exclusive; together they delineate the breadth and boundaries of the six categories.

CATEGORIES OF THE COGNITIVE PROCESS DIMENSION

In the discussion that follows, we define the cognitive processes within each of the six categories in detail, making comparisons with other cognitive processes, where appropriate. We offer sample educational objectives and assessments in various subject areas as well as alternative versions of assessment tasks. Each illustrative objective in the following material should be read as though preceded by the phrase "The student is able to . . ." or "The student learns to. . . ."

1. REMEMBER

When the objective of instruction is to promote retention of the presented material in much the same form as it was taught, the relevant process category is *Remember.* Remembering involves retrieving relevant knowledge from long-term memory. The two associated cognitive processes are *recognizing* and *recalling.* The relevant knowledge may be *Factual, Conceptual, Procedural,* or *Metacognitive,* or some combination of these.

To assess student learning in the simplest process category, the student is given a recognition or recall task under conditions very similar to those in which he or she learned the material. Little, if any, extension beyond those conditions is expected. If, for example, a student learned the English equivalents of 20 Spanish words, then a test of remembering could involve requesting the student to match the Spanish words in one list with their English equivalents in a second list (i.e., *recognize*) or to write the corresponding English word next to each of the Spanish words presented in the list (i.e., *recall*).

Remembering knowledge is essential for meaningful learning and problem solving as that knowledge is used in more complex tasks. For example, knowledge of the correct spelling of common English words appropriate to a given grade level is necessary if the student is to master writing an essay. Where teachers concentrate solely on rote learning, teaching and assessing focus solely on remembering elements or fragments of knowledge, often in isolation from their context. When teachers focus on meaningful learning, however, re-

5.1 THE COGNITIVE PROCESS DIMENSION

CATEGORIES & COGNITIVE PROCESSES	ALTERNATIVE NAMES	DEFINITIONS AND EXAMPLES
1. REMEMBER—Retrieve relevant knowledge from long-term memory		
1.1 RECOGNIZING	Identifying	Locating knowledge in long-term memory that is consistent with presented material (e.g., Recognize the dates of important events in U.S. history)
1.2 RECALLING	Retrieving	Retrieving relevant knowledge from long-term memory (e.g., Recall the dates of important events in U.S. history)
2. UNDERSTAND—Construct meaning from instructional messages, including oral, written, and graphic communication		
2.1 INTERPRETING	Clarifying, paraphrasing, representing, translating	Changing from one form of representation (e.g., numerical) to another (e.g., verbal) (e.g., Paraphrase important speeches and documents)
2.2 EXEMPLIFYING	Illustrating, instantiating	Finding a specific example or illustration of a concept or principle (e.g., Give examples of various artistic painting styles)
2.3 CLASSIFYING	Categorizing, subsuming	Determining that something belongs to a category (e.g., concept or principle) (e.g., Classify observed or described cases of mental disorders)
2.4 SUMMARIZING	Abstracting, generalizing	Abstracting a general theme or major point(s) (e.g., Write a short summary of the events portrayed on a videotape)
2.5 INFERRING	Concluding, extrapolating, interpolating, predicting	Drawing a logical conclusion from presented information (e.g., In learning a foreign language, infer grammatical principles from examples)
2.6 COMPARING	Contrasting, mapping, matching	Detecting correspondences between two ideas, objects, and the like (e.g., Compare historical events to contemporary situations)
2.7 EXPLAINING	Constructing models	Constructing a cause-and-effect model of a system (e.g., Explain the causes of important 18th-century events in France)
3. APPLY—Carry out or use a procedure in a given situation		
3.1 EXECUTING	Carrying out	Applying a procedure to a familiar task (e.g., Divide one whole number by another whole number, both with multiple digits)
3.2 IMPLEMENTING	Using	Applying a procedure to an unfamiliar task (e.g., Use Newton's Second Law in situations in which it is appropriate)

CATEGORIES & COGNITIVE PROCESSES	ALTERNATIVE NAMES	DEFINITIONS AND EXAMPLES
4. ANALYZE—Break material into its constituent parts and determine how the parts relate to one another and to an overall structure or purpose		
4.1 DIFFERENTIATING	Discriminating, distinguishing, focusing, selecting	Distinguishing relevant from irrelevant parts or important from unimportant parts of presented material (e.g., Distinguish between relevant and irrelevant numbers in a mathematical word problem)
4.2 ORGANIZING	Finding coherence, intergrating, outlining, parsing, structuring	Determining how elements fit or function within a structure (e.g., Structure evidence in a historical description into evidence for and against a particular historical explanation)
4.3 ATTRIBUTING	Deconstructing	Determine a point of view, bias, values, or intent underlying presented material (e.g., Determine the point of view of the author of an essay in terms of his or her political perspective)
5. EVALUATE—Make judgments based on criteria and standards		
5.1 CHECKING	Coordinating, detecting, monitoring, testing	Detecting inconsistencies or fallacies within a process or product; determining whether a process or product has internal consistency; detecting the effectiveness of a procedure as it is being implemented (e.g., Determine if a scientist's conclusions follow from observed data)
5.2 CRITIQUING	Judging	Detecting inconsistencies between a product and external criteria, determining whether a product has external consistency; detecting the appropriateness of a procedure for a given problem (e.g., Judge which of two methods is the best way to solve a given problem)
6. CREATE—Put elements together to form a coherent or functional whole; reorganize elements into a new pattern or structure		
6.1 GENERATING	Hypothesizing	Coming up with alternative hypotheses based on criteria (e.g., Generate hypotheses to account for an observed phenomenon)
6.2 PLANNING	Designing	Devising a procedure for accomplishing some task (e.g., Plan a research paper on a given historical topic)
6.3 PRODUCING	Constructing	Inventing a product (e.g., Build habitats for a specific purpose)

membering knowledge is integrated within the larger task of constructing new knowledge or solving new problems.

1.1 RECOGNIZING

Recognizing involves retrieving relevant knowledge from long-term memory in order to compare it with presented information. In *recognizing*, the student searches long-term memory for a piece of information that is identical or extremely similar to the presented information (as represented in working memory). When presented with new information, the student determines whether that information corresponds to previously learned knowledge, searching for a match. An alternative term for *recognizing* is identifying.

SAMPLE OBJECTIVES AND CORRESPONDING ASSESSMENTS In social studies, an objective could be for students to recognize the correct dates of important events in U.S. history. A corresponding test item is: "True or false: The Declaration of Independence was adopted on July 4, 1776." In literature, an objective could be to recognize authors of British literary works. A corresponding assessment is a matching test that contains a list of ten authors (including Charles Dickens) and a list of slightly more than ten novels (including *David Copperfield*). In mathematics, an objective could be to recognize the numbers of sides in basic geometric shapes. A corresponding assessment is a multiple-choice test with items such as the following: "How many sides does a pentagon have? (a) four, (b) five, (c) six, (d) seven."

ASSESSMENT FORMATS As illustrated in the preceding paragraph, three main methods of presenting a recognition task for the purpose of assessment are verification, matching, and forced choice. In verification tasks, the student is given some information and must choose whether or not it is correct. The true-false format is the most common example. In matching, two lists are presented, and the student must choose how each item in one list corresponds to an item in the other list. In forced choice tasks, the student is given a prompt along with several possible answers and must choose which answer is the correct or "best answer." Multiple-choice is the most common format.

1.2 RECALLING

Recalling involves retrieving relevant knowledge from long-term memory when given a prompt to do so. The prompt is often a question. In *recalling*, a student searches long-term memory for a piece of information and brings that piece of information to working memory where it can be processed. An alternative term for *recalling* is retrieving.

SAMPLE OBJECTIVES AND CORRESPONDING ASSESSMENTS In *recalling*, a student remembers previously learned information when given a prompt. In social studies, an objective could be to recall the major exports of various South American countries. A corresponding test item is "What is the major export of Bolivia?" In literature, an objective could be to recall the poets who wrote various poems. A corresponding test question is "Who wrote *The Charge of the Light Brigade*?" In mathematics, an objective could be to recall the whole-number multiplication facts. A corresponding test item asks students to multiply 7×8 (or "$7 \times 8 = ?$").

ASSESSMENT FORMATS   Assessment tasks for *recalling* can vary in the number and quality of cues that students are provided. With low cueing, the student is not given any hints or related information (such as "What is a meter?"). With high cueing, the student is given several hints (such as "In the metric system, a meter is a measure of _____.").

Assessment tasks for *recalling* can also vary in the amount of embedding, or the extent to which the items are placed within a larger meaningful context. With low embedding, the recall task is presented as a single, isolated event, as in the preceding examples. With high embedding, the recall task is included within the context of a larger problem, such as asking a student to recall the formula for the area of a circle when solving a word problem that requires that formula.

2. UNDERSTAND

As we indicated, when the primary goal of instruction is to promote retention, the focus is on objectives that emphasize *Remember*. When the goal of instruction is to promote transfer, however, the focus shifts to the other five cognitive processes, *Understand* through *Create*. Of these, arguably the largest category of transfer-based educational objectives emphasized in schools and colleges is *Understand*. Students are said to *Understand* when they are able to construct meaning from instructional messages, including oral, written, and graphic communications, however they are presented to students: during lectures, in books, or on computer monitors. Examples of potential instructional messages include an in-class physics demonstration, a geological formation seen on a field trip, a computer simulation of a trip through an art museum, and a musical work played by an orchestra, as well as numerous verbal, pictorial, and symbolic representations on paper.

Students understand when they build connections between the "new" knowledge to be gained and their prior knowledge. More specifically, the incoming knowledge is integrated with existing schemas and cognitive frameworks. Since concepts are the building blocks for these schemas and frameworks, *Conceptual knowledge* provides a basis for understanding. Cognitive processes in the category of *Understand* include *interpreting, exemplifying, classifying, summarizing, inferring, comparing,* and *explaining.*

2.1 INTERPRETING

Interpreting occurs when a student is able to convert information from one representational form to another. *Interpreting* may involve converting words to words (e.g., paraphrasing), pictures to words, words to pictures, numbers to words, words to numbers, musical notes to tones, and the like.

Alternative terms are translating, paraphrasing, representing, and clarifying.

SAMPLE OBJECTIVES AND CORRESPONDING ASSESSMENTS   In *interpreting*, when given information in one form of representation, a student is able to change it into another form. In social studies, for example, an objective could be to learn to paraphrase important speeches and documents from the Civil War period in U.S. history. A corresponding assessment asks a student to paraphrase a famous speech, such as Lincoln's Gettysburg Address. In science, an objective could be to learn to draw pictorial representations of various natural phenomena. A corresponding assessment item asks a student to draw a series of diagrams illustrating photosynthesis. In mathematics, a sample objective could be to learn to translate number sentences expressed in words into algebraic equations expressed in symbols. A corresponding assessment item asks a student to write an equation (using B for the number of boys and G for the number of girls) that corresponds to the statement "There are twice as many boys as girls in this class."

ASSESSMENT FORMATS   Appropriate test item formats include both constructed response (i.e., supply an answer) and selected response (i.e., choose an answer). Information is presented in one form, and students are asked either to construct or to select the same information in a different form. For example, a constructed response task is: "Write an equation that corresponds to the following statement, using T for total cost and P for number of pounds. The total cost of mailing a package is \$2.00 for the first pound plus \$1.50 for each additional pound." A selection version of this task is: "Which equation corresponds to the following statement, where T stands for total cost and P for number of pounds? The total cost of mailing a package is \$2.00 for the first pound plus \$1.50 for each additional pound. (a) $T = \$3.50 + P$, (b) $T = \$2.00 + \$1.50(P)$, (c) $T = \$2.00 + \$1.50(P - 1)$."

To increase the probability that *interpreting* rather than *remembering* is being assessed, the information included in the assessment task must be new. "New" here means that students did not encounter it during instruction. Unless this rule is observed, we cannot ensure that *interpreting* rather than *remembering* is being assessed. If the assessment task is identical to a task or example used during instruction, we are probably assessing *remembering*, despite our efforts to the contrary.

Although we will not repeat this point from here on, it applies to each of the process categories and cognitive processes beyond *Remember*. **If assessment tasks are to tap higher-order cognitive processes, they must require that students cannot answer them correctly by relying on memory alone.**

2.2 EXEMPLIFYING

Exemplifying occurs when a student gives a specific example or instance of a general concept or principle. *Exemplifying* involves identifying the defining features of the general concept or principle (e.g., an isosceles triangle must have two equal sides) and using these features to select or construct a specific instance (e.g., being able to select which of three presented triangles is an isosceles triangle). Alternative terms are illustrating and instantiating.

SAMPLE OBJECTIVES AND CORRESPONDING ASSESSMENTS   In *exemplifying*, a student is given a concept or principle and must select or produce a specific example or instance of it that was not encountered during instruction. In art history, an objective could be to learn to give examples of various artistic painting styles. A corresponding assessment asks a student to select which of four paintings represents the impressionist style. In science, a sample objective could be to be able to give examples of various kinds of chemical compounds. A corresponding assessment task asks the student to locate an inorganic compound on a field trip and tell why it is inorganic (i.e., specify the defining features). In literature, an objective could be to learn to exemplify various play genres. The assessment may give the students brief sketches of four plays (only one of which is a romantic comedy) and ask the student to name the play that is a romantic comedy.

ASSESSMENT FORMATS   *Exemplifying* tasks can involve the constructed response format—in which the student must create an example—or the selected response format—in which the student must select an example from a given set. The science example, "Locate an inorganic compound and tell why it is inorganic," requires a constructed response. In contrast, the item "Which of these is an inorganic compound? (a) iron, (b) protein, (c) blood, (d) leaf mold" requires a selected response.

2.3 CLASSIFYING

Classifying occurs when a student recognizes that something (e.g., a particular instance or example) belongs to a certain category (e.g., concept or principle). *Classifying* involves detecting relevant features or patterns that "fit" both the specific instance and the concept or principle. *Classifying* is a complementary process to *exemplifying*. Whereas *exemplifying* begins with a general concept or principle and requires the student to find a specific instance or example, *classifying* begins with a specific instance or example and requires the student to find a general concept or principle. Alternative terms for *classifying* are categorizing and subsuming.

SAMPLE OBJECTIVES AND CORRESPONDING ASSESSMENTS   In social studies, an objective could be to learn to classify observed or described cases of mental disorders. A corresponding assessment item asks a student to observe a video of the behavior of a person with mental illness and then indicate the mental disorder that is displayed. In the natural sciences, an objective could be to learn to categorize the species of various prehistoric animals. An assessment gives a student some pictures of prehistoric animals with instructions to group them with others of the same species. In mathematics, an objective could be to be able to determine the categories to which numbers belong. An assessment task gives an example and asks a student to circle all numbers in a list from the same category.

ASSESSMENT FORMATS   In constructed response tasks, a student is given an instance and must produce its related concept or principle. In selected response tasks, a student is given an instance and must select its concept or principle from a list. In a sorting task, a student is given a set of instances and must determine which ones belong in a specified category and which ones do not, or must place each instance into one of multiple categories.

2.4. SUMMARIZING

Summarizing occurs when a student suggests a single statement that represents presented information or abstracts a general theme. *Summarizing* involves constructing a representation of the information, such as the meaning of a scene in a play, and abstracting a summary from it, such as determining a theme or main points. Alternative terms are generalizing and abstracting.

SAMPLE OBJECTIVES AND CORRESPONDING ASSESSMENTS   In *summarizing*, when given information, a student provides a summary or abstracts a general theme. A sample objective in history could be to learn to write short summaries of events portrayed pictorially. A corresponding assessment item asks a student to watch a videotape on the French Revolution and then write a short summary. Similarly, a sample objective in the natural sciences could be to learn to summarize the major contributions of famous scientists after reading several of their writings. A corresponding assessment item asks a student to read selected writings about Charles Darwin and summarize the major points. In computer science, an objective could be to learn to summarize the purposes of various subroutines in a program. An assessment item presents a program and asks a student to write a sentence describing the subgoal that each section of the program accomplishes within the overall program.

ASSESSMENT FORMATS   Assessment tasks can be presented in constructed response or selection formats, involving either themes or summaries. Generally speaking, themes are more abstract than summaries. For example, in a constructed response task, the student may be asked to read an untitled passage on the California Gold Rush and then write an appropriate title. In a selection task, a student may be asked to read a passage on the California Gold Rush and then select the most appropriate title from a list of four possible titles or rank the titles in order of their "fit" to the point of the passage.

2.5 INFERRING

Inferring involves finding a pattern within a series of examples or instances. *Inferring* occurs when a student is able to abstract a concept or principle that accounts for a set of examples or instances by encoding the relevant features of each instance and, most important, by noting relationships among them. For example, when given a series of numbers such as 1, 2, 3, 5, 8, 13, 21, a student is able to focus on the numerical value of each digit rather than on irrelevant features such as the shape of each digit or whether each digit is odd or even. He or she then is able to distinguish the pattern in the series of numbers (i.e., after the first two numbers, each is the sum of the preceding two numbers).

The process of *inferring* involves making comparisons among instances within the context of the entire set. For example, to determine what number will come next in the series above, a student must identify the pattern. A related process is using the pattern to create a new instance (e.g., the next number on the series is 34, the sum of 13 and 21). This is an example of *executing*, which is a cognitive process associated with *Apply*. *Inferring* and *executing* are often used together on cognitive tasks.

Finally, *inferring* is different from *attributing* (a cognitive process associated with *Analyze*). As we discuss later in this chapter, *attributing* focuses solely on the pragmatic issue of determining the author's point of view or intention, whereas *inferring* focuses on the issue of inducing a pattern based on presented information. Another way of differentiating between these two is that *attributing* is broadly applicable to situations in which one must "read between the lines," especially when one is seeking to determine an author's point of view. *Inferring*, on the other hand, occurs in a context that supplies an expectation of what is to be inferred. Alternative terms for *inferring* are extrapolating, interpolating, predicting, and concluding.

SAMPLE OBJECTIVES AND CORRESPONDING ASSESSMENTS   In *inferring*, when given a set or series of examples or instances, a student finds a concept or principle that accounts for them. For example, in learning Spanish as a second language, a sample objective could be to be able to infer grammatical principles from examples. For assessment, a student is given the article-noun pairs "la casa, el muchacho, la señorita, el pero" and asked to formulate a principle for when to use "la" and when to use "el." In mathematics, an objective could be to learn to infer the relationship expressed as an equation that represents several observations of values for two variables. An assessment item asks a student to describe the relationship as an equation involving x and y for situations in which if x is 1, then y is 0; if x is 2, then y is 3; and if x is 3, then y is 8.

ASSESSMENT FORMATS   Three common tasks that require *inferring* (often along with *implementing*) are completion tasks, analogy tasks, and oddity tasks. In completion tasks, a student is given a series of items and must determine what will come next, as in the number series example above. In analogy tasks, a student is given an analogy of the form A is to B as C is to D, such as "nation" is to "president" as "state" is to _____. The student's task is to produce or select a term that fits in the blank and completes the analogy (such as "governor"). In an oddity task, a student is given three or more items and must determine which does not belong. For example, a student may be given three physics problems, two involving one principle and another involving a different principle. To focus solely on the inferring process, the question in each assessment task could be to state the underlying concept or principle the student is using to arrive at the correct answer.

2.6 COMPARING

Comparing involves detecting similarities and differences between two or more objects, events, ideas, problems, or situations, such as determining how a well-known event (e.g., a recent political scandal) is like a less familiar event (e.g., a historical political scandal). *Comparing* includes finding one-to-one correspondences between elements and patterns in one object, event, or idea and those in another object, event, or idea. When used in conjunction with *inferring* (e.g., first, abstracting a rule from the more familiar situation) and *implementing* (e.g., second, applying the rule to the less familiar situation), *comparing* can contribute to reasoning by analogy. Alternative terms are contrasting, matching, and mapping.

SAMPLE OBJECTIVES AND CORRESPONDING ASSESSMENTS   In *comparing,* when given new information, a student detects correspondences with more familiar knowledge. For example, in social studies, an objective could be to understand historical events by comparing them to familiar situations. A corresponding assessment question is "How is the American Revolution like a family fight or an argument between friends?" In the natural sciences, a sample objective could be to learn to compare an electrical circuit to a more familiar system. In assessment, we ask "How is an electrical circuit like water flowing through a pipe?"

Comparing may also involve determining correspondences between two or more presented objects, events, or ideas. In mathematics, a sample objective could be to learn to compare structurally similar word problems. A corresponding assessment question asks a student to tell how a certain mixture problem is like a certain work problem.

ASSESSMENT FORMATS   A major technique for assessing the cognitive process of *comparing* is mapping. In mapping, a student must show how each part of one object, idea, problem, or situation corresponds to (or maps onto) each part of another. For example, a student could be asked to detail how the battery, wire, and resistor in an electrical circuit are like the pump, pipes, and pipe constructions in a water flow system, respectively.

2.7 EXPLAINING

Explaining occurs when a student is able to construct and use a cause-and-effect model of a system. The model may be derived from a formal theory (as is often the case in the natural sciences) or may be grounded in research or experience (as is often the case in the social sciences and humanities). A complete explanation involves constructing a cause-and-effect model, including each major part in a system or each major event in the chain, and using the model to determine how a change in one part of the system or one "link" in the chain affects a change in another part. An alternative term for *explaining* is constructing a model.

SAMPLE OBJECTIVES AND CORRESPONDING ASSESSMENTS   In *explaining*, when given a description of a system, a student develops and uses a cause-and-effect model of the system. For example, in social studies, an objective could be to explain the causes of important eighteenth-century historical events. As an assessment, after reading and discussing a unit on the American Revolution, students are asked to construct a cause-and-effect chain of events that best explains why the war occurred. In the natural sciences, an objective could be to explain how basic physics laws work. Corresponding assessments ask students who have studied Ohm's law to explain what happens to the rate of the current when a second battery is added to a circuit, or ask students who have viewed a video on lightning storms to explain how differences in temperature affect the formation of lightning.

ASSESSMENT FORMATS   Several tasks can be aimed at assessing a student's ability to explain, including reasoning, troubleshooting, redesigning, and predicting. In reasoning tasks, a student is asked to offer a reason for a given event. For example, "Why does air enter a bicycle tire pump when you pull up on the handle?" In this case, an answer such as "It is forced in because the air pressure is less inside the pump than outside" involves finding a principle that accounts for a given event.

In troubleshooting, a student is asked to diagnose what could have gone wrong in a malfunctioning system. For example, "Suppose you pull up and press down on the handle of a bicycle tire pump several times but no air comes out. What's wrong?" In this case, the student must find an explanation for a symptom, such as "There is a hole in the cylinder" or "A valve is stuck in the open position."

In redesigning, a student is asked to change the system to accomplish some goal. For example, "How could you improve a bicycle tire pump so that it would be more efficient?" To answer this question, a student must imagine altering one or more of the components in the system, such as "Put lubricant between the piston and the cylinder."

In predicting, a student is asked how a change in one part of a system will effect a change in another part of the system. For example, "What would happen if you increased the diameter of the cylinder in a bicycle tire pump?" This question requires that the student "operate" the mental model of the pump to see that the amount of air moving through the pump could be increased by increasing the diameter of the cylinder.

3. APPLY

Apply involves using procedures to perform exercises or solve problems. Thus, *Apply* is closely linked with *Procedural knowledge*. An exercise is a task for which the student already knows the proper procedure to use, so the student has developed a fairly routinized approach to it. A problem is a task for which the student initially does not know what procedure to use, so the student must locate a procedure to solve the problem. The *Apply* category consists of two cognitive processes: *executing*—when the task is an exercise (familiar)—and *implementing*—when the task is a problem (unfamiliar).

When the task is a familiar exercise, students generally know what *Procedural knowledge* to use. When given an exercise (or set of exercises), students typically perform the procedure with little thought. For example, an algebra student confronted with the 50th exercise involving quadratic equations might simply "plug in the numbers and turn the crank."

When the task is an unfamiliar problem, however, students must determine what knowledge they will use. If the task appears to call for *Procedural knowledge* and no available procedure fits the problem situation exactly, then modifications in selected *Procedural knowledge* may be necessary. In contrast to *executing*, then, *implementing* requires some degree of understanding of the problem as well as of the solution procedure. In the case of *implementing*, then, to *understand conceptual knowledge* is a prerequisite to being able to *apply procedural knowledge*.

3.1 EXECUTING

In *executing*, a student routinely carries out a procedure when confronted with a familiar task (i.e., exercise). The familiarity of the situation often provides sufficient clues to guide the choice of the appropriate procedure to use. *Executing* is more frequently associated with the use of skills and algorithms than with techniques and methods (see our discussion of *Procedural knowledge* on pages 52–53). Skills and algorithms have two qualities that make them particularly amenable to *executing*. First, they consist of a sequence of steps that are generally followed *in a fixed order*. Second, when the steps are performed correctly, the end result is a predetermined answer. An alternative term for *executing* is carrying out.

SAMPLE OBJECTIVES AND CORRESPONDING ASSESSMENTS   In *executing*, a student is faced with a familiar task and knows what to do in order to complete it. The student simply carries out a known procedure to perform the task. For example, a sample objective in elementary level mathematics could be for students to learn to divide one whole number by another, both with multiple digits. The instructions to "divide" signify the division algorithm, which is the necessary *Procedural knowledge*. To assess the objective, a student is given a worksheet that has 15 whole-number division exercises (e.g., 784/15) and is asked to find the quotients. In the natural sciences, a sample objective could be to learn to compute the value of variables using scientific formulas. To assess the objective, a student is given the formula Density = Mass/Volume and must answer the question "What is the density of a material with a mass of 18 pounds and a volume of 9 cubic inches?"

ASSESSMENT FORMATS   In *executing*, a student is given a familiar task that can be performed using a well-known procedure. For example, an execution task is "Solve for x: $x^2 + 2x - 3 = 0$ using the technique of completing the square." Students may be asked to supply the answer or, where appropriate, select from among a set of possible answers. Furthermore, because the emphasis is on the procedure as well as the answer, students may be required not only to find the answer but also to show their work.

3.2 IMPLEMENTING

Implementing occurs when a student selects and uses a procedure to perform an unfamiliar task. Because selection is required, students must possess an understanding of the type of problem encountered as well as the range of procedures that are available. Thus, *implementing* is used in conjunction with other cognitive process categories, such as *Understand* and *Create*.

Because the student is faced with an unfamiliar problem, he or she does not immediately know which of the available procedures to use. Furthermore, no single procedure may be a "perfect fit" for the problem; some modification in the procedure may be needed. *Implementing* is more frequently associated with the use of techniques and methods than with skills and algorithms (see the discussion of *Procedural knowledge* on pages 52–53). Techniques and methods have two qualities that make them particularly amenable to *implementing*. First, the procedure may be more like a "flow chart" than a fixed sequence; that is, the procedure may have "decision points" built into it (e.g., after completing Step 3, should I do Step 4A or Step 4B?). Second, there often is no single, fixed answer that is expected when the procedure is applied correctly.

The notion of no single, fixed answer is especially applicable to objectives that call for *applying conceptual knowledge* such as theories, models, and structures (subtype Cc), where no procedure has been developed for the application. Consider an objective such as "The student shall be able to apply a social psychological theory of crowd behavior to crowd control." Social psychological theory is *Conceptual* not *Procedural knowledge*. This is clearly an *Apply* objective, however, and there is no procedure for making the application. Given that the theory would very clearly structure and guide the student in the application, this objective is just barely on the *Apply* side of *Create*, but *Apply* it is. So it would be classified as *implementing*.

To see why it fits, think of the *Apply* category as structured along a continuum. It starts with the narrow, highly structured *execute*, in which the known *Procedural knowledge* is applied almost routinely. It continues through the broad, increasingly unstructured *implement*, in which, at the beginning, the procedure must be selected to fit a new situation. In the middle of the category, the procedure may have to be modified to *implement* it. At the far end of *implementing*, where there is no set *Procedural knowledge* to modify, a procedure must be manufactured out of *Conceptual knowledge* using theories, models, or structures as a guide. So, although *Apply* is closely linked to *Procedural knowledge*, and this linkage carries through most of the category of *Apply*, there are some instances in *implementing* to which one applies *Conceptual knowledge* as well. An alternative term for *implementing* is using.

SAMPLE OBJECTIVES AND CORRESPONDING ASSESSMENTS   In mathematics, a sample objective could be to learn to solve a variety of personal finance problems. A corresponding assessment is to present students with a problem in which they must choose the most economical financing package for a new car. In the natural sciences, a sample objective could be to learn to use the most effective, efficient, and affordable method of conducting a research study to address a specific research question. A corresponding assessment is to give students a research question and have them propose a research study that meets specified criteria of effectiveness, efficiency, and affordability. Notice that in both of these assessment tasks, the student must not only apply a procedure (i.e., engage in *implementing*) but also rely on conceptual understanding of the problem, the procedure, or both.

ASSESSMENT FORMATS   In *implementing*, a student is given an unfamiliar problem that must be solved. Thus, most assessment formats begin with specification of the problem. Students are asked to determine the procedure needed to solve the problem, solve the problem using the selected procedure (making modifications as necessary), or usually both.

4. ANALYZE

Analyze involves breaking material into its constituent parts and determining how the parts are related to one another and to an overall structure. This process category includes the cognitive processes of *differentiating, organizing,* and *attributing*. Objectives classified as *Analyze* include learning to determine the relevant or important pieces of a message (*differentiating*), the ways in which the pieces of a message are organized (*organizing*), and the underlying purpose of the message (*attributing*). Although learning to *Analyze* may be viewed as an end in itself, it is probably more defensible educationally to consider analysis as an extension of *Understanding* or as a prelude to *Evaluating* or *Creating*.

Improving students' skills in analyzing educational communications is a goal in many fields of study. Teachers of science, social studies, the humanities, and the arts frequently give "learning to analyze" as one of their important objectives. They may, for example, wish to develop in their students the ability to:

- distinguish fact from opinion (or reality from fantasy);
- connect conclusions with supporting statements;

- distinguish relevant from extraneous material;

- determine how ideas are related to one another;

- ascertain the unstated assumptions involved in what is said;

- distinguish dominant from subordinate ideas or themes in poetry or music; and

- find evidence in support of the author's purposes.

The process categories of *Understand, Analyze,* and *Evaluate* are interrelated and often used iteratively in performing cognitive tasks. At the same time, however, it is important to maintain them as separate process categories. A person who understands a communication may not be able to analyze it well. Similarly, someone who is skillful in analyzing a communication may evaluate it poorly.

4.1 DIFFERENTIATING

Differentiating involves distinguishing the parts of a whole structure in terms of their relevance or importance. *Differentiating* occurs when a student discriminates relevant from irrelevant information, or important from unimportant information, and then attends to the relevant or important information. *Differentiating* is different from the cognitive processes associated with *Understand* because it involves structural organization and, in particular, determining how the parts fit into the overall structure or whole. More specifically, *differentiating* differs from *comparing* in using the larger context to determine what is relevant or important and what is not. For instance, in *differentiating* apples and oranges in the context of fruit, internal seeds are relevant, but color and shape are irrelevant. In *comparing,* all of these aspects (i.e., seeds, color, and shape) are relevant. Alternative terms for *differentiating* are discriminating, selecting, distinguishing, and focusing.

SAMPLE OBJECTIVES AND CORRESPONDING ASSESSMENTS   In the social sciences, an objective could be to learn to determine the major points in research reports. A corresponding assessment item requires a student to circle the main points in an archeological report about an ancient Mayan city (such as when the city began and when it ended, the population of the city over the course of its existence, the geographic location of the city, the physical buildings in the city, its economic and cultural function, the social organization of the city, why the city was built and why it was deserted).

Similarly, in the natural sciences, an objective could be to select the main steps in a written description of how something works. A corresponding assessment item asks a student to read a chapter in a book that describes lightning formation and then to divide the process into major steps (including moist air rising to form a cloud, creation of updrafts and downdrafts inside the cloud, separation of charges within the cloud, movement of a stepped leader downward from cloud to ground, and creation of a return stroke from ground to cloud).

Finally, in mathematics, an objective could be to distinguish between relevant and irrelevant numbers in a word problem. An assessment item requires a student to circle the relevant numbers and cross out the irrelevant numbers in a word problem.

ASSESSMENT FORMATS   *Differentiating* can be assessed with constructed response or selection tasks. In a constructed response task, a student is given some material and is asked to indicate which parts are most important or relevant, as in this example: "Write the numbers that are needed to solve this problem: Pencils come in packages that contain 12 each and cost $2.00 each. John has $5.00 and wishes to buy 24 pencils. How many packages does he need to buy?" In a selection task, a student is given some material and is asked to choose which parts are most important or relevant, as in this example: "Which numbers are needed to solve this problem? Pencils come in packages that contain 12 each and cost $2.00 each. John has $5.00 and wishes to buy 24 pencils. How many packages does he need to buy? (a) 12, $2.00, $5.00, 24; (b) 12, $2.00, $5.00; (c) 12, $2.00, 24; (d) 12, 24."

4.2 ORGANIZING

Organizing involves identifying the elements of a communication or situation and recognizing how they fit together into a coherent structure. In *organizing*, a student builds systematic and coherent connections among pieces of presented information. *Organizing* usually occurs in conjunction with *differentiating*. The student first identifies the relevant or important elements and then determines the overall structure within which the elements fit. *Organizing* can also occur in conjunction with *attributing*, in which the focus is on determining the author's intention or point of view. Alternative terms for *organizing* are structuring, integrating, finding coherence, outlining, and parsing.

SAMPLE OBJECTIVES AND CORRESPONDING ASSESSMENTS   In *organizing*, when given a description of a situation or problem, a student is able to identify the systematic, coherent relationships among relevant elements. A sample objective in social studies could be to learn to structure a historical description into evidence for and against a particular explanation. A corresponding assessment item asks a student to write an outline that shows which facts in a passage on American history support and which facts do not support the conclusion that the American Civil War was caused by differences in the rural and urban composition of the North and South. A sample objective in the natural sciences could be to learn to analyze research reports in terms of four sections: hypothesis, method, data, and conclusion. As an assessment, students are asked to produce an outline of a presented research report. In mathematics, a sample objective could be to learn to outline textbook lessons. A corresponding assessment task asks a student to read a textbook lesson on basic statistics and then generate a matrix that includes each statistic's name, formula, and the conditions under which it is used.

ASSESSMENT FORMATS   *Organizing* involves imposing a structure on material (such as an outline, table, matrix, or hierarchical diagram). Thus, assessment can be based on constructed response or selection tasks. In a constructed response task, a student may be asked to produce a written outline of a passage. In a selection task, a student may be asked to select which of four alternative graphic hierarchies best corresponds to the organization of a presented passage.

4.3 ATTRIBUTING

Attributing occurs when a student is able to ascertain the point of view, biases, values, or intention underlying communications. *Attributing* involves a process of deconstruction, in which a student determines the intentions of the author of the presented material. In contrast to *interpreting,* in which the student seeks to *Understand* the meaning of the presented material, *attributing* involves an extension beyond basic understanding to infer the intention or point of view underlying the presented material. For example, in reading a passage on the battle of Atlanta in the American Civil War, a student needs to determine whether the author takes the perspective of the North or the South.
An alternative term is deconstructing.

SAMPLE OBJECTIVES AND CORRESPONDING ASSESSMENTS   In *attributing,* when given information, a student is able to determine the underlying point of view or intention of the author. For example, in literature, an objective could be to learn to determine the motives for a series of actions by characters in a story. A corresponding assessment task for the students having read Shakespeare's *Macbeth* is to ask what motive(s) Shakespeare attributed to Macbeth for the murder of King Duncan. In social studies, a sample objective could be to learn to determine the point of view of the author of an essay on a controversial topic in terms of his or her theoretical perspective. A corresponding assessment task asks a student whether a report on Amazon rain forests was written from a pro-environment or pro-business point of view. This objective is also applicable to the natural sciences. A corresponding assessment task asks a student to determine whether a behaviorist or a cognitive psychologist wrote an essay about human learning.

ASSESSMENT FORMATS   *Attributing* can be assessed by presenting some written or oral material and then asking a student to construct or select a description of the author's or speaker's point of view, intentions, and the like. For example, a constructed response task is "What is the author's purpose in writing the essay you read on the Amazon rain forests?" A selection version of this task is "The author's purpose in writing the essay you read is to: (a) provide factual information about Amazon rain forests, (b) alert the reader to the need to protect rain forests, (c) demonstrate the economic advantages of developing rain forests, or (d) describe the consequences to humans if rain forests are developed." Alternatively, students might be asked to indicate whether the author of the essay would (a) strongly agree, (b) agree, (c) neither agree nor disagree, (d) disagree, or (e) strongly disagree with several statements. Statements like "The rainforest is a unique type of ecological system" would follow.

5. EVALUATE

Evaluate is defined as making judgments based on criteria and standards. The criteria most often used are quality, effectiveness, efficiency, and consistency. They may be determined by the student or by others. The standards may be either quantitative (i.e., Is this a sufficient amount?) or qualitative (i.e., Is this good enough?). The standards are applied to the criteria (e.g., Is this process sufficiently effective? Is this product of sufficient quality?). The category *Evaluate* includes the cognitive processes of *checking* (judgments about the internal consistency) and *critiquing* (judgments based on external criteria).

It must be emphasized that not all judgments are evaluative. For example, students make judgments about whether a specific example fits within a category. They make judgments about the appropriateness of a particular procedure for a specified problem. They make judgments about whether two objects are similar or different. Most of the cognitive processes, in fact, require some form of judgment. What most clearly differentiates *Evaluate* as defined here from other judgments made by students is the use of standards of performance with clearly defined criteria. Is this machine working as efficiently as it should be? Is this method the best way to achieve the goal? Is this approach more cost effective than other approaches? Such questions are addressed by people engaged in *Evaluating*.

5.1 CHECKING

Checking involves testing for internal inconsistencies or fallacies in an operation or a product. For example, *checking* occurs when a student tests whether or not a conclusion follows from its premises, whether data support or disconfirm a hypothesis, or whether presented material contains parts that contradict one another. When combined with *planning* (a cognitive process in the category *Create*) and *implementing* (a cognitive process in the category *Apply*), checking involves determining how well the plan is working. Alternative terms for *checking* are testing, detecting, monitoring, and coordinating.

SAMPLE OBJECTIVES AND CORRESPONDING ASSESSMENTS   In *checking,* students look for internal inconsistencies. A sample objective in the social sciences could be to learn to detect inconsistencies in persuasive messages. A corresponding assessment task asks students to watch a television advertisement for a political candidate and point out any logical flaws in the persuasive message. A sample objective in the sciences could be to learn to determine whether a scientist's conclusion follows from the observed data. An assessment task asks a student to read a report of a chemistry experiment and determine whether or not the conclusion follows from the results of the experiment.

ASSESSMENT FORMATS   *Checking* tasks can involve operations or products given to the students or ones created by the students themselves. *Checking* can also take place within the context of carrying out a solution to a problem or performing a task, where one is concerned with the consistency of the actual implementation (e.g., Is this where I should be in light of what I've done so far?).

5.2 CRITIQUING

Critiquing involves judging a product or operation based on externally imposed criteria and standards. In *critiquing*, a student notes the positive and negative features of a product and makes a judgment based at least partly on those features. *Critiquing* lies at the core of what has been called critical thinking. An example of *critiquing* is judging the merits of a particular solution to the problem of acid rain in terms of its likely effectiveness and its associated costs (e.g., requiring all power plants throughout the country to restrict their smokestack emissions to certain limits). An alternative term is judging.

SAMPLE OBJECTIVES AND CORRESPONDING ASSESSMENTS   In *critiquing*, students judge the merits of a product or operation based on specified or student-determined criteria and standards. In the social sciences, an objective could be to learn to evaluate a proposed solution (such as "eliminate all grading") to a social problem (such as "how to improve K–12 education") in terms of its likely effectiveness. In the natural sciences, an objective could be to learn to evaluate the reasonableness of a hypothesis (such as the hypothesis that strawberries are growing to extraordinary size because of the unusual alignment of the stars). Finally, in mathematics, an objective could be to learn to judge which of two alternative methods is a more effective and efficient way of solving given problems (such as judging whether it is better to find all prime factors of 60 or to produce an algebraic equation to solve the problem "What are the possible ways you could multiply two whole numbers to get 60?").

ASSESSMENT FORMATS   A student may be asked to critique his or her own hypotheses or creations or those generated by someone else. The critique could be based on positive, negative, or both kinds of criteria and yield both positive and negative consequences. For example, in *critiquing* a school district's proposal for year-round schools, a student would generate positive consequences, such as the elimination of learning loss over summer vacation, and negative consequences, such as disruption of family vacations.

6. CREATE

Create involves putting elements together to form a coherent or functional whole. Objectives classified as *Create* have students make a new product by mentally reorganizing some elements or parts into a pattern or structure not clearly present before. The processes involved in *Create* are generally coordinated with the student's previous learning experiences. Although *Create* requires creative thinking on the part of the student, this is not completely free creative expression unconstrained by the demands of the learning task or situation.

To some persons, creativity is the production of unusual products, often as a result of some special skill. *Create*, as used here, however, although it includes objectives that call for unique production, also refers to objectives calling for production that all students can and will do. If nothing else, in meeting these objectives, many students will create in the sense of producing their own synthesis of information or materials to form a new whole, as in writing, painting, sculpting, building, and so on.

Although many objectives in the *Create* category emphasize originality (or uniqueness), educators must define what is original or unique. Can the term *unique* be used to describe the work of an individual student (e.g., "This is unique for Adam Jones") or is it reserved for use with a group of students (e.g., "This is unique for a fifth-grader")? It is important to note, however, that many objectives in the *Create* category do not rely on originality or uniqueness. The teachers' intent with these objectives is that students should be able to synthesize material into a whole. This synthesis is often required in papers in which the student is expected to assemble previously taught material into an organized presentation.

Although the process categories of *Understand, Apply,* and *Analyze* may involve detecting relationships among presented elements, *Create* is different because it also involves the construction of an original product. Unlike *Create*, the other categories involve working with a given set of elements that are part of a given whole; that is, they are part of a larger structure the student is trying to understand. In *Create*, on the other hand, the student must draw upon elements from many sources and put them together into a novel structure or pattern relative to his or her own prior knowledge. *Create* results in a new product, that is, something that can be observed and that is more than the student's beginning materials. A task that requires *Create* is likely to require aspects of each of the earlier cognitive process categories to some extent, but not necessarily in the order in which they are listed in the Taxonomy Table.

We recognize that composition (including writing) often, but not always, requires the cognitive processes associated with *Create*. For example, *Create* is not involved in writing that represents the remembering of ideas or the interpretation of materials. We also recognize that deep understanding that goes beyond basic understanding can require the cognitive processes associated with *Create*. To the extent that deep understanding is an act of construction or insight, the cognitive processes of *Create* are involved.

The creative process can be broken into three phases: problem representation, in which a student attempts to understand the task and generate possible solutions; solution planning, in which a student examines the possibilities and devises a workable plan; and solution execution, in which a student successfully carries out the plan. Thus, the creative process can be thought of as starting with a divergent phase in which a variety of possible solutions are considered as the student attempts to understand the task (*generating*). This is followed by a convergent phase, in which the student devises a solution method and turns it into a plan of action (*planning*). Finally, the plan is executed as the student constructs the solution (*producing*). It is not surprising, then, that *Create* is associated with three cognitive processes: *generating, planning,* and *producing.*

6.1 GENERATING

Generating involves representing the problem and arriving at alternatives or hypotheses that meet certain criteria. Often the way a problem is initially represented suggests possible solutions; however, redefining or coming up with a new representation of the problem may suggest different solutions. When *generating* transcends the boundaries or constraints of prior knowledge and existing theories, it involves divergent thinking and forms the core of what can be called creative thinking.

Generating is used in a restricted sense here. *Understand* also requires generative processes, which we have included in *translating, exemplifying, summarizing, inferring, classifying, comparing,* and *explaining.* However, the goal of *Understand* is most often convergent (that is, to arrive at a single meaning). In contrast, the goal of *generating* within *Create* is divergent (that is, to arrive at various possibilities). An alternative term for *generating* is hypothesizing.

SAMPLE OBJECTIVE AND CORRESPONDING ASSESSMENT   In *generating,* a student is given a description of a problem and must produce alternative solutions. For example, in the social sciences, an objective could be to learn to generate multiple useful solutions for social problems. A corresponding assessment item is: "Suggest as many ways as you can to assure that everyone has adequate medical insurance." To assess student responses, the teacher should construct a set of criteria that are shared with the students. These might include the number of alternatives, the reasonableness of the various alternatives, the practicality of the various alternatives, and so on. In the natural sciences, an objective could be to learn to generate hypotheses to explain observed phenomena. A corresponding assessment task asks students to write as many hypotheses as they can to explain strawberries growing to extraordinary size. Again, the teacher should establish clearly defined criteria for judging the quality of the responses and give them to the students. Finally, an objective from the field of mathematics could be to be able to generate alternative methods for achieving a particular result. A corresponding assessment item is: "What alternative methods could you use to find what whole numbers yield 60 when multiplied together?" For each of these assessments, explicit, publicly shared scoring criteria are needed.

ASSESSMENT FORMATS   Assessing *generating* typically involves constructed response formats in which a student is asked to produce alternatives or hypotheses. Two traditional subtypes are consequences tasks and uses tasks. In a consequences task, a student must list all the possible consequences of a certain event, such as "What would happen if there was a flat income tax rather than a graduated income tax?" In a uses task, a student must list all possible uses for an object, such as "What are the possible uses for the World Wide Web?" It is almost impossible to use the multiple-choice format to assess *generating* processes.

6.2 PLANNING

Planning involves devising a solution method that meets a problem's criteria, that is, developing a plan for solving the problem. *Planning* stops short of carrying out the steps to create the actual solution for a given problem. In *planning*, a student may establish subgoals, or break a task into subtasks to be performed when solving the problem. Teachers often skip stating *planning* objectives, instead stating their objectives in terms of *producing*, the final stage of the creative process. When this happens, *planning* is either assumed or implicit in the *producing* objective. In this case, *planning* is likely to be carried out by the student covertly during the course of constructing a product (i.e., *producing*). An alternative term is designing.

SAMPLE OBJECTIVES AND CORRESPONDING ASSESSMENTS   In *planning*, when given a problem statement, a student develops a solution method. In history, a sample objective could be to be able to plan research papers on given historical topics. An assessment task asks the student, prior to writing a research paper on the causes of the American Revolution, to submit an outline of the paper, including the steps he or she intends to follow to conduct the research. In the natural sciences, a sample objective could be to learn to design studies to test various hypotheses. An assessment task asks students to plan a way of determining which of three factors determines the rate of oscillation of a pendulum. In mathematics, an objective could be to be able to lay out the steps needed to solve geometry problems. An assessment task asks students to devise a plan for determining the volume of the frustrum of a pyramid (a task not previously considered in class). The plan may involve computing the volume of the large pyramid, then computing the volume of the small pyramid, and finally subtracting the smaller volume from the larger.

ASSESSMENT FORMATS   *Planning* may be assessed by asking students to develop worked-out solutions, describe solution plans, or select solution plans for a given problem.

6.3 PRODUCING

Producing involves carrying out a plan for solving a given problem that meets certain specifications. As we noted earlier, objectives within the category *Create* may or may not include originality or uniqueness as one of the specifications. So it is with *producing* objectives. *Producing* can require the coordination of the four types of knowledge described in Chapter 4. An alternative term is constructing.

SAMPLE OBJECTIVES AND CORRESPONDING ASSESSMENTS   In *producing*, a student is given a functional description of a goal and must create a product that satisfies the description. It involves carrying out a solution plan for a given problem. Sample objectives involve producing novel and useful products that meet certain requirements. In history, an objective could be to learn to write papers pertaining to particular historical periods that meet specified standards of scholarship. An assessment task asks students to write a short story that takes place during the American Revolution. In science, an objective could be to learn to design habitats for certain species and certain purposes. A corresponding assessment task asks students to design the living quarters of a space station. In English literature, an objective could be to learn to design sets for plays. A corresponding assessment task asks students to design the set for a student production of *Driving Miss Daisy*. In all these examples, the specifications become the criteria for evaluating student performance relative to the objective. These specifications, then, should be included in a scoring rubric that is given to the students in advance of the assessment.

ASSESSMENT FORMATS   A common task for assessing *producing* is a design task, in which students are asked to create a product that corresponds to certain specifications. For example, students may be asked to produce schematic plans for a new high school that include new ways for students to conveniently store their personal belongings.

DECONTEXTUALIZED AND CONTEXTUALIZED COGNITIVE PROCESSES

We have examined each cognitive process in isolation (i.e., as decontextualized processes). In the next section we examine the processes within the context of a particular educational objective (i.e., as contextualized processes). In this way, we are reuniting cognitive processes with knowledge. Unlike decontextualized processes (e.g., planning), contextualized processes occur within a specific academic context (e.g., planning the composition of a literary essay, planning to solve an arithmetic word problem, or planning to perform a scientific experiment).

Although it may be easier to focus on decontextualized cognitive processes, two findings from research in cognitive science point to the important role of context in learning and thinking (Bransford, Brown, and Cocking, 1999; Mayer, 1992; Smith, 1991). First, research suggests that the nature of the cognitive process depends on the subject matter to which it is applied (Bruer, 1993; Mayer, 1999; Pressley and Woloshyn, 1995). For example, learning to plan solutions to mathematics problems is different from learning to plan the composition of literary essays. Consequently, experience in planning in mathematics does not necessarily help a student learn to plan essay compositions. Second, research on authentic assessment suggests that the nature of a process depends on the authenticity of the task to which it is applied (Baker, O'Neil, and Linn, 1993; Hambleton, 1996). For example, learning to generate writing plans (without actually writing an essay) is different from learning to generate plans within the context of actually producing an essay.

Although we have described the cognitive processes individually, they are likely to be used in coordination with one another to facilitate meaningful school learning. Most authentic academic tasks require the coordinated use of several cognitive processes as well as several types of knowledge. For example, to solve a mathematical word problem, a student may engage in:

- *interpreting* (to understand each sentence in the problem);
- *recalling* (to retrieve the relevant *Factual knowledge* needed to solve the problem);
- *organizing* (to build a coherent representation of the key information in the problem, that is, *Conceptual knowledge*);
- *planning* (to devise a solution plan); and
- *producing* (to carry out the plan, that is, *Procedural knowledge*) (Mayer, 1992).

Similarly, to write an essay, a student may engage in:

- *recalling* (to retrieve relevant information that may be included in the essay);
- *planning* (to decide what to include in the essay, determine what to say, and how to say it);
- *producing* (to create a written product); and
- *critiquing* (to make sure the written essay "makes sense") (Levy and Ransdell, 1996).

AN EXAMPLE OF EDUCATIONAL OBJECTIVES IN CONTEXT

In simplest terms, our revised framework is intended to help teachers teach, learners learn, and assessors assess. Suppose, for example, that a teacher has a very general objective for her students: She wants them to learn about Ohm's law. She devises an instructional unit accordingly. Because of the vagueness of the objective, this unit potentially includes all four types of knowledge: *Factual, Conceptual, Procedural,* and *Metacognitive*. An example of *Factual knowledge* is that current is measured in amps, voltage in volts, and resistance in ohms. An example of *Procedural knowledge* is the steps involved in using the formula for Ohm's law (voltage = current × resistance) to compute a numerical value.

Although these two types of knowledge are the most obvious to include in this unit, a deeper understanding of Ohm's law requires the other two types of knowledge: *Conceptual* and *Metacognitive*. An example of *Conceptual knowledge* is the structure and workings of an electrical circuit that consists of batteries, wires, and a light bulb. An electrical circuit is a conceptual system in which there are causal relations among the elements (e.g., if more batteries are added in serial, the voltage increases, which causes an increase in the flow of electrons in the wires as measured by an increase in current). As an example of *Metacognitive knowledge,* the teacher may intend students to know when to use mnemonic strategies for memorizing the name of the law, the formula, and similar relevant items. She also may want them to establish their own goals for learning Ohm's law and its applications.

REMEMBERING WHAT WAS LEARNED

A restricted set of objectives for the unit on Ohm's law could focus solely on promoting retention. Objectives for promoting retention are based primarily on the cognitive process category *Remember,* which includes *recalling* and *recognizing factual, procedural, conceptual,* and *metacognitive knowledge.* For example, an objective for *recalling factual knowledge* is that students will be able to *recall* what the letters stand for in the formula for Ohm's law. An objective for *recalling procedural knowledge* is that students will be able to *recall* the steps involved in applying Ohm's law.

Although these are the obvious kinds of retention-type objectives to include in the unit, it is also possible to develop retention-type objectives that involve *Conceptual* and *Metacognitive knowledge.* For *Conceptual knowledge,* an objective is that students will be able to draw, from memory, a picture of an electrical circuit. Because this objective focuses on *recalling,* each student's drawing is evaluated in terms of how closely it corresponds to a picture presented in the textbook or previously on the chalkboard. Students may answer questions about *Conceptual* and *Metacognitive knowledge* in a rote manner, relying exclusively on previously presented material. When the overall purpose of the unit is to promote transfer of learning, *Remember* objectives need to be supplemented with objectives that involve more complex cognitive processes.

Finally, an objective pertaining to *recalling metacognitive knowledge* is that students remember "When stuck in a hole, stop digging." In other words, when their first approach to solving a problem or arriving at an answer is not succeeding, they remember to stop and assess other possible approaches. Again, with the emphasis on *Remember,* students may be queried about whether, when their first approach to a problem bogged down, they remembered the slogan. If student answers are being graded, students will give the response they know the teacher desires (i.e., "Of course, I did"), so this assessment task works only where students realize its purpose is to help them improve their learning.

MAKING SENSE OF AND USING WHAT WAS LEARNED

When the concern of the teacher turns to promoting transfer, he or she needs to consider the full range of cognitive process categories. Consider the myriad of possibilities inherent in the following list:

- An objective for *interpreting factual knowledge*: "Students should be able to define key terms (e.g., *resistance*) in their own words."

- An objective for *explaining conceptual knowledge*: "Students should be able to explain what happens to the rate of current in an electrical circuit when changes are made in the system (e.g., two batteries that were connected in serial are reconnected in parallel)."

- An objective for *executing procedural knowledge*: "The student will be able to use Ohm's law to compute the voltage when given the current (in amperes) and the resistance (in ohms)."

- An objective for *differentiating conceptual knowledge*: "The student will be able to determine which information in word problems involving Ohm's law (e.g., wattage of light bulb, thickness of wire, voltage of battery) is needed to determine the resistance."

- An objective for *checking procedural knowledge*: "The student will be able to determine whether a worked-out solution to a problem involving Ohm's law is likely to be effective in solving it."

- An objective for *critiquing metacognitive knowledge*: "The student will be able to choose a plan for solving problems involving Ohm's law that is most consistent with his or her current level of understanding."

- An objective for *generating conceptual knowledge*: "The student will be able to generate alternative ways of increasing the brightness of the light in a circuit without changing the battery."

We can summarize the entire set of objectives in this instructional unit on Ohm's law using the Taxonomy Table (see Table 5.2). The Xs indicate objectives that are included in this unit based on the examples we gave. Not all cells are filled; thus, not all possible combinations of cognitive process and knowledge are included in the unit. Nonetheless, it is clear that the unit includes a variety of objectives that go beyond *remember factual knowledge*. Our focus on objectives in instructional units suggests that the most effective way of teaching and assessing educational objectives may be to embed them within a few basic contexts (such as an instructional unit) rather than to focus on each in isolation. We return to this theme later.

CONCLUSION

A major goal of this chapter is to examine how teaching and assessing can be broadened beyond an exclusive focus on the cognitive process *Remember*. We described 19 specific cognitive processes associated with six process categories. Two of these cognitive processes are associated with *Remember*; 17 are associated with the process categories beyond it: *Understand, Apply, Analyze, Evaluate*, and *Create*.

Our analysis has implications for both teaching and assessing. On the teaching side, two of the cognitive processes help to promote retention of learning, whereas 17 of them help to foster transfer of learning. Thus, when the goal of instruction is to promote transfer, objectives should include the cognitive processes associated with *Understand, Apply, Analyze, Evaluate*, and *Create*. The descriptions in this chapter are intended to help educators generate a broader range of educational objectives that are likely to result in both retention and transfer.

On the assessment side, our analysis of cognitive processes is intended to help educators (including test designers) broaden their assessments of learning. When the goal of instruction is to promote transfer, assessment tasks should tap cognitive processes that go beyond remembering. Although assessment tasks that tap *recalling* and *recognizing* have a place in assessment, these tasks can (and often should) be supplemented with those that tap the full range of cognitive processes required for transfer of learning.

5.2 COMPLETED TAXONOMY TABLE FOR HYPOTHETICAL OHM'S LAW UNIT

THE KNOWLEDGE DIMENSION	THE COGNITIVE PROCESS DIMENSION					
	1. REMEMBER	2. UNDERSTAND	3. APPLY	4. ANALYZE	5. EVALUATE	6. CREATE
A. FACTUAL KNOWLEDGE	X	X				
B. CONCEPTUAL KNOWLEDGE	X	X		X		X
C. PROCEDURAL KNOWLEDGE	X		X		X	
D. META-COGNITIVE KNOWLEDGE	X				X	

The Taxonomy in Use

CHAPTER 6

Using the Taxonomy Table

In this major section we demonstrate how educators can use the Taxonomy Table to help teachers and other educators in at least three ways. First, it can help them gain a more complete understanding of their objectives (both those they choose for themselves and those that are provided by others); that is, the table can help educators answer what we refer to as the "learning question" (see page 6). Second, from this understanding, teachers can use the table to make better decisions about how to teach and assess their students in terms of the objectives; that is, the table can help educators answer the "instruction question" and the "assessment question" (see pages 7–8). Third, it can help them determine how well the objectives, assessments, and instructional activities fit together in a meaningful and useful way; that is, the table can help educators answer the "alignment question" (see page 10). In this initial chapter we address these questions in the context of an example that involves the teaching of science to illustrate how using the Taxonomy Table can help educators.

USING THE TAXONOMY TABLE IN ANALYZING YOUR OWN WORK

Before we revisit the Taxonomy Table and explore how it can be helpful, we have an important word for teachers who are planning to use the framework to guide the development of curriculum units: Your use of the framework will be less complex than what is presented in this and the following chapters because we are analyzing units prepared by others. This requires us to take the stance of an observer attributing intended meaning to objectives, instructional activities, and assessments. The result appears complicated because we make hypotheses about what was meant and then we have to check them against other evidence for confirmation.

As an example, we interrupt the narrative of Chapter 8, the first vignette, with analyses that make trial inferences about what Ms. Nagengast, the teacher, meant by certain actions so that we can relate them to the Taxonomy. If Ms. Nagengast had done the analysis herself, the vignette would have looked quite different and been much simpler. It would also have been less instructive about the Taxonomy framework, however (which is why we didn't present it that way). The trial inferences illustrate the distinctions among categories and show how the various categories are used.

If she were doing the analysis herself, Ms. Nagengast would have an internal idea of what she is seeking to teach. Then the framework would become a reference to use as she develops the unit. As part of the unit development process, she would reflect on her actions and decisions by answering questions such as those that follow.

"In stating my objective, do the words I use describe what I intend?" A teacher may use the word "explain" when she does not mean "to construct a causal model" (our definition). Rather, she might mean interpret or summarize. Although all three of these cognitive processes are in the category *Understand*, the choice of one over the other has different implications for instruction and assessment. Using the Taxonomy's terms can add precision.

"Is the objective that can be inferred from my instructional activities consistent with my statement of the objective?" When both objectives and instructional activities are translated into the Taxonomy framework, do they point to the same types of knowledge and the same cognitive processes? Several factors can guide a teacher's choice of instructional activities. Are students interested in them? Do they enjoy them? Are they likely to engage in them? Do I have the resources I need to support them (e.g., the equipment needed for a laboratory experiment)? If activities are selected mainly on these criteria, their link with the stated objective may become eroded. Thus, inferring objectives from instructional activities and relating them to the intended objective are the means to ensure that instructional activities are "on target."

"Are my assessments valid?" When one classifies the assessments in the Taxonomy framework, do they align with the stated objectives? At the very least, validity means that the assessment used by the teacher provides him or her with information about how well the students achieved (or are achieving) the objective. Inferences about objectives based on assessments can come from two sources. The first is the actual assessment tasks (e.g., test items, project directions). This source is sufficient when select-type formats with correct answers are used (e.g., multiple choice, matching). The second source is the criteria used to score or evaluate student performance on the assessment tasks (e.g., scoring keys, rating scales, scoring rubrics). This source becomes necessary when extended-response formats are used (e.g., essays, research reports). The question here is whether inferences based on the assessments lead back to the stated objectives.

USING THE TAXONOMY TABLE IN ANALYZING THE WORK OF OTHERS

When anyone uses the framework to analyze the work of others, they encounter the same complexities we faced in our vignette analyses. Teachers may be handed objectives (e.g., state or local standards) or assessments prepared by others (e.g., statewide or standardized tests). They may be asked to analyze another teacher's units or conduct observations in fellow teachers' classrooms. These analyses all require attributions of intent, which are difficult when objectives lack important words or phrases or when peripheral words or phrases are misleading. Even the key words and phrases do not always mean what they seem to mean. In addition, words (i.e., the statement of the objective) and actions (i.e., the instructional activities and assessments related to the objective) may be inconsistent. For all these reasons, placing an objective in the Taxonomy Table requires that one determine the intentions of the teacher [or author(s) in the case of materials prepared by others] in relation to the meaning of the objective, the purpose of the instructional activities, and the aim of the assessments.

On page 34, we stated that the use of multiple sources of information is likely to result in the most valid and defensible classification of objectives. In the next section we begin to explore why this is so.

THE TAXONOMY TABLE REVISITED

The two-dimensional Taxonomy Table, shown earlier as Table 3.1, is reproduced on the inside front cover of this book. Tables 4.1 and 5.1, which summarize the knowledge and cognitive process dimensions, are printed on the front and back covers, respectively and on the next page. We encourage you to refer to these tables while reading the remainder of this chapter.

THE LEARNING QUESTION

Let us begin with a seemingly straightforward objective: "Students should learn to use laws of electricity and magnetism (such as Lenz' law and Ohm's law) to solve problems." To place this objective in the Taxonomy Table, we must examine the verb and noun phrase in relation to the categories of the table. Specifically, we must relate the verb, "use," to one of the six major cognitive process categories and the noun phrase, "laws of electricity and magnetism," to one of the four types of knowledge. The verb is fairly easy: "use" is an alternative name for *implement* (see inside back cover), which is associated with the category *Apply*. With respect to the noun, laws are principles or generalizations, and knowledge of principles and generalizations is *Conceptual knowledge*. If our analysis is correct, then, this objective should be placed in the cell of the Taxonomy Table that corresponds to the intersection of *Apply* and *Conceptual knowledge* (cell B3; see Table 6.1. Note in Table 6.1 that the four types of knowledge form the rows labeled A through D, and the six processes form the columns labeled 1 through 6. A cell can thus be designated by a letter and a number to indicate its intersection of a row and a column). Now we have answered the "learning question." We want students to learn to *apply conceptual knowledge*.

In this analysis we relied on knowledge subtypes (e.g., *knowledge of principles and generalizations*) and specific cognitive processes (e.g., *implementing*) rather than on the four major types of knowledge and the six cognitive process categories. Based on our collective experience, we believe subtypes and specific processes provide the best clues to the proper placement of objectives in the Taxonomy Table. Note also that we based our decisions on assumptions we

6.1 PLACEMENT OF THE OBJECTIVE IN THE TAXONOMY TABLE

THE KNOWLEDGE DIMENSION	THE COGNITIVE PROCESS DIMENSION					
	1. REMEMBER	2. UNDERSTAND	3. APPLY	4. ANALYZE	5. EVALUATE	6. CREATE
A. FACTUAL KNOWLEDGE						
B. CONCEPTUAL KNOWLEDGE			Objective			
C. PROCEDURAL KNOWLEDGE						
D. META-COGNITIVE KNOWLEDGE						

Key.
Objective = the objective, "Students should learn to use laws of electricity and magnetism (such as Lenz' law and Ohm's law) to solve problems."

made about the teacher's intention. For example, our inference that we are dealing with *implementing* rather than *executing* is supported not only by the inclusion of the verb "use" but also by the phrase "in problems" in the statement of the objective. Because problems are unfamiliar (rather than familiar) tasks (see page 77), *implementing* seems more appropriate than *executing* (see inside back cover).

THE INSTRUCTION QUESTION

Although the objective can be classified in one cell (see Table 6.1), when we consider different instructional activities a teacher may use, we see a much more complex and differentiated picture. For example, in general, if students are to implement scientific laws, they might (1) determine the type of problem they are confronting, (2) select a law that will likely solve that type of problem, and (3) use a procedure in which the law is embedded to solve the problem. As we described on pages 78–79, then, *implementing* involves both *Conceptual knowledge* (i.e., knowledge of the type or category of problem) and *Procedural knowledge* (i.e., knowledge of the steps to follow to solve the problem). Instructional activities might help students develop both types of knowledge.

Note the verbs used in the decomposition of this single objective: "determine," "select," and "use." From Table 5.1, inside back cover, we see that determining that something belongs to a category is the definition of *classifying (Understand)*, selecting is an alternative term for *differentiating (Analyze)*, and using is an alternative term for *implementing (Apply)*. The instructional activities should help students engage in *classifying* and *differentiating* as well as *implementing*.

Because students may make errors in *classifying, differentiating*, and *implementing*, it also seems reasonable to emphasize *Metacognitive knowledge* during instruction. For example, students might be taught strategies for monitoring their decisions and choices to see whether they "make sense." "How do I know this problem is a certain type?" "If it is, how do I know which laws to use?" In addition to being able to *recall* these strategies, students may be taught to *implement* them.

Finally, it may be advisable to focus some of the instructional activities on so-called higher-order cognitive processes. Because *implementation* often involves making choices along the way, students should be taught to check as they go and critique the final result or solution. Both *checking* and *critiquing* fall in the *Evaluate* category.

The answer to the "instruction question," then, is far more complicated that it would appear to be at first blush. Instructional activities might provide opportunities for students to develop at least three types of knowledge (*Conceptual, Procedural*, and *Metacognitive*) and engage in at least six cognitive processes (*recalling, classifying, differentiating, implementing, checking*, and *critiquing*) associated with five process categories (*Remember, Understand, Apply, Analyze*, and *Evaluate*). An analysis of the instructional activities in terms of the Taxonomy Table, then, results in many more cells being included (see Table 6.2).

6.2 PLACEMENT OF THE OBJECTIVE AND INSTRUCTIONAL ACTIVITIES IN THE TAXONOMY TABLE

THE KNOWLEDGE DIMENSION	THE COGNITIVE PROCESS DIMENSION					
	1. REMEMBER	2. UNDERSTAND	3. APPLY	4. ANALYZE	5. EVALUATE	6. CREATE
A. FACTUAL KNOWLEDGE						
B. CONCEPTUAL KNOWLEDGE		*Activity 1*	**Objective**	*Activity 2*	*Activity 7*	
C. PROCEDURAL KNOWLEDGE			*Activity 3*		*Activity 6*	
D. META-COGNITIVE KNOWLEDGE	*Activity 4*		*Activity 5*			

Key.
Objective = the objective, "Students should learn to use laws of electricity and magnetism (such as Lenz' law and Ohm's law) to solve problems."
Activity 1 = activities intended to help students classify types of problems
Activity 2 = activities intended to help students select appropriate laws
Activity 3 = activities intended to help students implement proper procedures
Activity 4 = activities intended to help students recall metacognitive strategies
Activity 5 = activities intended to help students implement metacognitive strategies
Activity 6 = activities intended to help students check their implementation of the procedure
Activity 7 = activities intended to help students critique the correctness of their solution

An examination of the relationship of the single cell that contains the objective (B3) to the seven cells that contain the instructional activities (B2, B4, B5, C3, C5, D1, and D3) produces an interesting result; namely, none of the instructional activities pertains directly to the objective. The reason for this is clear from our definition of *Apply* (see inside back cover). *Apply* means to carry out or use a procedure in a given situation. In other words, *Apply* requires *Procedural knowledge*. Therefore, if laws of electricity and magnetism (*Conceptual knowledge*) are to be applied, they must be embedded within a procedure (*Procedural knowledge*). The procedure typically "unpacks" the laws in a way that facilitates their application (e.g., first, calculate or estimate the electromotive force in volts; second, calculate or estimate the current in amperes; third, divide the electromotive force by the current to yield the resistance). Earlier consideration of the relationship between *Apply* and *Procedural knowledge* might have suggested that we initially classify the objective as *apply procedural knowledge* (C3) instead of *apply conceptual knowledge* (B3).

THE ASSESSMENT QUESTION

Suppose a teacher has spent several days of instruction on this objective and wants to know how well her students are learning. She has a number of decisions to make, including these three important ones: Does she focus her assessment only on the cell that contains the objective, or does she assess the effectiveness of the various instructional activities as well? Does she integrate assessment with her instruction (i.e., formative assessment), or does she conduct a more independent assessment for the purpose of assigning grades (i.e., summative assessment)? How does she know that her assessment tasks require the students to engage in *implementing* rather than *executing* (or some other cognitive process)?

FOCUSED VERSUS DISTRIBUTED ASSESSMENT   Our initial analysis, based solely on the statement of the objective, suggests that the teacher focus her assessment on the extent to which students have learned to *apply conceptual knowledge* (cell B3). In contrast, our more detailed analysis, based on relevant and appropriate instructional activities, suggests the teacher assess the wide variety of cells related to attaining the primary objective (B2, B4, B5, C3, C5, D1, and D3). The trade-off seems to be breadth versus depth. On the one hand, the focused assessment permits the teacher to probe the depths of student learning relative to a single objective. A variety of different problems related to this objective can be included on a single assessment. On the other hand, a more distributed assessment permits the teacher to examine broadly the processes involved in the attainment of the target objective. The broader testing not only assesses the primary objective in the context of related knowledge and cognitive processes, but also may permit a diagnosis of the student's underlying difficulties where, for example, a contributing aspect of *Procedural knowledge* is not adequately learned.

FORMATIVE VERSUS SUMMATIVE ASSESSMENT   Formative assessment is concerned with gathering information about learning as learning is taking

place, so that "in-flight" instructional modifications may be made to improve the quality or amount of learning. In contrast, summative assessment is concerned with gathering information about learning after the learning should have occurred, usually for the purpose of assigning grades to students. Thus, formative assessment is used primarily to improve student learning; summative assessment is used primarily to assign grades. Class work and homework are often used in formative assessment; more formal tests are used as a means of summative assessment.

ASSESSING IMPLEMENTING VERSUS EXECUTING   Because *implementing* and *executing* are both associated with *Apply*, it is important to distinguish between them if the results of the assessment are to be valid. If assessment tasks do not include unfamiliar tasks and/or do not require students to select relevant and appropriate *Procedural knowledge*, then it is more likely that *executing* rather than *implementing* is being assessed. As we mentioned in the discussion of *interpreting* (see page 71), using assessment tasks that are new to the student is a primary method of ensuring that students respond to the assessments at the most complex cognitive process called for in the objective.

ASSESSMENT AND THE TAXONOMY TABLE   Continuing with our example, let us suppose that the teacher decides she is as concerned about students using the correct procedure as she is about their getting the right answer. The teacher sees the assessment as formative in nature. She gives her students ten electrical and mechanical problems and asks them to solve each problem, showing their work.

As we did for the objective and the instructional activities, we can examine the assessment in terms of the Taxonomy Table. In this case, we would focus on the assigned point values. For each of the ten problems, score points are given for "selecting a correct procedure." The teacher's scoring rubric requires that students are able to classify the problem correctly (*understanding conceptual knowledge*, one point), select the appropriate law (*analyzing conceptual knowledge*, one point), and select a procedure that follows from the law and is likely to solve the problem (*analyzing procedural knowledge*, one point). Since she considers the procedure and the result to be equally important, having given three points for selecting the correct procedure for solving each problem, she gives three points for arriving at the correct solution to the problem (i.e., *implementing procedural knowledge*). Once again, the results of our analysis can be summarized in terms of the Taxonomy Table (see Table 6.3).

THE ALIGNMENT QUESTION

Since the entries in Tables 6.1 and 6.2 are reproduced in Table 6.3, we can address the alignment question by focusing on Table 6.3. Specifically, one can examine the cells that contain the objective, the instructional activities, the assessments, and various combinations of these. Cells that contain an objective, one or more instructional activities, and some aspect of assessment indicate a high degree of alignment. In contrast, cells that contain only the objective or only an instructional

6.3 PLACEMENT OF THE OBJECTIVE, INSTRUCTIONAL ACTIVITIES, AND ASSESSMENT IN THE TAXONOMY TABLE

THE KNOWLEDGE DIMENSION	THE COGNITIVE PROCESS DIMENSION					
	1. REMEMBER	2. UNDERSTAND	3. APPLY	4. ANALYZE	5. EVALUATE	6. CREATE
A. FACTUAL KNOWLEDGE						
B. CONCEPTUAL KNOWLEDGE		Activity 1 Test 1A	Objective	Activity 2 Test 1B	Activity 7	
C. PROCEDURAL KNOWLEDGE			Activity 3 Test 2	[Objective as Refocused— See Page 104] Test 1C	Activity 6	
D. META-COGNITIVE KNOWLEDGE	Activity 4		Activity 5			

Key
Objective = the objective, "Students should learn to use laws of electricity and magnetism (such as Lenz' law and Ohm's law) to solve problems."
Activity 1 = activities intended to help students classify types of problems
Activity 2 = activities intended to help students select appropriate laws
Activity 3 = activities intended to help students implement proper procedures
Activity 4 = activities intended to help students recall metacognitive strategies
Activity 5 = activities intended to help students implement metacognitive strategies
Activity 6 = activities intended to help students check their implementation of the procedure
Activity 7 = activities intended to help students critique the correctness of their solution
Test 1A, Test 1B, Test 1C = cells associated with the procedural aspect of each problem, Test 2 = cell associated with the correct "answer"

activity or only some aspect of assessment indicate weak alignment. This interpretation, however, requires that a basic assumption be made. Because the completed table represents our inferences, we must assume that we made reasonably valid inferences on the statement of objective, our analysis of the instructional activities, and our examination of the assessment. This assumption enables us to differentiate misclassification from misalignment.

If we assume correct classification from these three sources (i.e., the statement of objective, the instructional activities, and the assessment), then Table 6.3 presents evidence of both alignment and misalignment. For example, cell C3 (*apply procedural knowledge*) includes both an instructional activity and a score point on the assessment. If the objective were properly classified, in line with our earlier discussion, this would increase the alignment. Similar alignment appears in cells B2 and B4, which also contain an instructional activity and a score point on the assessment.

At the same time, looking at Table 6.3, we see misalignment, which appears to stem from three sources.

- Having a "disconnect" between the verb and noun in the statement of the objective. "Use," being an alternative term for *implement*, is associated with the category *Apply* (see the inside back cover). *Procedural knowledge* is typically associated with *Apply*. We approached the analysis of the noun phrase "laws of electricity and magnetism" with this in mind. Thus, rather than focusing on knowledge of "laws" as *Conceptual knowledge* (which it is), we should focus on procedures for using the laws to solve problems— *Procedural knowledge*. In light of this "re-focus" on the procedures instead of the laws, the objective should be classified in cell C3 (*apply procedural knowledge*), rather than in cell B3 (*apply conceptual knowledge*). That classification gives the strongest possible alignment in cell C3: The objective, instructional activity, and assessment would all be present there.

- Including instructional activities that are not assessed and thus provide no information for the diagnosis of learning problems. Examples in Table 6.3 include ACT4 (remembering they should check their progress as they work on each problem), ACT6 (determining whether their progress is satisfactory), ACT5 (making modifications based on their "progress checks," if needed), and ACT7 (checking the accuracy of their final solution). All four relate to the process of reviewing work "in progress." Simply asking students whether they had done the reviews would reinforce the importance of doing so. Furthermore, individually querying those students who reported reviewing but still arrived at the wrong solution might help them find mistakes in their own work and how they typically attack such problems.

- Awarding points (cell C4) based on the problem-solving process that either was not emphasized during the instructional activities or, if it was, was not linked with any stated objective.

Based on the analysis using the Taxonomy Table, the teacher can make changes in the statement of the objective, the instructional activities, or the assessment tasks or evaluation criteria to increase the overall alignment.

PROBLEMS IN CLASSIFYING OBJECTIVES

Because the classification of objectives, whether the objectives are stated, implicit in instructional activities, or deduced from assessments, requires that inferences be made, there are many instances in which the classification is not easy. The editors of the original *Handbook* noted problems inherent in the classification of objectives. We pose these problems as questions:

- Am I working at the level of specificity at which the Taxonomy Table is most useful?
- Have I made correct assumptions about students' prior learning?
- Does the objective as stated describe an intended learning result, not activities or behaviors that are "means to an end"?

THE LEVEL OF SPECIFICITY PROBLEM

As we discussed on page 15, educational objectives can be written at three levels of specificity. They can be general program goals to be achieved over a year or a number of years, objectives for a particular course or unit within a course, or objectives for a particular lesson within a unit (Krathwohl, 1964; Krathwohl and Payne, 1971). The Taxonomy is designed to be most useful in planning instruction and assessment at the course or unit level. As we demonstrate in the vignette analyses, however, the Taxonomy has implications for learning activities and assessment tasks at the daily lesson level as well.

A useful test of the specificity of an objective is to ask whether, after having read it, you can visualize the performance of a student who has achieved it. "What would a student have to do to demonstrate that he or she has learned what I intended him or her to learn?" If you envision a variety of different performances, you probably ought to ask, "What performance is the most representative of the achievement of this objective?" Discerning this central performance narrows broad objectives down to the more specific ones that are needed to use the Taxonomy Table.

Consider, for example, this global objective: "The student should learn to be a good citizen in a democracy." What pictures come to mind when you try to visualize the actions of a student who has mastered this global objective? Probably lots of things: Voting? Protection of minority viewpoints? Acceptance of majority rule? Each of these suggests a more specific objective that, in combination, could help the student move toward the broad citizenship goal. An example might be: "The student will learn a variety of strategies for resolving group conflicts (e.g., voting, mediation)." The somewhat more specific objectives are the most appropriate for use with the Taxonomy Table.

THE PRIOR LEARNING PROBLEM

To classify an objective correctly, one must make assumptions about students' prior learning. This is most obvious when a student experiences an instructional activity or assessment task that he or she has encountered before. In such cases, an activity or task that is intended to evoke a more complex cognitive process (e.g., *Analyze*) will not do so because the student has only to *Remember* the prior experience. If we intend students to learn to *Analyze*, we must do what we can to ensure that instructional activities and assessments evoke the complex processes intended.

In the same vein, an objective may fall into different cognitive process categories with increasing grade levels. What is a more complex objective in the early grades may become a less complex objective in later grades. For example, a mathematics objective in grade 3 that requires *differentiating* in order to painstakingly sort out what is needed to solve a particular problem type may require in grade 4 *implementing* because the identification of that problem type has become routine. By grade 5, this same objective may require *executing* because problem solution is almost automatic, and by grade 6, the objective may require simple *recalling* because all the common problem types likely to be used in instruction and assessment have already been encountered.

Thus, to reach agreement about the classification of objectives, teachers must have some knowledge or make an assumption about the students' prior learning. This is probably the single most common and most difficult problem to overcome when trying to classify an objective in the abstract without reference to any specific group and/or grade level or when using the Taxonomy Table with no information provided about students' prior learning.

DIFFERENTIATING OBJECTIVES FROM ACTIVITIES

In working with the Taxonomy Table, one sometimes finds (as those of us who worked on this project often did) that it is easy to slip into the mode of trying to categorize learning activities rather than intended learning outcomes. To test the framework, one of us would suggest a verb—for instance, "estimating"—and ask where it belongs. Initially, we found that estimating was difficult to categorize. When we paired it with knowledge so that it became an objective, however, classifying became much easier. Consider the following: "Students should learn to estimate the product of two large numbers." This objective reduces to students learning a three-step procedure: (1) rounding to the nearest power of ten, (2) multiplying the remaining one-digit, non zero numbers, and (3) adding the correct number of zeros. In this context, estimating means *executing* an estimation procedure, or *applying procedural knowledge*.

Sometimes one of us would suggest a silly activity like "doodling" and ask where it would fit. Not only is "doodling" unlikely to appear in an educational objective, but if it were to appear, it once again would have to be in a knowledge context to be classifiable. For example, "The student will learn that doodling helps him or her to relieve stress temporarily when working on difficult problems." This might be a strategy within *Metacognitive knowledge*. The phrase "learn that" suggests simple *recall* (i.e., "know that"). The objective, then, would take the form *remember metacognitive knowledge*. The point is that it makes sense to try to classify "doodling" when it is placed in a knowledge context; without that context, it makes no sense.

We have one final point in this regard: Many "verbs," particularly those associated with undesirable student behavior (e.g., disrupt, agitate), are not likely to be included in statements of educational objectives. Consequently, they are not usefully classified within our framework.

SOME HELPFUL HINTS

In light of the problems and based on our combined experience in the field, we offer four helpful hints that should increase your probability of classifying objectives correctly: (1) consider the verb-noun combination, (2) relate the knowledge type to the process, (3) make sure you have the right noun or noun phrase, and (4) rely on multiple sources.

CONSIDER THE VERB-NOUN COMBINATION

As we mentioned earlier, verbs by themselves can be misleading. Consider this objective: "Students should be able to identify various literary devices (e.g., similes, metaphors, hyperbole, personification, alliteration) used in novels." Clearly, the verb is "identify." In Table 5.1, inside back cover, identifying is an alternative term for *recognizing*, which is in the process category *Remember.* If we categorized this as a *Remember* objective, however, it would be inappropriate. A more complete reading of this objective suggests that the intention is for students to learn to identify examples of literary devices in novels. Finding examples is *exemplifying*, which is associated with the process category *Understand.* This inference is consistent with the fact that literary devices are concepts (that is, classes of things sharing common attributes). More likely, then, the objective has the form *understand conceptual knowledge.*

RELATE TYPE OF KNOWLEDGE TO PROCESS

For objectives that involve *Remember, Understand,* and *Apply,* there generally is a direct correspondence between process category and type of knowledge. We do intend, for example, students to recall facts (*remember factual knowledge*), interpret principles (*understand conceptual knowledge*), and execute algorithms (*apply procedural knowledge*).

When *Analyze, Evaluate,* and *Create* are involved, however, the correspondence between process category and type of knowledge is less predictable. Consider, for example, *evaluate conceptual knowledge.* We typically do not intend students to learn to *critique* (*Evaluate*) a set of criteria (*Conceptual knowledge*). Rather, we intend them to learn to *critique* **something** based on or in terms of the criteria. The something might be a hypothesis advanced by a scientist or a solution to a problem proposed by a legislator. The criteria on which the evaluation is based may include reasonableness and cost effectiveness, respectively. Thus, *evaluate conceptual knowledge* becomes in essence *evaluate* [based on] *conceptual knowledge* or *evaluate* [in terms of] *conceptual knowledge.*

Now consider *Create*. Again, we intend for students to learn to *create* something—poems, novel solutions to a problem, research reports. Students typically are expected to rely on more than one type of knowledge during the creative process. Suppose, for example, we intend for students to learn to write original research reports about famous Americans in history based on themes and supporting details derived from materials about them. We could classify this objective as *Create* (write original research reports) *Conceptual knowledge* (themes) and *Factual knowledge* (supporting details). This classification would be not only confusing but also likely incorrect. We do not necessarily intend for students to *create conceptual* and *factual knowledge*. However, we do intend them to *create* [original research reports based on] *conceptual* and *factual knowledge*. As in the preceding case of *Evaluate*, students are to *Create* something based on some knowledge. With *Create*, students may well use all the knowledge at their disposal (*Factual, Conceptual, Procedural*, and *Metacognitive*).

The point here is simple but important. When objectives involve the three most complex cognitive processes, knowledge provides the basis for the cognitive processes and often multiple types of knowledge are required. This idea is exemplified in several of the vignettes.

MAKE SURE YOU HAVE THE RIGHT NOUN

As we worked with various drafts of the Taxonomy Table, we encountered statements of objectives in which the nouns and noun phrases did not help us determine the appropriate type of knowledge. In general, the verbs in these objectives indicated more complex cognitive process categories (i.e., *Analyze*, *Evaluate*, and *Create*). Consider the following examples:

- Students should learn to outline textbook lessons.
- Students should learn to critique proposed solutions to social problems.
- Students should learn to design sets for various plays.

In each case, the verb is easily identifiable and quite easily classified. Outlining is an alternative term for *organizing* [*Analyze*], *critiquing* is associated with *Evaluate*, and constructing is an alternative term for *producing* [*Create*]. The noun phrases in these cases are "textbook lessons," "proposed solutions to social problems," and "sets for various plays." What is missing from these statements, and what must be made explicit before the objectives can be classified correctly, is the knowledge that students need to organize lessons (e.g., the organizing principles), critique proposed solutions (e.g., the evaluation criteria), or plan sets (e.g., the design parameters).

Now consider a second set of objectives:

- Students should learn to analyze in a work of art <u>the relationship of the materials used to the rendition of color</u>.
- Students should learn to evaluate commercials seen on television or read in newspapers/magazines from the standpoint of a <u>set of principles pertaining to "appeals."</u>

- Students should learn to design habitats for certain species <u>so their survival is ensured</u>.

Like the objectives in the first set, these three objectives are concerned with *Analyze*, *Evaluate*, and *Create*, respectively. Unlike the objectives in the first set, however, the knowledge needed is contained in the objectives (as underlined). In the first objective, students need knowledge of the relationship of the materials used to the rendition of color. In the second objective, students need knowledge of the set of principles pertaining to "appeals." Finally, in the third objective, students need sufficient knowledge of a particular species so they can design a habitat to ensure their survival. The point here is that not all nouns and noun phrases provide useful clues to the proper classification of the objective in terms of the knowledge component. Particularly for objectives that focus on developing more complex cognitive processes, the clues pertaining to knowledge may be found in:

- the definition or description of the cognitive process itself (see, for example, our discussion of *differentiating* on pages 80–81); and/or
- the evaluation criteria or scoring rules used with the assessment.

If clues are not given in either of these sources, then there is a need to further clarify, or spell out, the knowledge in the statement of the objective.

RELY ON MULTIPLE SOURCES

As we began to analyze the vignettes, we learned that our understanding of the objectives of the unit increased as we considered multiple sources: the statements of the objectives, the instructional activities, and the assessment tasks and evaluation criteria. This was particularly important in those cases in which one or more of the stated objectives was a bit vague or more global than those we could classify easily. The value of multiple sources will be seen in the vignettes. Before we move to the individual vignettes, however, we explore in the next chapter how the vignettes were put together, what they "look like," and how they were analyzed.

CHAPTER 7

Introduction to the Vignettes

Based in large measure on our collective experiences in working with the original *Handbook*, we believe that a framework such as the Taxonomy Table requires numerous illustrations and a great deal of discussion before it can be adequately understood and ultimately used in classroom settings. To this end, we have developed six vignettes (see Table 7.1).

In combination, the vignettes were selected to ground the propositions advanced in the earlier chapters and to illustrate the key concepts and elements in the Taxonomy Table. The purpose of this chapter is to characterize the vignettes in our collection, spell out their central components, and suggest ways in which the Taxonomy Table can be used to aid in understanding the complex nature of classroom instruction. With increased understanding may come opportunities to improve the quality of instruction provided in our classrooms.

CHARACTERIZATION OF THE VIGNETTES

It is instructive to begin with what the vignettes are **not**. First, they do not necessarily represent "best practice," excellent teaching, or models of instruction for others to adopt or emulate. Looking at the vignettes in such an evaluative light will likely undermine our purpose for including them in this volume. We urge readers to suspend their need to evaluate and instead see the vignettes as a collection of teaching episodes within larger curriculum units written by teachers.[1] The question for the reader is not whether the vignettes represent good or bad teaching. Rather, the question is how the Taxonomy Table can help the reader make sense of the objectives, instructional activities, and assessments described by the teachers with the intent of improving their own teaching and the students' learning.

---

[1] Chapter 12, the Volcanoes? Here? vignette, was taught by an experienced teacher, but the vignette was prepared by Dr. Michael Smith, who observed the teaching as part of a National Science Foundation study.

TABLE 7.1 Our Collection of Vignettes

CHAPTER NUMBER	TITLE	GRADE LEVEL(S)	SUBJECT AREA
8	Nutrition	5	Health
9	*Macbeth*	12	English literature
10	Addition Facts	2	Mathematics
11	Parliamentary Acts	5	History
12	Volcanoes? Here?	6–7	Science
13	Report Writing	4	Language arts

Second, these vignettes certainly do not represent all approaches to classroom instruction at all grade levels in all subject matters in all countries of the world. Stated somewhat differently, the collection is intended to be illustrative, not exhaustive. However, we believe that our analysis of the vignettes can enable readers to analyze their own and others' learning expectations, instruction, and assessment, and to consider alternative approaches to instruction and assessment that may be more appropriate and effective in light of what students are expected to learn.

Having discussed what the vignettes are not, we now turn to what they are. First, and perhaps most important, the vignettes are real. They represent curriculum units taught in American schools by practicing teachers. The initial drafts of these vignettes varied from being fairly brief to quite expansive—almost 20 pages. Because of space limitations, the longer vignettes were edited. Nonetheless, they all contain essential descriptions of curriculum units told in the language of the teachers who taught them.

Second, the vignettes represent high levels of verisimilitude. They capture some of the complexity, ambiguity, and problematic nature of classroom instruction. These qualities should add to the wonderment the reader brings to the descriptions and allow us to show the usefulness of the Taxonomy Table. Simple linear teaching over extremely short periods of time requires little in the way of analysis.

Third, we asked the teachers to describe curriculum units, rather than briefer one- or two-day lessons. Our rationale for this decision is presented in the next section.

THE CURRICULUM UNIT

A curriculum unit consists of one or more educational objectives that require approximately two to three weeks to achieve. If there is more than one educational objective, the objectives are related in some way, often in that they pertain to the same topic (e.g., Chapter 8, Nutrition; Chapter 9, *Macbeth;* Chapter 12,

Volcanoes? Here?). Interdisciplinary units (e.g., a unit on airplanes involving history, science, mathematics, and literature) and integrative units (e.g., Chapter 11, Parliamentary Acts; Chapter 13, Report Writing) are also examples of curriculum units. Within a curriculum unit, there may be several instructional objectives, each associated with a lesson that lasts one, two, or perhaps three days. In other cases, no instructional objectives are stated (although they may be implied).

A focus on curriculum units offers four advantages over a focus on daily lessons. First, curriculum units provide the time needed for more integrated, holistic learning. Over time students can be helped to see relationships and connections among ideas, materials, activities, and topics; that is, the unit structure helps them see the forest as well as the trees.

Second, curriculum units provide more flexibility in the use of available time. If a teacher runs out of time on a particular day, the activity can be carried out the next day. The availability of "flexible time" in a curriculum unit is important because, as we shall see in the vignettes, activities do not always go as planned. In addition, some students may need more time to learn than other students. Curriculum units allow teachers to accommodate these classroom realities.

Third, curriculum units provide a context for interpreting daily objectives, activities, and assessments. For example, the importance of a lesson on writing declarative sentences is often better understood in the context of a unit on writing paragraphs. Similarly, understanding the concepts of ratios and proportions can be enhanced in the context of a unit on painting and sculpture.

Finally, the larger curriculum units provide sufficient time for instructional activities that allow for the development and assessment of student learning of more complex objectives. Objectives that involve *Analyze*, *Evaluate*, and *Create* typically require longer time periods for students to learn.

CENTRAL COMPONENTS OF THE VIGNETTE DESCRIPTIONS

To provide a common structure, one that permits comparisons to be made across the vignettes, each vignette begins with a description of the classroom context and then is divided into three major components: (1) objectives, (2) instructional activities, and (3) assessment. For each component a series of questions was written to guide teachers in the preparation of the vignettes.

For the classroom context description and the objectives component, our questions included the following:

- What are the unit objectives and how were they determined?

- How does the unit fit into the larger scheme of things (e.g., statewide standards or testing program, district curriculum, prior and/or future units, age or grade level of students)?

- What materials (e.g., texts, software, maps, videos) and equipment (e.g., computers, television, laboratory equipment) were available to you and the students?

- How much time was allocated to the unit? On what basis did you decide on the temporal length of the unit?

For the instructional activities component, we asked teachers questions such as the following:

- How was the unit introduced to the students (e.g., Was an overview of the entire unit given? Was the need for or purpose of the unit discussed with the students?)?
- In what activities were students engaged during the unit? Why were these activities selected?
- What assignments were given to students? Why were specific assignments selected?
- How did you monitor the engagement and success of students in the activities and on the assignments?

Finally, for the assessment component, we asked teachers to consider questions such as these:

- How did you determine whether students were, in fact, learning? How did you assess what your students learned?
- Did you make use of rubrics, scoring keys or guides, criteria, and standards for judging the quality of student work? If so, what were they and how were they used?
- How did you inform students about how well they were doing (or did) on the unit?
- How were grading decisions made? What grading standards were used?

The teachers were told that the questions were guides, not requirements. Even a cursory examination of the vignettes will indicate that our prompts were used precisely in this way. Not all of our questions were relevant to all teachers, and teachers did not address those they believed to be irrelevant. Regardless of the questions considered, however, each teacher wrote a reasonably comprehensive account of each of the four central components. In all six vignettes, the components are presented and discussed in a fixed order: classroom context, objectives, instructional activities, and assessment.

We must emphasize that this order is not meant to convey a linear perspective on planning. We are well aware of the research suggesting that teachers often begin their planning with instructional activities, not with objectives or assessments. We assume that planning might begin with any of the three components: objectives, instructional activities, or assessment. Planning that is "objective-driven" begins with specifying instructional objectives. "Activity-driven" planning gives initial emphasis to the instructional activities. Finally, a teacher operating from a "test-driven" perspective starts with concerns for assessment. Regardless of the starting point, however, virtually all teachers are also concerned with the other two components as well as materials that are needed to support the activities and the amount of time that is available for the unit.

We anticipated that the description of instructional activities within the unit might take different forms. One was to convey a day-to-day chronology of events that took place in the classroom as the unit progressed. Another possibility was a little less sequential and more episodic, with descriptions of salient events related to key issues and concerns. Most teachers chose combinations of these approaches, focusing on salient events within a chronological time frame.

USING THE TAXONOMY TABLE TO ANALYZE THE VIGNETTES

We began our analysis by reading through the descriptions provided by the teachers, searching for clues that would enable us to make sense of these descriptions in the context of the Taxonomy Table. Consistent with the structure of our objectives (see Chapter 2), these clues came primarily from nouns and verbs. As we demonstrated in Chapter 6, we used Table 4.1 (see also the front inside cover) to make sense of the nouns we encountered and Table 5.1 (see also the back inside cover) to help us with the verbs.

The term *clues* in the preceding paragraph is used intentionally. We were never certain at any one time exactly where a specific descriptive element fit within the Taxonomy Table. Sometimes our initial placement became increasingly clear and more defensible the farther into the vignette we read. At other times later descriptions provided by the teacher contradicted our initial placement.

To understand our problem, consider the following example. One of the stated objectives in the Nutrition vignette (Chapter 8) is for students to "acquire knowledge of a classification scheme of appeals that describes the common targets commercial writers take into account in writing commercials." The verb "acquire" is nowhere to be found in our list of cognitive processes. However, the phrase "classification scheme" suggests *Conceptual Knowledge.* At this point, we assumed that "acquire" meant either *Remember* or *Understand*, and we made our initial classification of the objective in terms of the Taxonomy Table, namely, *remember* or *understand conceptual knowledge.*

With this initial placement in mind, we moved on to the description of the instructional activities. Early in the unit, Ms. Nagengast, the teacher, presented six "appeals" made by writers of commercials (i.e., ease, economy, health, love/admiration, fear, and comfort/pleasure) and students were expected to remember the **names** of the six appeals. Because the emphasis is on the names of the appeals rather than on their underlying **categories**, we classified the intent of this activity as *remember factual knowledge.* Note that this emphasis on *Factual knowledge* does not match our initial placement based on the stated objective. Shortly thereafter, however, students spent time with examples and nonexamples of each appeal and were asked to give examples to illustrate their understanding. The use of examples and nonexamples suggests two things: first, categories are being formed; second, students are engaged in *exemplifying.* Because knowledge of categories is *Conceptual knowledge* and *exemplifying* is associated with *Understand*, the inferred objective would be classified as *understand conceptual knowledge.* This inference is partially consistent with our initial placement (with a focus on *Understand* rather than *Remember*).

Finally, we moved on to assessment. Ms. Nagengast used two assessment tasks with this objective. In the first, she asked students to "identify a commercial, describe it, and then attribute to the commercial writers what appeal [i.e., the type or category of appeal] they were working with." In the second, she asked students to "develop a claim for a given product that would match the [type of] appeal she (the teacher) had advanced." To perform these assessment tasks well, students would need to do more than simply remember the names of the six types of appeals (i.e., *remember factual knowledge*). They would need to understand each type (i.e., category) of appeal in terms of its defining attributes or features so they could correctly place new examples in the proper category (task 1) or come up with new examples for a given category (task 2). In combination, then, the clues taken from the objectives, instructional activities, and assessments led us to believe that Ms. Nagengast's intention is for students to learn to *understand conceptual knowledge* (i.e., cell B2 of the Taxonomy Table).

In a similar way, we read each vignette component by component. In each component, we paid particular attention to those elements most likely to provide us with the necessary clues. These elements are summarized in Table 7.2.

In the objectives component, we focused on statements of general purpose, lists of included topics, and explicit objectives. In the Parliamentary Acts vignette (Chapter 11), for example, the teacher's general purpose is to "integrate students' persuasive writing with their knowledge of historical persons and events." The verb "integrate" and the noun phrases "persuasive writing" and "knowledge of historical persons and events" provided clues to the placement of intended student learning in the Taxonomy Table. Similarly, in the Volcanoes? Here? vignette (Chapter 12), the teacher indicates that the unit was predicated on the "dominant research paradigm in geology, the theory of plate tectonics." In combination with the unit title, this statement provides a clear topical emphasis for the unit—the role of plate tectonics in explaining volcanic activity. Topical emphases help us place objectives in the proper rows (i.e.,

TABLE 7.2 Elements Relevant to Taxonomic Analysis of the Vignettes

COMPONENT	ELEMENTS
Objectives	General purposes/aims
	Stated objectives
	Topics
Instructional activities	Teachers' comments
	Teachers' questions
	Student assignments
Assessment	Assessment tasks (e.g., test items, portfolio requirements)
	Scoring keys, guides, and rubrics
	Evaluation criteria and standards

types of knowledge) of the Taxonomy Table. Placement in the proper columns (i.e., kinds of cognitive processes), however, is virtually impossible when only a topical orientation is given.

In the instructional activities component, clues were provided by comments made by the teachers (particularly the way activities were introduced to the students or their descriptions of the activities), the questions teachers asked of students (and students of teachers), and the assignments students were given as part of or as a follow-up to the activity. In the Addition Facts vignette (Chapter 10), for example, the teacher tells her students that "if they learn one of the facts in a family (e.g., 3 + 5 = 8), they'll know the other (e.g., 5 + 3 = 8). Therefore, fact families make the job of memorizing easier because they have to remember only half of the facts." From the first statement we learn that the teacher is using categories (i.e., fact families) to reduce the amount of memorization that students need to do. Knowledge of the categories themselves is *Conceptual knowledge*. Unlike the Nutrition example, however, the categories are not intended to aid in understanding. Thus, the goal is **not** *understanding conceptual knowledge*. Rather, as the teacher makes clear in the second sentence, the categories are intended to reduce students' "memory load." The verb here is quite clearly "remember." The ultimate goal of this activity, then, is for students to memorize the addition facts (i.e., *remember factual knowledge*). As we read through the remainder of the vignette, our attention turned to the interesting relationship the teacher establishes between *Conceptual knowledge* and *Factual knowledge*, and between *Understand* and *Remember*.

In the *Macbeth* vignette (Chapter 9), clues came from the questions the teacher asks her students. As she leads the discussion of Act II, for example, she asks, "Why does Macbeth refuse to return to Duncan's room in order to plant the bloody dagger on the guards?" To answer this question, students must search for the underlying motive for a specific action (or, more specifically, inaction). That is, they must construct a mental model that explains the inaction in terms of one or more causes. Therefore, we would classify this question as explaining, which is associated with process category *Understand*.

Finally, in the assessment component, our clues came from the assessment tasks as well as the evaluation criteria (e.g., rating scales, scoring rubrics) used to judge the adequacy of student performances on the tasks. In the Parliamentary Acts vignette (Chapter 11), the teacher provides students with an "Evaluation Form" to use in evaluating their editorials, editorials that were to be written from the perspective of a historical figure. The form contains a set of evaluation criteria (e.g., the student has at least three reasons to support the character's point of view, at least one of which is not from the textbook or class discussion; the reasons are appropriate to the character and historically accurate). In combination, the criteria suggest a concern for both *Factual knowledge* (e.g., historical accuracy, reasons taken from the textbook or discussion) and *Conceptual knowledge* (e.g., appropriate to the character, at least one reason NOT taken from the textbook or discussion). When these criteria are examined within the context of the vignette as a whole, we would argue that students were expected to *remember factual knowledge* and *understand conceptual knowledge*.

Finally, in the Addition Facts vignette (Chapter 10), the ultimate assessment is a timed test of addition facts. The "timed" aspect of the assessment provided another clue that the teachers' concern is indeed memorization. Students who attempted to use the various memorization strategies included in the unit activities would be unable to complete the assessment in the time allotted. Thus, the primary unit objective is to recall the addition facts (i.e., *remember factual knowledge*), and all the activities are simply different ways of helping students attain that objective.

THE ANALYTIC PROCESS: A SUMMARY

After a great deal of discussion and much trial, error, and revision, we arrived at a four-step process for analyzing the vignettes. The first step was to identify and highlight the elements in the vignettes that lent themselves to analysis in terms of the Taxonomy Table. The entries in Table 7.2 proved useful in this regard. The second step required that we focus on the relevant nouns and verbs. Referring frequently to Table 4.1 (for the nouns) and Table 5.1 (for the verbs), we jotted down our "best guesses" about the type of knowledge and cognitive process underlying the objectives, instructional activities, and assessments described by the teacher. When possible and useful, we made a tentative placement of our "best guesses" in the Taxonomy Table at this point. In actuality, we completed three separate Taxonomy Tables: one for our analysis of the statement of objectives, one for our analysis of the instructional activities, and one for our analysis of the assessments. In the third step we re-read our entire set of notes and relevant portions of the vignette descriptions to see if we could make better guesses. In almost all cases we found this re-reading and re-examination very useful. We revised our notes and the Taxonomy Tables accordingly. Finally, we examined the consistency across the three tables, comparing the classifications of objectives, instructional activities, and assessments to determine whether they were in alignment. Having completed the analysis, we translated our notes into narrative form as they are contained in the vignette chapters.

It was during this final step that we began to come to grips with some of the major issues and concerns that confronted the teachers as they planned and implemented their units. These are discussed in Chapter 14. Not surprisingly, the issues and concerns we identified have troubled teachers for some time. We believe that serious consideration of these key issues and concerns along with serious and sustained attempts to deal with them holds great potential for the improvement of educational quality.

ORGANIZATION AND STRUCTURE OF THE VIGNETTE CHAPTERS

As we mentioned earlier, we use a common format for the vignettes to allow the reader to not only make sense of each vignette but also make comparisons across the vignettes.

The descriptive portions of each vignette, as prepared by the teachers themselves, are printed in the same font and size of type as this sentence and inset from the left margin as is this paragraph.

Periodically, you will encounter a commentary based on our analysis. All such commentaries are set off with headings printed in the same style of type as the rest of this book.

Following each major component (that is, objectives, instructional activities, and assessments), we summarize our analysis in terms of the Taxonomy Table. As we mentioned earlier, the end result is three completed Taxonomy Tables for each vignette. The first summarizes our analysis based on the objectives. The **objectives** are indicated in **bold type**. The second summarizes our analysis based on the instructional activities. The *activities* are given in *italics*. For ease of comparison, the **objectives** are carried over in **bold type** to this second table. The third table summarizes our analysis based on the assessments. The analysis based on the assessments is shown in regular type. Again, the **objectives** (**bold**) and the *instructional activities* (*italics*) are carried over.

We conclude our discussion of each vignette by examining it in terms of the four guiding questions: the learning question, the instruction question, the assessment question, and the alignment question. We also raise a few "closing questions" about the unit as designed and implemented by the teacher. The questions can be used as "starting points" for an open discussion of the unit as described in the vignette.

To get the reader started, we describe our analytic process in more detail in the first vignette (Chapter 8, Nutrition). The clues we use are shown in bold type. Specific relationships between these clues and our interpretation of them in terms of types of knowledge and/or specific cognitive processes are made explicit. In addition, connections between specific cognitive processes (e.g., *classify*) and process categories (e.g., *Understand*) are highlighted. Finally, we describe the reasoning behind our classifications when we believe such a description is necessary and appropriate.

In Chapter 5 we use the standard verb form to refer to process categories and gerunds to refer to specific cognitive processes. In the vignettes we deviate from this distinction from time to time only in order to adhere to basic rules of grammar. However, we continue to capitalize the first letter of each of the six process categories to differentiate them from the 19 specific cognitive processes, which are not capitalized. Both are italicized.

A CLOSING COMMENT

We close this chapter by reminding the reader of our purpose for including the vignettes. Although we hope they will enhance the credibility of our framework and approach, their primary purpose is to increase readers' understanding and thus to provide a means to analyze and ultimately improve the quality of education students receive.

CHAPTER 8

Nutrition Vignette

This vignette describes a two-week unit on commercials developed and taught by Ms. Nancy C. Nagengast. It is part of a larger nine-week unit on nutrition.

Most recently, I taught this unit to a second-grade class consisting of 13 boys and 13 girls. In general, the students were very distractible, but whenever they got "into" something, whether it had to do with school or not, they were motivated and enthusiastic. This unit, taught toward the end of the school year, capitalized on the study skills and cooperative learning dispositions the students had acquired during their year's experience.

The plan called for 30 minutes a day to be spent on the unit. On some days, when the children became engrossed in an activity, I extended the time allotted for this unit. On other days, when the assignment for the day had been completed after 30 minutes or so, we turned our attention away from commercials and nutrition until the next day.

PART 1: OBJECTIVES

Four objectives were established for the unit. Students were expected to:

1. **acquire knowledge** of a **classification scheme of "appeals"**[1] that describes the common targets that commercial writers take into account in writing commercials;

2. **check** the influences that commercials have **on their own "senses"** and **understand** how those influences work **on them**;

3. **evaluate** commercials seen on TV or read in newspapers/magazines **from the standpoint of a set of principles pertaining to "appeals";** and

4. **create** a commercial about a common food product that reflects **understandings of how commercials are designed to influence potential clients**.

---

[1]Attention is directed to clues used in the analysis of the appropriate Taxonomy classification by setting them in bold type. Intended to help readers get started on the analysis process, this convention appears in only this, the first of the vignettes.

We begin our analysis of this vignette by looking for clues in the statements of objectives. In the first objective, the primary clue is the phrase "classification scheme of appeals." In terms of the knowledge dimension, knowledge of classification schemes is *Conceptual knowledge*. The verb phrase "acquire knowledge" is ambiguous in relation to the cognitive processes. It might refer to *Remember*, *Understand*, or one of the other process categories. At this point, we withhold judgment and seek additional information.

In the second objective, the primary clues come from the verbs: "check" and "understand." In Table 5.1 *checking* is one of the cognitive processes in the category *Evaluate*. On the surface, "understand" corresponds to the process category *Understand*. We are not sure at this point whether the teacher is using the term in the same way it is used in the Taxonomy Table, but our initial assumption is that she is. In terms of the knowledge dimension, the focus seems to be on the students' knowledge of themselves (i.e., the way in which students are influenced by commercials). This emphasis on self suggests *Metacognitive knowledge*.

In the third objective, the students are expected to evaluate the appeals made in commercials "from the standpoint of a set of principles." In the language of the Taxonomy Table, knowledge of principles is *Conceptual knowledge* (see Table 4.1). In terms of the objective, the principles become evaluation criteria. It is important to note that the "noun" in this objective is the principles, not the commercials; the commercials are merely the materials used to teach the objective. (The reader is encouraged to re-read our discussion of this important difference on pages 17–18.)

In the fourth objective, the emphasis is on creating commercials based on students' "understandings of how commercials are designed to influence potential clients." The verb is "create." As in the third objective, the noun is not the commercials; rather, it is "understandings of how commercials are designed," For the time being, we classify this as *Procedural knowledge*.

Now we can restate the four objectives in terms of the classifications of the Taxonomy Table. Students should learn to:

1. *remember* and *understand conceptual knowledge* (i.e., the classification scheme of appeals);

2. *evaluate* and *understand metacognitive knowledge* (i.e., how students are influenced by commercials);

3. *evaluate* [based on] *conceptual knowledge* (i.e., "appeals" principles); and

4. *create* [based on] *procedural knowledge* (i.e., knowledge of how commercials are designed).

We then place these objectives in the corresponding cells of the Taxonomy Table as shown in Table 8.1. Because two verbs are included in the first two objectives, Objectives 1 and 2 are placed in two cells of the table.

PART 2: INSTRUCTIONAL ACTIVITIES

After reviewing what we discussed about the **four food groups** and **nutritious food** earlier in the larger unit (see, for example, Attachment A at the end of

8.1   ANALYSIS OF THE NUTRITION VIGNETTE IN TERMS OF THE TAXONOMY TABLE BASED ON STATED OBJECTIVES

THE KNOWLEDGE DIMENSION	THE COGNITIVE PROCESS DIMENSION					
	1. REMEMBER	2. UNDERSTAND	3. APPLY	4. ANALYZE	5. EVALUATE	6. CREATE
A. FACTUAL KNOWLEDGE						
B. CONCEPTUAL KNOWLEDGE	Objective 1	Objective 1			Objective 3	
C. PROCEDURAL KNOWLEDGE						Objective 4
D. META-COGNITIVE KNOWLEDGE		Objective 2			Objective 2	

Key
Objective 1 = Acquire knowledge of a classification scheme of "appeals."
Objective 2 = Check the influences commercials have on students' "senses."
Objective 3 = Evaluate commercials from the standpoint of a set of principles.
Objective 4 = Create a commercial that reflects understandings of how commercials are designed to influence people.

the chapter), I mentioned foods seen on television. I suggested that some commercials aim at the idea of economy (i.e., trying to convince people that buying the product will save money), while others focus on ease (e.g., trying to convince people that buying the product will save time and effort over alternatives). I then summarized by stating that these were **examples of appeals** that commercials make to the television viewer/potential consumer.

COMMENTARY

Once again we look for clues in the teacher's description of her instruction activities (see **bold** type). The teacher is presenting a variety of *Factual knowledge* related to the first objective. In addition, the exercises in Attachment A focus on *Factual knowledge* (e.g., locate and circle the fat grams, locate and circle the calories). The activity either (1) is preparatory to the first objective or (2) suggests that *Factual knowledge* is an important component of the first objective. We opt for the first choice because the teacher immediately begins to discuss each specific food in terms of one (or more) category of appeals.

Six such appeals were presented. In addition to **ease and economy, the others were health, fear, love/admiration, and comfort/pleasure**. Over the next few days, students spent time with **examples and nonexamples** of each appeal and gave examples to illustrate their **understanding**.

COMMENTARY

At this point the teacher completes the shift to *Conceptual knowledge*. The clue to this shift is the use of examples and nonexamples (a recognized approach to teaching *Conceptual knowledge*). Apparently Ms. Nagengast intends her students to acquire a classification system that includes six types of appeals. These activities, in addition to her use of the word "understanding," clarify the meaning of the first objective. The emphasis is on *understanding conceptual knowledge*.

To assess how well students had acquired the concepts in this scheme, I asked them to **describe a commercial** and then to **attribute to the commercial writers the appeal** they were making to the audience. Alternatively, I **gave students an appeal** as a prompt and asked them to **develop a claim** for a given product **that would match that appeal**.

COMMENTARY

These tasks also contribute to our understanding of the first objective. The first task is a form of *classifying* (placing specific commercials into the proper appeals category). The alternative task is a form of *exemplifying* (giving an example of a commercial for a specific type of appeal). Although both of these cognitive processes fall into the same category *Understand* (see inside the back cover), they are not identical.

One phrase used by the teacher requires additional consideration: "attribute to the commercial writers." This phrase suggests that students are not to classify the commercials based on the appeal-effect the commercial has on them; rather, they are to classify commercials on the basis of the appeal **intended by** the developer of the commercial. As we show in Table 5.1, *attributing* is a cognitive process associated with the category *Analyze*, which is a more complex category than *Understand*.

Some students were imaginative and fluent in matching commercials with appeals. Others had difficulty, and often the appeal they identified as the target of the ad writer was, at least from my point of view, decidedly off target.

COMMENTARY

Is there an explanation for this "learning problem"? Ms. Nagengast is discussing the instructional activities related to the first objective. But students may have the second objective in their minds as well, which would make them aware of the effect of the appeals on themselves. Consistent with her first objective, Ms. Nagengast is asking about the intended appeal of the writer. The students, however, realizing that the unit is also about the second objective, may miss this distinction. Therefore, those operating from an analytic (attributional) framework will more likely produce "proper" classifications. In contrast, students who respond in terms of their own understanding (its effect on them) can be expected to produce fewer correct classifications.

From these exercises, I was able to determine which students had and had not mastered the concept of appeal as it applied to nutritional commercials. To be successful, students not only had to **recall the names of all six appeals** but also had to **understand the concept of appeals well enough to classify commercials appropriately**.

COMMENTARY

Ms. Nagengast is making an important distinction here. Students may be able to remember the name of the class to which the appeal was assigned (*Factual knowledge*), but they may not be able to classify examples of appeals correctly (*Conceptual knowledge*). Ms. Nagengast is concerned with both types of knowledge. Thus, the activities related to Objective 1 focus on both *Remember* and *Understand* and on both *Factual* and *Conceptual knowledge* (see Table 8.2).

My second objective was for students to examine the impact that commercials have **on their own decisions**. Students were asked to respond to the impact that various "hooks" had **on their own thinking**. A first step was to get students to examine the phrases they associated with various products (see Attachment B) and then to reflect on the impact those commercials had **on their feelings**.

8.2 ANALYSIS OF THE NUTRITION VIGNETTE IN TERMS OF THE TAXONOMY TABLE BASED ON INSTRUCTIONAL ACTIVITIES

THE KNOWLEDGE DIMENSION	THE COGNITIVE PROCESS DIMENSION					
	1. REMEMBER	2. UNDERSTAND	3. APPLY	4. ANALYZE	5. EVALUATE	6. CREATE
A. FACTUAL KNOWLEDGE	*Activities during teaching of Objective 1*					
B. CONCEPTUAL KNOWLEDGE	**Objective 1**	**Objective 1** *Activities during teaching of Objective 1*		*Activities during teaching of Objective 1*	**Objective 3** *Activities during teaching of Objective 3*	*Activities during teaching of Objective 4*
C. PROCEDURAL KNOWLEDGE			*Activities during teaching of Objective 4*			**Objective 4**
D. META-COGNITIVE KNOWLEDGE		**Objective 2** *Activities during teaching of Objective 2*		*Activities during teaching of Objective 2*	**Objective 2**	

Key
Objective 1 = Acquire knowledge of a classification scheme of "appeals."
Objective 2 = Check the influences commercials have on students' "senses."
Objective 3 = Evaluate commercials from the standpoint of a set of principles.
Objective 4 = Create a commercial that reflects understandings of how commercials are designed to influence people.

COMMENTARY

Consistent with the stated intent of Objective 2, these activities focus on the impact of the commercials on the students themselves. The initial "matching exercise" (Attachment B) is an attempt to determine the students' *Factual knowledge* about commercials. The questions asked by the teacher appear to be intended to stimulate *Metacognitive knowledge*.

In class discussion, students were asked questions such as "**What did you think** when you heard this commercial?" and "What was the commercial **writer expecting you to think** when the ad said that Michael Jordan uses the product?" The comments, questions, and observations shared in this discussion served as the evidence bearing on my second objective.

COMMENTARY

The first question reinforces our belief that Objective 2 emphasizes *understanding metacognitive knowledge* (i.e., to understand the impact that commercials have on the students). The second question asks for more than *Understanding*. Students are expected to examine the commercial from the point of view of the writer/designer of the commercial (i.e., attribute). This question reinforces our belief that the teacher wants students to *Analyze* commercials by making attributions about the motives of their writers/designers. This also is consistent with our commentary on the activities related to the first objective.

Once the students had mastered the idea of the appeals and discussed the effects of those appeals on themselves, I played three or four commercials on the VCR, asking students, working in groups, to evaluate how well the commercials "worked." Specifically, students were to **judge how well the commercial made the appeal and how convincing and compelling** it was. **Students generated criteria for "being convincing"** through a teacher-pupil planning session. The criteria were incorporated into an initial draft of a scoring guide. After a few revisions, the scoring guide became more useful to the students in registering their evaluations of the commercial (see Attachment C at the end of the chapter). One of the major differences in the drafts was that the early versions of the scoring guide reflected too much of my own language and not enough of that of the students.

COMMENTARY

Here the focus shifts to *Evaluate*. In order to *Evaluate*, students must possess knowledge of the criteria that they generated to define "being convincing" (*Conceptual knowledge*). Again, we must emphasize that the commercials themselves are simply the materials used to teach the knowledge; they are not the knowledge to be learned per se. Ms. Nagengast clearly intends the students to use their knowledge with commercials encountered outside of class and in the future.

The culminating activity in this unit had students, in groups of two to four, working to create their own commercials. Each group was to select a food product and to **prepare a tentative advertising plan** for the product. These plans would then be shared with another group in the class and **feedback would be provided using the scoring rubric developed for evaluating commercials**, along with the nutrition concepts from earlier lessons in the larger unit.

COMMENTARY

In Table 5.1 *planning* is a cognitive process in the category *Create*. Because the students are to plan their commercials based on their knowledge of how to design commercials to influence potential clients, the knowledge component of the objective would fall into the *Procedural knowledge* category. Because the plans are to be evaluated on the basis of explicit criteria, *Conceptual knowledge* is also involved. Nonetheless, we would classify this objective as *Create* [based on] *Procedural knowledge*.

After receiving feedback about their planning from their peers and from me, the students rehearsed their commercials and then presented them to the whole class. Subsequently, the groups presented their commercials to a larger audience including parents, teachers, and other second-grade classes. Each effort was videotaped so that I could analyze it carefully at my leisure rather than "on the fly" while it was being presented.

Once all the commercials were performed, I convened the groups again and asked them to **summarize what things they had done as a group that had been particularly useful in producing the commercials and what things the group might have done to do a better job**. Students were reminded **not to blame individuals** within their group but instead to focus on those elements of the group process that might be useful to remember the next time they worked in groups. Each group reported the products of their thinking to the entire class, and I recorded the insights generated by the class on a sheet of poster paper.

COMMENTARY

We assume that the scoring guide in Attachment C provides the criteria used to *Evaluate* the final commercials. Note that Ms. Nagengast avoids the word *Evaluate*, choosing *Analyze* instead. Clearly, the scoring guide requires analysis; however, the analysis performed provides the basis for evaluating the quality of the commercials. In addition to the criteria included in Attachment C, students are asked to evaluate the group process according to three criteria:

(1) areas of strength, (2) ways of improving the process, and (3) avoidance of the placement of blame. Because these are "non-cognitive" criteria, we do not classify them in the Taxonomy Table.

Throughout this final segment of the nutrition unit, the **purpose of each activity became more clear to the students**. Students became enthralled in singing and/or reciting commercials verbatim and consequently completing the worksheet.

COMMENTARY

The students themselves are learning the difference between the activities and the objective (i.e., the purpose of the activity in terms of the intended learning outcome).

Our analysis of the entire set of instructional activities over the ten-day period was summarized in Table 8.2 shown earlier. To aid in comparing the activities with the stated objectives, the objectives from Table 8.1 were reproduced in **bold** type in Table 8.2. The instructional activities were *italicized*.

PART 3: ASSESSMENT

I assessed the students in various ways. Class discussions provided useful information as to whether the students were grasping the objectives. As the students began working in groups, I would walk around the room monitoring their progress and checking to make sure each person in the group was contributing to the project. These unobtrusive observations provided me a true indicator of their progress.

In addition to monitoring the discussion in which students were engaged, I read the worksheets the students generated as part of their study (e.g., their plans for their commercials). Ultimately, I did a **rigorous evaluation of the commercials** the students prepared for signs of understanding of the **principal ideas associated with nutrition.**

I graded them for completion of class work and homework. Throughout the unit, I kept a record of each student's effort in this regard with the distinctions of a check-plus, check, or check-minus entered into the grade book.

Finally, the students engaged in an oral evaluation of both their final commercials and their work as cooperative groups. After they had completed the unit, students occasionally commented on the commercials they saw on television and often wrote about the unit as one of the favorite activities done that year.

COMMENTARY

The vast majority of Ms. Nagengast's discussion of assessment pertains to informal assessment and grading. She developed separate assessment tasks for only the first objective. For all other objectives she used selected instructional activities as assessment tasks; that is, the activities were intended to help students learn **and** to allow Ms. Nagengast to assess students' learning. This dual function of instructional activities (for facilitating both learning and assessment) is fairly common for the teachers who prepared the vignettes. In most instances, although it may contribute to student grades, the assessment is considered formative because its primary purpose is to put students "on the right track."

The one aspect of assessment that lends itself to analysis in terms of the Taxonomy Table is Ms. Nagengast's "rigorous evaluation of the commercials" prepared by the students. The scoring guide used to evaluate the commercials contains six criteria ("scoring elements") (see Attachment C). The first scoring element (A) pertains to the general appropriateness of the commercial to the unit (i.e., nutrition) and so was not classified. The second scoring element (B) is tangentially related to Objective 1. Rather than identify the type of appeal (i.e., *Conceptual knowledge*), the emphasis is on whether the commercial appealed to "wants and needs" (a more affective than cognitive concern). The third scoring element (C) is the one related most directly to the knowledge contained in Objective 4 (i.e., *Procedural knowledge*). The scoring element criterion (D) pertains to realism (and therefore is tangentially to the objectives as stated). However, we place this in cell B6 (*create* [based on] *conceptual knowledge*). Both the fifth (E) and sixth (F) criteria address the audience of the commercial. Did the commercial make the audience want to buy the food? Was the commercial aimed at the intended audience? These criteria are related to Objective 2, if one assumes the students see themselves as the intended audience.

Our analysis of the assessments in terms of the Taxonomy Table is presented in Table 8.3. Again, for comparison purposes, the entries from Tables 8.1 (**objectives**) and Table 8.2 (*instructional activities*) are reproduced in Table 8.3.

PART 4: CLOSING COMMENTARY

In this section we examine the vignette in terms of our four basic questions: the learning question, the instruction question, the assessment question, and the alignment question.

THE LEARNING QUESTION

The overall purpose of the unit is for students to learn to create commercials about common food products that reflect their understanding of how commercials are designed to influence potential consumers (Objective 4). As mentioned in our summary of the instructional activities, the unit builds from objective to objective, culminating in Objective 4. In terms of emphasis, fully five of the ten days spent on the unit are devoted to the fourth objective. In addition, the fourth objective is the only one subjected to formal assessment and evaluation.

THE INSTRUCTION QUESTION

It is interesting that the order of the instructional activities corresponds to the sequence of the stated objectives. That is, the activities are used to move

8.3 ANALYSIS OF THE NUTRITION VIGNETTE IN TERMS OF THE TAXONOMY TABLE BASED ON ASSESSMENTS

THE KNOWLEDGE DIMENSION	THE COGNITIVE PROCESS DIMENSION					
	1. REMEMBER	2. UNDERSTAND	3. APPLY	4. ANALYZE	5. EVALUATE	6. CREATE
A. FACTUAL KNOWLEDGE	Activities during teaching of Objective 1					
B. CONCEPTUAL KNOWLEDGE	Objective 1	Objective 1 Activities during teaching of Objective 1 Assess 1		Activities during teaching of Objective 1	Objective 3 Activities during teaching of Objective 3 Assess 3	Activities during teaching of Objective 4 Assess 4; Element C, D
C. PROCEDURAL KNOWLEDGE			Activities during teaching of Objective 4			Objective 4
D. META-COGNITIVE KNOWLEDGE		Objective 2 Activities during teaching of Objective 2		Activities during teaching of Objective 2 Assess 2	Objective 2	Assess 4 Elements E, F

Key
Objective 1 = Acquire knowledge of a classification scheme of "appeals."
Objective 2 = Check the influences commercials have on students' "senses."
Objective 3 = Evaluate commercials from the standpoint of a set of principles.
Objective 4 = Create a commercial that reflects understandings of how commercials are designed to influence people.
Assess 1 = Classroom exercise—classifying and exemplifying.
Assess 2 = "Higher-order" classroom questions.
Assess 3 = Commercials on videotapes.
Assess 4 = Scoring guide.
Dark shading indicates the strongest alignment—an objective, an instructional activity, and an assessment are all present in the same cell. Lighter shading indicates two of the three are present.

students from *remembering* and *understanding conceptual knowledge* (Objective 1) to *understanding* and *analyzing metacognitive knowledge* (Objective 2) to *evaluating* commercials based on *conceptual knowledge* (Objective 3) to *creating* commercials based on *procedural knowledge* (Objective 4).

Generally speaking, the activities in which Ms. Nagengast engaged her students are consistent with her learning intentions. She used positive and negative examples to teach types (categories) of appeals (*Conceptual knowledge*). She gave students practice in classifying and exemplifying (*Understand*). She used so-called higher-order questions in her pursuit of *Metacognitive knowledge* (e.g., "What do you think?"). She worked with the students to develop the criteria (*Conceptual knowledge*) used to evaluate the commercials, and students practiced using the criteria in *Evaluating*. Finally, with respect to *Creating* commercials, she asked students to prepare plans, provide and receive feedback on the plans, rehearse the plans "in action," and ultimately implement the plans in front of several audiences.

THE ASSESSMENT QUESTION

The teacher used both informal and formal assessments. As shown in Table 8.3, she used the informal assessments to determine students' progress on the first three objectives. Thus, these assessments were formative in nature. The scoring guide used in the informal assessment relative to Objective 3 was developed in part by the students. Once developed, it formed the basis for the more formal assessment of Objective 4.

There was both a formative and summative assessment of the fourth objective. Both assessments relied on the aforementioned scoring guide. The formative assessment was a peer assessment of the plans for the commercials. The summative assessment was a teacher assessment of the production of the commercial.

THE ALIGNMENT QUESTION

Overall, the alignment among objectives, instructional activities, and assessments is quite strong. This alignment is most evident for Objectives 1 and 3 (see Table 8.3). If we look at the cells of the table, the alignment is less clear for the other objective. By focusing on the rows of the table, however, we see a reasonable degree of alignment for the second objective. The emphasis on *Metacognitive knowledge* is clear in Objective 2 and in the related instructional activities and assessments. The misalignment stems from a slight difference in the process categories *Analyze* and *Evaluate*. A similar point can be made for the fourth objective. This time, however, the misalignment comes from the columns of Table 8.3. The stated objective, instructional activities, and assessments all focus on *Create*. The differences pertain to the types of knowledge tapped by the formal assessment. In addition to *Procedural knowledge*, the scoring guide includes criteria relating to *Conceptual knowledge* and *Metacognitive knowledge*.

Most of the anomalies in Table 8.3 may be explained fairly easily. For example, Objective 1 is placed in two cells: *remember conceptual knowledge* and *understand conceptual knowledge*. After reviewing the entire unit, we believe our initial classification of the stated objective as *remember conceptual knowledge* is inaccurate. Similarly, although some of the instructional activities related to Objective 1 are placed in the cell corresponding to *remember factual knowledge*, these activities involve associating the names of the appeals (*Factual knowledge*) with the categories of appeals (*Conceptual knowledge*). This activity is important, but it may not justify an objective in and of itself (or a formal assessment). Finally, some activities related to Objective 1 are placed in the cell corresponding to *analyze conceptual knowledge* rather than *understand conceptual knowledge*. The difference between *attribute* and *classify* is substantial and worthy of discussion (see below). In retrospect, then, we would eliminate the entries in cells A1 (*remember factual knowledge*) and B1 (*remember conceptual knowledge*), but keep the entry in cell B4 (*analyze conceptual knowledge*).

PART 5: CLOSING QUESTIONS

As with the analysis of all our vignettes, we were left with a few unanswered questions. We raise three of the most interesting in this closing section.

1. **Is it sufficient to align objectives, instructional activities, and assessments in terms of the rows or columns alone?** This question comes from our examination of Table 8.3 (see above) coupled with our analysis of the activities related to the first objective. It seems clear to us that the objective and activities focus on *Conceptual knowledge*. There is, however, a difference between *Understand* (*exemplifying* and *classifying*) and *Analyze* (*attributing*), which is implicit in the objective and is made explicit in the teacher's reaction to student performance of the assessment tasks. As we mentioned on our commentary on the activities related to Objective 1, students who classify based on their own reactions to a commercial (*Understand*) are likely to arrive at appeals that are different from those of students who classify based on appeals they attribute to the writers/designers of the commercials (*Analyze*). This question is important because, in common practice, alignment decisions are often based solely on the knowledge dimension or the cognitive process dimension. Alignment decisions based on either dimension alone may be misleading in terms of the interaction between the two dimensions that, we believe, define intended student learning.

2. **Is it possible that student input into developing scoring rubrics produced rubrics with less than optimum validity?** On the one hand, it is difficult to criticize teachers who involve students in setting criteria for evaluating their own work. On the other, a problem may result if too much reliance is placed on student input. Of the six criteria developed by the students, only two (A and E) or three (C) relate clearly to the knowledge intended to be developed in the instructional unit. The other criteria

are a bit vague (B), or tangentially related (D and F) to nutrition, the content of the unit. As a consequence, students who master the *Conceptual knowledge* (e.g., the classification of appeals) and *Procedural knowledge* (e.g., the "technical" aspects of designing "appealing" commercials) may still receive low overall evaluations based on the less than optimally valid criteria used to evaluate the prepared commercials. One way of preempting this problem may be to establish a set of meta-criteria, that is, a set of criteria to be used jointly with the students in determining the criteria to include on the scoring rubric. Alternatively, the teacher may critique the criteria along with the students, leading them to recognize any problems with the criteria (e.g., irrelevancy).

3. **What are the advantages and disadvantages of having instructional activities serve both a learning and an assessment function?** The practice of using instructional activities for both learning and assessment purposes, though fairly common, causes at least two problems. The first is blurring the distinction between objectives and instructional activities; that is, students who perform well on a single activity (i.e., the production of a single commercial) are assumed to have mastered the objective (i.e., the ability to produce commercials that meet specified criteria) when the activity is but a single example of the realm of activities circumscribed by the objective.

   The second problem comes in delineating where teaching ends and assessment begins. Traditionally, teachers help students with instructional activities, whereas students are "left alone" when performing assessment tasks. Assessment tasks, then, provide an "independent estimate" of learning (that is, independent of teacher assistance and involvement). When instructional activities serve both learning and assessment functions, this independence is lost. The result is that an assessment is made of both teaching and learning for that individual, not of learning alone. It may be difficult, even impossible, for teachers to separate these functions in their own minds.

   The primary advantage of using instructional activities for both purposes is a general increase in the authenticity of the assessment and, hence, its instructional validity. The issue to be addressed is whether this trade-off is reasonable. Probably teachers are less focused on keeping instruction and assessments independent than are supervisors and administrators, who are concerned about the impact on their schools if students do poorly. Where punishment of low-scoring schools is a real concern, then perhaps the trade-off balance involved in combining instruction and assessment needs to be adjusted.

Read the Label!

Read these food labels to find out the nutritional value of the food shown on this page.

NUTRITION INFORMATION
SERVING SIZE ....1 CUP
CALORIES 120
PROTEIN ....8 GRAMS
CARBOHYDRATE ..11 GRAMS
FAT ....5 GRAMS
SODIUM ....125 mg

NUTRITION INFORMATION – PER 1/2 CUP SERVING
SERVINGS PER CONTAINER .... APPROX. 4
CALORIES 60   FAT ....0 g
PROTEIN ....0 g   SODIUM 20mg
CARBOHYDRATE ...16 g   CHOLESTEROL ....0 g

Use a red crayon to circle the fat found in each food. Use a blue crayon to circle the calories found in each food.

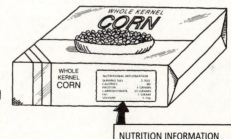

NUTRITION INFORMATION
SERVING SIZE ....3.3 OZ.
CALORIES 80
PROTEIN ....3 GRAMS
CARBOHYDRATE ... 20 GRAMS
FAT ....1 GRAM
SODIUM ....5 mg

NUTRITION INFORMATION
CALORIES ..250 PROTEIN ..5 g CARBOHYDRATE ..20
FAT ..2 g   SODIUM ..25 mg

Read the food labels on the food you eat at home. Can you find the nutrition information?

ATTACHMENT B   IDENTIFICATION OF PRODUCTS FROM THEIR "HOOKS"

Can you identify the following products from their hooks?

1. Have you had your break today?   _____

2. Where a kid can be a kid   _____

3. Just do it   _____

4. Pizza Pizza   _____

5. I love what you do for me   _____

6. Melts in your mouth, not in your hand   _____

ATTACHMENT C   SCORING GUIDE

Performance Task: Working as a team from an advertising agency, study a food product that you eat every day in terms of its nutritional values. Plan and present a compelling yet truthful commercial aimed at your classmates to induce them to eat more of your product. Promote your product by appealing to their individual needs and wants. Use various techniques to convince your viewers that your product is worth buying, but make sure your claims are accurate and your techniques realistic.

Scoring Element	Performance Levels
A. Did the commercial focus on nutrition and the nutritional value of food?	4—Principal focus was on food and nutrition. 3—Nutrition was only one of many ideas in the commercial—the others were a distraction. 2—Nutrition was mentioned but drowned out by other topics. 1—Nutrition was ignored in the commercial.
B. Did the commercial appeal to individual's wants and needs?	4—Message grabbed kids in class. 3—Message caused most kids to sit up and notice. 2—Message caught some students' attention. 1—Message was hard to follow or to engage.
C. Did the commercial make use of techniques to convince viewers?	4—Techniques were thoughtful and distinctive. 3—Techniques were copy-cat of commercials on TV. 2—Techniques were included but were not really a part of the design; they seemed simply added on. 1—No techniques.
D. Did the commercial use realism in its techniques?	4—Very realistic. It was like "being there!" 3—One (or two) unrealistic elements, but on the whole quite real. 2—Many unrealistic elements in the commercial. 1—Hard to find what's real.
E. Did the commercial make the audience want to buy the food?	4—Members of the audience would rush out to buy the product. 3—Members will buy the product during the next shopping trip. 2—Members might consider buying it. 1—Probably not.
F. Was the commercial aimed at the intended audience?	4—Commercial was right on target. 3—Some elements of the commercial would have gone over their heads, but on the whole all right. 2—A large part of the audience was lost. 1—Almost no one got the message.

CHAPTER 9

Macbeth *Vignette*

This instructional unit, developed and taught by Ms. Margaret Jackson, is intended for "low-level" high school seniors.

> I had my first experience teaching Shakespeare to these students when I decided to quit torturing myself with what passed for a literature text for these students. The educational philosophy reflected in the literature text was predicated on the assumption that students, particularly those labeled "educationally challenged," could neither comprehend nor appreciate literature that was not "relevant" to their particular situation.
>
> In contrast, I believe that great literature is everyone's birthright because it does not require that "relevancy" be externally imposed. Rather, a street-wise teenager from the projects—which these students were—can possess Shakespeare as completely and comfortably as a college professor.
>
> I initially had some misgivings about the language—many students were reading below a fifth-grade level and had difficulty writing coherent sentences. But they had less trouble and complained far less than my college-bound students. I realized that these students considered English in any form to be completely beyond their ken; a modern novel was as unintelligible to them as a 16th-century drama! They also immediately understood Macbeth's character and motivations; the world they live in has some striking similarities to 11th-century Scotland. In both places, if someone gets in the way of an ambitious person, he or she is likely to get knifed.
>
> I felt under a certain amount of self-imposed pressure to reduce the amount of time on this unit. My general experience had been that if *Macbeth* isn't finished by Christmas, I won't get to the Romantics until just before the May examination. However, these students put up definite resistance to being rushed and I was unable to pare the unit down to less than five weeks. This schedule allowed for a little under one week per act, leaving time at the end for review and testing.

PART 1: OBJECTIVES

The major objective of this five-week unit is that students will learn to see the relevance of literary works such as *Macbeth* to their own lives. A secondary objective is for students to remember important details about the play (e.g., specific events, characters, and their relationships).

COMMENTARY

In the major objective, the verb phrase is "see the relevance" and the noun phrase is "literary works in their own lives." In order to "see the relevance," it seems likely that students will compare characters and events in the play with characters and events from their own experience. In Table 5.1 (see inside back cover) *compare* is a cognitive process in the category *Understand*. With respect to the noun phrase, the emphasis is on literary works, with *Macbeth* being one example ("such as"). Because "literary works" denotes a category of writings, knowledge of literary works is *Conceptual knowledge*). Furthermore, because literary works contain concepts such as "character," "plot," and "setting," knowledge of these concepts is also classified as *Conceptual knowledge*. *Macbeth* is a specific literary work. Within *Macbeth* there are specific characters, a specific plot (and subplots), and specific settings. Knowledge of these specifics is *Factual knowledge*.

Because the second objective clearly emphasizes the details of a specific literary work, we classify it as *remember factual knowledge*. The first objective, on the other hand, suggests a more general concern of the teacher. Consequently, we classify it as *understand conceptual knowledge*.

The placement of these two objectives in the cells of the Taxonomy Table is shown in Table 9.1.

PART 2: INSTRUCTIONAL ACTIVITIES

Introductory Activity

The first day I focused on what I considered some of the play's primary concepts. I put the words "ambition," "temptation," and "fear" on the board and divided the class into three groups. The individuals in each group were asked to write for five minutes on one of the three words. They very quickly understood how ambition can help or hinder a person, how temptation can be resisted, and how fear can be handled or conquered. This led into a discussion of how these three terms are central to an understanding of *Macbeth*.

I then told the students that Shakespeare would have been dealing with an extremely diverse audience whose attention was difficult to capture and hold; therefore, he would have found it necessary to hit the ground running, establishing in the opening scene a mood that would permeate the entire play. Students were then asked to follow along in their books while I read Act I, scene i aloud, paying particular attention to the key words that aid in creating

9.1 ANALYSIS OF THE *MACBETH* VIGNETTE IN TERMS OF THE TAXONOMY TABLE BASED ON STATED OBJECTIVES

THE KNOWLEDGE DIMENSION	THE COGNITIVE PROCESS DIMENSION					
	1. REMEMBER	2. UNDERSTAND	3. APPLY	4. ANALYZE	5. EVALUATE	6. CREATE
A. FACTUAL KNOWLEDGE	Objective 2					
B. CONCEPTUAL KNOWLEDGE		Objective 1				
C. PROCEDURAL KNOWLEDGE						
D. META-COGNITIVE KNOWLEDGE						

Key
Objective 1 = Students will see the relevance of literary works such as *Macbeth* to their own lives.
Objective 2 = Students will remember important details about the play.

the predominant mood. (The scene is only 11 lines long, but almost every word is loaded with significance.)

I drew the students' attention to the line "Fair is foul and foul is fair" and asked them to put it in their own words. They ended up with the paradoxical concept: "Good is bad and bad is good," which led into a discussion of how something good could be bad and vice versa. Examples included alcohol, drugs, and sex. I stressed, as I continued to do throughout the unit, how this seemingly contradictory statement begins to develop what I see as the play's principal theme: Things are not as they seem.

COMMENTARY

The emphasis in this introductory activity is on *understanding conceptual knowledge*. Key concepts include ambition, temptation, fear (in the first paragraph of the Introductory Activity Section), mood (in the second paragraph), and paradox (in the third paragraph). In addition to the knowledge clues, students are asked to "put things in their own words" (third paragraph) and come up with contemporary examples (third paragraph). In Table 5.1 (see inside back cover), "paraphrase" is associated with *interpreting* and "generating examples" is *exemplifying*. Both *interpreting* and *exemplifying* are cognitive processes associated with the category *Understand*.

Activities Related to Act I

I began by telling students they had to write scene-by-scene synopses. Next, I initiated a discussion of the "tragic hero"—a person of great stature and distinction who is destroyed as a result of a character defect. The students all had observed first hand the "pity and fear" engendered by someone who sows the seeds of his or her own destruction while pursuing a dream. Students were helped to see the relevance of *Macbeth* to their own lives in that, given the right circumstances, the same thing could happen to many of them.

Students were assigned parts and the play was read aloud, stopping after each scene for whatever explication was necessary. I asked questions which focused primarily on understanding (e.g., "What are Macbeth's strengths of character?" "What would have happened if Macbeth had never met the witches?").

Despite initial reluctance and self-consciousness on the part of students, I insisted that students "act out" key scenes, with the class assuming the role of director. Initially I had to do almost all the directing, but once the students grasped the concept of there being actions behind the words, the effect was energizing.

After reading and discussing Act I, students were shown three different film versions: the 1940s version directed by and starring Orson Welles; Roman Polanski's graphic and bloody 1972 treatment; and the BBC version from "The Shakespeare Plays" series. Before I showed Act I of these three versions, students were asked to write for five minutes on what a good movie version of *Macbeth* should include by way of cinematography and characterization. I then distributed a chart (see Attachment A at the end of the chapter) to be used to compare the three films. Following the viewing of the three versions of Act I, I distributed an outline for a comparison/contrast paper on the three film versions (see Attachment B at the end of the chapter), with the introduction to be written the next day in the writing lab and the rough draft due the next week.

The activities relative to Act I took about one week to complete.

COMMENTARY

As in the introductory activity, the focus is on *Conceptual knowledge*. Key concepts include tragic hero, character defects, cinematography, and characterization. The nature of Ms. Jackson's questions is consistent with *Understand* (e.g., *exemplifying* and *inferring*). The chart (Attachment A) contains seven key concepts that are used as the basis for comparing and contrasting three film versions of the play. The first four concepts (setting, sound, lighting, and special effects) concern elements of the films; the last three concepts pertain to the characterization of the witches, Macbeth, and Lady Macbeth. Since comparing is a cognitive process in the category *Understand*, the focus of these activities is, once again, *understanding conceptual knowledge*.

Activities Related to Act II

I allowed the class to select the film version they would continue to view act by act throughout the unit. After some deliberation they cautiously agreed on Polanski's (although they were less enthusiastic about his depiction of the witches). Students were expected to keep a film journal (see Attachment C at the end of the chapter), an expectation which required rather close guidance from me.

I began the study of Act II by introducing the concept of *motif*. Students were asked to be aware of three *motifs* as they read Act II: blood, sleep, and darkness. They were asked to write for five minutes on these three terms and the feelings they engendered, both singly and in combination.

Class sessions consisted of reading and discussion. Again, I used questions to guide the discussion (e.g., "Why does Macbeth refuse to return to Duncan's room in order to plant the bloody dagger on the guards?" "What difference would it have made if Lady Macbeth had been able to murder Duncan herself?")

I divided the class into three equal groups; each group was assigned one of the three motifs. The only instruction given to the groups was to find every mention of their motif in scenes i and ii of Act II and to arrive at a consensus regarding the significance of the motif in the context of the play.

The activities related to Act II took about a week to complete.

COMMENTARY

The emphasis on *understanding conceptual knowledge* continues. The film journal requires comparing and contrasting (hence *Understanding*). Two superordinate concepts—cinematography and characterization—are used to organize the journal. In the study of Act II, the major concept is motif. Specifically, students are to examine three motifs as they read Act II: blood, sleep, and darkness. The affective aspect of concepts is acknowledged when Ms. Jackson has the students write about the "feelings [that each concept] engendered."

The final activity also emphasizes *understanding conceptual knowledge*. Students are asked to find instances of the specific motifs in the play and describe each motif's significance in the context of the play. Finding instances is *exemplifying* (hence *Understand*). The concern for the significance of the motifs as well as Ms. Jackson's questions during the discussion of Act II require process categories beyond *Understand*. Determining significance "in the context of the play" is *attributing*. Similarly, the question pertaining to Macbeth's refusal to return to Duncan's room requires that attributions be made.

Finally, the question asking students to speculate on what would have happened if Lady Macbeth had murdered Duncan requires *generating*. In Table 5.1 (see inside back cover), *attributing* is associated with *Analyze*, whereas *generating* is related to *Create*. Thus, although the emphasis on *understanding conceptual knowledge* continues throughout these activities, two additional cognitive process categories are involved: *Analyze* and *Create*. Several knowledge types are likely to be involved in *Analyzing* and *Creating* in this instance; *Factual* and *Conceptual knowledge* seem particularly relevant.

Activities Related to Act III

I began the discussion of Act III by asking the students to predict what direction Macbeth would take now that he is well versed in murder. Most agreed that he would most likely kill again, that killing would become easier and easier for him. Some were able to predict Banquo's murder, sensing that Macbeth would begin to be uncomfortable with how much his friend already knew.

All of Act III was read and then discussed. Once again, I used questions to guide the discussion (e.g., "How would you direct an actor to portray a man feeling the constant fear that Macbeth obviously feels?" "Is the murder of Banquo more or less understandable than the murder of Duncan? Why or why not?").

At this point in time, I took class time to allow students to work on their group projects. (See Section III, Assessment, for examples and Attachment D at the end of the chapter for scoring criteria.)

The activities related to Act III took about three days to complete, with the projects requiring an additional five days.

The discussion of Act III begins by asking students to predict what will happen next. In terms of the process dimension, "predicting" is an alternative name for *inferring*, and *inferring* is a cognitive process in the category *Understand* (see Table 5.1). As the class begins to read and discuss Act III, Ms. Jackson once again uses questions to guide the discussion. The first discussion question ("How would you direct?") is quite complex, requiring concepts from cinematography and from the play itself. In terms of the cognitive process dimension, the focus is on the category *Create*. The second discussion question requires *Evaluating*, with the tag "Why or why not?" asking students to state the criteria they are using to make their judgments. Five additional days are spent in class on the major project, which is also the major unit assessment. Ms. Jackson is borrowing instructional time for the purpose of assessment, believing that her students need structured classroom time, with supervision, to complete their projects. *Creating* and *Evaluating* in this context quite likely require some combination of *Conceptual* and *Factual knowledge*.

Activities Related to Act IV

Because of the time lag between finishing Act III and taking up Act IV, I felt the need to do a fairly extensive review of the previous three acts before beginning Act IV. By way of preparation, I asked the students to consider Act IV in the light of a steady downward progression for Macbeth, who at this point is becoming overwhelmed with his fears and the increasing number of murders they inspire.

Following the reading of Act IV, I engaged students in a class discussion. Again, a series of questions served as a guide (e.g., "Explain Macbeth's reasoning in having MacDuff's family killed. How does this murder differ in character and motivation from others?" "Can the scene between Malcolm and MacDuff be rightly criticized for its lack of credibility? Why or why not?").

The review period lasted about a day, with an additional four days spent on Act IV.

Once again the major clues for classifying in the Taxonomy Table come from Ms. Jackson's questions. She asks students to "explain" (*Understand*), "compare" (*Understand*), and "critique" (*Evaluate*). Unlike in the previous evaluation question, however, the criterion to be used by the students in making their judgments (i.e., credibility) is given by Ms. Jackson.

Activities Related to Act V

Despite the fact that Act V is composed of a large number of short scenes, each involving complicated action and a bewildering influx of numerous minor characters, students enjoyed the fast pace and appreciated the rapidity with which the play hurtles toward its end. Almost every scene unravels more and more of the false securities with which Macbeth has surrounded himself.

The class delighted in the fiendish ironies in the fulfillment of the witches' prophecies, and it took very little prompting for them to see that Macbeth, who had confounded other characters throughout the play with the differences between what he seemed to be and what he actually was, is now himself the victim of appearance vs. reality. (Although I mentioned the term *irony* in passing, I considered it to be more important that these students recognize it rather than label it. Macbeth has a "right" ending, and this all of the students could understand and appreciate.)

Following the reading aloud of Act V, questions such as the following were used to guide the concluding discussion. "What is Macbeth's frame of mind in his famous 'Tomorrow' soliloquy?" "Predict what would happen if Macbeth had refused to fight MacDuff once he learned the truth of MacDuff's birth?" "What is the effect of Malcolm's speech at the end of the play?"

COMMENTARY

Continuing with her emphasis on *Conceptual knowledge*, Ms. Jackson introduces the concept of "irony." It is important to note that she is more interested in having students understand the concept than in having them remember the label attached to it. In Ms. Jackson's words, students should "recognize it rather than label it." To foster the development of *Conceptual knowledge*, her questions ask students to *Understand* (*inferring* and *explaining*) and to *Analyze* (*attributing*).

Our analysis of the instructional activities in terms of the Taxonomy Table is summarized in Table 9.2.

PART 3: ASSESSMENT

The primary assignment was a group project to complete and present to the class. A group consisted of two to four students. Examples include: "Choose any scene from the play and rewrite it, using a modern setting and language but retaining the sense of what is said. Present the scene before the class." "Create an edition of *The Scotland Chronicle* which deals with the news-worthy events of the play. Use a combination of news articles, feature articles, editorials, and special features such as political cartoons, advice columns, and want ads." The criteria for scoring the projects are shown in Attachment D at the end of the chapter.

9.2 ANALYSIS OF THE *MACBETH* VIGNETTE IN TERMS OF THE TAXONOMY TABLE BASED ON INSTRUCTIONAL ACTIVITIES

THE KNOWLEDGE DIMENSION	THE COGNITIVE PROCESS DIMENSION					
	1. REMEMBER	2. UNDERSTAND	3. APPLY	4. ANALYZE	5. EVALUATE	6. CREATE
A. FACTUAL KNOWLEDGE	Objective 2			Activities for Act II	Activities for Act III	Activities for Acts II and III
B. CONCEPTUAL KNOWLEDGE		Objective 1 *Introductory activity and activities for Acts I–V; Film journal; Film comparison*		Activities for Acts II, IV, and V	Activities for Acts III and IV	Activities for Acts II and III
C. PROCEDURAL KNOWLEDGE						
D. META-COGNITIVE KNOWLEDGE						

Key
Objective 1 = Students will see the relevance of literary works such as *Macbeth* to their own lives.
Objective 2 = Students will remember important details about the play.

COMMENTARY

The clues to the proper placement of this assignment in the Taxonomy Table come from two sources: (1) the directions given to the students and (2) the five criteria used to score the projects. The first example requires *interpreting* (*Understand*) and *producing* (*Create*), whereas the second example requires *differentiating* (*Analyze*) and *producing* (*Create*). Although both examples require students to *Create*, different projects require different additional process categories to be used by the students prior to or in conjunction with the act of creating. Thus, by virtue of student choice, some students are likely to work on projects that are more complex cognitively and, hence, likely to be more difficult. Also, consistent with the first objective, the examples attempt to get students to place *Macbeth* in a modern context (e.g., modern settings, a newspaper format).

If we consider the five criteria, accuracy (and perhaps thoroughness) seems to call for *remembering factual knowledge*. Creativity seems to call for *creating* [based on] *factual and conceptual knowledge*. The other three criteria—thoroughness, attractiveness, and correct form—all seem to require *understanding conceptual knowledge*. Students need to know what makes a project thorough, attractive, and in correct form. Other than accuracy, then, the criteria are unrelated to the content of the play; rather, they are related to desired qualities of the project per se.

I also administered a final test over Macbeth. The test includes three sections: (1) matching descriptions with specific characters; (2) short answers to "what," "where," "when," "who," "why," and "how many" questions; and (3) quotations (for which students have to write who says it, to whom it is said, and what the circumstances surrounding it are). (See Attachment E at the end of the chapter.) The test was strongly "factually based"—I considered it important that students remain aware of the specific events in the play and could keep the characters and their relationships straight.

COMMENTARY

Both Ms. Jackson's discussion about the test and a cursory examination of the the test itself suggest that the final test clearly falls into cell A1 of the Taxonomy Table: *remember factual knowledge*.

At the same time, however, I was more pleased with the group projects and class dramatizations, which I felt were longer-lasting learning experiences. Over the unit, I saw improvement in the ease with which students could come up with a finished product, either a long-term project or dramatization based on only 15 minutes of planning.

I have always based the "bottom line" success or failure of any classroom enterprise on student responses, less formal measures such as enthusiastic discussion and participation. As the unit progressed, students became less reluctant to venture opinions and to volunteer to read and act out scenes (which I took as a definite sign that they were not only learning but enjoying the challenge).

Apparently, challenging work was something that happened all too infrequently in their academic careers. One student actually said to me, "I wish we had read some hard stuff before this year!" I took this comment as a measure of the unit's success.

COMMENTARY

Ms. Jackson "puts more faith" in projects than in tests. Thus, her first objective is the "real" objective of the unit, whereas her second objective is included primarily because it is "expected" by the students and/or the school system. She also assessed the unit's effectiveness in terms of the students' affective responses (i.e. increase in ease, increase in enthusiasm, enjoyment in challenging work).

Our analysis of the assessments in terms of the Taxonomy Table is provided in Table 9.3.

PART 4: CLOSING COMMENTARY

In this section we examine the vignette in terms of our four basic questions: the learning question, the instruction question, the assessment question, and the alignment question.

THE LEARNING QUESTION

In terms of intended student learning, this unit clearly focuses on helping students *understand conceptual knowledge*. It is through concepts such as tragic hero, character defects, and irony that Ms. Jackson believes students will "see the relevance of literary works . . . in their own lives." At the same time, however, Ms. Jackson is somewhat of a pragmatist. She believes it is important for students to remember particular details about *Macbeth*. Students may need to remember these details on later tests; furthermore, there is a certain "social value" in being able to "talk about" *Macbeth*.

THE INSTRUCTION QUESTION

The vast majority of the time spent on this unit was devoted to activities that relate directly or indirectly to the first objective. For most acts of the play, students were engaged in activities related to the more complex cognitive process categories: *Analyze* (Acts II, IV, and V); *Evaluate* (Acts III and IV); and *Create* (Acts II and III). The stimulus for this engagement was teacher questioning.

9.3 ANALYSIS OF THE *MACBETH* VIGNETTE IN TERMS OF THE TAXONOMY TABLE BASED ON ASSESSMENTS

THE KNOWLEDGE DIMENSION	THE COGNITIVE PROCESS DIMENSION					
	1. REMEMBER	2. UNDERSTAND	3. APPLY	4. ANALYZE	5. EVALUATE	6. CREATE
A. FACTUAL KNOWLEDGE	**Objective 2** Final test; Project C1	Project In1		*Activities for Act II* Project In2	*Activities for Act III*	*Activities for Acts II and III* Project In1; Project In2
B. CONCEPTUAL KNOWLEDGE		**Objective 1** *Introductory activity and activities for Acts I–V; Film journal; Film comparison* Project In1; Project C2, 4, and 5		*Activities for Acts II, IV, and V* Project In2	*Activities for Acts III and IV*	*Activities for Acts II and III* Project In1; Project In2; Project C3
C. PROCEDURAL KNOWLEDGE						
D. META-COGNITIVE KNOWLEDGE						

Key
Objective 1 = Students will see the relevance of literary works such as *Macbeth* to their own lives.
Objective 2 = Students will remember important details about the play.
Project In1 = Instructions: Choose any scene and rewrite with modern language in modern setting.
Project In2 = Instructions: Create an edition of *The Scotland Chronicle* dealing with newsworthy events.
Project C1 = Criteria: accuracy.
Projects C2, 3, 4, and 5 = Criteria: thoroughness, creativity, attractiveness, correct form.
Dark shading indicates the strongest alignment—an objective, an instructional activity, and an assessment are all present in the same cell. Lighter shading indicates two of the three are present.

Because these cognitive process categories are not included in the statement of objectives or on the assessment, we believe Ms. Jackson used them in an attempt to increase her students' understanding of the play. This is a good illustration of the use of more complex cognitive processes in an effort to help students more thoroughly achieve less complex objectives. The intent in such instances is not mastery of the complex processes sufficient for them to be included as unit objectives, but just enough practice with them to result in deeper processing of the students' understanding.

It is interesting to note that not a single instructional activity related directly to the second objective (i.e., Students will remember important details of the play). Students apparently were expected to acquire this knowledge as they watched the film, read and acted out the play, and participated in the various activities.

THE ASSESSMENT QUESTION

The two formal assessments were the group project and the final unit test. These two assessments lay at opposite ends of the cognitive process continuum, with the group project requiring *Create* and the test *Remember*. Only one of the five criteria used to evaluate the group project focuses on *Create*. Two of the criteria focus on the content of the play: accuracy and thoroughness. The other two criteria emphasize the form of the finished product: attractiveness and correct form.

Table 9.3 shows some inconsistency between the instructions given to the students for completing the project (In1 and In2), which appear in cells A2, B2, A4, B4, A6, and B6, and the criteria used to evaluate the completed projects (C1 through C5), which appear in cells A1, B2, and B6. One would expect the instructions and criteria to be classified in the same cell. Instead, they are in two cells: B2 (*understand conceptual knowledge*) and B6 (*create [based on] conceptual knowledge*). However, the instructions are placed in four cells that have no criteria: A2 (*understand factual knowledge*), A4 (*analyze [based on] factual knowledge*), B4 (*analyze [based on] conceptual knowledge*), and A6 (*create [based on] factual knowledge*). Further, one criterion is in a cell that has no instructions: A1 (*remember factual knowledge*). Students could thus have trouble if their expectations for what counts toward a grade lead them to concentrate their efforts to the exclusion of other important aspects, such as not studying the factual knowledge aspects of the play.

THE ALIGNMENT QUESTION

We can clearly see the alignment of objectives, instructional activities, and assessments in Table 9.3. The final test is aligned with the second objective, remembering important facts about the play. As mentioned above, however, no instructional activities relate directly to either the objective or the final test.

There is reasonable alignment between the instructional activities and the group project. As mentioned earlier, Ms. Jackson allocated five days of classroom time for students to work on the project. In addition, most of the instructional activities focused on helping students develop *Conceptual knowledge* (row B of the Taxonomy Table).

The misalignment is more evident when we consider the cells of Table 9.3 rather than the rows and columns. For example, although most of the instructional activities emphasize *Conceptual knowledge*, they differ in the cognitive processes they demand from students. In many cases, these demands are beyond *Understanding*, which is the target of the second objective. As we mentioned earlier, however, it may well be that Ms. Jackson was attempting to develop a deeper and more enduring understanding by getting students to work at the so-called higher cognitive levels. Similarly, although the *Create* column contains both instructional activities and assessments, it does not contain an objective. It seems reasonable that *Understand* (the cognitive process in the objective) should be one of the criteria used to assess the group project.

PART 5: CLOSING QUESTIONS

As with the analysis of all our vignettes, we were left with a few unanswered questions. We raise two of the most important in this closing section.

1. **What is the role of the more complex cognitive process categories in the development of *Conceptual knowledge*?** Ms. Jackson wanted to help students see relationships between the play and their own lives. The pathway to accomplishing this objective was to use *Conceptual knowledge*. Most students know "tragic heroes"; they experience "irony." Concepts such as these enable them to make the connections desired by Ms. Jackson. Although her focus was on *understanding conceptual knowledge*, Ms. Jackson engaged her students in discussions at higher levels of cognitive processing (e.g., *Analyze*, *Evaluate*, and *Create*). It seems reasonable to assume that *Conceptual knowledge* can be developed via these activities.

2. **What are the advantages and disadvantages of student choice of activities and assignments?** Ms. Jackson gave her students choices several times during the unit. For example, she let them choose which film to watch for the entire unit. This was an informed choice; that is, it was based on a comparison of the same scene presented in three different film versions of *Macbeth* (see Attachment A). Students also had a choice of group projects. In this case, however, students were undoubtedly unaware of the differences in cognitive demands among the projects as suggested by our analysis (see Table 9.3). Quite by accident, different groups of students could have chosen less complex or more complex assignments, less difficult or more difficult ones. Because the same scoring guide was used for all assignments, this choice of assignments could result in differences in the grades students earned simply because of the assignments, not

because of the quality of their work. Teachers often try to compensate for this in assessment, but it is difficult.

The two instances of student choice are quite different. In the first case, student choice of film is based on information and group consensus. As such, it quite likely contributed to increased interest and ownership on the part of students. In the second instance, choice of group project is perhaps a confounding factor in the grades assigned to them. The proper use of student choice and the amount of information students need to make "good" choices, as well as the implications of different student choices for achieving various objectives and for grading, are issues that need additional consideration by teachers and researchers.

ATTACHMENT A CHART COMPARING THREE FILM VERSIONS OF *MACBETH*

	Roman Polanski	Orson Welles	BBC
Setting			
Sound			
Lighting			
Special Effects			
Witches			
Macbeth			
Lady Macbeth			

ATTACHMENT B A COMPARISON/CONTRAST ESSAY ON THREE FILM VERSIONS OF WILLIAM SHAKESPEARE'S *MACBETH*

1. The **introduction** should address the questions of what a good film version of *Macbeth* should contain. The introduction should also take steps to engage the interest of the reader.

2. The **thesis statement** is the most important part of the introduction. The thesis should focus on cinematic effects (setting, sound, lighting, special effects) and characterization (Macbeth, Lady Macbeth, the witches) in the scenes viewed from each of the three films. Statements should be made regarding the relative merits of each film.

3. The **body** of the essay should develop the ideas established in the thesis statement. Use either the block form (each film discussed separately) or the subject form (the cinematics effects of each film are discussed, then the characterization).

4. The **conclusion** should restate the main idea and end with a statement as to which film version is the most effective and true to the play's purpose.

Write introduction here:

Approximately five class sessions will be devoted to watching the selected film version of *Macbeth*, one viewing session after we finish reading and discussing each act in class. Each student is asked to keep a journal of his or her impressions, opinions, and questions about the film. There should be one entry for each day of reviewing, each of 1 to 2 paragraphs.

The content of the journal is primarily up to you, but effort should be made to address certain criteria. As was done in the comparison/contrast essays written earlier, students should comment regarding the cinematography (setting, lighting, sound, special effects) and characterization (especially Macbeth, Lady Macbeth, Banquo, MacDuff, and the witches). Other points to consider would be how certain episodes are staged—for example, the dagger scene, the banquet scene, the sleepwalking scene, and Macbeth's murder. Also, if there are any scenes left out or changed in any significant way, this needs to be addressed in the journal.

The last journal entry should state what you found most effective in the movie and what you objected the most. Remember there are no right or wrong opinions, but any opinion must be based on evidence.

Research   _____

Accuracy (30%)   _____

Thoroughness (30%)   _____

Presentation   _____

Creativity (15%)   _____

Attractiveness (15%)   _____

Correct Form (10%)   _____

TOTAL   _____

I. Matching: Match the following with the names to the right. Some names will be used more than once. (2 points each)

_____	1. Is executed and forfeits his title to Macbeth.
_____	2. Reveals his suspicion of Macbeth's guilt by not attending the coronation.
_____	3. Is seen approaching Macbeth's castle, to his great horror and disbelief.
_____	4. Is the cause of Macbeth's "fit" at the banquet.
_____	5. Claims to be even more evil than Macbeth.
_____	6. Is the Thane of Fife.
_____	7. Names Malcolm, Prince of Cumberland.
_____	8. Often brings bad news to the other characters.
_____	9. Macbeth's castle.
_____	10. Is killed by Macbeth during Macbeth's final battle.
_____	11. Will "get" kings.
_____	12. Smears blood on King Duncan's sleeping guards.
_____	13. Gives instructions to trap Macbeth with a false sense of security.
_____	14. Flees to Ireland to avoid being unjustly accused of murder.
_____	15. Is angry at being left alone without protection.
_____	16. Kills Duncan's guards.
_____	17. Is reported to have committed suicide at the end of the play.
_____	18. Was "untimely ripp'd" from his mother's womb.
_____	19. Barely escapes being murdered at the same time as his father.
_____	20. Is with Macbeth when he first sees the witches.

A. Hecate

B. Duncan

C. Malcolm

D. Banquo

E. Lady Macbeth

F. Lady MacDuff

G. Dunsinane

H. Macbeth

I. MacDuff

J. Ross

K. Young Siward

L. Fleance

M. Thane of Cawdor

N. Banquo's ghost

O. Birnam Wood

P. Donalbain

(continued)

II. Short Answer. Fill in the blanks with the correct word or phrase. (3 points each)

1. What country is the main setting of *Macbeth*?

   _____

2. What is Macbeth's tragic flaw?

   _____

3. What does the helmeted head tell Macbeth to beware of?

   _____

4. Why does Lady Macbeth not kill Duncan herself?

   _____

5. How many apparitions do the witches show Macbeth?

   _____

6. What is the only comic scene in *Macbeth*?

   _____

7. What does Macbeth think he sees just before Duncan's murder?

   _____

8. When does the old man report that there were great disturbances in nature?

   _____

9. Where does Malcolm go after his father is killed?

   _____

10. Who observes Lady Macbeth walking in her sleep?

    _____

III. Quotes. In complete sentences tell (1) who says it, (2) to whom it is said, and (3) what the circumstances are. (5 points each)

1. "Lay on, MacDuff, and damned be him that first cries, 'Hold, enough!'"

2. "Fair is foul, and foul is fair."

3. "Fail not our feast."

4. "Is this a dagger I see before me, the handle toward my hand?"

5. "Look like the innocent flower, but be the serpent under it."

6. "Out, damned spot! Out, I say!"

CHAPTER 10

Addition Facts Vignette

This unit on strategies for memorizing addition facts that sum to 18 or less was developed and taught by Ms. Jeanna Hoffman.

The unit is part of the school district's second-grade core curriculum, and addition facts are included on the currently used standardized test. The unit is taught early in the year. There is so much to teach in the core curriculum that it is beneficial to teach students how to memorize these facts early in the year. It is more efficient for students to have the basic facts memorized before they move on to the whole-number addition (and subtraction) algorithms. Students already have been exposed to the concept of addition (in first grade and again earlier in second grade) through the use of manipulatives. Memorizing addition facts is difficult for many students. Usually, a handful of students begin second grade knowing all of the addition facts to 18. Most students have a good understanding of addition facts to 10. Once sums to 18 are begun, however, well over half the students use their fingers. Some still do by the end of second grade.

Generally, the class of second graders contains from 20 to 24 students. The classes tend to be heterogeneous in terms of achievement, and the students, for the most part, are motivated. The unit lasts approximately three weeks depending on the students' previous experiences with memorizing addition facts. It would be better to spend more time on this objective, but there are so many other objectives to cover in the curriculum. Review of many of the memorization strategies will take place throughout the school year to remind students of them and to see whether they are retained and being used.

PART 1: OBJECTIVES

The major objective of this three-week unit is that students will recall addition facts (sums to 18) without manipulatives. The longer-term objectives are to help students (1) understand the efficiency of memorization (in certain circumstances) and (2) gain a working knowledge of various memorization strategies. In concrete terms, students should be able to compute horizontal and vertical sums. The sums are of both two and three single-digit whole numbers (provided they do not exceed 18). Examples would include:

$$6 + 7 = \qquad 5 + 7 + 3 = \qquad \begin{array}{r} 7 \\ +9 \\ \hline \end{array} \qquad \begin{array}{r} 4 \\ +5 \\ +5 \\ \hline \end{array}$$

COMMENTARY

In terms of the Taxonomy Table, the major objective of the unit is straightforward: *remember factual knowledge*. The other two "longer-term" objectives are examples of *understand metacognitive knowledge* (specifically, knowledge of general strategies and knowledge about cognitive tasks) and *apply procedural knowledge* (assuming that "working knowledge" refers to knowledge that can be used or applied). The "various memorization strategies" constitute *Procedural knowledge*. Note that we classify this third objective as *Procedural knowledge* rather than *Metacognitive knowledge* because the "strategies" are specific to memorizing "math facts" (including addition, subtraction, multiplication, and division). Thus, the "strategies" have limited generalizability. The *Metacognitive knowledge* component comes from students understanding which strategies are most and least effective for them personally.

The placement of these three objectives in the Taxonomy Table is shown in Table 10.1.

PART 2: INSTRUCTIONAL ACTIVITIES

"Pocket facts" is an activity that begins the unit and is ongoing throughout it. Each day, as students enter the classroom, they pick a "fact strip" from a basket. Each student is expected to memorize this fact. Periodically, during the day, students are asked to recite their facts. Parents, the principal, custodians, cafeteria workers, and others know about the facts and can ask the students to recite them. The next morning each student writes his or her facts in his or her "pocket facts" book and picks a new fact.

COMMENTARY

"Pocket facts" emphasizes *remembering factual knowledge*. This activity takes place every day.

"Mad Math Minute" is an activity that begins the second week of school and continues daily throughout the school year. The students have one minute to complete 30 addition exercises. Halfway through the year, this is increased to 35. Mad Math Minute sheets are constructed so that within an eight-day period, students begin with exercises having a 2 as one of the addends, then

10.1 ANALYSIS OF THE ADDITION FACTS VIGNETTE IN TERMS OF THE TAXONOMY TABLE BASED ON STATED OBJECTIVES

THE KNOWLEDGE DIMENSION	THE COGNITIVE PROCESS DIMENSION					
	1. REMEMBER	2. UNDERSTAND	3. APPLY	4. ANALYZE	5. EVALUATE	6. CREATE
A. FACTUAL KNOWLEDGE	Objective 1					
B. CONCEPTUAL KNOWLEDGE						
C. PROCEDURAL KNOWLEDGE			Objective 3			
D. META-COGNITIVE KNOWLEDGE		Objective 2				

Key
Objective 1 = Recall addition facts (sums to 18).
Objective 2 = Understand the efficiency of memorization (in certain circumstances).
Objective 3 = Gain a working knowledge of various memorization strategies.

move to 3, then to 4, and so on. Once the +9 facts are done, the process begins again with +1. The number of exercises each student gets correct is posted daily in the room.

COMMENTARY

This year-long activity also focuses on *remembering factual knowledge*. The strict time limit (30 to 35 facts in one minute) virtually requires memorization.

Days 1–4

After these initial daily activities have been performed, the first four days of the unit are spent completing the Great Addition Wall Chart. In advance, I prepare an outline for the chart using 3' × 7' butcher paper. The numbers 0 through 9 are written along the top and left side. The students use two colors of Linker Cubes to make sticks and learn to say the addition facts they represent. They then write the facts in the appropriate cells of the chart. By the end of the second day, the chart is filled in completely. I tell the students there are 100 facts they will need to learn by the end of second grade and over the next several days they'll be learning strategies to help them memorize these facts.

COMMENTARY

Although the major objective states "without manipulatives," Ms. Hoffman uses manipulatives early in the unit. The manipulatives enable students to "see" concrete examples of the addition facts. The emphasis is on the meaning of 5, the meaning of 3, the meaning of 8, and so on. Thus, the activity promotes *understanding conceptual knowledge*.

During the third and fourth days I ask students to look for patterns and relationships among the facts included on the Great Addition Wall Chart. For example, the +0 row and column are pointed out. Students are asked to explain how they already know these facts without counting. Similarly, the +1 row and column are examined.

Also, the commutative property is illustrated (e.g., $5 + 8 = 13$ and $8 + 5 = 13$). I tell the students that if they know one of the two facts, they know the other. I conclude the activity by pointing out how many facts they already know by virtue of the +0 row and column, the +1 row and column, and the commutative property. They will need to memorize the rest.

COMMENTARY

This activity, in part, has a motivational purpose. Ms. Hoffman wants to show students how much they already know and, thus, how "little" they have yet to learn. In terms of the Taxonomy Table, the search for patterns involves comparing and the commutative property is a principle. Thus, the emphasis here is on *understanding conceptual knowledge*. Note that Ms. Hoffman does not use the phrase "commutative property" with the students. She is more interested in students understanding that "the order of numbers is not important when you add" than recalling the name "commutative property."

Days 5–6

"Fact Friends" is an activity that takes place on the fifth and sixth days. In this activity students use "doubles facts" (which they usually know) to help them remember other addition facts. I ask students to look for patterns in the Great Addition Wall Chart, in the rows, and in the columns. I choose one student to point out the doubles facts (e.g., 3 + 3, 4 + 4) and to circle them. I tell the students that on the chart there are special "fact friends." I use the doubles fact 4 + 4 = 8 as an example and write it on the board. On either side I write 3 + 4 = 7 and 5 + 4 = 9.

I ask the students why I call these "fact friends." (The answer is that they all have +4 in them.) I repeat this illustration with other doubles facts. Students are asked what they notice about the placement of these fact friends on the chart. (The answer is that they touch either on the sides or at the top and bottom.)

I then ask students how knowing one "fact friend" helps to know the others. As students share their thoughts, other students begin to catch on. I refer back to the Great Addition Wall Chart and have different students point out the fact friends around all of the doubles facts. I place check marks accordingly. I believe that this activity introduces the idea that mathematics is a network of relationships. It helps make facts and mathematics operations easier to remember and a lot more sense.

COMMENTARY

Like the preceding activity, these activities involve students looking for patterns and relationships. In terms of the Taxonomy Table, then, the emphasis is on *understanding conceptual knowledge* (more specifically, comparing knowledge of structures).

Days 7–8

On the seventh and eighth days, I introduce students to "fact families." In this activity, students are asked to look closely at three numbers in an equation and explore other arrangements of these numbers to see relationships. I write an equation on the board (e.g., 2 + 3 = 5). Students are asked if they can change it around to make another addition fact (e.g., $3 + 2 = 5$). Students are then asked if they can make a subtraction fact with these same numbers (e.g., $5 - 2 = 3$). (Students generally need help with this. Clues such as "start with the largest number" are helpful.)

I then draw an outline of a house around the two addition facts and the two subtraction facts and write the numerals 2, 3, and 5 in the "attic." I tell the students that these four equations (facts) belong to the same fact family and are the only facts that can live in this house. I then draw an outline of a house and place the numerals 4, 5, and 9 in the attic. Students are asked to work in pairs to identify the fact family for the house. Students continue to work in pairs to draw other houses. ("Doubles" live in apartments since there are only two numbers, e.g., 8, 16.)

I remind students that if they learn one of the facts in a family they'll know the others. Therefore, fact families make the job of memorizing easier because they only have to remember half of the facts. During the second day of this activity, I lead a closing discussion that is intended to help students realize that subtraction is the opposite of addition.

COMMENTARY

As on the earlier days, students are asked to explore the relationships inherent in equations (e.g., change them around, seek connections). Without using the phrase "additive inverse," Ms. Hoffman introduces students to this important concept within the equations. This activity is classified as *understanding conceptual knowledge*. Ms. Hoffman's prompt—"start with the largest number"—can be viewed as the first step in a procedure that students can use to transform addition facts into subtraction facts. If she continues to build this procedure, the classification would be *applying procedural knowledge*.

The reminder in the closing paragraph returns the students to Ms. Hoffman's main objective: remembering addition facts that sum to 18 or less. Nonetheless, the instruction during the first eight days has emphasized *understanding conceptual knowledge*. Her final discussion on Day 8 reinforces the concept of "additive inverse."

Days 9–10

On the ninth and tenth days, I engage students in a procedure that I call "make-a-ten." I begin by writing several addition exercises with 9 as the addend on the board. Each student is given a "ten-frame" (a piece of paper with two rows of five boxes). I ask the students to use two ten-frames to find a way to quickly figure out the answer to the first exercise (e.g., $9 + 7 =$). [The answer is that this is $(9 + 1)$ on one ten-frame, $+ 6$ on the other, which is $10 + 6$ or 16.] I continue with all the exercises in which 9 and 8 are addends.

I ask the students to record both the exercises and their answers on a separate piece of paper. We then discuss how the make-a-ten strategy works. I then point to the Great Addition Wall Chart and ask them how the make-a-ten procedure can help them memorize their addition facts.

COMMENTARY

This is a "cognitively rich" activity. Students are asked to *apply procedural knowledge* (i.e., carry out the make-a-ten procedure), *understand procedural knowledge* (i.e., discuss how the make-a-ten procedure works), and *understand metacognitive knowledge* (i.e., describe how procedures like make-a-ten can help them memorize knowledge like their addition facts).

Days 11–13

During the 11th through 13th days, I explore with the students the use of various approaches for memorizing addition facts whose sums are greater than 10. I begin by writing the exercise 5 + 8 on the board and ask the students how they could find the answer. Answers should include counting up; using fingers, objects, a calculator, or number line; using the make-a-ten strategy; relying on fact families; and memorizing through practice (e.g., pocket facts, Mad Math Minute). Each student is asked to either suggest an approach or choose one of those already suggested.

Each student then uses the approach he or she suggested (or chose) to perform the exercise (i.e., 5 + 8) and shares the strategy as it applies to that exercise with the class. As students explore and use the different strategies, I believe they will see that the fastest way to get the answer is having memorized it.

COMMENTARY

The focus of these three days is on the many ways students can approach learning addition facts that sum to 18 or less. Both *Conceptual knowledge* (e.g., fact families) and *Procedural knowledge* (e.g., make-a-ten) are available for students' use. Regardless of the type of knowledge, there is little doubt that the cognitive process is *Apply*. Thus, students are to *apply conceptual* and/or *procedural knowledge*. In Chapter 5, *Apply* is defined in terms of *Procedural knowledge*; that is, *Conceptual knowledge* is generally "unpacked" as embedded in a series of steps (i.e., *Procedural knowledge*) before it is applied. Thus, we classify this activity (or set of activities) as *applying procedural knowledge*.

Ultimately, however, Ms. Hoffman wants individual students to know which approach works best for them and come to the realization that the most efficient means of performing the addition exercises in the time available is to memorize them. With this intent, the goal has become *understanding metacognitive knowledge*.

10.2 ANALYSIS OF THE ADDITION FACTS VIGNETTE IN TERMS OF THE TAXONOMY TABLE BASED ON INSTRUCTIONAL ACTIVITIES

THE KNOWLEDGE DIMENSION	THE COGNITIVE PROCESS DIMENSION					
	1. REMEMBER	2. UNDERSTAND	3. APPLY	4. ANALYZE	5. EVALUATE	6. CREATE
A. FACTUAL KNOWLEDGE	**Objective 1** *Days 1–15 activities*					
B. CONCEPTUAL KNOWLEDGE		*Days 1–10 activities*				
C. PROCEDURAL KNOWLEDGE		*Days 9–10 activities*	**Objective 3** *Days 9–13 activities*			
D. META-COGNITIVE KNOWLEDGE		**Objective 2** *Days 9–13 activities*				

Key
Objective 1 = Recall addition facts (sums to 18).
Objective 2 = Understand the efficiency of memorization (in certain circumstances).
Objective 3 = Gain a working knowledge of various memorization strategies.

Days 14–15

The final activity takes place during the final two days of the unit. This activity requires students to put their memorization work into practice in a relay race format. In advance, I prepare strips of paper containing all the addition facts and place them randomly into four baskets. The class is divided into four teams and each team is in a line facing their basket. Each student draws a strip from the basket, studies it, and puts it away. The first student in line walks backward to the board, writes the fact, returns to the line, and taps the shoulder of the next person. This student then picks another fact from the basket and begins memorizing it. After a specified amount of time, "time" is called and the game ends. All teams with all correct facts win! The game is repeated.

COMMENTARY

In large part because the element of speed has been introduced, the final activity is classified as *remember factual knowledge*. Considering all of the unit activities, we produced Table 10.2. For ease of comparison, the stated objectives from Table 10.1 are listed in **bold** type in Table 10.2. The instructional activity analysis is *italicized*.

PART 3: ASSESSMENT

To assess student progress, I observed students, asked them questions, noted changes in the results of the daily Mad Math Minute, and scored their weekly quizzes. I observed students to determine which approaches they were using to arrive at answers. I noted that those students who completed the assignments quickly were beginning to memorize the addition facts. Slower students often began by counting on their fingers and then moved to "counting up." For these students, I try to get them to use fact friends and fact families.

During class, I often ask students how they figured out an answer. As the unit progresses, students more often report they knew because of fact families or fact friends and, ultimately, because they had it memorized.

Daily Mad Math Minute scores gradually improve for most students. This finding also suggests that students are memorizing the facts. Mad Math Minute scores are posted daily so students can see how many they answered correctly the previous day and, thus, chart their progress. As mentioned earlier, Mad Math Minute is used throughout the year.

The weekly quizzes provide the least information on the approaches that students use to get the answers. They are direct assessments of the unit objective, however, and are useful in providing information to students' parents. Initially I use a simple rubric (i.e., "is beginning to memorize addition facts" or "needs work memorizing addition facts") to inform students and their parents how the students are progressing.

10.3 ANALYSIS OF THE ADDITION FACTS VIGNETTE IN TERMS OF THE TAXONOMY TABLE BASED ON ASSESSMENTS

THE KNOWLEDGE DIMENSION	THE COGNITIVE PROCESS DIMENSION					
	1. REMEMBER	2. UNDERSTAND	3. APPLY	4. ANALYZE	5. EVALUATE	6. CREATE
A. FACTUAL KNOWLEDGE	**Objective 1** *Days 1–15 activities* Assess 3; Assess 4					
B. CONCEPTUAL KNOWLEDGE		*Days 1–10 activities*				
C. PROCEDURAL KNOWLEDGE		*Days 9–10 activities*	**Objective 3** *Days 9–13 activities* Assess 1; Assess 2			
D. META-COGNITIVE KNOWLEDGE		**Objective 2** *Days 9–13 activities*				

Key
Objective 1 = Recall addition facts (sums to 18).
Objective 2 = Understand the efficiency of memorization (in certain circumstances).
Objective 3 = Gain a working knowledge of various memorization strategies.
Assess 1 = Observations of students.
Assess 2 = Questions to students in class.
Assess 3 = Mad Math Minutes.
Assess 4 = Weekly quizzes.
Dark shading indicates the strongest alignment—an objective, an instructional activity, and an assessment are all present in the same cell. Lighter shading indicates two of the three are present.

Ms. Hoffman's questions focus on *applying procedural knowledge*. Through these assessments she is able to determine which procedures students are using. The changes in Mad Math Minute scores over time provide evidence of student improvement in *remembering factual knowledge*. Unlike the Mad Math Minutes, which are organized around a single addend, exercises on the weekly quizzes are drawn somewhat randomly from the universe of addition facts. Also, unlike the Mad Math Minute, the quizzes have more liberal time allocations. As a consequence, students have sufficient time to use a variety of approaches. Nonetheless, the emphasis remains on *remembering factual knowledge*.

The results of our analysis are shown in Table 10.3. Once again, initial analysis of the stated objectives is shown in **bold** type and analysis of the instructional activities is shown in *italics*.

PART 4: CLOSING COMMENTARY

In this section we examine the vignette in terms of our four basic questions: the learning question, the instruction question, the assessment question, and the alignment question.

THE LEARNING QUESTION

In terms of the learning question, we distinguish between what we term "focus" and "emphasis." The focus is clearly on *remembering factual knowledge*. This is quite clearly the desired end result of the three-week unit. The focus is evident in both the stated objectives and the assessments. In contrast, the emphasis is on *understanding conceptual knowledge*. With the brief exception of the Mad Math Minute, virtually all the activities in which students engaged during the first two weeks (approximately two-thirds) of the unit emphasize *understanding conceptual knowledge*. This discrepancy between focus and emphasis can perhaps best be explained by the difference between means and ends. For Ms. Hoffman, the end (her focus) is clear: students are to *remember factual knowledge*. On the knowledge dimension, *Conceptual*, *Procedural*, and to a certain extent *Metacognitive knowledge* are means to this end. Similarly, on the cognitive process dimension, *Understand* and *Apply* are the means. Thus, the emphasis in the unit reflects the means by which the end will be achieved.

THE INSTRUCTION QUESTION

Primarily because of the Mad Math Minute activity, some instructional activities related to the major objective (*remember factual knowledge*) took place every day. Activities related to the two longer-term objectives were reserved for the end of the unit (i.e., Days 9–13). As shown in Table 10.2, numerous activities are placed in cells of the Taxonomy Table that do not contain the stated objectives. In her description of these activities, Ms. Hoffman suggested that they were intended to help students develop a framework for efficient memorization. The activities during the first two weeks, for example, focused largely on *understanding conceptual knowledge*. Inherent in the structure of the Great Addition Wall Chart, for example, were patterns and connections that could make memorization easier.

Similarly, Ms. Hoffman introduced a variety of memorization strategies to her students. Her intention was for students to (1) choose the one or ones most useful to them, and (2) come to realize that memorization is more efficient than alternative ways of arriving at an answer. These activities had a dual focus: *apply procedural knowledge* and *understand metacognitive knowledge*.

Finally, what is interesting here is what Ms. Hoffman did not do. She did not give students a steady diet of "drill and practice." Rather, she made use of five cells of the Taxonomy Table (see Table 10.2) even though her intended learning for her students fell into a single cell.

THE ASSESSMENT QUESTION

Ms. Hoffman used both informal and formal assessments. She observed her students and asked them questions in class to gather information about the procedures they used to remember the addition facts. She used Mad Math Minutes and weekly quizzes to get at the "bottom line"—had students memorized the addition facts? Thus, the informal assessments were intended to get information about the process; the formal assessments were intended to get information about the outcome.

THE ALIGNMENT QUESTION

As we show in Table 10.3, the alignment of assessments and instructional activities with the stated objectives is fairly strong. Cells A1 and C3 include an objective, several activities, and assessments. As described above, the assessments in cell A1 (*remember factual knowledge*) were more formal; those in cell C3 (*apply procedural knowledge*) were more informal.

Only a few examples of misalignment occur. Ms. Hoffman has no formal assessment of *understanding metacognitive knowledge*, although she did informally assess how students were arriving at answers and inferring processes. It is not clear if she evaluated (or taught) whether students saw using analogies as applicable to other than addition facts. Several activities in cells B2 (*understand conceptual knowledge*) and C2 (*understand procedural knowledge*) have no associated objective or assessment. The latter supports the distinction between emphasis and focus that we made in our discussion of the learning question.

PART 5: CLOSING QUESTIONS

As with the analysis of all our vignettes, we were left with a few unanswered questions. We raise three of the most important in this closing section.

1. **What is the relationship between *understanding conceptual knowledge* and *remembering factual knowledge*?** The assumption that *understanding* underlying *conceptual knowledge* helps one to *remember factual* knowledge lies at the heart of Ms. Hoffman's approach to planning and teaching this unit. Would a constant emphasis on memorization strategies (such as rehearsal strategies) prove to be equally or more effective in producing the desired result? An answer to this question would help us understand the relationship between *Factual* and *Conceptual knowledge* as well as the role of *Understanding* in *Remembering*.

   Consistent with our emphasis on the importance of the more complex cognitive processes, Ms. Hoffman introduced students to these processes early in their school careers. Furthermore, she helped them learn early that as complex material is mastered conceptually, its use often becomes automatic. (Incidentally, in doing so, she used interesting and motivating activities that relieve the tedium of drill and practice—an insight that may come in handy in other heavy memorization subjects such as foreign languages.)

   Finally, Ms. Hoffman introduced her students to mathematical concepts they will encounter in later grades, an aspect not examined when we focus the Taxonomy Table on the unit level. The Taxonomy Table can be used, however, for grade-level planning and even multigrade planning. Indeed, when one is dealing with objectives that require lengthy periods of development, the table may be an especially helpful tool for examining when, where, and how efforts to develop them should be scheduled.

2. **Would direct assessment of *understanding conceptual knowledge* have been useful in separating what students understand from what they are able to do?** It is hard to determine whether the students are really developing a conceptual knowledge of number relationships and mathematical procedures. They clearly are learning their number facts, but are they learning about number concepts? Stated somewhat differently, is it likely that students who do not understand "fact families" would use "fact families" to aid their memorization of addition facts? A set of exercises that focus exclusively on "fact families" would allow the teacher to distinguish between students who understand but do not use a strategy and those who do not understand and therefore, perhaps, cannot use it. This information would help us understand the role of *understanding conceptual knowledge* in *applying procedural knowledge*.

3. **What information would a direct assessment of *understanding metacognitive knowledge* have yielded?** Inherent in the information that Ms. Hoffman obtained from her observations and questions of students is a continuum of development that begins with "counting on fingers," moves to "counting up," moves further (generally with her assistance) to examining the structure of addition facts, and culminates with memorization. Interviews with students at various stages may provide useful information about the progression toward memorization and the role of *Metacognitive knowledge* in this progression.

CHAPTER 11

Parliamentary Acts Vignette

This vignette, developed and taught by Ms. Gwendolyn K. Airasian, describes a unit that integrates colonial history prior to the Revolutionary War and a persuasive writing assignment.

I have taught for 17 years, the past 10 in fifth grade in a suburban middle school. Students are heterogeneously grouped into classes, with 26 students in my class, 16 males and 10 females. Five students have special learning needs and receive part-time support from aides when they are with me. The remaining students present a broad range of abilities, interests, and motivation.

Both persuasive writing and colonial history are required topics in the district's fifth-grade curriculum. I teach persuasive writing at various junctures from the middle to the end of the school year. As part of our writing program, students are taught to assess their own as well as others' writing. Colonial history in the 1760s and 1770s is taught in social studies in April, after study of early exploration of the "new world." My prior experience teaching this unit, along with the characteristics of my class (their prior writing experience, observed library skills, attention span, and ability to work together in groups), guided the number and selection of my objectives. I estimated that the unit would take from 10 to 12 days given an instructional period of 45 minutes three times a week and 90 minutes twice a week. If students caught on quickly to the most conceptual aspect of the unit, it would likely take 10 days. If students did not and/or if they had difficulty writing their editorials, it likely would be a 12- to 14-day unit.

PART 1: OBJECTIVES

My general objective for this unit is to have students gain knowledge of Colonial America in the 1760s and 1770s, particularly knowledge of King George's various taxes and the American colonists' reactions to them. More specific objectives are needed to clarify the meaning of this general objective. I want my students to:

1. remember the specifics about the Parliamentary Acts (e.g., the Sugar, Stamp, and Townshend Acts);

2. explain the consequences of the Parliamentary Acts for different colonial groups;

3. choose a colonial character or group and write a persuasive editorial stating his/her/its position on the acts (the editorial must include at least one supporting reason not specifically taught or covered in the class); and

4. self and peer edit the editorial.

COMMENTARY

Rather than starting with the four specific unit objectives, Ms. Airasian begins with an overarching objective: to gain knowledge about a particular period in American history. To provide the focus needed to plan instruction and assessment, she states four more focused objectives.

In the first specific objective, the verb is "remember" and the noun phrase is "specifics about the Parliamentary Acts." Thus, we classify this first objective as *remember factual knowledge.*

The essence of the second objective is to explain the effect of the acts on various colonial groups. In Table 5.1 (see back inside cover), *explaining* means constructing a cause-and-effect model and is a cognitive process in the category *Understand.* In terms of knowledge, "consequences for different colonial groups" most closely resembles "theories, models, and structures." Thus, we classify this second objective as *understand conceptual knowledge.*

The third objective resembles an activity or assessment task more than an objective. The verb is "write a persuasive editorial"; the noun is "colonial character or group." If we assume, however, that Ms. Airasian expects students to learn to write persuasive editorials on a variety of topics during the year, we can classify this objective. "Write persuasive editorials" suggests *Create.* "Variety of topics" suggests some combination of *Factual* and *Conceptual knowledge.* Thus, we place this objective in cells A6 (*create* [based on] *factual knowledge*) and B6 (*create* [based on] *conceptual knowledge*) of the Taxonomy Table.

A similar argument can be made for the fourth objective. The verbs are "self edit" and "peer edit"; the noun is "the editorial." We can proceed in two ways (assuming Ms. Airasian's intent is for students to learn to edit rather than simply engage in the editing activity). We can assume that editing, particularly self-editing and peer-editing, is a form of evaluation. Hence, *Evaluate* is the process category. The evaluation would be based on some criteria; hence, we have *evaluate* [based on] *conceptual knowledge.* Alternatively, one might think of editing as *Applying,* that is, applying the rules of punctuation and grammar. This is a frequent classification problem, where a less complex process, *Apply,* is involved in a more complex one, *Evaluate.* We solve this problem by arbitrarily classifying the objective in the more complex of the levels—in this case, *Evaluate.*

Still another way of looking at editing is as one step in the process of writing the editorial. Then we would be back to the previous objective: *create* [based on] *factual* and *conceptual knowledge*. For the time being, we follow our first instinct and place this objective in cell B5 (*evaluate* [based on] *conceptual knowledge*).

The placement of these objectives in the cells of the Taxonomy Table is shown in Table 11.1.

PART 2: INSTRUCTIONAL ACTIVITIES

Day 1

I considered a number of ways to teach my general objective, including having students write a letter to a relative in England describing the impact of the Parliamentary Acts on his/her family or having students write petitions against the taxes. In the end, I decided to have students write a newspaper editorial from the perspective of either a Patriot or a Tory colonial. To obtain editorials written from both a Patriot and Tory perspective, I randomly selected two student groups based on the total number of letters in their first and last names. Odd-numbered students were Patriots (cheers) and even-numbered students Tories (grumbles). Randomizing student groups provided balanced ability groups and peer support for students who needed it. I then reconvened the entire class and talked with them about the nature of the unit: a combination of social studies and persuasive writing requiring a number of steps to complete. Students were told that the unit would last approximately 10 days. I gave each student a copy of the checklist I would use when assessing the editorials (Attachment A at the end of the chapter). I read each criterion aloud and asked individual students to explain in their own words what each criterion meant.

COMMENTARY

Ms. Airasian recognizes that many instructional activities could form the basis for the unit, and she selects one. Her recognition points up the difference between objectives and instructional activities; stated somewhat differently, it points out the flexibility and creativity teachers have in planning, teaching, and assessing after they have identified specific objectives.

The phrase "a combination of social studies and persuasive writing requiring a number of steps to complete" suggests *Procedural knowledge*. Thus, we assume that students are going to *apply procedural knowledge* as they complete their primary task, writing the editorial. However, for the time being, none of the activities is related to such an objective. Overall, on the first day Ms. Airasian provides students with an overview of the unit, including the expected final product and the criteria that will be used to evaluate it. Since the set of criteria constitute *Conceptual knowledge*, we classify Day 1's activities as ultimately related to *understanding conceptual knowledge* (because students have to "explain in their own words what each criterion meant").

11.1 ANALYSIS OF THE PARLIAMENTARY ACTS VIGNETTE IN TERMS OF THE TAXONOMY TABLE BASED ON STATED OBJECTIVES

THE KNOWLEDGE DIMENSION	THE COGNITIVE PROCESS DIMENSION					
	1. REMEMBER	2. UNDERSTAND	3. APPLY	4. ANALYZE	5. EVALUATE	6. CREATE
A. FACTUAL KNOWLEDGE	Objective 1					Objective 3
B. CONCEPTUAL KNOWLEDGE		Objective 2			Objective 4	Objective 3
C. PROCEDURAL KNOWLEDGE						
D. META-COGNITIVE KNOWLEDGE						

Key
Objective 1 = Remember specifics about the Parliamentary Acts.
Objective 2 = Explain the consequences of the Parliamentary Acts on different colonial groups.
Objective 3 = Choose a colonial character or group and write a persuasive editorial stating his/her/its position.
Objective 4 = Self and peer edit the editorial.

Day 2

I began the second day with the social studies unit. I showed a video of the colonial period that described the tax acts and gave a sense of the attitudes of the colonists toward England. I followed the video with a class discussion of the various taxes (listed on the board for students) and the attitudes of different groups of colonists toward the taxes. ("How do you think people in the colonies felt about the taxes? Did everyone feel the same? Why?") For homework students read their textbook chapter on the tax acts.

COMMENTARY

Instruction on the first two objectives has begun. The video provides information on both the tax acts (Objective 1) and the attitudes of the colonists toward England (Objective 2). The textbook chapter provides additional information pertaining to the first two objectives. With respect to knowledge, the emphasis is primarily on *Factual knowledge*. Although Ms. Airasian introduces different groups of colonists, the key word is *introduce*. Thus, we suggest that these activities relate primarily to the first objective, *remember factual knowledge*.

Day 3

The third day was spent reviewing the homework. Class discussion of the various tax acts, the reasons for them, and their impact on the colonists occupied the whole class period. Students were told to prepare for a quiz on the various tax acts the next day. They were to reread the prior day's chapter and review their notes. I told them that the quiz would require them to match parts of a tax act to the name of the tax act.

COMMENTARY

The continued emphasis on *Factual knowledge* is evident. Ms. Airasian believes that *Factual knowledge* provides a "scaffold" for the other objectives. She believes that without *Factual knowledge* of the tax acts, students will have difficulty explaining the consequences of the acts and writing an editorial from a given colonist's point of view. The "matching" quiz is consistent with our classification of these activities as *remembering factual knowledge*.

Day 4

The fourth day began with a quiz that counted one-fifth of the final unit grade. After the quiz, I started a review of persuasive writing. I reminded the students that persuasive writing tries to make the reader agree with the writer's opinion, so the writer must provide facts and examples to back up the opinion.

Otherwise the writer would not persuade or convince the reader. Students were referred to their writing portfolios to examine their prior persuasive writing. I emphasized the difference between opinion (what one believes is true) and facts (what can be supported by evidence). I told them that an editorial is a type of persuasive writing and showed examples of student editorials from *Scholastic Magazine*. I outlined criteria for the editorial: a strong and clear opening sentence stating a position; at least three supporting reasons for that position based on facts, not opinions; and a convincing ending (Attachment A). I also had the School District's Grade 5 Focus Correction Areas (FCAs) (Attachment B at the end of the chapter), but did not find them sufficient without adding my own assessment criteria. I reminded students that one of their reasons had to be original, a reason they identified on their own, not one discussed in class or in the textbook.

COMMENTARY

Attention shifts to a review of persuasive writing. Clearly, writing an editorial requires *Procedural knowledge* (i.e., how to write persuasive essays) and *Conceptual knowledge* (i.e., the criteria used to evaluate a piece of persuasive writing). Chapter 4 explained that criteria are associated with *Procedural knowledge* (p. 54). Those criteria, however, are of a particular kind. They are used to determine when specific *Procedural knowledge* should be put to use. Criteria used to evaluate, as in this instance, are different. They tend to be classifications and categories (here, for example, "supporting reasons" or "character-appropriate reasons"). Because they are classifications and categories, we consider them *Conceptual knowledge*. Because persuasive writing had been introduced and practiced earlier in the school year, Ms. Airasian chooses to review persuasive writing conceptually (e.g., what makes persuasive writing persuasive writing, examples of persuasive editorials) and procedurally (e.g., three-step sequence). She also reviews a set of criteria for evaluating writing in general (also *Conceptual knowledge*). The Day 4 activities relate primarily to *understand conceptual knowledge* and secondarily to *apply procedural knowledge*.

Day 5

On the fifth day the whole class brainstormed about specific taxes and the colonists' reactions to them. I wrote their ideas on the board and students took notes. In preparing students for selecting a character whose views the editorial would represent, the larger Patriot and Tory groups were broken into small subgroups of three to five to discuss how the taxes and events affected different groups in the colonies (e.g., merchants, farmers, bankers, housewives, etc.). After 15 minutes of small group discussion, the class was called together to share the results of these discussions.

COMMENTARY

The focus returns to the tax acts and the colonists' reactions to them. During the brainstorming and small group discussions, students are asked to make inferences. According to Table 5.1, *inferring* means drawing a logical conclusion from presented data. Inferences are to be made based on students' *Conceptual knowledge* of Patriots and Tories (i.e., beliefs and attitudes of two different categories of colonists) and their *Factual knowledge* of the tax acts. Thus, these activities relate to *understand conceptual knowledge* and *remember factual knowledge*.

Days 6 and 7

The sixth and seventh days focused on students selecting a colonial character who would "author" their editorial and identifying reasons to support that character's position in the editorial. I provided social studies texts, trade books, classroom encyclopedias, and books containing brief biographies of colonial people and descriptions of life in the colonies. The materials presented a range of reading levels and content related to the effects of the Parliamentary Acts on different colonial characters. I passed out guidelines to help students think about and identify their character (Attachment C at the end of the chapter). Before identifying their character, I required students to read at least two short biographies of colonists representing their Patriot or Tory designation.

COMMENTARY

Here students select the character or group to "author" their editorials. This activity is clearly related to Objective 3. Students are given some latitude in selecting their characters or groups, but they must provide specific information about their choice. Attachment C provides criteria to guide students in making their choices—hence, *Conceptual knowledge*. Implicit in the selection of a character, however, is analyzing prior information in the unit as well as the readings for Days 6 and 7. In particular, to make their selection and respond to Attachment C, students must differentiate (that is, distinguish relevant from irrelevant or important from unimportant parts—see Table 5.1). *Differentiate* is a cognitive process in the category *Analyze*. Thus, these activities relate to *understand conceptual knowledge* and *analyze* [based on] *conceptual knowledge*, respectively.

At the end of the seventh day, students were required to submit a written description of their character, why they chose that character, what position he/she would take in the editorial, and one reason that supported that position. I read each student's description and made suggestions, usually about the appropriateness of his/her choice or the quality of his/her novel reason. I provided suggestions for the few students who had difficulty choosing a character.

COMMENTARY

Ms. Airasian is making a formative assessment of student learning, presumably to check students' status and completeness before allowing them to begin their editorials. Some students had difficulty finding a novel reason to support their character's or group's position. Coming up with a new example of an element within a category is *exemplifying*, a process in the category *Understand* (see Table 5.1). Thus, the students' task is classified as *understand conceptual knowledge* (with Patriots and Tories representing two categories).

Days 8–10

On the succeeding three days, students worked individually on their own editorials, starting with an outline and using the evaluation form (Attachment A) for guidance. During the writing, I moved around the room answering students' questions, helping them identify issues for their draft, guiding a few students in beginning their writing, asking questions to focus students on needed historical information, and listening to students' thoughts and problems. I often prompted students to help them solidify the sense of their character. For example, if the character was a printer, I might ask, "What taxes were most important to the character and how did they affect him or her?" I also referred students to the guidelines for identifying a colonial character (Attachment C). Some students were able to begin writing their draft almost immediately, while others needed more discussion.

COMMENTARY

During these three days students are expected to produce their editorials. Since *produce* is a cognitive process in the category *Create*, we classify this activity as *create* [based on] *factual knowledge* (i.e., specific knowledge about the colonists and the Parliamentary Acts) and *conceptual knowledge* (i.e., knowledge about Patriots vs. Tories; knowledge of the evaluation criteria).

At this time, objectives, instructional activities, and assessments are interacting simultaneously in the classroom. Although the main emphasis is on Objective 3, writing a persuasive editorial, Ms. Airasian spends most of her time helping students with Objectives 1 and 2. Mastery of these objectives provides the "raw material" for the editorials. Unfortunately, Ms. Airasian finds that some students still have questions about their character or group or have not even selected a character or group.

As expected, the time needed to complete a first draft varied considerably among the students. Some writers completed a first draft in one class period, while others needed all three periods. When several students completed their drafts, I stopped the class and did a mini-review of the evaluation checklist

11.2 ANALYSIS OF THE PARLIAMENTARY ACTS VIGNETTE IN TERMS OF THE TAXONOMY TABLE BASED ON INSTRUCTIONAL ACTIVITIES

THE KNOWLEDGE DIMENSION	THE COGNITIVE PROCESS DIMENSION					
	1. REMEMBER	2. UNDERSTAND	3. APPLY	4. ANALYZE	5. EVALUATE	6. CREATE
A. FACTUAL KNOWLEDGE	**Objective 1** *Days 2, 3, 5 activities*					**Objective 3** *Days 8–10 activities*
B. CONCEPTUAL KNOWLEDGE		**Objective 2** *Days 1, 4–7 activities*		*Days 6–7 activities*	**Objective 4** *Days 8–10 activities*	**Objective 3** *Days 8–10 activities*
C. PROCEDURAL KNOWLEDGE			*Day 4 activities*			
D. META-COGNITIVE KNOWLEDGE						

Key
Objective 1 = Remember specifics about the Parliamentary Acts.
Objective 2 = Explain the consequences of the Parliamentary Acts on different colonial groups.
Objective 3 = Choose a colonial character or group and write a persuasive editorial stating his/her/its position.
Objective 4 = Self and peer edit the editorial.

(Attachment A), since it would guide both self and peer review of the drafts. First, each student reviewed his or her draft using the checklist. After the self review, the student's partner also reviewed the draft using the checklist. (In this classroom students served as reviewing partners on a regular basis.) After identified corrections and/or additions were discussed between the partner and the author, the necessary changes were made as part of a second draft. Next, the student scheduled a private conference with me to review the second draft. Each student brought his or her redrafted editorial and the checklist completed by the student and partner. Each student read the second draft to me while I made notes about the content, writing style, and mechanics. Suggestions related to style, appropriateness of supporting information, and historical accuracy were provided. My written checklist notes, my oral comments, and the student's and partner's reviews guided the independent writing of the final draft. In general, writing the final draft took one class period. During this stage of writing I continued to hold conferences with students, mainly aiding those still working on an early draft. I held another mini-review for the last group of writers when their drafts were finished to review the checklist and/or revision and for grading.

COMMENTARY

When a group of students complete their first draft of the editorial, Ms. Airasian prepares them for the fourth objective, self and peer editing of the draft editorial. Because students rely on the evaluation checklist (Attachment A) as they edit the editorials, the emphasis in the review appears to be on *Evaluating* the editorial based on the *Conceptual knowledge* included in Attachment A. As we mentioned earlier, editing also can be viewed as *Procedural knowledge*. A major distinction between the two is whether students use the criteria "on their own" (*Conceptual knowledge*) or follow a series of steps in conducting the review, with at least some of the steps containing the criteria (*Procedural knowledge*). Although Attachment A is a checklist, there is no evidence that students must follow the checklist in a specified order (nor are they taught to do so). Thus, our classification of the activity as *evaluating* [based on] *conceptual knowledge* seems reasonable.

The third formative assessment of the editorials (self and peer review being the first two) is performed by Ms. Airasian. The use of the same evaluation criteria increases the likelihood of consistency across these three sources of feedback.

Our analysis of the instructional activities in terms of the Taxonomy Table is shown in Table 11.2.

PART 3: ASSESSMENT

I assessed my students during and at the end of the unit. Much of my assessment was informal and individual, noting student questions, requests for help, and response to my questions. I used these assessments mainly to help individuals or groups of students to be sure everyone was clear on the area of concern. I also used assessments that were individual and somewhat more formal, for example, my conferences with individual students to discuss the second draft of their editorial. The answers and suggestions students received from these two forms of individual assessment helped them to understand and improve their editorials. I did not grade students on these "helping" assessments, although it was clear from the conferences that there was a range in depth of understanding among the students.

COMMENTARY

All this assessment is formative. From the closing sentence, Ms. Airasian's emphasis seems to be on *Understanding*. However, we are not certain what type of knowledge is involved. Most likely, the comments made by Ms. Airasian focus on *Conceptual knowledge* (e.g., the evaluation criteria) as well as *Factual knowledge* (e.g., the specific historical details included in the editorial).

My quiz on the tax acts and the final grades I assigned to students' completed editorials constituted the more formal, group-based assessments. For grading purposes, I reviewed students' first draft, the self and peer reviews, the second draft, and the final product. I was interested in both the process of creating an editorial and the quality of the finished product. I think it is important for students to follow the various steps so they recognize that a number of activities and products are required to produce the finished editorial. Two-fifths of the final grades were allocated to whether students completed the drafts, peer and self reviews, redrafts, and a final draft of the editorial, that is, whether they completed the entire process. Most students did complete the process. Two-fifths of the final grade was based on the quality of the unit's product, the final editorial (see Attachment A). I reviewed what students presented, compared it to the checklist, assigned a grade, and wrote a note to each student explaining the basis for the grade (Attachment D at the end of the chapter). The quiz accounted for the final fifth of the grade.

COMMENTARY

The quiz focuses on the specifics of the various tax acts and, hence, relates to *remember factual knowledge*. In grading the editorial, Ms. Airasian is concerned with both the process (i.e., *apply procedural knowledge*) and the product (i.e., *creating* [based on] *factual* and *conceptual knowledge*). She expects all students to follow a nine-step procedure: (1) select a character, (2) read about the character, (3) prepare an outline, (4) write a draft, (5) self and peer review the draft, (6) revise the draft, (7) submit the editorial to Ms. Airasian, (8) receive feedback, and (9) possibly revise again. This is the procedure Ms. Airasian wants students to follow not only on this project but on future projects as well. The editing process involves *Evaluating* the editorial based on the criteria (*Conceptual knowledge*) in Attachment A.

I was generally pleased with the editorials my students produced. They completed them in a reasonable time, except for two students who needed extra time. I judged that students had done very well in identifying and using historical facts. They also did well in identifying and selecting supporting reasons to justify the position adopted in their editorials. For the most part, students' supporting reasons were accurate and appropriate to their chosen character. They followed the procedures required. However, it was also quite clear that many students had substantial difficulty inferring a supporting reason that was not taught in class or found in the text. This difficulty was evident in both the draft and completed editorials. Next time I teach this unit I would put more instructional emphasis on higher-level processes like interpreting and inferring.

COMMENTARY

Our analysis of the assessments in terms of the Taxonomy Table is presented in Table 11.3.

PART 4: CLOSING COMMENTARY

In this section we examine the vignette in terms of our four basic questions: the learning question, the instruction question, the assessment question, and the alignment question.

THE LEARNING QUESTION

This instructional unit has a dual focus. The first is on the Parliamentary Acts as seen through the eyes of various American colonists. The second is on persuasive writing. The first two objectives pertain to the first focus; the last two objectives are concerned with both foci. We can see the dual focus of the last two objectives most clearly by examining the criteria used to evaluate the editorial (Attachment A). The first two "content" criteria have to do with persuasive writing (i.e., stating a point of view and supporting that point of view). The last three "content" criteria have to do with the Parliamentary Acts (i.e., appropriate reasons, historically accurate reasons, and can tell whether character is a Patriot or a Tory). The remaining "content" criterion is a requirement that *Understanding* in addition to *Remembering* is displayed in the editorial.

11.3 ANALYSIS OF THE PARLIAMENTARY ACTS VIGNETTE IN TERMS OF THE TAXONOMY TABLE BASED ON ASSESSMENTS

THE KNOWLEDGE DIMENSION	THE COGNITIVE PROCESS DIMENSION					
	1. REMEMBER	2. UNDERSTAND	3. APPLY	4. ANALYZE	5. EVALUATE	6. CREATE
A. FACTUAL KNOWLEDGE	**Objective 1** *Days 2, 3, 5 activities* Assessment B	Assessment A				**Objective 3** *Days 8–10 activities* Assessment C
B. CONCEPTUAL KNOWLEDGE		**Objective 2** *Days 1, 4–7 activities* Assessment A		*Days 6, 7 activities*	**Objective 4** *Days 8–10 activities*	**Objective 3** *Days 8–10 activities* Assessment C
C. PROCEDURAL KNOWLEDGE			*Day 4 activities* Assessment C			
D. META-COGNITIVE KNOWLEDGE						

Key
Objective 1 = Remember specifics about the Parliamentary Acts.
Objective 2 = Explain the consequences of the Parliamentary Acts on different colonial groups.
Objective 3 = Choose a colonial character or group and write a persuasive editorial stating his/her/its position.
Objective 4 = Self and peer edit the editorial.
Assessment A = Classroom questions and observations; informal assessments.
Assessment B = Quiz
Assessment C = Editorial (with ten evaluation criteria—Attachment A).
Dark shading indicates the strongest alignment—an objective, an instructional activity, and an assessment are all present in the same cell. Lighter shading indicates two of the three are present.

THE INSTRUCTION QUESTION

The dual focus of this unit results in an interesting pattern of instructional activities. After a general orientation day, the next two days were spent on the Parliamentary Acts and the colonists; then the focus shifted to persuasive writing for a day. During the following two days, the focus was back on the Parliamentary Acts and the colonists. In the final three days, the focus returned to persuasive writing. The instructional activities addressed all six of the process categories (see Table 11.2). In the first week, the activities emphasized *Remember*, *Understand*, and *Apply*. During the second week, the activities moved from *Analyze* to *Evaluate* and *Create*.

THE ASSESSMENT QUESTION

Ms. Airasian used three different assessments for three different purposes. Classroom questions and observations were used to check students' *understanding conceptual knowledge*. Do students understand the differences between Patriots and Tories? Do they understand the criteria that will be used to evaluate their editorials? The quiz focused exclusively on *remembering factual knowledge*. Do students know the details of the various Parliamentary Acts? Both of these are classified as formative assessments. The summative assessment was the editorial. As mentioned earlier, the editorial assessed in part *creating* based on *factual* and *conceptual knowledge*.

THE ALIGNMENT QUESTION

Strong alignment is evident in cells A1 (*Remember Factual knowledge*), B2 (*Understand Conceptual knowledge*), and a combined A6/B6 (*Create* [based on] *Factual knowledge* and *Conceptual knowledge*). Each of these cells contains an objective, several days of activities, and some sort of assessment. We find minor indicators of misalignment: cells A2 (*Understand Factual knowledge*), B4 (*Analyze* [based on] *Conceptual knowledge*), B5 (*Evaluate* [based on] *Conceptual Knowledge*), and C3 (*Apply Procedural knowledge*). One of these cells is worthy of comment. The *Procedural knowledge* in cell C3 (*Apply Procedural knowledge*) is a "meta" procedure that applies to all writing: get information, prepare an outline, write a draft, review the draft and have a peer review the draft, revise the draft, submit the draft to the teacher, and prepare a final draft. Because this procedure had been emphasized throughout the school year, it was reviewed only briefly in this unit, with no objective stated and no assessment made.

PART 5: CLOSING QUESTIONS

As with the analysis of all our vignettes, we were left with a few unanswered questions. We raise two of the most important in this closing section.

1. **What are the advantages and disadvantages of integrated (or cross-disciplinary) instructional units?** This is a very nice example of an in-

structional unit linking history with language arts. This approach offers some advantages. For example, persuasive writing can make history "come to life"; students must put themselves in the place of historical characters in order to write the editorial. Similarly, integrated units help students see that real-world problems frequently require knowledge and skills from multiple academic disciplines or subject areas.

At the same time, however, this unit illustrates potential problems in designing and delivering such units. How should teachers sequence activities related to the dual focus of such units? How should teachers score and grade assessments that require integration of the two disciplines? How can teachers best deal with the individual differences among students on both dimensions: historical facts and concepts, and persuasive writing concepts and procedures? To fully understand the last question, consider that integrated units contain two sets of *Factual knowledge*, two sets of *Conceptual knowledge*, and two sets of *Procedural knowledge*. Finally, what role do cognitive process categories play in fully integrating cross-disciplinary units? Answers to these questions will go a long way toward designing "workable" interdisciplinary or cross-disciplinary units.

2. **What are the dangers of using generic rating scales or scoring rubrics in assessment?** Ms. Airasian was expected to use a district-adopted set of Focus Correction Areas (FCAs) to evaluate her students' writing of persuasive editorials. In addition, she included four generic writing criteria on her own evaluation form. The result was four sets of criteria on the evaluation form: (1) criteria pertaining to persuasive writing, (2) criteria pertaining to ensuring understanding rather than remembering, (3) criteria pertaining to the content of the editorial, and (4) criteria pertaining to writing in general. How are these four sets of criteria to be weighted in determining the quality of the editorial? How much value do generic writing criteria have in evaluating the quality of the editorial? These questions (and others) are worth addressing when multiple evaluation criteria are used with writing assignments.

Name _____ Date _____

Read the editorial and decide if the content and writing conventions are met.
Put a check mark for Yes and leave a blank for No.

	Author	Partner	Teacher

Content

1. The author states a clear point of view at the beginning of the editorial.

2. The author has at least three reasons to support the character's point of view.

3. The author includes one reason that is not from the textbook or class discussion.

4. The reasons given are appropriate to the character.

5. The reasons given are historically accurate.

6. The reader can tell whether the character writing is a Patriot or a Tory.

Writing Conventions

7. The author writes in complete sentences.

8. The author punctuates correctly.

9. The author uses correct spelling.

10. The author writes legibly.

ATTACHMENT B   GRADE 5 FOCUS CORRECTION AREAS (FCAs)

1. Use complete sentences (no sentence fragments or run-on sentences).

2. Write proper paragraphs.

    a. Indent the first line.

    b. Write a topic sentence.

    c. Write supporting details.

    d. Write all sentences on the same topic.

    e. Write a concluding sentence.

3. Use correct spelling.

4. Write legibly.

Here are some questions that can help you identify a character for your editorial:

Are you a man or a woman, a boy or a girl?

In which of the colonies do you live? Do you live in a city, in a small town, or on a farm?

How many people are in your family?

How long has your family been in the colony?

Does your family have a trade or occupation?

Do you have any ties to England, such as a cousin, grandparent, brother, or aunt?

How important are the things that the Parliament taxes (sugar, stamps, tea, glass, paper) for you or your family?

John, your editorial was excellent. The writing was clear throughout. I understood exactly why Thomas Goodson, the Boston banker, was a supporter of King George and the Parliamentary actions. You have carefully explained the position of Mr. Goodson and his ties to his family in London. This writing shows significant improvement over your last editorial. Keep up the good work.

I read your editorial, Karen, and knew very clearly why Abigail Jones was a supporter of the Patriots. This Cambridge widow certainly had her reasons to feel the actions of King George were unjust. You have explained why her husband grew so despondent after the establishment of the Stamp Act impacted so harshly on his printing business. Be sure to proof your writing carefully to avoid run-on sentences. This is an area in which you can improve.

Ben, I still do not understand your reasoning in this editorial. Andrew Dennis, as a Charleston landowner and cousin of the Duke of Lancaster, had many reasons to support the position of the English government. He shipped rice from his low country plantation to Europe for sale. He maintained close ties with his family in England and secured many loans from the family bank. Even when you have mentioned all of this, you have made him a Patriot and not supported his position with reasons. We discussed this during our conference. It appears to me that your final copy is basically the same as the rough draft we examined. It is important that you make necessary changes on the final copy. Also, Ben, the writing mechanics have not been polished. There are still many spelling errors, as well as sentence fragments. Please meet with me again to discuss how this editorial can be improved.

CHAPTER 12

Volcanoes? Here? Vignette

This vignette describes a unit on volcanoes that was taught to a seventh-grade science class in a large school district in Pennsylvania by Mr. Duane Parker. (The vignette was written by Dr. Michael Smith.)

> This class, comprised of 15 boys and 12 girls, met five times per week for 45-minute periods. In terms of their science achievement, I would rate 4 of the students as "high achievers," 11 as "low achievers," and the remaining 12 students as "average achievers."
>
> I planned the unit to last eight days. It actually lasted twice as long (16 class sessions)—almost a month of the school year.

PART 1: OBJECTIVES

The unit was designed to promote conceptual restructuring and meaningful learning in earth science. It was based on the dominant research paradigm in geology, the theory of plate tectonics. In contrast to the memorization of information about volcanoes, the emphasis was on "reasoned argument" which integrated evidence with theory. The major goal of the unit was for the students to "get smarter about volcanoes."

COMMENTARY

In the vocabulary of the Taxonomy Table, "conceptual restructuring" probably is similar in meaning to *understand conceptual knowledge*. More specifically, the *Conceptual knowledge* the students encounter in the unit is intended to "shape" or "modify" the conceptual framework that students bring to the unit. As used in Chapter 5, the phrase "meaningful learning" captures all of the cognitive process categories beyond *Remember*. Finally, unlike the objectives that follow, the stated goal ("get smarter about volcanoes") is extremely vague (as is true of most goals—see Chapter 2).

More specifically, the students were to achieve four objectives:

1. understand the theory of plate tectonics as an explanation for volcanoes;

2. examine and interpret a set of data on the geology of the local region (geologic maps, oil well drill records, and rock samples);

3. compare the geology of the local region to places that have volcanoes, such as the states of Hawaii and Washington; and

4. taking into account the learning reflected in Objectives 1 through 3, write a letter to the County Commissioner that is responsive to his request (see Attachment A at the end of the chapter).

COMMENTARY

This set of objectives is interesting. The verbs in the first three objectives ("understand," "interpret," and "compare") are all associated with the cognitive process category *Understand* (see Table 5.1 inside the back cover). The noun phrases ("theory of plate tectonics," "geology of the local regions," "places that have volcanoes") are more difficult to classify. "Theory" is clearly related to *Conceptual knowledge* (see Table 4.1 inside the front cover). The focus on *Conceptual knowledge* in the first objective is also supported by the phrase "as an explanation of volcanoes." Explaining requires the construction of a causal model (see Table 5.1). Thus, we classify the first three objectives as *understand conceptual knowledge*.

The fourth objective is a culminating activity, not an objective, so it will not be classified. However, in the third section on assessment we classify the components of the scoring rubric.

In summary, then, we place the first three objectives in a single cell of the Taxonomy Table, B2 (*understand conceptual knowledge*). Table 12.1. shows the placement.

PART 2: INSTRUCTIONAL ACTIVITIES

Day 1

I began the unit by presenting the students with a letter from County Commissioner Fred Luckino that posed a problem for them to consider. The letter (Attachment A) asked whether it would be prudent to develop, at considerable cost, a plan for evacuating the county in case a volcanic eruption occurred in the region. The Commissioner was asking for their help in making this decision. I told the students they were to submit a written recommendation based on scientific thinking and evidence by the end of the unit. I reminded them that three general criteria, emphasized throughout the course, were to be used in this regard: clarity, relationships among parts, and consistency with evidence. I told them they were required to prepare a portfolio of facts, analyses, findings, and authoritative statements to support their recommendation.

12.1 ANALYSIS OF THE VOLCANOES VIGNETTE IN TERMS OF THE TAXONOMY TABLE BASED ON STATED OBJECTIVES

THE KNOWLEDGE DIMENSION	THE COGNITIVE PROCESS DIMENSION					
	1. REMEMBER	2. UNDERSTAND	3. APPLY	4. ANALYZE	5. EVALUATE	6. CREATE
A. FACTUAL KNOWLEDGE						
B. CONCEPTUAL KNOWLEDGE		Objective 1; Objective 2; Objective 3				
C. PROCEDURAL KNOWLEDGE						
D. META- COGNITIVE KNOWLEDGE						

Key
Objective 1 = Understand the theory of plate tectonics as an explanation for volcanoes.
Objective 2 = Examine and interpret a set of data on the geology of the local region.
Objective 3 = Compare the geology of the local region to places that have volcanoes.

Furthermore, their recommendation should be based on the likelihood that the region would experience a volcanic eruption in the next several decades. This introduction took the better part of the first day.

COMMENTARY

In combination, the three criteria provide a framework to be used by students throughout the unit. The framework provides the link between the Commissioner's letter and the data examined during the unit. Because this is a general introduction to the unit, we do not classify it in the Taxonomy Table.

Day 2

On the second day, the students were asked to respond to two questions: (1) What am I being hired to do? and (2) What do I need to know? I asked the students to read silently through the letter and underline unfamiliar words and phrases. When a student asked, "Why are we talking about volcanoes when we don't have any here?" I responded by distributing a newspaper article dated February 1, 1986, reporting on volcanic activity in a nearby metropolitan area.

COMMENTARY

The two questions require that students analyze the information in the letter. Within the process category *Analyze*, the emphasis here is on *differentiating*—that is, distinguishing relevant from irrelevant or important from unimportant parts (see Table 5.1). We consider knowledge of the details presented in the letter to be *Factual knowledge*. Thus, we place this activity in cell A4, *Analyze Factual knowledge*.

Days 3, 4

The lessons on Days 3 and 4 were designed to determine students' current conceptions about how volcanoes "work." I asked them to draw what a volcano looks like above and below the ground and to explain why volcanoes erupt. After students had been engaged in their work for some time, I interrupted their efforts to set the stage for the next assignment—the creation of a class word bank relevant to a discussion of volcanoes. Students were asked to nominate words for inclusion in the word bank. As the class on Day 3 ended, I asked students to read about volcanoes in selected references and to come to class ready to discuss the material they read.

On Day 4, the students developed a 32-item word bank. The students then resumed work on the drawing task that had been suspended overnight. I urged them to use the word bank vocabulary to label elements of their drawings. They also were to identify needed additions to the word bank. I reviewed with them how the three criteria—clarity, relationships among the parts of the volcano, and consistency with the evidence—were to be applied to their drawings.

I instructed the students to write an explanation of how a volcano works to go along with their drawings and to complete the task without looking at each others' papers. I wanted to know what each student knew about volcanoes. Their work revealed a diversity of conceptions about underground structure and the causes of volcanic eruption.

COMMENTARY

In terms of cognitive processes, the emphasis is on *explaining* (*Understand*). *Explaining* requires constructing a cause-and-effect model of a system—in this case, a system that produces a volcanic eruption. The model itself is *Conceptual knowledge* (see Table 4.1). Therefore, we classify the drawing and writing activity as *understand conceptual knowledge*.

To talk about their models, the students need a vocabulary. In the Taxonomy Table, vocabulary is the same as knowledge of terminology. Thus, the emphasis here is on *Factual knowledge* (see Table 4.1). Since the terminology is to be used with the drawings, we see this activity as *understanding factual knowledge*. The word bank serves as a memory aid; thus, *recalling* is downplayed and the emphasis shifts to *recognize*.

This activity is a nice illustration of the difference between knowledge of terminology (*Factual knowledge*) and knowledge of categories the terminology represents (*Conceptual knowledge*). For example, "magma" is a term for "volcanic rock." Placing the label "magma" on their drawings enables students to talk about their drawings. Without proper labels, students would be forced to point to various aspects of the drawing and make references to "this" and "that."

In many ways, the activity on Days 3 and 4 serves as a pre-assessment. The teacher is interested in knowing what students understand about the causes of volcanic eruptions before instruction really begins. Since each picture invites numerous explanations, a written explanation is needed to get at student understanding. Thus, we are dealing with two related cells of the Taxonomy Table: *understand conceptual knowledge* and *remember factual knowledge*.

Day 5

The entire class session on the fifth day consisted of a class discussion about students' conceptions of the causes of volcanic eruptions. Having carefully examined the student work, I selected five diverse, high-quality pieces for students to present and "defend" to their classmates. I handed out photocopies of the selected work and told students that the goal of the discussion was to consider all possible explanations of what makes volcanoes erupt. The discussion turned out to be incredibly challenging to direct. Even with careful planning, the scene was full of improvisation, both on my part and on the part of the students.

In the midst of the debate I reminded students that consensus about why volcanoes erupt was not the goal of the conversation. Rather, the goal was to explore the diversity of drawings and ideas to find out why students understand what they do. The real battles would have to be fought with evidence and arguments; these would have to wait.

COMMENTARY

At this point, Mr. Parker recognizes the diversity of individual student knowing, rather than shared knowledge. Although this is consistent with his emphasis ("all possible explanations of what makes volcanoes erupt"), it is not consistent with his intent as expressed in the first objective (i.e., explanations consistent with the theory of plate tectonics). Eventually, the shift to a common understanding will be made based on "evidence and arguments." Thus, although all the activities on Day 5 are tangentially related to the first objective, *understand conceptual knowledge*, the first objective remains (purposely) unattained.

Day 6

On the sixth day, students began their work on the major task at hand: the examination of the geological evidence for volcanoes in their county. I began by asking questions such as "What kinds of rocks are volcanic?" "What do they look like?" "Do we have any old magma around here?" Students worked on this task for the next six days.

COMMENTARY

The emphasis now shifts to the second objective. The focus is on classifying rocks (*understanding conceptual knowledge*).

I introduced a geologic map that could be used to search for evidence of volcanism. Holding up the map, I directed students' attention to the variety of colors (a different color for each type of rock), acquainted them with the scale of the map, and described how the map key relates the colors to the rock names. I also told them how the map relates to the videotape on local geology I was about to show them. Next, I led the class through a page-by-page overview of their Research Materials Packet, a 20-page text containing background information and newspaper clippings about earthquakes.

COMMENTARY

These activities are intended to provide students with an accumulation of *Factual knowledge*. Cognitively, the focus seems to be on *remembering factual knowledge*. Eventually, students may have to select the relevant knowledge (*Analyze*), but we have to wait and see.

I then talked to them about the theory of plate tectonics, using three-dimensional models and a filmstrip to convey its major elements. I asked questions throughout the presentation, honing in on the utility of the information for the overall task.

COMMENTARY

Knowledge of theories and models is *Conceptual knowledge* (see Table 4.1). Eventually, Mr. Parker intends for students to use this theory and these models to explain what happens when volcanoes erupt. Thus, the implicit objective once again takes the form *understand conceptual knowledge*.

Finally, I played a 15-minute videotape on earthquakes and geological work. The first part of the video contained footage from recent earthquakes and a seismogram from a local museum. The second part showed a local geologist on a rock exposure in the northern part of the county. The geologist described how geologists collect and log rock samples. He also discussed how geologic maps are used to determine the age of rocks and concluded by telling the students that the rocks he has collected are the ones they will be examining in class. I provided a running commentary during the videotape, informing students of important features related to their task (e.g., the examination of evidence, the use of maps, the dating of rocks).

COMMENTARY

The first part of the videotape contains a great deal of *Factual knowledge*. Rather than having students remember this knowledge, however, the purpose seems to be motivational (i.e., to "legitimize" the task the students are facing). The second part of the videotape shifts to *Procedural knowledge* (e.g., how to collect and log rock samples, how to determine the age of rocks). Eventually, the students will be expected to *Apply* at least some of this as *Procedural knowledge*; however, the primary focus at this point seems to be *remember procedural knowledge*.

Day 7

On the seventh day, I led a more extensive discussion of the state geologic map, teaching students how to use the map, and making sure they knew that igneous rocks are critical evidence for volcanism. I then set them to work in groups on a task that took the remainder of the seventh day and most of the eighth. The task was to complete a data table according to rock type (e.g., igneous, sedimentary, and metamorphic), listing every kind of rock that appears in the state.

COMMENTARY

The focus shifts to *apply procedural knowledge* (i.e., how to use the map) as well as *remember factual knowledge* (e.g., igneous rocks are critical evidence for volcanism). The task, when completed, produces a written classification system of rocks. Thus, we move back to *understanding* (e.g., classifying) *conceptual knowledge*.

After the students completed this group task, they were to answer four questions:

1. What are the major rock types found in our county?
2. What kinds of igneous rocks are in the county (intrusive or extrusive)?
3. According to the geologic map, how far from our city are the closest igneous rocks? How old are they?
4. What conclusions can you draw from the data in terms of the possibility of volcanic activity in our county?

COMMENTARY

These questions tap a variety of types of knowledge and cognitive process categories. The first requires *remembering* (i.e., recalling) *factual knowledge*, the second *understanding conceptual knowledge*, and the third *applying procedural knowledge* (i.e., how to determine distances on maps using their scales). The fourth question requires students to make inferences. *Inferring* lies in the category *Understand* (see Table 5.1). These inferences are to be based on students' knowledge of the data (i.e., *Factual knowledge*)—hence, *understand factual knowledge*.

Day 8

On the eighth day, I led an "assessment conversation." I selected a volunteer from each group to come to the board to write the group's responses to one of the four questions. When each had done so, I asked the class to either confirm or challenge the responses. Whereas the responses to the first two questions were confirmed with little argument, the responses to question 3 created controversy. To answer this question, students had to measure the distance between their county and the closest igneous rocks. The groups came up with quite different answers, ranging from 120 to 250 miles. In a move to save time, I measured the distance on an overhead transparency of the map and arrived at an answer of 150 miles for intrusive igneous rocks that are 570 million years old.

COMMENTARY

Based on this "assessment conversation," Mr. Parker learns that the students are able to *remember* the relevant *factual knowledge* (question 1) and they *understand* the important *conceptual knowledge* (question 2). The problem resides in *applying procedural knowledge* (question 3).

At this point I was ready to elicit students' responses to the fourth question. There was quick consensus that volcanic activity in the county was highly unlikely. Nevertheless, they agreed with me that it could not be conclusively ruled out. I then proceeded to introduce students to the next task: comparing rocks collected in their region of the country with rocks collected at Mt. St. Helens.

COMMENTARY

After addressing the problem with *applying procedural knowledge,* students are able to make a proper inference about the likelihood of a volcanic eruption in their community (evidence that they *understand conceptual knowledge*).

I distributed ten rock samples to groups of students, five from a volcanic region and five collected locally. Students were asked to match the rock samples to descriptions of different types of rocks. Students completed this task within 15 minutes, but as I circulated around the room, I noticed that many had confused pumice with sandstone, a critical misinterpretation since pumice is volcanic rock and is not found in their county. As a result I decided to lead a brief "assessment conversation" to attain consensus about the identities of the samples and what these "findings" indicated about the local geology.

COMMENTARY

This activity involves *classifying*—hence, *Understand* (see Table 5.1). The classifying involves rock samples and rock "types" (i.e., categories). Types, classifications, and categories all suggest *Conceptual knowledge* (see Table 4.1).

Days 9–12

The next four days presented my students and me with the greatest challenge. Students were required to search for evidence of volcanic rocks on the geologic maps of five states surrounding their state, transfer igneous rock locations to a base map of the six-state region, measure the distance to the closest igneous rocks, and decide what this implied about the likelihood of volcanic activity affecting their county.

COMMENTARY

The activities during these four days are a repetition of those on Days 7 and 8 within a larger geographic context. The focus on the county is enlarged to multiple states, including one with recent volcanic activity. Therefore, our earlier analysis of the activities in terms of the Taxonomy Table applies here.

I began the ninth day by getting the students to think about the extensiveness of volcanic eruptions and the fact that their county is only 30 miles away from three other states, yet they have only looked at the geologic map of their own state. When students' responses indicated they did not seem to understand the magnitude of volcanic eruptions, I reminded them that when Mt. St. Helens erupted, cities 100 miles away were covered with ash. Once convinced that the students understood why they were doing the task, I gave them specific instructions about how to complete it. These instructions included warnings about the different colors and different scales used on different states' maps, suggestions as to how to measure distances on their base maps, and a reminder that the table of major rock types they had constructed should be used as a key in determining whether or not a specific rock is igneous.

COMMENTARY

The instructions given to the students are a combination of *Factual knowledge* ("warnings"), *Procedural knowledge* ("how to"), and *Conceptual knowledge* ("table of rock types"). Students are expected to *remember factual knowledge, apply procedural knowledge,* and *understand conceptual knowledge.*

The next three days (Days 10–12) I spent nearly all my time visiting groups and assisting students with difficulties. Among the major difficulties I noted were the following:

large amounts of data to be searched;

determining the "status" of metamorphosed igneous rocks;

differences in map keys between states;

differences in map scales;

variable methods of plotting data on base maps; and

variable methods of measuring the distance of the closest igneous rocks.

In combination, these difficulties suggest problems with *Factual knowledge* (e.g., the sheer amount of data), *Conceptual knowledge* (e.g., rock types, map scales), and *Procedural knowledge* (e.g., methods of plotting data and measuring distances on different maps). Any and all of these difficulties are likely to interfere with the primary unit goal, *understanding conceptual knowledge.*

Day 13

On Day 13, as part of an "assessment conversation," I selected several of the base maps prepared by the students and projected them on the wall using an opaque projector. As I projected each map, one student from the group that prepared it was asked to describe it. I spent most of my time helping students resolve discrepancies and disagreements about the types and ages of the rocks, as well as the distance of the closest igneous rocks from their county. Unfortunately, the time and effort required to evaluate and improve the quality of each map prevented me from helping students realize the limitations inherent in the evidence they were examining.

The conflicts among students seem to relate to the areas of *Conceptual knowledge* (types of rocks) and *Procedural knowledge* (how to determine the ages of rocks; how to determine distances of rocks from the county). Unfortunately, data on type, age, and distance are perhaps the key factors in determining the likelihood of volcanic activity in their county.

The time came to ask students about the likelihood of volcanoes in their county given the new evidence they had considered. About one in eight students said they did not have sufficient evidence to make a decision about the potential for volcanic activity. The rest of the students were ready to do so. About half of these students said it was possible that a volcano could affect the local region, citing the distant old igneous rocks as evidence to support their conclusion. The other half said that a volcano was not possible because the volcanic rocks from the past were too far away to affect them now.

The net result of the activities on Days 9–12 is to move students from consensus (*understand conceptual knowledge*) to disagreement and dissension.

Day 14

By Day 14 I felt pressured for time. I hastened students through a portfolio item in which they examined the location of their city in relation to the boundaries between tectonic plates. They examined a cross-section through the earth's crust and mantle from the Pacific Ocean to the Atlantic Ocean. Mt. St. Helens was near a plate boundary; their county was roughly 2,000 miles away from the nearest plate boundary.

COMMENTARY

At this point in the unit, Mr. Parker re-introduces the theoretical basis for examining and discussing the evidence: the theory of plate tectonics (*Conceptual knowledge*). In addition, he provides one key piece of *Factual knowledge*: the students' county is nowhere near a plate boundary. Thus, he refocuses students on the primary objective: *understand conceptual knowledge*.

I managed to direct students' attention to the fact that Mt. St. Helens and Yellowstone, two volcanic regions in the continental United States, have something in common: rising magma. I also directed students to the first pages of the Research Materials Packet, which showed a map of the world's tectonic plates and a cross-section through the crust and mantle which shows how magma rises near plate boundaries. With these materials, students proceeded to answer questions about the implications of the theory of plate tectonics for the argument they were to construct.

COMMENTARY

This is more *Factual knowledge* ("volcanic regions have rising magma," "magma rises near plate boundaries"). *Factual knowledge* is intended to help clarify key issues and thus enhance *understanding conceptual knowledge*.

A summary of our analysis of the instructional activities in terms of the Taxonomy Table is shown in Table 12.2.

PART 3: ASSESSMENT

On the fifteenth day, I realized that the class remained split about the possibility of a volcano affecting the area. Some students were convinced that ancient igneous rocks located 150 miles away are still a possible threat. Nonetheless, I was ready to have students begin drafting their letter to the County Commissioner. My instructions to the class emphasized the importance of coming to an agreement within each group and persuasively arguing for whatever position they took.

I evaluated each of the letters the students drafted to submit to Mr. Luckino according to a rubric (see Attachment B at the end of the chapter). Before

12.2 ANALYSIS OF THE VOLCANOES VIGNETTE IN TERMS OF THE TAXONOMY TABLE BASED ON INSTRUCTIONAL ACTIVITIES

THE KNOWLEDGE DIMENSION	THE COGNITIVE PROCESS DIMENSION					
	1. REMEMBER	2. UNDERSTAND	3. APPLY	4. ANALYZE	5. EVALUATE	6. CREATE
A. FACTUAL KNOWLEDGE	*Days 3, 4, 6–14 activities*	*Days 3, 4, 7 activities*		*Day 2 activity*		
B. CONCEPTUAL KNOWLEDGE		**Objective 1; Objective 2; Objective 3** *Days 3–14 activities*				
C. PROCEDURAL KNOWLEDGE	*Day 6 activities*		*Days 7–13 activities*			
D. META-COGNITIVE KNOWLEDGE						

Key
Objective 1 = Understand the theory of plate tectonics as an explanation for volcanoes.
Objective 2 = Examine and interpret a set of data on the geology of the local region.
Objective 3 = Compare the geology of the local region to places that have volcanoes.

applying this rubric, however, I invited students to share their letters with the other groups. Students in those groups were to use the rubric to evaluate each letter they read. After this exercise, some student groups sought permission to revise their letters and were permitted to do so. Even though the letters represented a wide range of opinion about the central question and contained recommendations that were diverse and divergent, I was pleased with the high level of thinking and understanding they reflect.

COMMENTARY

The rubric contains four criteria. The first criterion, "accuracy of information in summary," pertains primarily to *remembering factual knowledge*. The second criterion, "consistency with the evidence," requires *understanding conceptual knowledge*. A recommendation can only be consistent with evidence that is interpreted in some way. The theory of plate tectonics provides the conceptual framework for that interpretation. The third and fourth criteria are difficult to classify. The third is "acknowledgment of alternative explanations." Explanations, as mentioned earlier, require the construction of cause-and-effect models. The constructed model is a form of *Conceptual knowledge*. The word "alternative," however, suggests that multiple models can be constructed and students can generate alternatives from the various models. If this is the case, the verb would be "generating" (*Create*), with "alternative models" (*Conceptual knowledge*) as the noun. The generation of models different from the theory of plate tectonics contradicts the first objective, however. Finally, the fourth criterion is equally challenging. If we assume that a procedure for writing such a letter was taught to students in advance, then this criterion requires *applying procedural knowledge*. If, however, students have to "figure it out on their own," then *planning* and *producing* are more likely the cognitive processes involved. In this case, then, the fourth criterion requires *creating* [based on] the vast array of *Factual*, *Conceptual*, and *Procedural knowledge* included in the unit.

In addition to this formal assessment, I engaged in two "assessment conversations" during the unit. The first took place on Day 8 following the assignment in which students answered four questions about rock types and volcanism. The second took place on Day 13 and involved a class discussion of the students' base map projects.

COMMENTARY

As mentioned in our analysis of the instructional activities, the questions included in the first assessment conversation can be classified as (1) *remember factual knowledge*, (2) *understand conceptual knowledge*, and (3) *apply procedural knowledge*. In addition, the discussion of the base maps focuses on (1) *understanding conceptual knowledge* and (2) *applying procedural knowledge*.

The summary of our analysis of the assessments in terms of the Taxonomy Table is presented in Table 12.3.

12.3 ANALYSIS OF THE VOLCANOES VIGNETTE IN TERMS OF THE TAXONOMY TABLE BASED ON ASSESSMENTS

THE KNOWLEDGE DIMENSION	THE COGNITIVE PROCESS DIMENSION					
	1. REMEMBER	2. UNDERSTAND	3. APPLY	4. ANALYZE	5. EVALUATE	6. CREATE
A. FACTUAL KNOWLEDGE	*Days 3, 4, 6–14 activities* Assess A1; Assess B(1)	*Days 3, 4, 7 activities*		*Day 2 activity*		Assess B(4)
B. CONCEPTUAL KNOWLEDGE		**Objective 1; Objective 2; Objective 3** *Days 3–14 activities* Assess A1, 2; Assess B(2)				Assess B(3, 4)
	Day 6 activities		*Days 7–13 activities* Assess A1, 2			Assess B(4)
D. META-COGNITIVE KNOWLEDGE						

Key
Objective 1 = Understand the theory of plate tectonics as an explanation for volcanoes.
Objective 2 = Examine and interpret a set of data on the geology of the local region.
Objective 3 = Compare the geology of the local region to places that have volcanoes.
Assess A = Assessment conversations 1 and 2.
Assess B = Scoring rubric for letter to commissioner; criteria 1, 2, 3, and 4.
Dark shading indicates the strongest alignment—an objective, an instructional activity, and an assessment are all present in the same cell. Lighter shading indicates two of the three are present.

PART 4: CLOSING COMMENTARY

In this section we examine the vignette in terms of our four basic questions: the learning question, the instruction question, the assessment question, and the alignment question.

THE LEARNING QUESTION

The actual focal point of this unit is the culminating activity, the letter to the County Commissioner. In the letter the students were to offer their recommendation concerning the need for a "volcano emergency" plan. Objective 1 is intended to provide the theoretical basis for the recommendation; Objectives 2 and 3 are intended to provide the empirical support for the recommendation. Whether the data do or do not lend support, however, the students must interpret the data. Interpretation requires some combination of *Procedural knowledge* (i.e., how to read geologic maps), *Conceptual knowledge* (i.e., types of rocks), and *Factual knowledge* (i.e., igneous rocks are critical evidence for volcanism).

THE INSTRUCTION QUESTION

After the first few lessons, Mr. Parker relied extensively on "hands-on" activities. For the last half of the unit, or about seven days, students were working simultaneously on *remembering factual knowledge, understanding conceptual knowledge*, and *applying procedural knowledge*. Unfortunately, these activities took so long that Mr. Parker had to move to a lecture mode near the end of the unit (Day 14) and students had only two class sessions to complete their projects (Days 15 and 16).

THE ASSESSMENT QUESTION

Mr. Parker used what he referred to as "assessment conversations" to determine whether students were making progress toward achieving the unit objectives. Both assessment conversations contained questions that addressed *remembering factual knowledge, understanding conceptual knowledge*, and *applying procedural knowledge*. The questions served a formative assessment purpose.

The major unit assessment was the group project. Each group had to prepare a letter to send to the County Commissioner indicating whether he should or should not fund an evacuation plan and giving reasons for the specific recommendation. Each group's project was evaluated in terms of a set of criteria. The criteria fell into five cells of the Taxonomy Table: A1 (*remember factual knowledge*), B2 (*understand conceptual knowledge*), A6 (*create* [based on] *factual knowledge*), B6 (*create* [based on] *conceptual knowledge*), and C6 (*create* [based on] *procedural knowledge*).

THE ALIGNMENT QUESTION

If all three objectives are related to *understand conceptual knowledge*, as our initial analysis of the statements of the objectives suggests, then several alignment problems are evident in this unit (see Table 12.3). Reclassifying the second and third objectives would produce a better alignment. Both of these objectives can be written in a "how to" form: Students will learn **how to** examine and interpret a set of data on the geology of the local region. Students will learn **how to** compare the geology of the local region to places that have volcanoes. In fact, when we consider the instructional activities themselves, **how to** is what students were expected to learn. As restated, these objectives now fall into cell C3 (*apply procedural knowledge*). As such, both would be aligned with the activities on Days 7–13 and the two assessment conversations.

Even with this change, however, other alignment problems are evident in Table 12.3. For example, only one of the criteria on the scoring rubric relates directly to the "theoretical" objective (Objective 1). The other criteria are associated with *remembering factual knowledge* and *creating* [based] on *factual*, *conceptual*, and *procedural knowledge*.

Similarly, the alignment would be strengthened if students had spent more class time "pulling things together" in preparing the group project. Apparently, the project was done with little, if any, input from the teacher. As such it was clearly an assessment of student learning independent of teacher guidance and assistance, unlike so many of the projects in the other vignettes.

PART 5: CLOSING QUESTIONS

As with the analysis of all our vignettes, we were left with a few unanswered questions. We raise three of the most important in this closing section.

1. **What is the proper role of pre-instructional activities in the overall delivery of instruction?** Mr. Parker planned a unit that was supposed to last eight days. By the end of the first four days, halfway through the "planned" unit, he had provided an orientation to the students about the unit, had them determine their task, and had them draw their conceptualization of a volcano (labeling it appropriately and explaining how it "works"). These activities, though important, are not truly instructional activities. We consider them "pre-instructional activities"; that is, they are a "jumping off" point for instruction. In light of Mr. Parker's perceived need for these activities, he should have extended the initial time estimates for the unit. This extension would likely have reduced the time constraints that he felt later in the unit. Finally, it is somewhat surprising that students were not asked to re-draw their conceptualization of a volcano as a post-assessment. That would have been a direct assessment of learning relative to the initial unit objective.

2. **Should instructional units be planned primarily in terms of the achievement of objectives or the completion of activities?** All available evidence suggests that midway through the eighth day the students agreed that volcanoes were very unlikely to occur in their community. On that basis, they could have begun to write their letters to the County Commissioner. Mr. Parker had more activities planned for the students, however, that re-

quired students to enlarge the scope of their investigation beyond the county lines. Enlarging the scope was certainly a worthwhile activity, but the result in relation to attaining the overall unit goal seems negative. The consensus achieved at the end of Day 8 was replaced by a diversity of opinion by the end of Day 12. The additional activities interfered with the consensual understanding each group needed to write the letter to the County Commissioner. This example raises the issue of the proper relationship between objectives and instructional activities in planning and, perhaps more important, in delivering an instructional unit.

3. **What role can the Taxonomy Table play in diagnosing learning problems?** On the seventh day, Mr. Parker's students were given four questions to answer. The first concerned *remembering factual knowledge*, the second and fourth questions pertained to *understanding conceptual knowledge*, and the third question asked students to *apply procedural knowledge*. The next day, Mr. Parker engaged in an "assessment conversation" with his students based on their answers to these four questions. During this conversation he learned that students did *remember* the *factual knowledge* and had achieved some degree of *understanding* of the *conceptual knowledge*. But they apparently had difficulty *applying procedural knowledge*. Once this problem was addressed, students gained the level of understanding that Mr. Parker sought. This example points to the possibility of using the Taxonomy Table to pinpoint deficiencies in student learning. When deficiencies are identified, future instruction can be altered to help students overcome them.

Department of Engineering and Public Safety
County Commissioner's Office
Anytown, USA 12345

April 10

Re: Earthquake and Volcano Hazard Study for Our County

It is well known that earthquakes and volcanoes can destroy property and injure or even kill people. In January, a major earthquake rocked Los Angeles, California. The earthquake killed many people and caused an estimated 30 billion dollars in damage to homes, businesses, roads, and bridges. In May of 1980, the Mt. St. Helens Volcano in Washington erupted violently. The force of the volcanic eruption tore trees out of the ground 15 miles away. Closer to home, two earthquakes struck a town 100 miles from us in January, and an earthquake shook Metropolis in 1986. Could an earthquake strong enough to destroy bridges and buildings strike our county? Need we be concerned about a volcano?

We need you to study the geology of our area and tell us whether or not a damaging earthquake or volcano might happen here. Your results will help us decide if our county should prepare a plan for a geologic hazard. Such a plan would involve preparing for an evacuation and making emergency medical plans.

This challenging and important problem will require effort and creativity to solve. To assist you in this task, we gathered geologic data from federal and state geological offices. This information includes geologic maps, cross-sections, oil well drilling records, and rock samples. We also asked that a *Research Materials Packet* be sent to you. We think it will help you to interpret geologic evidence. The packet has a summary of the theory of plate tectonics, which will help you understand the causes of earthquakes and volcanoes. It also contains newsclippings about recent earthquakes and volcanoes, and information on the geology of places that have frequent earthquakes and volcanic eruptions.

Your task is to use this information to interpret the geology of our area, compare your results to places that have many earthquakes (California) and volcanoes (Mt. St. Helens, Washington), and decide if our county needs a safety and evacuation plan.

The final report that you submit to our office should include:

A. Your *decision* as to the likelihood that a damaging earthquake and/or a volcano will affect our county.
B. An *explanation* of your decision that is supported by comparing the *evidence* you have studied to *scientific theory* for the causes of earthquakes and volcanoes.
C. Maps that show any volcanic rocks and past earthquakes in our region.
D. A geologic cross-section through our county showing the underground structure of rocks.
E. Any other items and explanations that you think support your decision.

During the next several weeks, professional geologists may visit your classroom to look at your work. They may ask you to talk about the way you are thinking and reasoning about this problem. These scientists will be involved in the review of your final report.

Thank you for your attention to this most important matter. Good luck!

Sincerely yours,

Fred Luckino
County Commissioner

ATTACHMENT B RUBRIC FOR SCORING PERFORMANCE ON THE EARTHQUAKE UNIT TERMINAL TASK

Definition of the task: Acting in the capacity of a scientist who understands volcanoes and theories concerning their causes and geographical distribution, examine the geological data of our region and compare those data with corresponding data from California. Based on your findings, write a letter to our County Commissioner that includes a summary of your findings that is accurate and a recommendation concerning the need to invest money in preparing an Earthquake Evacuation Plan for our region. The recommendation should be consistent with the evidence you have collected and it should acknowledge alternative explanations.

Criteria	Levels of Performance
Accuracy of information in summary	3—The information in the summary is complete and accurate. 2—Some important information is missing, misconstrued, misrepresented in the summary. 1—Significant portions of the summary are inaccurate and/or important data are missing.
Consistency with the evidence	3—Recommendations are consistent with the evidence that is available. 2—Recommendations are generally consistent with the evidence that is available—slight inconsistencies are ignored in the letter. 1—Recommendations are in large part inconsistent with the evidence.
Acknowledgment of alternative explanations	3—Recommendations are nicely qualified in terms of rival explanations for the findings of the study. 2—Recommendations are advanced, with a caveat added to acknowledge rival explanations, but the caveat appears more as an "add-on" than as a fully integrated piece of thinking. 1—Recommendations appear to be shrill and definite—with only little (or no) acknowledgment of rival explanations.
Clarity	3—Recommendations are stated succinctly and presented in a logical order. Diagrams and drawings are labeled and easy to understand. 2—The link between narratives and diagrams is difficult to make. Recommendation is vague. 1—Recommendation is not responsive to the task. Recommendation is not supported with evidence.
Perfect Score = 12	

CHAPTER 13

Report Writing Vignette

This vignette describes a unit on report writing developed by Ms. Christine Evans and Ms. Deanne McCreadie, both of whom also taught it. Ms. Colleen Vandie, the teacher in the vignette, represents them and their experiences.

This unit was taught to a class of fourth-grade children during the early spring, after the class members had learned to work with one another and after some basic writing criteria had been studied and mastered by most of the class. The class included 28 students, 13 boys and 15 girls. About half of the class were minorities—Asian Americans, African Americans, and Hispanic Americans. The class represented a considerable spread in academic ability. However, none of the children was identified as needing special education services.

There is a strong sense of educational accountability in the state, with students, teachers, and parents being very conscious of the state content standards and the consequences of not meeting those standards. As a consequence, I carefully selected the objectives for this unit so they closely corresponded with the state Content Standards for English Language Arts. Indeed, even the language in which the objectives are phrased reflects the standards. My students will be assessed on these standards at the close of the fifth-grade year, and students who fail to meet the standards will be required to attend summer school and/or be retained in fifth grade until they meet them. Thus, I was concerned about preparing all the students for this "high stakes" assessment. Finally, because of the state emphasis on teaching thematically, in ways that integrate various disciplines, this unit emphasizes language arts topics while at the same time addressing important fourth-grade social studies topics.

Based on my previous experience with this unit, I allocated six weeks to complete it. Each day, we spent about 90 minutes on the unit.

PART 1: OBJECTIVES

There were four principal objectives. The students should learn to:

1. identify, locate, and select sources of information related to writing a report on a famous person in American history;

2. select information about a famous person in American history that is relevant to the purposes of their written and oral reports;

3. write informative text that communicates to classmates and other appropriate audiences in the school important aspects of the life of a famous person in American history and which includes students' opinions of how the famous American's contributions impacted society; and

4. deliver a talk to the class about a portion of the written report. (The talk should include the essential information pertaining to the segment of the famous person's life the student has elected to share, and be well organized and delivered in an effective manner.)

COMMENTARY

Objective 1 contains three verbs: "identify," "locate," and "select." The key to classifying this objective is the verb "select." In Table 5.1, on the back inside cover, selecting is an alternative name for *differentiating*, which is a cognitive process in the category *Analyze*. From all available materials, students are to differentiate those that are relevant to writing a report on a person famous in American history from those that are not. The noun phrase in Objective 1 is "sources of information." As noted in previous vignettes, sources of information are materials. Thus, the noun phrase provides us with little help in determining the relevant type of knowledge. One scenario is that students will learn (or have learned) criteria for distinguishing relevant from irrelevant materials. This suggests *Conceptual knowledge* (e.g., "What makes relevant materials relevant materials?"). A second scenario is that students will be taught a procedure for identifying, locating, and selecting relevant materials. This case involves *Procedural knowledge*. If *Procedural knowledge* is at issue here, however, then students would be expected to *apply procedural knowledge* (i.e., carry out the steps). If we stay with *Analyze*, the most appropriate placement of the objective in the Taxonomy Table is in cell B4, *analyze* [based on] *conceptual knowledge* (although the alternative inference, *apply procedural knowledge*, is certainly not unreasonable).

Objective 2 contains the single verb "select." Again, then, we are dealing with *differentiating* (*Analyze*). The noun is "information" (rather than "sources of information"). The statement of the objective includes qualifiers that pertain to the information to be selected from the located sources. The information must be (1) about a famous person in American history and (2) relevant to preparing written and oral reports. The first qualifier is simply a restatement of what was already included in the first objective. The second qualifier, however, is unique. Of all the information available about the famous American, students must select the most relevant—relevant to the preparation of written and oral reports. In combination, all of these clues support the placement of Objective 2 in the same cell as the first one, B4 (*analyze* [based on] *conceptual knowledge*).

For her last two objectives, Ms. Vandie is interested in having her students learn to construct products: a manuscript ("informative text") for Objective 3 and a talk (based on the written text) for Objective 4. Thus, the meaning of the two ambiguous verbs, "write" and "deliver," is clarified within the context of the entire objective. They both signify "constructing," an alternative term for *producing*, which is a cognitive process in the *Create* category.

Much of the information contained in these two objectives pertains to the criteria that will be used to evaluate the products. The manuscript will be evaluated in terms of (1) communication with an identified audience, (2) important aspects of the person's life, and (3) the writer's opinions of the impact of the person's contributions on society. The talk will be evaluated according to whether it (1) includes essential information, (2) is well organized, and (3) is delivered in an effective manner. Because these are the criteria used for the purpose of evaluation, knowledge of them constitutes *Conceptual knowledge*. In addition to this *Conceptual knowledge*, students need to have knowledge of fairly specific details about the person being written or spoken about (i.e., *Factual knowledge*). Thus, these last two objectives are placed in two cells of the Taxonomy Table: A6 (*create* [based on] *factual knowledge*) and B6 (*create* [based on] *conceptual knowledge*).

A summary of the analysis of the objectives in terms of the Taxonomy Table is provided in Table 13.1.

PART 2: INSTRUCTIONAL ACTIVITIES

Lesson 1

I introduced the unit to the students by describing in some length what comprises the format of a written and an oral informative report. Through class discussion, and using the blackboard to record relevant contributions from the class, emphasis was given to purpose, audience, sources of information, and other elements derived from the state standards document and elsewhere. In combination, these criteria were adapted from the Delaware General Rubric for Writing. I ended the discussion by displaying a "kid-friendly" rubric for the written report (Attachment A) and set of rating scales for the oral presentation (Attachment B). These were to be used by students as they planned their reports and by me as I assessed the quality of their work.

COMMENTARY

As shown in Attachment A (at the end of the chapter), the rubric contains five criteria for guiding and evaluating written reports: development, organization, word choice, sentence formation, and writing rules. The class discussion guidelines include other criteria: purpose, audience, and sources of information. Finally, the ratings scales in Attachment B (at the end of the chapter) provide a third set of criteria. In our framework, knowledge of criteria is associated with

13.1 ANALYSIS OF THE REPORT WRITING VIGNETTE IN TERMS OF THE TAXONOMY TABLE BASED ON STATED OBJECTIVES

THE KNOWLEDGE DIMENSION	THE COGNITIVE PROCESS DIMENSION					
	1. REMEMBER	2. UNDERSTAND	3. APPLY	4. ANALYZE	5. EVALUATE	6. CREATE
A. FACTUAL KNOWLEDGE						Objective 3 Objective 4
B. CONCEPTUAL KNOWLEDGE				Objective 1 Objective 2		Objective 3 Objective 4
C. PROCEDURAL KNOWLEDGE						
D. META-COGNITIVE KNOWLEDGE						

Key
Objective 1 = Select sources of information related to writing a report on a famous person in American history.
Objective 2 = Select information about a famous person in American history that is relevant to the purposes of students' written and oral reports.
Objective 3 = Write informative text that communicates to classmates and other appropriate audiences in the school important aspects of the life of a famous person in American history and that includes students' opinions of how the famous American's contributions impacted society.
Objective 4 = Deliver a talk to the class about a portion of the written report.

Conceptual knowledge. At this point, we are not certain of the appropriate cognitive process to use with *Conceptual knowledge.* It seems reasonable to assume, however, that because Lesson 1 is introductory, the teacher's intent is simply to provide an overview of the criteria. Consequently, the objective we infer from this activity falls into the process category *Remember;* that is, students should *remember conceptual knowledge.*

Lesson 2

The second lesson dealt with "taking notes" and identifying themes. I began by showing the class a short video, asking the students to take notes on large pieces of construction paper, cut into fourths. (I believed that using the video instead of a passage from a book as a prompt decreased the chances that students would elect to copy passages straight from the text.) The plan was to post the notes the students took on the blackboard so that the whole class could see them and comment on them. Students shared their notes and as I taped them to the blackboard, the class discussed the fact that some notes could be grouped together on the same topic or theme. I moved the notes around on the blackboard at the direction of class members until there were several groupings. The students were then invited to give each grouping a title.

COMMENTARY

It seems fairly clear that the cognitive process emphasized is *classifying* (*Understand*). Since students are placing specific "notes" into thematic categories and then naming them, two types of knowledge are involved: *Conceptual knowledge* and then *Factual knowledge.* The *Conceptual knowledge* is for *Understanding;* the *Factual knowledge* is to be *Remembered.*

Ms. Vandie begins to implement a sequence of activities often used in connection with producing (*Create*) a product. The procedure illustrates scaffolding and modeling. Scaffolding is seen in moving the task from scaled-down simpler versions of the materials under study to "the real thing" when students are working on their class projects. Ms. Vandie's modeling procedures show the students how to proceed and also prompt them by "thinking aloud" behaviors on the teacher's part.

Lesson 3

During the next lesson, I read a book aloud and modeled how I would take notes on the passages that I read. The students also took notes as I was reading. As before, the notes were posted on the blackboard, placed into groups, and the groups of notes were given titles. Students then read in unison a passage displayed on the overhead projector. They watched as I modeled note taking and the classification of notes. As I was pasting my notes on the board, I prompted the students by "thinking aloud" about the decisions I was making about grouping the notes and about titling the groups.

After a question-and-answer session, I engaged the students in note taking with another common reading, one that was considerably longer than the passage on the overhead projector. Each student had a photocopy of a four-page essay about George Washington Carver, and they were instructed to take notes on the passage. Working in small groups, with approximately four students in each group, students entered the notes they had taken on "Post-It" slips and grouped them on a large sheet of poster paper. As a group, the students classified their notes and attempted to name the groups they formed.

As I observed the students' progress at this point, I decided the students needed additional instruction in note taking. I called the class back together and once again modeled note-taking procedures. The students then returned to working within their groups. When the lesson was complete, the groups reported the results of their work to the entire class. In the discussion that ensued, the class identified those groupings that seemed to be most helpful in learning about George Washington Carver.

COMMENTARY

In this lesson the teacher is teaching by modeling. The issue becomes what students are expected to learn from this approach to teaching. Are they to develop *Procedural knowledge*, which they are then to *Apply* to the note-taking–grouping–naming sequence? Are they to develop *Metacognitive knowledge* (i.e., their own unique strategy) for performing the task? To complicate matters further, the second step of the sequence involves cognitive processes in the category *Analyze*. At present, then, we opt for two objectives: *apply procedural knowledge* and *analyze conceptual knowledge.* Although not an objective in its own right, *apply metacognitive knowledge* may be part of the *analyze conceptual knowledge* activity.

Lesson 4

During the next lesson, I asked the students, still working in groups, to read a book that focused on the life of Matthew Henson, a famous American. All the children in the class were expected to read the same book. Students who were not reading at grade level were paired with a partner or listened to the book on audiotape. The members of each group were then asked to select as a group the aspect of his life they would like to emphasize and describe to the class. Each group needed to choose one aspect of Matthew Henson's life—childhood, adulthood, awards, contributions to society, and so forth. Each group used the note-taking–grouping–naming approach to record and to organize the important facts concerning their single aspect of Henson's life. I made overhead transparencies of each group's "final" product, and the notes and classifications with titles were shared in class and critiqued by the class. I made a point to commend those elements apparent in the groups' work that complied with my standards of good note taking.

COMMENTARY

At least four verbs help us decide on the cognitive processes being sought by the teacher: "select" (*Analyze*), "use" (*Apply*), "organize" (*Analyze*), and "critique" (*Evaluate*). The first three verbs suggest that Lesson 4 is a follow-up activity to Lesson 3. Thus, we continue with *analyze conceptual knowledge* and *apply procedural knowledge*. We add *evaluate* [based on] *conceptual knowledge*. Students are evaluating based on the categories (concepts), not on the process (procedure) students use to arrive at them.

Lessons 5–8

During the next several lessons the emphasis shifted to having students identify famous persons they wanted to nominate to their group members as an object of intense study. I gave them a list of famous Americans from which they could choose. The list included men, women, Whites, African Americans, Asian Americans, Native Americans, Hispanic Americans, Presidents, inventors, civil rights workers, and many others. Besides making an effort to allow students to make choices from options that reflected the cultural and ethnic diversity of the United States, I was careful to see to it that the school library had several appropriate books for each of the names on my list.

Students were given time to explore the options available to them. Some students had never heard of the "famous" people on the list. Some students looked them up on the Internet or in the library, or asked me questions about them.

After several class periods of exploration, the students were ready to engage in a process for making group decisions about the person they would be studying. Interestingly, some boys chose to report on women and some girls elected to write about men. Both white and black students opted to study famous Americans of different races. Although their reasons were not clear to me, I was pleased with the variety of student choices. In their groups, students tried to "sell" their preferred choice to the others in the group. Using democratic procedures, each group chose one famous American to study for the purposes of addressing the objectives of this unit.

COMMENTARY

This four-day process of choosing a person for study does not relate directly to any of the objectives associated with this unit. Certainly, though, learning to work together, learning to take the views of others into account, and learning to value democratic processes are important outcomes of schooling. In fact, the teacher may well have course or year-long objectives that deal with these intended outcomes. The point is that we will not attempt to classify these activities in terms of the Taxonomy Table for this unit.

Lesson 9

The next lesson dealt with preparing a bibliography. Students were encouraged to search their family's libraries, the school library, the Internet, and other sources to find books and articles on the famous American they had selected. I helped students with reading difficulties to locate appropriate resources. I began this lesson by sharing books about George Washington Carver, describing how this first collection of books could be sorted in terms of usefulness and how they might be entered into a bibliography. One or two books were clearly quite difficult and included information not accessible to fourth-grade students. Another was a picture book written for primary students that included very little text about George Washington Carver. Four or five books were "on target" in terms of their appropriateness for the assignment. The students watched as I sorted the books and discussed why some of the sources were more useful than were others. I then demonstrated how to prepare a bibliography chart for the sources deemed most useful.

COMMENTARY

Two objectives seem important here. The first is learning to differentiate books (i.e., sources of information) in terms of their usefulness for the project (the criteria on which to differentiate them). This objective is classified as *analyze* [based on] *conceptual knowledge*. The second objective is learning how to prepare a bibliography chart. Without more information, we classify this objective as *apply procedural knowledge*. If it were taught as a generic strategy rather than as unique to social studies, however, the activity would be *apply metacognitive knowledge*.

Lessons 10–16

Beginning with Lesson 10 and lasting about five days, the students began researching the famous American their group had selected for study. Students searched in the library and on computers to find relevant sources. Working closely with the Media Specialist in the school, I had arranged for the class to spend several periods in the library. Students pored over the sources that were available to them, determining whether the sources provided potentially useful information about their famous American.

My intent was that students would behave as "real" researchers and determine topics as they began the research process. For the first two days (Lessons 10 and 11), the students only reviewed books and took notes on Post-It notes.

It was a quiet time for everyone to do some reading and to take notes. At the end of each day, the group members simply stuck the notes onto their poster board. At the end of these two days, the group members began to review their notes and began moving them around to determine the themes that individual group members might address. I emphasized the importance of cooperation during group work so that all group members were able to participate. Post-It notes that included several ideas often needed to be rewritten so the notes fit only one category. These categorization activities lasted another three days (Lessons 12–14).

In monitoring their work, I found that some groups of students were unable to locate themes—even after preparing as many as 50 Post-It notes. When the students tried to sort the cards into themes, no common threads seemed apparent to them. After they had struggled with the "finding themes" assignment unsuccessfully for two days, I elected to help students. Either I would suggest a theme or two that I saw reflected in the group's notes or I would urge the student to reread particular passages from the books they had located.

COMMENTARY

The emphasis in this set of seven lessons is on students using the three-step procedure they had been taught in Lessons 3 and 4: (1) take notes, (2) categorize notes according to themes, and (3) name the theme. Here we have *Analyze* embedded within *Procedural knowledge*; that is, the second step of the procedure requires that students engage in the process of differentiating. Because this step is a part of the application process, we categorize the objective here as *apply procedural knowledge*.

Now, after several days of note taking, the groups' reading and research became more focused as group members began reading more deeply into the themes that had "bubbled up" from the note-taking process. By Lesson 15, I asked the groups to determine how the themes would be divided among the group members for presentation. Each group member was to be assigned a unique theme. In this way, the individual student reports were less likely to be overlapping in content and each would be more likely to look and sound quite different.

After reviewing the sources pertinent to the selected themes, each student prepared a carefully constructed bibliographical chart, as they had been previously taught (Lessons 15 and 16). These were given to me at the end of Lesson 16. I found that some of them were skimpy, listing only one or two sources. I tried to help these students either to find more material or to choose another famous person. Other students included books or other materials that were well beyond their reading levels. I assisted these students in finding more appropriate sources.

COMMENTARY

The phrase that helps us categorize this activity is "as they had been previously taught." The students were taught a particular procedure for preparing their bibliographic chart and are expected to follow it. Thus, we place this activity in the Taxonomy Table in cell C3 (*apply procedural knowledge*).

In Lesson 15, the students determined how the themes would be divided among the group members for presentation. This activity falls in the same category as the activities of Lessons 5–8 and so also is not classified in the Taxonomy Table for this unit (see the discussion on pages 216–217).

Lessons 17–20

Beginning with Lesson 17 and continuing through Lesson 20, we moved into a "Writers' Workshop" mode. Students drafted their written reports on the themes reflected in the lives of their famous persons. I held conferences with individual students on the content and organization of their written reports. Several students needed more than one conference. Early drafts were read by fellow students who gave suggestions in peer conferences about how the reports could be improved. In reading the drafts, the students used the "kid-friendly" rubrics that were introduced to them on the first day of the unit to guide their comments and suggestions. The rubric was somewhat confusing to some students, so I brought them together in a small group to explicitly teach the criteria and descriptors that were designed to guide their writing. In addition, the students had access to a Revision and Editing Checklist (see Attachment C at the end of the chapter) that had been used often in previous Writers' Workshop activities in the class. After intensive work in class (and at home), the projects were handed in on time.

COMMENTARY

The activities during these four lessons focus on producing the written reports (*Create*) and critiquing early drafts of them (*Evaluate*). "Producing" requires both *Factual knowledge* (the specifics) and *Conceptual knowledge* (the themes). "Critiquing" requires primarily *Conceptual knowledge* (namely, the scoring rubric and the Revision and Editing Checklist). Thus, we place these activities in cells A6 (*creating* [based on] *factual knowledge*), B6 (*creating* [based on] *conceptual knowledge*), and B5 (*evaluating* [based on] *conceptual knowledge*).

Lessons 21–30

However, the unit was not finished when the written reports were submitted. What remained was the oral reporting! At this point, students were asked to review the rating scales used to evaluate oral reports (see Attachment B). Students were asked to select and share with their group members the aspect of their famous person's life they intended to present. The group listened to the plans each of its members had for sharing—and how they might make the oral presentation informative and interesting. Some students planned to wear a costume that would represent the person they were describing. Others planned to share various artifacts that would provide some concrete examples. Still others prepared displays. Each student understood that his/her report was to take no longer than five minutes. I allocated 25 minutes a day for 10 days to the oral reporting—giving students a brief time to respond to an oral report with questions and/or comments (Lessons 21–30). This activity culminated six weeks of instruction on the unit.

COMMENTARY

To analyze this activity in terms of the Taxonomy Table, we must rely on the rating scales used to evaluate oral reports (Attachment B). Because the rating scales are criteria, we suggest that they represent *Conceptual knowledge*. The presentations are based on *Factual knowledge*. We further suggest that students are expected to use the ratings scales in planning their oral presentations. Thus, we believe the appropriate cognitive process category is *Create*. The inferred objective, then, takes the form *create* [based on] *conceptual knowledge* and *factual knowledge* (since factual knowledge comprises the raw material for the written report).

A summary of our analysis of the entire set of instructional activities in terms of the Taxonomy Table is shown in Table 13.2.

PART 3: ASSESSMENT

I assessed and evaluated my students' learning throughout the unit. Specifically, I assessed and coached them in their use of research procedures, in their evaluations of materials, in their selections of themes, and in their writing assignments. When students needed more individual guidance, I provided them with explicit instruction to improve their understanding. In this effort, I relied on the judgments of my colleague, the Media Specialist, who also observed very carefully the progress the students were making.

I worked closely with the students as they located and selected information about the famous Americans they were studying. Some students were facile in using the library and the computer to locate information. Others were less resourceful. I continued to coach those students who were having difficulty and engaged the more sophisticated students in helping their fellow group members who were having some difficulty. After consulting with the Media Specialist and considering my own notes in my journal, I was convinced that almost everyone improved in this area by the end of the unit.

13.2 ANALYSIS OF THE REPORT WRITING VIGNETTE IN TERMS OF THE TAXONOMY TABLE BASED ON INSTRUCTIONAL ACTIVITIES

THE KNOWLEDGE DIMENSION	THE COGNITIVE PROCESS DIMENSION					
	1. REMEMBER	2. UNDERSTAND	3. APPLY	4. ANALYZE	5. EVALUATE	6. CREATE
A. FACTUAL KNOWLEDGE	Lesson 2 activities					**Objective 3; Objective 4** Lessons 17–20 activities; Lessons 21–30 activities
B. CONCEPTUAL KNOWLEDGE	Lesson 1 activities	Lesson 2 activities		**Objective 1; Objective 2** Lessons 3, 4, 9 activities	Lesson 4 activities; Lessons 17–20 activities	**Objective 3; Objective 4** Lessons 17–20 activities; Lessons 21–30 activities
C. PROCEDURAL KNOWLEDGE			Lessons 3, 4 activities; Lessons 9–14 activities; Lesson 16 activities			
D. META-COGNITIVE KNOWLEDGE						

Key
Objective 1 = Select sources of information related to writing a report on a famous person in American history.
Objective 2 = Select information about a famous person in American history that is relevant to the purposes of students' written and oral reports.
Objective 3 = Write informative text that communicates to classmates and other appropriate audiences in the school important aspects of the life of a famous person in American history and that includes students' opinions of how the famous American's contributions impacted society.
Objective 4 = Deliver a talk to the class about a portion of the written report.
Note: As discussed in the text, activities related to Lessons 5–8 and 15 are not analyzed in terms of the Taxonomy Table.

The Media Specialist and I paid strict attention to the judgments students made in selecting resources to use in their reports. As in most areas, some students needed more help than others. The selection process was confounded not only by the factor "relevance" but also by "accessibility." Some students were able to select relevant sources, but the reading levels of the sources were too difficult for them. Individual assistance at this time became very important. Nevertheless, by the end of the unit, we were confident that most of the students grasped the idea of "relevance" in making their choices of materials.

To evaluate the third and fourth objectives, I was able to use the Primary Trait Scoring Guide (see Attachment D) and the ratings scales for oral reports (Attachment B), respectively. The results suggest that while most of the students seemed to have met the standards set for these two objectives, some had not. I carefully studied the efforts of those who had not performed well to identify areas of weakness. Since the unit was taught in early March, there was time to re-teach some of these important skills and understandings in subsequent units.

COMMENTARY

Both informal and formal assessments are made of student learning. The informal assessments take place during Lesson 3, Lessons 10 and 11, and Lesson 16. In Lesson 3, the assessment focuses on students' note-taking skills (i.e., how to take notes). This represents *apply procedural knowledge*. In Lessons 10 and 11, the assessment focuses on students' ability to locate themes (i.e., to analyze the information on the Post-It notes). This represents *analyze conceptual knowledge* (with *Conceptual knowledge* used in the themes or categories formed by the students). Finally, the assessment during Lesson 16 focuses on the bibliography prepared by the students. Concerns are raised by the teacher over the number of entries and reading levels of the materials included. Since this assessment clearly relates to the first two objectives, we classify it as *analyze conceptual knowledge* (although, as mentioned in our discussion of these objectives, there is an element of *apply procedural knowledge* as well).

The two formal assessments are the written reports and oral presentations. To analyze these assessments, we focus first on the Primary Trait Scoring Guide (Attachment D) and the rating scales used to evaluate oral reports (Attachment B). Both are conceptual frameworks that can be used to evaluate the quality of the products produced by the students. It is important to note that the verb "evaluate" here pertains to the teacher, not the students. The issue for us is what is being evaluated, and simply stated, it is the products that the students have created. The products contain both *Factual knowledge* (details) and *Conceptual knowledge* (themes). We suggest, therefore, that we are dealing with *creating* [based on] *factual* and *conceptual knowledge*. Hence, we place our inferred objectives in two cells: A6 (*create* [based on] *factual knowledge*) and B6 (*create* [based on] *conceptual knowledge*).

A summary of our analysis of both the informal and formal assessments in terms of the Taxonomy Table is shown in Table 13.3.

PART 4: CLOSING COMMENTARY

In this section we examine the vignette in terms of our four basic questions: the learning question, the instruction question, the assessment question, and the alignment question.

THE LEARNING QUESTION

As the vignette title suggests, this is a unit on report writing. The overall purpose of the unit is for students to learn to write research papers and to learn to deliver portions of those papers orally. This purpose is best captured in Objectives 3 and 4 (see Table 13.1). In terms of the Taxonomy Table, this main purpose can be represented as *create* [written reports and oral presentations from] *factual* and *conceptual knowledge*. Within the context of the entire unit, Objectives 1 and 2 are best considered prerequisites to or facilitative of Objectives 3 and 4. They are very important prerequisites or facilitators, though. When students achieve the first two objectives, they have acquired the "raw material" they need for Objectives 3 and 4. Achieving Objectives 1 and 2, however, requires that students are able to *Analyze* material in terms of its relevance, importance, and, in the case of fourth-grade students, readability. To do this, they need to understand the meaning of "relevance," "importance," and "readability," which requires *Conceptual knowledge*.

THE INSTRUCTION QUESTION

The early activities (Lessons 1 and 2) were intended to introduce the unit to the students (see Table 13.2). Ms. Vandie told students about criteria that would be used to evaluate their final products, and the students began to explore how they were to go about choosing the information that would eventually find its way into the final products.

As shown in Table 13.2, many lessons were devoted to *applying procedural knowledge*. The teacher expected students to use a three-step procedure in moving from the available resources to preparation for writing the report: (1) take notes, (2) group the notes according to themes, and (3) assign a name to each theme. In these lessons, the teacher modeled the procedure. In addition, she provided individual assistance (i.e., "coaching") to those students who were unable to apply the procedure. It is instructive to note that the three-step procedure assumes that proper materials have been selected. The validity of this assumption is called into question by the teacher's descriptions of Lessons 15

13.3 ANALYSIS OF THE REPORT WRITING VIGNETTE IN TERMS OF THE TAXONOMY TABLE BASED ON ASSESSMENTS

THE KNOWLEDGE DIMENSION	THE COGNITIVE PROCESS DIMENSION					
	1. REMEMBER	2. UNDERSTAND	3. APPLY	4. ANALYZE	5. EVALUATE	6. CREATE
A. FACTUAL KNOWLEDGE	Lesson 2 activities					Objective 3; Objective 4 Lessons 17–2C activities; Lessons 21–3C activities Assess F1, F2
B. CONCEPTUAL KNOWLEDGE	Lesson 1 activities	Lesson 2 activities		Objective 1; Objective 2 Lessons 3, 4 activities Assess In2, In3	Lesson 4 activities; Lessons 17–20 activities	Objective 3; Objective 4 Lessons 17–2C activities; Lessons 21–3C activities Assess F1, F2
C. PROCEDURAL KNOWLEDGE			Lessons 3, 4 activities; Lessons 9–14 activities; Lesson 16 activities Assess In1, In3			
D. META-COGNITIVE KNOWLEDGE						

Key
Objective 1 = Select sources of information related to writing a report on a famous person in American history.
Objective 2 = Select information about a famous person in American history that is relevant to the purposes of students' written and oral reports.
Objective 3 = Write informative text that communicates to classmates and other appropriate audiences in the school important aspects of the life of a famous person in American history and that includes students' opinions of how the famous American's contributions impacted society.
Objective 4 = Deliver a talk to the class about a portion of the written report.
Assess In1, In2, and In3 refer to three separate informal assessments; assess F1 (written report) and F2 (oral presentation) refer to the tw formal assessments.
Note: As discussed in the text, activities related to Lessons 5–8 and 15 are not analyzed in terms of the Taxonomy Table.
Dark shading indicates the strongest alignment—an objective, an instructional activity, and an assessment are all present in the same cell. Lighter shading indicates two of the three are present.

and 16. Apparently, many students had not located a sufficient number of appropriate sources.

About halfway through the unit (Lessons 17–20), the emphasis shifted to the more complex objectives: *evaluate* [based on] *conceptual knowledge*, and *create* [based on] *factual* and *conceptual knowledge*. The format for these lessons was a "Writers' Workshop." Students worked on their written reports and critiqued the draft reports of other students.

Finally, the last ten days of the unit were given over to the oral presentations. Students had a set of rating scales to use in planning their oral presentations (see Attachment B). *Planning* is a cognitive process in the category *Create*; the rating scales represent criteria (*Conceptual knowledge*). Additionally, however, the students possess *Factual knowledge* about the famous Americans they have studied, which is organized around the themes they have identified (*Conceptual knowledge*). Thus, we classify this two-week-long activity as *create* [based on] *factual* and *conceptual knowledge*.

THE ASSESSMENT QUESTION

Both formal and informal assessments were used. As shown in Table 13.3, the informal assessments tapped some combination of *analyze conceptual knowledge* and *apply procedural knowledge*. It is interesting that *analyzing conceptual knowledge* was an integral part of the *Procedural knowledge* students were taught to apply. In this case, then, one objective (*analyze conceptual knowledge*) is embedded within the other (*apply procedural knowledge*). Table 13.3 shows that the informal assessments provided information to the teacher about student progress on the first two objectives.

In contrast with the informal assessments, the formal assessments focused on the second two objectives. What is interesting, however, is the use of fairly generic rating scales and scoring rubrics to assess Objectives 3 and 4. What gets lost in the generic approach is the specific criteria embedded within the statement of the objectives (e.g., "how the famous American's contributions impacted society" in Objective 3 and "essential information pertaining to the segment of the famous person's life the student has elected to share" in Objective 4).

THE ALIGNMENT QUESTION

Table 13.3 provides the information we need to address the alignment question. In fact, some of the alignment issues were either addressed or alluded to in our discussion of the previous questions. In our treatment of the instruction question, for example, we mentioned that the initial activities provided students with a general overview of the unit. It is not surprising, then, that they are not aligned with any of the specific objectives or with the assessments. Similarly, in our discussion of the assessment question, we noted that the informal assessments are aligned with the first two objectives, whereas the formal assessments are aligned with the last two objectives.

Strong alignment is evident in cells A6 (*create* [based on] *factual knowledge)*, B4 (*analyze* [based on] *conceptual knowledge*), and B6 (*create* [based on] *conceptual knowledge*). Each of these three cells has at least one entry from the objectives, the instructional activities, and the assessments. In contrast, the major misalignment seems to be in cell C3 (*apply procedural knowledge*) and, particularly, cell B5 (*evaluate* [based on] *conceptual knowledge*). But, while cell C3 contains nine lessons of activities, no explicit objective, and two informal assessments as noted above, it is integrally related to cell B4. Similarly, cell B5 relates to five lessons, has no explicit objective and no assessments, either informal or formal, but is linked to the activities in cell A6 and cell B6.

PART 5: CLOSING QUESTIONS

As with the analysis of all our vignettes, we were left with a few unanswered questions. We raise two of the most important in this closing section.

1. **What can be done to improve the learning of *Procedural knowledge* that involves more complex cognitive processes?** One of the major emphases in this unit is getting students to follow a three-step procedure in moving from "raw information" to information that is organized for the purpose of writing a report. The procedure is taking notes, organizing the notes around topics or themes, and then naming the theme. Taking notes involves *differentiating* relevant parts of the material from irrelevant parts. *Organizing* involves determining how the elements (e.g., notes) fit within a structure. Thus, two of the three steps involve cognitive processes associated with *Analyze*. At several points in her discussion, Ms. Vandie suggested that students were having difficulty applying the procedure. Based on our analysis, the difficulty most likely resides with *Analyze* rather than *Apply*. What can be done to help students develop the cognitive processes they need to successfully *apply procedural knowledge*?

2. **In assessing objectives that fit within the process category *Create*, how important is it to have evaluation criteria specific to the content knowledge component of the objective?** We mentioned earlier that the rating scales and scoring rubrics include fairly general criteria. Students would likely benefit from knowledge of these criteria as they work on their written reports or oral presentations. Within our framework, knowledge of criteria used to evaluate is *Conceptual knowledge*. Knowledge of evaluation criteria should not be confused with *knowledge of criteria for determining when to use appropriate procedures*, which is a component of *Procedural knowledge* (see page 54). Yet another type of *Conceptual knowledge* is relevant here. In organizing the information gleaned from reading about the famous Americans, the students placed the relevant information in categories called themes. Knowledge of these categories is also *Conceptual*

knowledge. The rating scales and scoring rubrics include criteria relevant to only knowledge of evaluation criteria, not knowledge of the content categories. Do the themes have a unity to them? Do the titles accurately and appropriately represent the underlying information? How important is it for rating scales and scoring rubrics to include at least some criteria relevant to this second type of *Conceptual knowledge*—knowledge of principles and generalizations?

	DEVELOPMENT	ORGANIZATION	WORD CHOICE	SENTENCE FORMATION	WRITING RULES
4	☐ I have excellent details. ☐ My details are well explained. ☐ My details stick to the topic.	☐ I have an introduction, a body, and a conclusion. ☐ I use transition words to connect the beginning, middle, and end in a logical order.	☐ I vary my word choices. ☐ I use descriptive adjectives, action verbs, and adverbs.	☐ I write complete sentences. ☐ I begin my sentences in different ways. ☐ My sentences make sense.	I use correct: ☐ capitals ☐ punctuation—end marks, commas, apostrophes, and quotation marks ☐ subjects, verbs, and pronouns that agree ☐ spelling
3	☐ I have specific details. ☐ My details are usually well explained. ☐ My details usually stick to the subject.	☐ I have an introduction, a body, and an end. ☐ My details are in an order that makes sense.	☐ I usually vary my word choices. ☐ I use some descriptive adjectives, action verbs, and adverbs.	☐ I usually write complete sentences. ☐ I usually begin my sentences in different ways. ☐ My sentences always make sense.	I usually use correct: ☐ capitals ☐ punctuation—end marks, commas, apostrophes, and quotation marks ☐ subjects, verbs, and pronouns that agree ☐ spelling
2	☐ I have some details. ☐ Some of my details may not belong. ☐ Some of my details need more explanation. ☐ I sometimes stay on topic.	☐ My writing may be missing a beginning, a middle, or an end. ☐ Some of my details are in order.	☐ I sometimes repeat words or ideas. ☐ I need more descriptive and action words.	☐ I sometimes write complete sentences. ☐ I often start my sentences in the same way.	I sometimes use correct: ☐ capitals ☐ punctuation—end marks, commas, apostrophes, and quotation marks ☐ subjects, verbs, and pronouns that agree ☐ spelling
1	☐ I have few or no details. ☐ My piece is very short. ☐ I do not stay on the topic.	☐ My writing has no clear beginning, middle, or end. ☐ My writing is not in order.	☐ I often repeat the same words. ☐ I leave out words. ☐ I need to use descriptive and action words.	☐ My sentences are not complete.	I forget to use correct: ☐ capitals ☐ punctuation—end marks, commas, apostrophes, and quotation marks ☐ subjects, verbs, and pronouns that agree ☐ spelling

ATTACHMENT B SPEAKING

Student Name _____ **Assessment Context(s)** _____

Directions: Rate the student's speaking skills by assigning a score of 1–4 on each criterion listed below. Record any additional comments at the bottom of the page.

Speaking Skills	Needs to Improve	Fair	Good	Excellent
Looks at audience while speaking	1	2	3	4
Maintains good posture	1	2	3	4
Speaks clearly	1	2	3	4
Varies tone and volume appropriately	1	2	3	4
Pronounces words clearly	1	2	3	4
Uses pauses and gestures effectively	1	2	3	4
Does not fidget while speaking	1	2	3	4
Avoids hesitation (e.g., "uh," "er")	1	2	3	4
Speaks in turn	1	2	3	4
Speaks for a specific purpose:				
to inform	1	2	3	4
to entertain	1	2	3	4
to give directions	1	2	3	4
to persuade	1	2	3	4
to express personal feelings and opinions	1	2	3	4

Oral Composition Strategies				
Chooses appropriate topics and material	1	2	3	4
Prepares presentation effectively	1	2	3	4
Organizes information in an effective way	1	2	3	4
Uses visual aids appropriately	1	2	3	4
Achieves purpose of presentation	1	2	3	4
Uses appropriate vocabulary	1	2	3	4
Adapts speaking to purpose and audience	1	2	3	4
Expresses self effectively	1	2	3	4

Comments

_____ Did I write about the **topic**?

_____ Did I **stay on the topic** that I was told to write about?

_____ Did I use **details** in my writing?

_____ Did I give **examples or ideas** for my details?

_____ Did I **organize** my writing?

_____ Did I **write** so that my ideas are **clear** to other people?

_____ Did I **choose words carefully** to express what I want to say?

_____ Did I use **complete sentences**?

_____ Did I use **correct spelling, grammar, capitalization, and punctuation**?

"Revision and Editing Checklist" from Delaware Department of Education. Copyright © Delaware Department of Education. Reprinted with permission.

Name: _____ Date: _____

Possible Points: **Scoring:**

Content:

4 = Always	40–37 = excellent
3 = Usually	36–34 = good
2 = Sometimes	33–31 = average
1 = Seldom	30–28 = needs improvement
0 = Never	27–0 = unsatisfactory

Form:

| 48–45 = excellent |
| 44–41 = good |
| 40–37 = average |
| 36–34 = needs improvement |
| 33–0 = unsatisfactory |

Content:

1. Is the topic focused or narrowed? _____
2. Will the audience be interested in the report? _____
3. Is the report organized (introduction, body, conclusion)? _____
4. Does the introduction reveal the main idea of the report? _____
5. Are the facts in the body relevant to the topic? _____
6. Does the ending summarize, solve the problem, or answer the questions? _____
7. Is the writer's voice evident? _____
8. Does the report make sense? _____
9. Is there evidence of research (sources cited, interviews)? _____
10. Are experiences or prior knowledge of the writer included? _____

                                        Total _____

Form:

1. Does the report have a title? _____
2. Is the first line of each paragraph indented? _____
3. Is every verb form correct? _____
4. Is every pronoun used correctly? _____
5. Do all important words in the title begin with capital letters? _____
6. Does each sentence begin with a capital letter? _____
7. Does every proper noun begin with a capital? _____
8. Does each sentence end with the correct end mark? _____
9. Are there punctuation marks where they are needed? _____
10. Is every word spelled correctly? _____
11. Is the correct format followed? _____
12. Are graphic aids included? (if appropriate, if not appropriate rate 4) _____

                                        Total _____

CHAPTER 14

Addressing Long-standing Problems in Classroom Instruction

We believe our revised Taxonomy can contribute usefully to the discussion of the four fundamental questions we raised in Chapter 1:

- What is important for students to learn in light of the limited school and classroom time available?   (the learning question)

- How does one plan and deliver instruction that will result in high levels of learning for students?   (the instruction question)

- How does one select or design assessment instruments and procedures that provide accurate information about how well students are learning?   (the assessment question)

- How does one ensure that objectives, instruction, and assessment are consistent with one another?   (the alignment question)

At the end of each of our six vignettes, we briefly addressed each of these four questions. Our analyses of the entire set of vignettes, coupled with a great deal of discussion at our meetings over the past several years, have led us to a set of generalizations that relate to these four questions. In this chapter we focus on nine of these generalizations.

Two of our generalizations are related to the learning question.

- Transfer and retention are important goals of instruction. The more complex cognitive processes are useful in this regard. They transfer to other contexts from the one in which they are learned; once developed, they are retained in memory for fairly long periods of time. They also can be used as activities to facilitate mastery of educational objectives that include the less complex cognitive processes. In this latter case, complex cognitive process learning is a means to an end, rather than an end in itself.

- Just as there are different cognitive processes, there are different types of knowledge. Together knowledge and cognitive processes define what students actually learn. The choice of a type of knowledge often suggests the accompanying cognitive process(es). Similarly, the choice of a cognitive process often suggests an accompanying types of knowledge.

Two of the generalizations are related to the instruction question.

• Certain types of knowledge regularly accompany certain cognitive processes. Specifically, *Remember* and *Factual knowledge*, *Understand* and *Conceptual knowledge*, and *Apply* and *Procedural knowledge* are often associated. Understanding and acting on these connections should enable teachers to better plan and deliver more effective instruction.

• Failing to differentiate instructional activities from educational objectives can have a negative impact on student learning. When the focus is placed on activities, students may be more interested in **performing** the activity than in **learning from** the activity. For experience to be an important teacher, students must learn from their experiences.

Two generalizations relate to the assessment question.

• Assessment serves a variety of purposes, of which two are primary: to improve student learning (formative assessment) and to assign grades to students that reflect degrees of learning (summative assessment). Both are important and useful for improving instruction and learning.

• External assessments (e.g., statewide tests, district scoring guidelines) affect classroom instruction in ways that are both positive and negative. Teachers need to find ways of incorporating these external assessments into classroom instruction that are positive and constructive.

Finally, three of our generalizations are related to the alignment question.

• If assessments are not aligned with objectives, then they do not provide clear evidence of intended student learning. Teachers should make sure that assessments are aligned with objectives.

• If instructional activities are not aligned with assessment, then the assessment results may underestimate the effectiveness of instruction. A teacher may be teaching superbly and students may be learning equally superbly, but nonaligned assessments do not capture evidence of that learning. Students are not learning things that will help them on the assessments. Indeed, students may be taught it is more important to learn what will be assessed than what goes on in the classroom.

• If instructional activities are not aligned with objectives, then students may be actively engaged in the activities but may not achieve the intended learning results. Objectives give purpose to instructional activities.

In the sections that follow, we discuss each generalization in some detail. For each generalization the organization of our discussion is essentially the same. We begin by grounding each generalization in teaching practice using examples from the vignettes. We then indicate why the generalization is important for teachers. Finally, we suggest the value of the Taxonomy Table in using the knowledge included in the generalization.

GENERALIZATIONS RELATED TO THE LEARNING QUESTION

USING COMPLEX PROCESSES TO FACILITATE MASTERY OF SIMPLER OBJECTIVES

In the Parliamentary Acts vignette (Chapter 11), the teacher chose to incorporate persuasive writing into a unit on the effects of King George's taxes on American colonists in the 1760s and 1770s. Why would she choose to do that? She believed that students would better understand the effects of the taxes if they placed themselves in the historical context by writing a persuasive editorial from the point of view of either a Patriot or a Tory. In addition to requiring the *Conceptual* and *Procedural knowledge* associated with persuasive writing, writing the editorial required students to *Analyze, Evaluate,* and *Create* based on the material contained in the unit. The activities that involved more complex process categories were not intended to be objectives, however. Rather, they were means by which students would more likely attain the primary unit objective—understand the effects of King George's taxes on the American colonists. In other words, *Analyze, Evaluate,* and *Create* activities were intended to increase students' *Understanding*.

The other vignettes contain similar examples. The focal point in the Volcanoes? Here? vignette (Chapter 12) was "conceptual restructuring and meaningful learning." The unit began with the teacher having students draw pictures of a volcano. Inherent in these pictures were students' initial conceptions of volcanoes. The teacher hoped that after reading various texts, examining a variety of data, and engaging in discussions with other students, students would modify their initial conceptions to conform more closely to the actual structure of volcanoes. Furthermore, this "conceptual restructuring" would enable students to address the probability of a volcano occurring in their community and to write a letter to the County Commissioner offering their recommendations on funding the proposed evacuation plan. The primary task of the unit, then, required students to *Analyze* (e.g., perform data analysis), *Evaluate* (e.g., judge how consistent their initial drawings were with the newly acquired information), and *Create* (e.g., combine information derived from multiple sources). Once again, however, the use of these more complex processes in instructional activities did not change the nature of the primary unit objective, *understanding conceptual knowledge*.

THE SIGNIFICANCE OF USING COMPLEX PROCESS CATEGORIES

Whereas *Remember, Understand,* and *Apply* are often tied to specific types of knowledge, *Analyze, Evaluate,* and *Create* tend to be more generalizable cognitive process categories. That is, they tend to be used with and on the full variety of knowledge types. As activities, they also can be used to facilitate *Remembering, Understanding,* and *Applying.* The vignettes contain examples of these various uses.

Using the more complex cognitive processes in learning is not a new idea. In the original *Handbook* the authors wrote about evaluation (our *Evaluate*):

> Although evaluation is placed last in the cognitive domain because it
> is regarded as requiring to some extent all the other categories of be-
> havior, it is not necessarily the last step in thinking or problem solv-
> ing. It is quite possible that the evaluative process will in some cases
> be the prelude to the acquisition of new knowledge, a new attempt at
> comprehension or application, or a new analysis and synthesis.
> (Bloom et al., 1956, p. 185)

We believe the same reasoning applies to *Analyze* and *Create.*

Furthermore, because of the wide applicability of these more complex cognitive processes, they hold the keys to the transfer of learning and problem solving. This is not to suggest that the transfer of learning and problem solving are "knowledge free." Rather, we suggest that students are increasingly likely to make connections between and among elements of knowledge when activities are used that involve more complex processes such as *Analyze, Evaluate,* and *Create.*

One way of directly teaching the more complex, generalizable process categories is to incorporate them into students' *Metacognitive knowledge.* As we mentioned in Chapter 4, *Metacognitive knowledge* is more strategic than the other types of knowledge. At the heart of *Metacognitive knowledge* lie analytic strategies, evaluative strategies, and creative strategies. Initially, these strategies may need to be imposed externally, that is, directly taught by teachers. Externally imposed strategies are inherent in the scoring rubric in the Volcanoes vignette, the scoring guide in the Nutrition vignette, the district writing guidelines in the Parliamentary Acts vignette, and the chart in the *Macbeth* vignette (Chapter 9). To facilitate the strategies becoming *Metacognitive knowledge,* teachers should help students reflect on these strategies and their relationship to their learning in general. Then, to the extent that these strategies are abstracted and learned by the student, they become part of his or her *Metacognitive knowledge* base.

The chart in the *Macbeth* vignette is a noteworthy example of a form that may be used as the basis for a discussion intended to facilitate metacognitive learning. Stripped of the specific instructional material, the left-hand column of the table contains the criteria on which comparisons are to be made. The top row contains the objects to be compared (in this case, video productions of *Macbeth*). This same format can be used with almost any objects and comparative criteria.

We emphasize that learning externally imposed strategies requires a great deal of time and many opportunities for practice. In this regard, Mr. Parker's comment in the Volcanoes vignette that he was interested in helping students "develop the habit of comparing their responses and those of their classmates to the available evidence" is noteworthy.

THE VALUE OF THE TAXONOMY TABLE   The value of the Taxonomy Table goes well beyond making us aware of the possibility and desirability of including more complex cognitive process categories in classroom instruction. The two-dimensional format of the table makes it clear that more complex process categories either may be taught directly as the basis of achieving "higher-order" objectives or may be used as activities by teachers to facilitate student learning of objectives that embody less complex process categories. The multiple uses of more complex cognitive processes give teachers additional tools in their teaching repertoire.

In addition, the Taxonomy Table points to the necessity of considering complex cognitive processes in terms of knowledge. Although we have had to talk about cognitive processes without reference to an accompanying type of knowledge, in our framework, complex processes are never taught as ends in themselves. To become "ends," they must be combined with some type of knowledge to form an objective.

Finally, because all of the cells in the Taxonomy Table offer possible answers to that most fundamental of all curriculum questions "What's worth learning?" the Taxonomy Table encourages educators to consider educational possibilities rather than to be channeled constantly within the constraints of school and classroom life.

CHOOSING VARIETIES OF KNOWLEDGE

The vignettes illustrate the four major types of knowledge that students may be expected to acquire or construct. In the Nutrition vignette (Chapter 8), students were expected to learn the names of six "appeals" used by designers of commercials. In the Volcanoes vignette (Chapter 12), students were to remember that "igneous rocks are critical evidence for volcanism." In the Parliamentary Acts vignette (Chapter 11), students were expected to know the specifics of the Sugar Act, the Stamp Act, and the Townshend Act. In the *Macbeth* vignette (Chapter 9), students were expected to remember important details of the play (e.g., what Macbeth thinks he sees before Duncan's murder). In the Addition Facts vignette (Chapter 10), students were to learn their addition facts with sums through 18. Finally, in the Report Writing vignette (Chapter 13), students were to learn details about famous Americans. These are all instances of *Factual knowledge*.

The vignettes also emphasize *Conceptual knowledge*. In the Nutrition vignette, each appeal (e.g., to love and admiration, to comfort and pleasure) is, in reality, a **category** of appeals. Within each category are a variety of instances and examples. The category is defined by common attributes that define the rules of inclusion and exclusion (e.g., What makes a specific appeal an appeal to love and admiration? How does an appeal to love and admiration differ from an appeal to comfort and pleasure?). In addition to **naming** the appeals (which is *Factual knowledge*), *Conceptual knowledge* requires that students know, at a minimum, the underlying **category.** Following are other examples of *Conceptual knowledge* in the vignettes:

- Igneous rocks and the theory of plate tectonics (Volcanoes vignette)

- Patriots and Tories (Parliamentary Acts vignette)

- Tragic hero, motif, and irony (*Macbeth* vignette)

- Additive inverse and commutative property—though not by these names (Addition Facts vignette)

- Themes (Report Writing vignette)

Most of these examples are self-explanatory; however, a comment on the commutative property and the theory of plate tectonics is in order. Properties and theories contain multiple concepts. The commutative property includes the concepts of "order" and "equality." Concepts associated with the theory of plate tectonics include "continental draft," "lithosphere," "asthenosphere," "faults," "earthquakes," and "volcanoes." Thus, principles and theories are built upon concepts and their relationships.

The vignettes also include *Procedural knowledge*. The *Procedural knowledge* in the Parliamentary Acts vignette pertains to how to write a persuasive editorial. It is important to note that a student can possess *Conceptual knowledge* of persuasive writing and yet not be able to write persuasively (i.e., he or she lacks *Procedural knowledge*). The following are examples of *Procedural knowledge* in the other vignettes:

- Knowing how to use geologic maps to determine the age of rocks (Volcanoes vignette)

- Knowing how to use the "make-a-ten" technique (Addition Facts vignette)

- Knowing how to design a commercial (Nutrition vignette) and

- Knowing how to complete a retrieval chart (*Macbeth* vignette)

Finally, the vignettes contain *Metacognitive knowledge* (although it appears less frequently than the other three types of knowledge). In the Volcanoes vignette, *Metacognitive knowledge* is inherent in the criteria that students are expected to use to check their progress in completing their assignments properly (i.e., accuracy, consistency with the evidence, acknowledgment of alternative explanations, clarity). The teacher hoped that students would learn these criteria and use them throughout the course and beyond. These are examples of *Metacognitive knowledge* in the other vignettes:

- Students examine the impact commercials have on their own decision making (Nutrition vignette)

- Students check their own editorials before submitting them to the teacher (Parliamentary Acts vignette)

- Students acquire various memory aids (Addition Facts vignette)

THE SIGNIFICANCE OF USING DIFFERENT TYPES OF KNOWLEDGE

The differences among the four types of knowledge are far more than semantic. Evidence indicates that educators should use different instructional strategies for teaching different types of knowledge (Anderson, 1995). *Factual knowledge* is usually taught through repetition and rehearsal. In contrast, some kinds of *Conceptual knowledge* are best taught through the use of positive and negative examples of the categories. Teaching *Procedural knowledge* is often more effective when visual displays such as flow charts are made available to or developed by the students. Finally, *Metacognitive knowledge* is often taught by means of a strategic, often self-regulatory emphasis. In addition, *Metacognitive knowledge* develops over a lengthy period of time, usually more than a single course or semester.

Switching from the teaching methods used for one type of knowledge to those used for another may be useful in helping students develop the more complex processes. For example, although teaching the **concept** of persuasive writing may help students **understand** it, this understanding may or may not enable them to write persuasively. Teaching them a **procedure** for persuasive writing may be needed before students can **apply** what they have learned. Similarly, a student may **remember** a dictionary or textbook definition of irony (*Factual knowledge*) but still not **understand** the meaning of irony (*Conceptual knowledge*).

To illustrate this point, *irony* can be defined as "an expression or utterance marked by a deliberate contrast between apparent and intended meaning" (*American Heritage Dictionary of the English Language*, 1992). Knowledge of this string of words constitutes *Factual knowledge*, which a student might remember. To help students better *understand conceptual knowledge*, the teacher might emphasize the defining features of irony (e.g., "deliberate opposite" or "contrast," "apparent vs. intended meaning") and give examples (e.g., "Even as the Prime Minister was urging resistance to the influence of American culture, he was unknowingly wearing American jeans"). Teaching irony as a concept, complete with defining features and positive and negative examples, is more likely to facilitate understanding.

THE VALUE OF THE TAXONOMY TABLE

As should be evident from the preceding discussion, teachers have a great deal to say about the type of knowledge they intend their students to acquire or work with. Considering the rows of the Taxonomy Table permits teachers to make choices about the type(s) of knowledge they judge to be most important. These decisions, together with the processes involved with the knowledge, enable teachers to plan more effective instruction and assessment.

A key issue confronting teachers, then, is to differentiate among the various types of knowledge and help students acquire or work with the type of knowledge that most likely will result in their mastery of the target objective.

GENERALIZATIONS RELATED TO THE INSTRUCTION QUESTION

RECOGNIZING LINKS BETWEEN KNOWLEDGE TYPES AND COGNITIVE PROCESSES

In several of the vignettes (particularly the Volcanoes vignette, but also the *Macbeth* vignette, the Addition Facts vignette, and the Parliamentary Acts vignette), there is a parallel relationship between the first three rows of the Taxonomy Table (*Factual, Conceptual*, and *Procedural knowledge*) and the first three columns (*Remember, Understand*, and *Apply*). Very often *Factual knowledge* is to be *Remembered, Conceptual knowledge* is to be *Understood*, and *Procedural knowledge* is to be *Applied*. As a consequence, for teachers who begin their planning with these parts of the knowledge dimension (e.g., "What facts, concepts, and procedures should I teach my students?"), the associated cognitive processes readily suggest themselves.

In the Addition Facts vignette, for example, the *Factual knowledge* consists of the addition facts with sums through 18. The related cognitive process is *Remember* and the objective becomes "Students will remember addition facts." Similarly, in the *Macbeth* vignette, *Conceptual knowledge* is emphasized: "tragic hero," "character defects," "motif," and "irony." Here the related cognitive process is *Understand* and the objective becomes "The students will understand the meaning of *Macbeth* in their own lives" (using the concepts of "tragic hero," "character defects," "motif," and "irony" to make the connection). Finally, in the Volcanoes vignette, students are taught **how** geologists collect and log rock samples and **how** they use geologic maps to determine the ages of the rocks they have collected. Hence, the focus is on *Procedural knowledge*. It is not a stretch to assume that the teacher wants students to *Apply* this *Procedural knowledge* to the rock samples and geologic maps they are given in class.

Given evidence of the frequent pairing of *Factual knowledge* with *Remember, Conceptual knowledge* with *Understand*, and *Procedural knowledge* with *Apply*, where does this leave *Metacognitive knowledge, Analyze, Create*, and *Evaluate*? There are at least two possible answers to this question.

The first is that the pairing continues; that is, *Metacognitive knowledge* is associated with the process categories of *Analyze, Evaluate*, and *Create*. Some support for this possibility comes from our examples of objectives that include

Metacognitive knowledge. Strategies (e.g., the Volcanoes? Here? and Addition Facts vignettes) almost always require that students *Analyze, Evaluate,* and/or *Create*. Self-examination (e.g., the Nutrition vignette), self-expression through journal writing (e.g., the *Macbeth* vignette), and monitoring of one's writing (e.g., the Parliamentary Acts vignette) likewise require one or more of these complex cognitive processes.

There is a second possible answer to the question of the pairing of the more complex processes with knowledge, one we discussed earlier in this chapter. Rather than stating these processes explicitly in objectives, teachers use instructional activities that incorporate or require either *Metacognitive knowledge* or the three most complex cognitive processes with the expectation that they will enable students to achieve "lower-level" objectives. For example, memorization strategies are used to help students *remember factual knowledge*. Similarly, self-regulation strategies are used to help students correctly *apply procedural knowledge*.

Although many objectives follow the pairing pattern we have described, many do not, especially those objectives aimed directly at achieving skills in the higher-order objectives. In these instances, *Analyze, Evaluate,* and *Create* are linked to all the kinds of knowledge.

THE SIGNIFICANCE OF RECOGNIZING THE LINKS BETWEEN KNOWLEDGE TYPES AND COGNITIVE PROCESS CATEGORIES

If, as we suggest, many school objectives fall into three cells of the Taxonomy Table (cells A1, B2, and C3), this has several implications for teachers. Two are discussed in this section. The first is similar to a point we made earlier. If a teacher knows that a specific objective is of the form *remember factual knowledge, understand conceptual knowledge,* or *apply procedural knowledge,* then the teacher may make some assumptions about how to teach and assess that objective. Consequently, rather than starting from scratch, the teacher can ground his or her plans in this prior knowledge.

If a teacher knows, for example, that an objective is of the form *understand conceptual knowledge* that relates to a concept class or category, then the teacher may facilitate learning by focusing the students' attention on the class or category's defining attributes and by using examples and nonexamples in teaching. With respect to assessment, students should be required to go beyond memorization. They might be asked to differentiate between **novel** positive and negative examples or to construct **novel** examples (i.e., those not included in the text or discussed in class), explaining why the examples are, in fact, examples. Note this does not indicate **which** specific positive and negative examples to use in teaching or assessment, but, in this instance, they do know that **some** would be helpful.

A second implication of this issue for teachers is the desirability of including explicit objectives that focus on *Metacognitive knowledge* in the curriculum. Although some students engage in metacognition on their own, not all students do. Stating metacognitive objectives, therefore, tends to level the playing field. All students are expected to use metacognitive knowledge to enhance their learning.

In general, *Metacognitive knowledge* is part of what sociologists have referred to as the "latent curriculum" (Dreeben, 1968). Now it may be time to make *Metacognitive knowledge* manifest. One important result of this change would be the shift from teacher authority in teaching to student empowerment in learning. *Metacognitive knowledge* enables students to learn to take greater control of their own learning; teachers become facilitators of learning rather than dispensers of knowledge.

THE VALUE OF THE TAXONOMY TABLE   The Taxonomy Table is a useful framework for analyzing a unit or course that is currently being taught or for planning a unit or course that will be taught in the future. In the first case, the analysis permits teachers to determine which types of objectives (that is, cells of the table) are emphasized, which are merely "mentioned," and which are omitted. This analysis may lead to either general satisfaction with the "state of affairs" or recognition of the need to modify the course or unit (e.g., the need to achieve a more appropriate balance among types of objectives).

Empty cells in the table may be viewed as "missed opportunities." Whether a teacher wishes to take advantage of these missed opportunities depends in large part on which cells are empty. If the overall goal of the teacher is retention of knowledge (see Chapter 5) and there are numerous empty cells in the *Remember* column, then this missed opportunity needs attention paid to it. Similarly, if the overall goal of the teacher is transfer of knowledge to fields other than those in which it was learned (again, see Chapter 5) and there are numerous empty cells in the columns to the right of *Remember*, then the teacher has a problem.

In the second case, the Taxonomy Table permits teachers to develop a unit or course that most closely reflects the philosophy of a teacher, a group of teachers (e.g., department, grade level), or some larger unit (e.g., community, school board). The authors of the original *Handbook* suggested that the Taxonomy was "value-free" (Bloom et al., 1956, p. 14). In this regard, the Taxonomy is perhaps best viewed as a conceptual framework that can be used within virtually any philosophical framework. We endorse this position, while recognizing at the same time that a great deal of curriculum discussion and work take place in the arena of values (Sosniak, 1994). In this regard, the Taxonomy Table is best seen as aiding the necessary transition from curriculum to instruction. The Taxonomy Table does not define curriculum; only people can do that. In Dewey's (1916) words, "Education as such has no aims; only persons, parents, teachers, etc., have aims" (p. 107). Rather, the Taxonomy Table helps "sort out" the complexities of the curriculum once it has been decided upon so that teaching is more likely to be successful and assessment is more likely to be appropriate and useful.

DIFFERENTIATING INSTRUCTIONAL ACTIVITIES FROM OBJECTIVES

Teacher educators and administrators who are responsible for supervising practicing teachers have long been impatient with teachers who fail to differentiate activities from objectives. Imagine this conversation between two teachers.

Teacher #1: My students are learning how dominant and recessive genes explain the differential inheritance of some characteristics in brothers and sisters. What objectives are you addressing in class today?

Teacher #2: My students are going on a field trip to the zoo.

Teacher #1: Good, but going to the zoo is an activity. Is there an objective for the lesson?

Teacher #2: That's it. Our objective is to visit the zoo!

As we emphasized in Chapter 2, objectives are statements that describe the desired results or "ends" of the instructional process. When we ask, "In which activities should students be engaged?" we are concerned with means. When we ask, "What should students learn from their involvement in these activities?" we are concerned with ends. In our hypothetical example, the real question in terms of objectives is "What are the students expected to learn from their visit to the zoo?"

Numerous activities are included in the vignettes. Here are some examples:

- Creating a word bank, watching a videotape (Volcanoes vignette)

- Reviewing the editorial checklist; taking a quiz (Parliamentary Acts vignette)

- Writing scene-by-scene synopses; working in groups on motifs (*Macbeth* vignette)

- Engaging in "fact friends" and "fact family" activities; participating in the relay race (Addition Facts vignette)

- Discussing popular commercials; videotaping students' original commercials (Nutrition vignette)

- Selecting sources of information (Report Writing vignette)

Notice that each of these activities can serve multiple learning ends. Students can "create a word bank" in order to memorize the words in the bank or to develop a conceptual framework for understanding the unit material. Students can review an editorial checklist to understand the criteria used to judge the quality of editorials or to learn how to write editorials of high quality.

In addition to cognitive "ends," activities may have intended purposes in the affective and/or behavioral realms. The decision to "play a videotape" may be made on the basis of a concern for students' interests. The teacher may believe that the videotape will be more interesting than lecturing students on the same material. Similarly, the use of a relay race in second-grade arithmetic may reflect the need as perceived by the teacher for children in this age group to move around periodically in the classroom.

Although there is a link between instructional activities and educational objectives, the strength of that link varies with the specificity of the objective. For example, an objective is for students to "recall addition facts to 18 without manipulatives" in the Addition Facts vignette. For many teachers, *recall* suggests that the instructional activities will likely involve repetition, redundancy, and perhaps memorization strategies. This is as far as the link goes, however. From there the ingenuity of the teacher takes over, as witnessed by the vignette's "Great Addition Wall Chart," "pocket facts," "Mad Math Minutes," "fact friends," "fact families," "houses with attics," "ten-frames," and relay race game.

Without teachers' ingenuity, objectives that are very specific can lead to tight links among the objective, instructional activities, and assessment tasks. The link may be so tight, in fact, that it is extremely difficult to differentiate objectives from assessment tasks, and assessment tasks from instructional activities. Thus, the teacher could use each student's success in the relay race as an assessment as well as an instructional activity. The vignettes contain several activities that serve as both assessments and instructional activities.

In contrast, consider the objective that students will learn to analyze poems. It is much more difficult to predict what the instruction will involve, and the link between objective and instructional activity is looser. Teachers may use many means to teach this objective to students. Similarly, the nature of assessment of this objective will vary among teachers. Consequently, teachers have great latitude in determining appropriate activities for teaching and assessing this objective.

One can ponder why some teachers frame their objectives as activities. We suggest at least three possible explanations. The first is that with the current emphasis on performance assessment, teachers may see the performances as the objectives. Teachers therefore write as their objectives "to write a letter to Congress," "to conduct an experiment," "to give a demonstration," "to write informative text," and "to deliver a talk." These are activities, however. If the students were taught **how to** write an effective letter, **how to** conduct a valid experiment, **how to** give a compelling demonstration, **how to** write informative text, and **how to** deliver a talk, these would be legitimate objectives with an emphasis on *applying procedural knowledge*. The statements of objectives, then, take the form: "The student will learn to write an effective letter."

A second explanation for confusing activities and objectives is that activities, being observable, allow the teacher to assess students' progress toward the objectives of the unit while the unit is being taught. A comment made by Ms. Marnie Jackson in discussing the *Macbeth* vignette is a wonderful illustration of this point. Ms. Jackson was asked how she determines how well students are learning while she is teaching them. She replied:

When the majority of these students get involved with an activity their facial expressions and body language are eloquent mirrors of their minds. In one discussion of ambition [**an activity**], for example, most students said initially that ambition was a positive attribute. I asked them, "Could it ever be a bad quality in an individual personality?" I could almost see the wheels turning as they processed this information. Then, as a revised concept of ambition began to form in their minds, one student said, "Well yeah! If it's too much." The student then glanced around the room at his or her peers, looking for validation. Another student chimed in, "Like J. R. Ewing of *Dallas*!" Nods of assent and scattered "Yeahs" around the room followed. Occasions such as this get me as energized as they do the students; when existing concepts are stretched or enriched with new data [**the objective**].

In cases like this, the activity is seen as a "proxy" for the objective. Perhaps giving an activity as an objective is a shorthand notation. The teacher is really saying, "*To assess my real objective, I will ask students to* give a demonstration, write a letter to Congress, conduct an experiment, and so on. *By watching and listening to them I will be able to determine how well they are progressing with respect to my real objective.*" (The italicized words are unspoken.) The criteria for judging the success of the activity are also implicit. For example, most teachers do not want students to write any old letter; they want them to write a **formal** letter or an **effective** letter. There are criteria that define a formal letter and an effective letter (although the latter may be somewhat more difficult to specify).

A final possible explanation for confusing activities and objectives is that there is no difference between them. Some teachers are convinced that there are educational activities (i.e., experiences) that have value in their own right. Experts have suggested that education is what is left after we have forgotten all the specifics we were taught in school. What do we remember about our school experiences? We are more likely to remember the trip to the zoo or our participation in a dramatic debate than the inert knowledge gained during those activities (i.e., the animals' eating habits, the issue under debate and the arguments made). This final possibility is often associated with teachers of the humanities. Just listening to Brahms, looking at a Picasso, or watching a performance of *The Firebird* has value in itself in terms of what individual students' take away from the experience.

THE SIGNIFICANCE OF DIFFERENTIATING ACTIVITIES FROM OBJECTIVES   The distinction between activities and objectives is important. Undue emphasis is often placed on the success of the teaching-learning activities (means) rather than success in terms of student learning (ends). This point was well made by Jackson (1968) in his now classic *Life in Classrooms*. Students are able to answer the question "What did you **do** in school today?" They often struggle, however, with the question "What did you **learn** in school today?"

This second question is often greeted with a shrug of the shoulders and a muttered "nothing."

One explanation for this difference is that activities are observable and can be recounted serially, whereas learning is unobservable and hence requires that inferences be made. In other words, although students know what they did, they may not know what, if anything, they learned by doing it. Reminding students of the links between activities and objectives may increase the likelihood that they make the proper inferences about learning. In addition, understanding this link between activities and objectives may help students see the connection between what they do and what they learn.

Equally important is ensuring that students know what the objective **is** and what it **means**. We believe that meaning is enhanced by, first, using verbs and nouns that are as specific as possible in stating the objectives and, second, showing students sample assessment tasks when the objective is introduced to them. In this way, the objective becomes more precise and more concrete. Simply stated, you are more likely to get there if you know where you are going.

THE VALUE OF THE TAXONOMY TABLE   Activities provide clues to the proper placement of objectives in the Taxonomy Table. Because actions (verbs) can be used to achieve a variety of ends, however, a taxonomic classification cannot be made based on the verb alone. For example, a student can write a set of notes recalled from a lecture (i.e., *Remember*), can write the differences between two objects or ideas (i.e., *Understand*), or can write an original essay on the value of spirituality in community life (i.e., *Create*). When the verbs used to describe activities are linked with the verbs associated with process categories as well as with the knowledge dimension, the purpose of the activities (that is, the intended learning outcomes) becomes clearer.

Furthermore, as illustrated in the vignettes, the Taxonomy Table provides an easy way for teachers to use activities to infer objectives. Confronted with an activity, teachers have to answer only one basic question: "What do I expect my students to learn as a result of participating in (or completing) this activity?" The answer to this question is quite frequently the objective.

GENERALIZATIONS RELATED TO THE ASSESSMENT QUESTION

USING SUMMATIVE AND FORMATIVE ASSESSMENTS

Teachers assess students for two basic reasons: (1) to monitor student learning and make necessary adjustments in instruction, both for individual students and for entire classes, and (2) to assign grades to students following some period of instruction. The former type of assessment is called formative because its primary function is to help "form" learning while there is still time and opportunity for students to improve. The latter type is called summative because its primary function is to "sum up" student learning at the end of some period of time (Scriven, 1967).

Although the interpretation of the assessment and the use to which it is put classify assessment as formative or summative, in practice there is another difference. Formative assessment is usually more informal, based on a variety of information sources (e.g., classroom questions, observations of students, homework, and quizzes). Summative evaluation, in contrast, is usually more formal, based on more focused information sources (e.g., tests, projects, and term papers). The reliance on formal means of summative assessment is consistent with the felt need of many teachers to be able to justify or defend the grades they assign to students. In addition, formal assessment often makes teachers aware of students whose learning they had underestimated on the basis of classroom interaction. Although the data from informal assessment, on the other hand, may, or, more likely may not, reach technical standards, they are timely and therefore far more useful in guiding instructional adjustments.

Despite these differences, formative and summative assessment are often intertwined in the classroom. Consider some examples from the vignettes. In the Parliamentary Acts vignette, the summative assessment was an editorial in which students were to "interpret the [Parliamentary] Acts from the perspective of a Patriot or Tory character." Students wrote drafts of their editorials; received feedback from themselves, their peers, and Ms. Airasian; and were expected to rewrite their drafts in line with the feedback they received. Two-fifths of the grade (summative) was based on their completion of this formative process. In this example, the lines between formative and summative assessment were blurred.

Examples of formative assessment in the Volcanoes? Here? vignette were the "assessment conversations," held twice during the unit. The first followed a homework assignment in which students had to answer four questions on rock types, igneous rocks, and volcanic activity. The second was a conversation about students' analysis and interpretation of data pertaining to rocks and volcanoes (an in-class assignment). The summative assessment was a letter written to the County Commissioner concerning the likelihood of a volcanic eruption affecting the local area. Following a peer assessment session, however, Mr. Parker gave those students who asked to do so an opportunity to revise their letters prior to submitting them for a grade. Thus, once again the formative and summative assessments were intertwined. (Emphasized in the summative assessment was the motivation to achieve because the opportunity to revise had to be requested by the student.)

THE SIGNIFICANCE OF USING FORMATIVE AND SUMMATIVE ASSESSMENT   Formative assessment provides teachers and students with information they need as the unit is being taught: for students, how to achieve the objective, and for teachers, what instructional decisions to make. Should I go over this material again? Do students need more time to complete their work? Should I just skip this session (because it appears too boring or confusing to students)? Should I add a few extra days to this unit? Should I plan a small group session with Bill, Latoya, Jean, and Carl to work on their misunderstandings? These are rather "low stakes" decisions; a wrong decision quickly becomes evident and can be corrected. In this context, teachers can afford to rely on students' expressions, persistence, responses to oral questions, and responses to a variety of short written assignments. Virtually every teacher in our vignettes engaged in formative assessment and relied on such information to guide their instructional decisions.

Summative assessment provides the data teachers need to make and justify the grades they assign students. Because these are "high-stakes" decisions for individual students, the data should have high technical quality. Furthermore, because grading decisions must be not only made but also justified, teachers may feel more comfortable relying on fairly traditional tests of *Factual knowledge* in summative assessment. The test questions have clear "right" and "wrong" answers that are easy to defend. Ms. Jackson's final examination in the *Macbeth* vignette is a vivid example.

To the extent that formative assessment and summative assessment are linked in some way, students are more likely to do better on the summative assessments. To the extent that formative and summative assessments are virtually identical (as when summative assessments are used formatively or when a series of formative assessments replace an independent summative assessment), the distinction between instruction and assessment becomes blurred. We say more about this later in the chapter.

THE VALUE OF THE TAXONOMY TABLE   In general, the Taxonomy Table is more relevant for summative assessment than for formative assessment. An exception to this generalization is when summative-like assessments are used for formative assessment purposes. We noted examples of this exception above, and they are evident in almost all of the vignettes.

In designing summative assessments, teachers can develop prototypical assessment tasks for each cell of the Taxonomy Table. Statements of *Factual knowledge*, for example, often take the form of sentences. Transforming the sentences into questions becomes the basis for assessing many *Factual knowledge* objectives. In the Volcanoes vignette, one important piece of *Factual knowledge* is that "igneous rocks are critical evidence for volcanism." Students are expected to *Remember* that *Factual knowledge*. Appropriate assessment questions include "What kind of rocks are critical evidence for volcanism?" and "Igneous rocks are critical evidence for what natural phenomenon?" If multiple-choice items are desired, the teacher can add a homogeneous set of response options to the questions.

When the emphasis is on *remembering factual knowledge*, the question is a verbatim transformation of the sentence. Using synonyms in the transformation moves the objective from *Remember* to *Understand* (e.g., "Magma is critical evidence for what natural phenomenon?"). To answer this question students need to know that magma is an example of the category of igneous rocks.

Developing prototypical assessment tasks for objectives that include more complex cognitive processes and different types of knowledge is likely to require more thought. Several examples of assessment tasks for sample objectives for each cognitive process were presented in Chapter 5. Many more models of items are found in the original *Handbook*, which gave greater emphasis to assessment. Once a set of prototypical tasks are designed, they can serve as format blueprints for preparing assessments for objectives in particular cells of the Taxonomy Table. In this context, the Taxonomy Table serves as a "labor-saving device" for preparing valid assessments.

Finally, teachers may place the proportion of assessment tasks (e.g., test items or score points in the case of performance assessments) along with the proportion of time spent on particular instructional activities in the appropriate cells of the Taxonomy Table. Assuming that these two proportions in each cell should be roughly the same, teachers can judge the instructional validity of the assessment(s). These proportions should also be the same as the relative emphasis intended for each objective.

DEALING WITH EXTERNAL ASSESSMENTS

Increasingly teachers are confronted with state curriculum standards and corresponding state testing programs, and with district core curriculums and corresponding district scoring guides for performance assessments. We refer to these testing programs and performance assessment scoring guides as external assessments because people who typically do not teach in classrooms mandate them. External assessments have flourished over the past several years, largely as a result of more education accountability measures. Generally, these assessments are referred to as "high-stakes" assessments because critical decisions about students, teachers, and, increasingly, schools are made based on their results. See, for example, the Report Writing vignette (page 210).

As might be expected, most teachers are less than enamored with external assessments. Consider the following letter to the editors of *Newsweek* magazine:

> Kudos for showing how dangerous these new standardized tests are.
> As a former English teacher who quit rather than "teach for the tests,"
> I applaud students who refuse to take these exams. Education officials
> need to find an alternative fast, before our kids grow up with no idea
> how to think without a No. 2 pencil and a multiple-choice bubble
> sheet. (Ellis, 1999, p. 15)

Many of the teachers who wrote our vignettes struggled with external assessments. Ms. Jeanna Hoffman (Addition Facts vignette), for example, gave two reasons for her choice of instructional unit. First, the "unit is part of the school district's second-grade core curriculum," and second, "addition facts are included on the currently used standardized test." Similarly, Ms.

Airasian (Parliamentary Acts vignette) indicated that "both persuasive writing and colonial history are required topics in the district's fifth-grade curriculum." In addition, she was expected to use a set of district-adopted Focus Correction Areas (FCAs), four criteria to be applied to all student writing (i.e., use complete sentences, write proper paragraphs, use correct spelling, and write legibly).

THE SIGNIFICANCE OF DEALING WITH EXTERNAL ASSESSMENTS

The significance of external assessments stems in large part from the seriousness of their consequences for students, teachers, and administrators (i.e., the fact that they are "high stakes"). Students may be retained at a particular grade level for a second or third year or denied a high school diploma. Schools may be identified publicly as "low performing" or, in South Carolina, "critically impaired." In some states, "critically impaired" schools are subject to being "taken over" by the state Board of Education.

A second reason external assessments are significant is that they are likely to be around for some time. The number of states that have enacted some form of accountability legislation has tripled in the past several years. In almost all cases, the legislation calls for the issuance of school report cards, based in large part on the results of external assessments.

Third, avoiding the consequences of high-stakes testing may depend, at least in part, on finding the balance between an appropriate interpretation of what is required by the combination of externally mandated standards with their accompanying assessments and the local school's interpretation of what is an appropriate education. External assessments are intended to be used with all students at selected grade levels in all schools in a district or state. But, schools do not provide identical curriculums or instruction (despite efforts to ensure they do). Therefore, the assessments will better fit the instruction received by certain students and in some schools than others. Consequently, it is quite possible that assessment results reflect differences in the interpretation of the standards and therefore the validity of the assessments. Finding a balance that meets both external mandated standards and local preferences will be increasingly important.

Simply stated, external assessments have become a way of life for students, teachers, and administrators. Rather than "rage against the dying of the light," it seems more reasonable to adopt the stance of a second teacher who sent a letter to *Newsweek:*

> The challenge for teachers of the 21st century is to provide mastery of those necessary test-taking skills **without losing sight of our deeper mission.** (Halley, 1999, p. 15, emphasis added)

THE VALUE OF THE TAXONOMY TABLE

As illustrated in the vignettes, teachers can use the Taxonomy Table to analyze assessments as well as instructional activities and objectives. Using the Taxonomy Table to analyze external assessments permits educators to look beneath the surface elements of the assessments to infer the deeper levels of student learning being assessed. Rather than "teach for the tests," teachers can then teach for the learning being tested.

When confronted by external assessments, teachers should prepare two Taxonomy Tables: one for the course objectives and the other for the external assessment. By comparing these two tables, teachers can estimate the extent of the match between the course objectives and the external assessment. Furthermore, they can note opportunities to link the course objectives with the external assessment. Ms. Airasian (Parliamentary Acts vignette) illustrated how this can be done with scoring rubrics for performance assessments. In evaluating the students' editorials, Ms. Airasian used two sets of criteria. The first was a generic set for all writing prepared by the school district, and the second was a set intended specifically for persuasive essays. In combination these two sets of criteria allowed her to conform to the district's expectations (i.e., the external assessment) while at the same time to incorporate more specific criteria related to the primary unit objective.

GENERALIZATIONS RELATED TO THE ALIGNMENT QUESTION

ALIGNING ASSESSMENTS WITH OBJECTIVES

Most of us know a mathematics teacher who says his or her "real" objective is problem solving but who tests students on factual recall. At the opposite extreme is the history teacher whose objective is stated as remembering "great men and big events" but who asks students to compose an essay explaining the role of religious differences in various conflicts. How can this misalignment of objectives and assessment be explained? The vignettes illustrate at least four answers to this question.

First, instructional units include complicated sets of events and experiences with twists and turns introduced as exigencies arise during their implementation. As teachers encounter difficulties teaching the unit, their objectives may change or their understanding of the previously stated objectives may change. The end-of-unit assessments may reflect the "new" objectives or evolved understandings rather than the objectives that were stated at the beginning of the unit.

Second, teachers may not possess a good grasp of their objectives at the beginning of the unit. Consider the language used by teachers who wrote the vignettes as they described their primary unit objective(s):

- The unit was designed to promote conceptual restructuring and meaningful learning in earth science.   (Volcanoes vignette)

- I want to integrate students' persuasive writing with their knowledge of historical persons and events.   (Parliamentary Acts vignette)

- Students will see the relevance of literary works in their own lives. (*Macbeth* vignette)

- It is a unit on teaching strategies for memorizing addition facts that sum to 18 or less.   (Addition Facts vignette)

- [Students should learn] to check the influences that commercials have on their own "senses" and to understand how those influences work on them.   (Nutrition vignette)

As a unit unfolds, the instructional activities make the objectives more concrete, which generally results in a greater understanding of the objectives on the part of the teacher (and, it is hoped, the students as well). When the time comes for formal assessment, the concrete understanding provided by the activities, rather than the abstract understanding inherent in the stated objectives, is more often mirrored in the assessment. The mismatch between abstract and concrete likely corresponds with the misalignment of objectives and assessment.

Third (and somewhat related to the second), some teachers may take a long-range perspective as they determine their objectives. They may focus on objectives that will be addressed in multiple units during the school year, with actual mastery of the objectives expected to occur only at the end of a course (or perhaps after several years of instruction). Teachers may feel it is premature to assess these long-range objectives after the completion of a single unit. Premature assessment may generate results that are technically unsound and, more important from the teacher's point of view, discouraging for the students. Thus, the teacher engages in what may be termed a "partial assessment," assessing only that knowledge and those cognitive processes that have been "covered" up to the time the assessment is made. The assessment, then, is far more specific than the general objective, and misalignment in the general-specific sense is often noted.

Fourth, and consistent with our discussion in the preceding section, the cause of misalignment may be external to the teacher. Two of the vignettes illustrate this situation. Ms. Airasian (Parliamentary Acts vignette) operated within the framework of the district writing guidelines. Since, as mentioned earlier, these writing conventions apply to all writing, they are not as aligned with the primary unit objective as conventions developed exclusively for persuasive writing would be. Similarly, it appears that Ms. Jackson's (*Macbeth* vignette) choice of her final examination was made primarily on the basis of her need to grade students, not her need validly to assess student learning with respect to her primary unit objective.

THE SIGNIFICANCE OF ALIGNING ASSESSMENTS WITH OBJECTIVES

Our placement of the terms *assessments* and *objectives* in the heading of this section is important and intentional. In those areas in which teachers can exercise discretion (i.e., those states not completely given to high-stakes testing and those assessments teachers construct themselves), assessments should be aligned with objectives, not vice versa. In our view, assessments provide evidence of how well students have learned what we intended them to learn. Intentions precede evidence! The more difficult question of What's worth learning? should not be replaced by the far easier question What can and/or must we assess?

Having said this, we recognize that teachers often find themselves in situations where they have to align their objectives with external assessments. Then the issue should be the alignment, not the above "chicken and egg" discussion. There are two major reasons for aligning assessment and objectives. First, alignment increases the probability that students will have an opportunity to learn the knowledge and cognitive processes included on the various assessments they will encounter. In today's world of high-stakes assessment, denying students opportunities to learn has serious consequences for them as well as for their teachers and administrators. At the very least, then, alignment ensures that teachers provide students with some minimum opportunity to learn what is required.

Second, for many students, objectives are defined by assessments, particularly when assessments determine the grades students receive. Their "job" becomes doing well on the assessments so as to get "good grades." When assessments and objectives are aligned, these "good grades" are more likely to translate into "good learning." When objectives and assessments are misaligned, however, students are more likely to put effort into learning what is assessed than to learn what is intended by the objectives.

THE VALUE OF THE TAXONOMY TABLE   The Taxonomy Table may have its greatest value in relation to this critical issue. We present one method for estimating the alignment between objectives and assessment using the Taxonomy Table: First, identify the major unit objectives and determine the cells of the Taxonomy Table to which they correspond. Second, identify the major assessments and determine the cells to which they correspond. Also note whether the emphasis intended for each objective is reflected in the assessment. If the cells and emphases derived from the first two steps do not match, misalignment is evident. If the cells are the same, further study of the alignment of instructional activities and assessment tasks is in order. (We will say more about this "further study" in the next section.)

Note that the Taxonomy Table provides a common basis for examining objectives and assessments. Alignment is not determined by a direct comparison of objectives with assessments; rather, objectives and assessments are independently placed in appropriate cells of the Taxonomy Table. To the extent that an objective and an assessment are placed in the same cell, alignment is evident. In this way, the comparison is made at a "deeper" level and is more likely to focus on student learning.

ALIGNING INSTRUCTIONAL ACTIVITIES WITH ASSESSMENTS

Traditionally, it has been assumed that assessments are valid if they match the unit or course objectives. This type of validity is known as content validity. Beginning in the 1970s, however, the assumption was questioned. Some argued that the validity of the assessments depended on what was taught in the classroom, not what was supposed to be taught in light of the objectives. This type of validity was referred to as instructional validity or instructional sensitivity (Thorndike, Cunningham, Thorndike, and Hagen, 1991).

The relationship between instructional activities and assessment tasks/score points can range from being so close as to be identical to being so distinct as to be completely out of alignment. Consider there closeness in the Parliamentary Acts vignette, for example. The activities on Days 2 and 3 were intended to provide the general knowledge needed for the major assessment (i.e., the editorial); those on Days 4 and 5 were designed to provide students with the persuasive writing knowledge and skills they would need to write the editorial. The activities on Days 6 and 7 allowed students to obtain the more specific knowledge they needed to complete their specific editorial. Finally, students spent the last three days of the unit in class writing their editorials, with teacher guidance and supervision. This final instructional activity, then, provided the data that would ultimately be used in making the assessment.

Alternatively, the relationship between instructional activities and assessment tasks may be a bit "looser." The instructional activities may be similar but not identical to the tasks included in the assessment. In the Nutrition vignette, for example, one of the instructional activities was for students to identify appeals made in familiar television commercials for foods. The first activity required students to place each appeal into one of six "type of appeal" categories. In the second activity, students watched commercials played on a videocassette recorder and, in groups, evaluated how well the commercial "worked." The end result of this activity was a set of criteria for "being convincing." The assessment task that followed required students, working in groups of two to four, to design a commercial that included one or more appeals and was "convincing." This assessment task required a conceptual understanding of the six appeal "types" (the first activity) as well as the criteria for "being convincing" (the second activity).

Finally, the instructional activities may be completely unrelated to the assessment tasks, as illustrated in the *Macbeth* vignette. None of the instructional activities focused solely or primarily on the details of the play. Rather, the activities emphasized basic concepts (e.g., motif, irony) and required students to make inferences (e.g., predict what would happen, explain the reasoning). In contrast, however, the end-of-unit test included questions that focused exclusively on the details of the play (e.g., matching activities for qualities with people, matching characters with familiar quotations). In this case, there were two assessments: the group project and the end-of-unit test. Whereas the first was not aligned with the instructional activities, the second was nicely aligned with them.

THE SIGNIFICANCE OF ALIGNING INSTRUCTIONAL ACTIVITIES WITH ASSESSMENTS   As we mentioned earlier, instructional activities and assessment tasks can be identical in terms of their substance (e.g., knowledge, cognitive process) and their form (e.g., multiple choice, performance assessments). They differ primarily in their function. Instructional activities are intended to help students learn, whereas assessment tasks are intended to determine whether or how well students have learned.

Ensuring that students encounter instructional activities that are similar to assessment tasks in substance increases the instructional validity of the assessment. Ensuring that students encounter instructional activities that are similar to assessment tasks in form increases the likelihood they will perform better on external assessments by getting them used to different task formats and different testing conditions (e.g., timed tests).

Another way to align assessments with instructional activities when performance assessment is used is to ensure that students *Remember*, *Understand*, and can *Apply* the evaluation criteria or scoring rubric. As in the Nutrition vignette, students can be involved in determining the criteria or rubric. This strengthens the link between instructional activities and assessment tasks even more.

When assessment tasks and instructional activities are severely out of alignment, teachers cannot properly estimate the effectiveness of the instructional activities. For example, Mr. Parker (Volcanoes vignette) may do a wonderful job of teaching conceptual understanding (the objective). If the formal assessment consisted of a series of facts about volcanoes in different regions of the country and throughout the world, however, students may not do very well on this assessment. Based on the data from the assessment, then, we might conclude that the instruction provided by Mr. Parker was ineffective. A somewhat more logical inference would be that the objective and the assessment were misaligned.

THE VALUE OF THE TAXONOMY TABLE   Once again, the value of the Taxonomy Table here stems largely from its use as an analytic tool. Within the context of more traditional assessment (e.g., a test), the correct placement of an objective in the Taxonomy Table provides clues to the appropriate assessment tasks for that objective. For example, an objective that focuses on *applying procedural knowledge* generally has assessment tasks that include (1) a new or novel problem situation, (2) a question to be answered or directions to be followed, and (3) a set of response options or a space within which student work can be demonstrated and the final answer given. Knowing this basic structure, the teacher can design or select a fairly large set of assessment tasks. Once this set is developed, some may be incorporated into the instructional activities (to facilitate learning) and others may be set aside exclusively for assessment purposes (to see how well learning occurred). In this way, the alignment between instruction and assessment is strengthened without compromising the integrity of the tasks used for assessment.

If, in this example, students are expected to demonstrate their work **and** write their answer, then some type of scoring guide (e.g., rating scales, scoring rubric) must be developed. This scoring guide should clarify the teacher's expectations in terms of performance when shared with the students and serve as a link between instructional activities and assessment tasks.

ALIGNING INSTRUCTIONAL ACTIVITIES WITH OBJECTIVES

One might think that if the assessments are aligned with the objectives and the instructional activities are aligned with the assessments, then the instructional activities will automatically be aligned with the objectives. This is usually, but not always, the case. It is possible for teachers to include instructional activities that are not directly related to either the objectives or assessments. In many cases, these activities are intended to provide students with the information they need to master an objective.

In the Report Writing vignette, for example, the first two objectives pertained to selecting sources of information and, ultimately, specific information about a famous person in American history. As written, the objectives assumed that the students already had a person in mind. That was not the case, however. Consequently, the activities in Days 5–8 related to the task of choosing a famous person. Certainly this is an important task because without it students could not progress toward the unit objectives; however, the activity is preparatory to, not aligned with, the objectives.

THE SIGNIFICANCE OF ALIGNING ACTIVITIES WITH OBJECTIVES   Our
final generalization suggests the value of checking alignment one more time. We believe this final check identifies instructional activities that are unrelated or, at best, tangentially related to the unit objectives. We do not believe the tangentially related activities should be discarded out of hand, however. Within the context of an instructional unit, activities play a variety of roles.

For example, some activities are intended to introduce the unit to students. The Nutrition vignette contained an activity in which students were to identify products from their "hooks," which focused on arousing student interest.

Other activities are intended to enhance student engagement or involvement in the unit. In the *Macbeth* vignette, students were given a choice among three film versions of the play.

Some activities foreshadow material that will be encountered later and so are intended to lay a foundation. An example comes from the Addition Facts vignette, in which the concept of "additive inverse" was explored (without ever using the name).

Finally, there are activities that function as pre-assessments; that is, determinations of what students "bring to" the unit in terms of their knowledge and cognitive processes. The activity in the Volcanoes? Here? vignette of having students draw their conceptions of volcanoes was one such example.

Knowing the function of the instructional activities within an instructional unit is essential to determining the activities that may seem irrelevant but that serve special functions not represented in the Taxonomy Table. Eliminating such activities can result in a "tighter," more efficient unit. And, in today's world, efficiency is indeed a virtue in light of the vast array of objectives that are competing for a limited amount of classroom time.

THE VALUE OF THE TAXONOMY TABLE   The value of the Taxonomy Table with respect to this final generalization is the same as we described for the other two generalizations pertaining to alignment. In summary, the Taxonomy Table is an analytic tool that enables teachers to conduct a "deeper" examination of alignment, one that goes beyond the surface features of activities and objectives to their common underlying meaning in terms of student learning.

A FINAL COMMENT

Teachers (and educators in general) have confronted the four questions posed at the beginning of this chapter since the publication of the original *Handbook* almost a half-century ago, and long before. Although the Taxonomy Table cannot provide answers to these questions, we believe the framework provides a basis for a useful discussion of them. More specifically, the Taxonomy Table can enable teachers and those who work with teachers to consider these long-standing questions in a different light—to gain new insights into them and, using the generalizations derived from the vignettes, gain a new understanding of them.

For example, when viewed through the lens of the Taxonomy Table, a relatively simple concept such as "alignment" takes on new meaning. It is not sufficient to align instruction and assessment based on only types of knowledge or cognitive process categories. It is only when alignment involves the intersection of knowledge with process (i.e., the objective) that it is likely to result in increased student learning. This added degree of precision helps us understand both why previous efforts at alignment may not have been successful and what kinds of future efforts need to be made. Once gained, these insights and this understanding can help teachers develop solution strategies not thought of before.

UNSOLVED PROBLEMS

Although we hope our revision is an improvement over the original *Handbook*, those who work on heuristic frameworks find that the quest for a better one never ends. With each attempt, one does the best one can with the approach chosen, while being aware of aspects that, could they be accommodated, would make the framework still more useful. Following are some issues that may provide challenges for those who seek to take the next steps.[1]

THE TIME DEMANDS OF ANALYSIS

The analysis proposed in the vignette chapters is labor intensive. We believe that it is worth the investment, however, as it helps one learn the analysis process, and where a unit or course is repeated, for very large classes, or for those involved in distance education. But for classes that require extensive updating every time they are taught, that are approached differently each time, that are very small, and/or that are offered irregularly, the investment may not be warranted. Even for these, however, having the categories of our framework in mind will likely spark efforts to broaden the range of knowledge and cognitive processes that are included and thereby strengthen what is offered. Other frameworks may be better alternatives for those cases where a heavy investment in planning and analysis is more difficult to justify.

THE LINKAGE OF OBJECTIVES AND INSTRUCTION

The linkage between objectives and instruction needs further study. Although we have noted instances where the characteristics of instructional activities are suggested by the nature of the educational objectives, specifying a learning objective does not automatically lead to a prescribed method of instruction. This, of course, was the expectation of the performance-based movement of the late 1960s and early 1970s. Researchers were to determine what teaching methods, instructional strategies, or teacher behaviors would produce particular learning under specified circumstances. They did not then, and they still haven't. In fact, many now believe it is unrealistic to expect they ever will. Until and unless the linkage of objectives to instructional activities can be markedly strengthened, we believe the current boundaries of how far a framework such as ours can usefully suggest appropriate instruction are illustrated by the examples in our vignette analyses.

What might help teachers is a framework that facilitates the transition from abstract goals to general teaching strategies to concrete instructional activities that can facilitate goal attainment by large numbers of students. Can a

---

[1] A more extensive discussion of unsolved problems appears in the complete edition of this book as Chapter 17.

framework be developed that is more facilitative than those now available? Obviously, this is an empirical question, but it will not be an easy task.

LACK OF PROGRESS IN MULTIPLE-CHOICE ITEM FORMATS

An important feature of the original *Handbook* was its extensive modeling of multiple-choice item formats for each taxonomic category. Although Chapter 5 is helpful in identifying assessment formats, the examples are more useful in illustrating and clarifying the kinds of cognitive processes to be expected in a given process category than they are in demonstrating the variety of ways student learning within a given category might be accomplished.

Although the technology of testing has made substantial advances in the years since the publication of the original *Handbook*, the field of item writing unfortunately has progressed little. In Sternberg's (1997) words: "There is one industry . . . that remains a glaring exception to the general rapid rate of technological progress. . . ." He continues in an ironic vein, "an example of innovation . . . (as announced fairly recently by one testing company) is including mathematical ability items that are not multiple-choice; they are fill-in-the-blank items" (p. 1137). Forty-four years after publication of the *Handbook*, we could add little that would show any advance in item writing. Educators should not forget the usefulness of portfolios and other performance assessments, but those seeking additional suggestions on test items appropriate for a given Taxonomy category should revisit the original *Handbook* as well as books like Smith and Tyler (1942). Paul and Nosich (1992) provide models for measuring higher-level thinking Haladyna (1997) intends to help individuals test for complex behaviors; and Hannah and Michaelis (1977) include sample items for their categories.

RELATIONSHIP TO A THEORY OF LEARNING AND COGNITION

Ideally, the dimensions of our framework and the ordering of its categories should be based on a single, widely accepted, and functional theory of learning. Advances in cognitive theories have contributed to our revision. Despite the many advances since the original *Handbook*, however, the single psychological theory that adequately provides a basis for all learning has yet to found.

RELATIONSHIPS AMONG THE DOMAINS

The authors of the *Handbook* divided objectives into three domains: cognitive, affective, and psychomotor. This decision has been justly criticized because it isolates aspects of the same objective—and nearly every cognitive objective has an affective component. For example, English teachers want a student not only to learn to critique good literature but also to value it, appreciate it, and seek opportunities to encounter it. Making affective aspects regularly planned parts of instruction would be facilitated if the Taxonomy were better integrated across the domains.

By intentionally focusing on the cognitive domain, this revision ignores this problem except for the fact, as noted earlier, that the *Metacognitive Knowledge* category in some respects bridges the cognitive and affective domains. However, a number of alternative frameworks include an affective component. Hauenstein (1998), for example, provided an affective taxonomy in addition to a cognitive one (and a psychomotor one too). None of the alternative frameworks seems to have drawn a wide following as yet. Our hope, however, is that by including a discussion of them in the complete edition of this book (see its Chapter 15), they may gain added visibility. Some of them may provide ideas that may prove attractive in the future.

IN CLOSING

Like the original framework, our revision will be most beneficial to those who adapt it to their purposes. Bloom, Hastings, and Madaus (1971) showed how the original framework could be adapted to better fit a number of fields: language arts (Moore and Kennedy, 1971), mathematics (J. W. Wilson, 1971), art education (B. G. Wilson, 1971), social studies (Orlandi, 1971), and science (Klopfer, 1971). McGuire (1963) modified the framework for medical education as well. These authors adjusted the breaks between categories to fit their subject matter fields and created subcategories to highlight important discipline-related distinctions. Some of those adjustments to the original framework would be equally applicable to this revision; some could be further altered to increase their effectiveness. Although the revision, of necessity, was developed as a generally applicable framework, we strongly encourage users to adapt it creatively to their particular requirements.

All frameworks such as the Taxonomy are abstractions of reality that simplify in order to facilitate perceptions of underlying orderliness. This framework is no exception. Just as the proof of good food is in the eating, the value of a conceptual framework such as this one lies in its applicability—the breadth and depth of its use and its impact on the field.

There is much in the original *Handbook* that is worth preserving. Its continuous and widespread citation attests to its perceived value over time. "In a field marked by wide pendulum swings, the likelihood of finding an idea, concept, or point of view that has remained constant in its acceptance and application is small indeed. Without doubt, the Taxonomy is one of these rarities" (Anderson and Sosniak, 1994, p. viii). We hope we have preserved the essentials of the original, have borrowed the best ideas from alternative frameworks and advances in cognitive theories and research, and have created a revision that is more serviceable and user-friendly—that our revision may become as familiar to educators as the original.

Appendixes

Summary of the Changes from the Original Framework

The original framework consisted of six major categories arranged in the following order: Knowledge, Comprehension, Application, Analysis, Synthesis, and Evaluation. The categories above Knowledge were collectively labeled "abilities and skills." It was understood that Knowledge is used in each of the abilities and skills because their effective use requires the appropriate knowledge.

Each category had subcategories: Knowledge and Comprehension, many; the rest, few. The categories and subcategories were presumed to lie along a continuum, from simple to complex and from concrete to abstract. The relationships among the categories along the continuum were presumed to constitute a cumulative hierarchy (see point 11 below).

Readers familiar with the original framework will recognize that we have made a number of changes, 12 in all: four changes in emphasis, four in terminology, and four in structure. Most important, we have changed the focus of the document.

FOUR CHANGES IN EMPHASIS

1. THE REVISION'S PRIMARY FOCUS IS ON THE TAXONOMY IN USE

The revision emphasizes the use of the Taxonomy in planning curriculum, instruction, assessment, and the alignment of these three. This emphasis is a major shift from the original focus on assessment, providing extensive examples of test items for each of the six categories. The contrast between the two versions is seen most sharply by comparing the proportions of the original version and of the revision given to examples of the use of the Taxonomy in curriculum planning and instruction. In the initial version, the proportion is small. In the revision, 11 of the 17 chapters describe the application of the framework. Chapters 1, 2, 3, and 6 introduce the use of the framework in planning and analyzing curriculum, instruction, assessment, and alignment. Chapter 7 describes its use in the preparation and analysis of classroom vignettes, and Chapters 8–13 present the vignettes and their analysis. Chapter 14 develops nine generalizations concerning critical educational issues that grow out of those analyses.

The group that developed the original *Handbook* was largely college and university examiners who anticipated that its initial use would be in the exchange of test items among institutions. However, as Ben Bloom indicated in his opening remarks to the originators at their first working conference (Bloom, 1949), he expected considerably broader use; the problems with which the Taxonomy deals are universal. This revision not only demonstrates that his perceptions were realistic but also modifies the Taxonomy in ways intended to make it increasingly and more broadly effective.

2. The Revision Is Aimed at a Broader Audience, Emphasizing Teachers

The revision is designed to be of use to teachers at all grade levels. Our group particularly kept the elementary and secondary classroom teacher in mind. The touchstone was: How would this change make the Taxonomy more useful for all teachers? The answers guided our decisions. Whereas the initial version was aimed largely at higher education, with almost no examples drawn from elementary and secondary education, instances from the latter predominate in the revision. Indeed, all of the vignettes are pre-college level.

3. Sample Assessment Tasks Are Included Primarily to Convey Meaning

The revision includes sample assessment tasks (e.g., performance tasks, test items) primarily to help illustrate and clarify the meaning of the various categories. Because of the amazing lack of progress in item writing between the original *Handbook* and our revision, there seemed no way we could improve on the original in this respect. Because of the considerable emphasis on model test items (primarily multiple choice) in the first edition—almost 40 percent of the pages—it is the better source of item formats. Many of the formats developed by Smith and Tyler (1942) for the Eight Year Study are still some of the cleverest devised for measuring complex cognitive processes.

4. The Revision Emphasizes the Subcategories

The original framework emphasized the six major categories rather than their subcategories, describing the former in considerable detail. In the revision, definitions of the major categories emerge most clearly from the extensive description and illustration of the subcategories (i.e., knowledge subtypes and specific cognitive processes) and their use in the analysis of the vignettes. (See Chapters 4 and 5 and all chapters in Section III.)

Four Changes in Terminology

5. Major Category Titles Were Made Consistent with How Objectives Are Framed

We adjusted the original terms to provide consistency with the way objectives are framed, which was missing in the initial framework. Educational objectives indicate that the student should be able to do something (verb) to or with something (noun)—a verb-noun relationship. The knowledge categories generally supply the nouns in objectives, and this was reflected in the original structure's first category, Knowledge, which was a noun. However, the remaining categories of the original framework were also nouns (e.g., Application, Analysis, etc.), whereas they take the verb form (e.g., apply, analyze, etc.) when used in objectives. We decided to relabel these categories in their verb forms (e.g., *Apply, Analyze,* etc.) to reflect the verb-noun relationship. For completeness, Knowledge was renamed *Remember.*

6. The Knowledge Subcategories Were Renamed and Reorganized

Because of the emphasis on the six categories in the original *Handbook,* some people forget there were subcategories of Knowledge. In the *Handbook,* these subcategories were delineated in an appendix. Our review of alternative frameworks devised since the publication of the *Handbook* (see Chapter 15) as well as research on learning led us to reframe the Knowledge subcategories as four types of knowledge: *Factual knowledge, Conceptual knowledge, Procedural knowledge,* and a new subcategory, *Metacognitive knowledge.* As we indicated in Chapter 4, one easily can locate the counterparts to *Factual, Conceptual, and Procedural knowledge* in the original Knowledge subcategories. We anticipate that the new category will bring needed attention to metacognitive objectives.

7. Subcategories of the Cognitive Process Categories Were Replaced by Verbs

In the original framework the subcategories of the five categories beyond Knowledge were either nouns or nominative phrases (e.g., translation, interpretation, extrapolation within Comprehension). Verbs of the kind used by teachers in statements of objectives and during instruction seemed more helpful in framing and categorizing objectives, instructional activities, and assessment tasks. We replaced the nouns with verbs (e.g., *interpreting, exemplifying, inferring*). To distinguish them from the major category verb names, we call them "cognitive processes." Why did we choose particular verbs to replace the original subcategories? The verbs selected met two criteria: (1) they represented cognitive processes incorporated within cognitive theory and research, and (2) they were the type of processes commonly encountered in statements of objectives and unit plans of teachers.[1]

8. COMPREHENSION AND SYNTHESIS WERE RETITLED

We retitled two of the major categories: Comprehension became *Understand* and Synthesis became *Create*. The reasons for these changes are discussed in Chapter 5 and, for *Understand*, in the last section of this chapter.

FOUR CHANGES IN STRUCTURE

9. THE NOUN AND VERB COMPONENTS OF OBJECTIVES BECAME SEPARATE DIMENSIONS

Advances in research on learning and distinctions made in alternative taxonomic frameworks caused us to rethink the role of knowledge in the original structure. Ultimately, we separated the noun and verb components implicit in the original Knowledge category. The noun aspect retained the label Knowledge but became a separate dimension with the four categories as noted in point 6 above. (See also the knowledge dimension on the inside front cover.)

The verb aspect of Knowledge became the category *Remember*, which replaced the original Knowledge classification in the six major categories, now all consisting of verbs. Its verb form describes the action implicit in the original Knowledge category; the first thing one does in learning knowledge is to remember it. Considered the least complex of the six process categories, *Remember* occupies the bottom rung originally occupied by Knowledge. Together the six major categories, expressed as verbs to describe what one does with or to Knowledge, form the cognitive process dimension (see inside back cover).

10. THE TWO DIMENSIONS ARE THE BASIS FOR OUR ANALYTICAL TOOL, THE TAXONOMY TABLE

Determining that knowledge would be a new dimension logically led us to make its relationship to the cognitive process dimension explicit in a two-dimensional structure we call the Taxonomy Table (see inside front cover). The cells of the Taxonomy Table contain the educational objectives. In addition to classifying objectives, the Taxonomy Table permits the analysis of instructional activities and assessment tasks (as shown in the vignettes, Chapters 8–13). When objectives,

---

[1] The necessity of translating the Taxonomy categories into the verbs used in objectives was recognized early by Metfessel, Michael, and Kirsner (1969). To facilitate the work of teachers, administrators, and other users of the framework, they provided a thesaurus-like list that suggested alternative verbs for each of the major Taxonomy categories.

instructional activities, and assessment tasks are examined in the context of the Taxonomy Table, issues of alignment can be addressed.

11. THE PROCESS CATEGORIES DO NOT FORM A CUMULATIVE HIERARCHY

The revised framework is a hierarchy in the sense that the six major categories of the cognitive process dimension are presumed to be ordered in terms of increasing complexity. The categories of the original scheme were claimed to be a cumulative hierarchy, however. This meant that mastery of a more complex category required prior mastery of all the less complex categories below it—a stringent standard. Subsequent research provided empirical evidence for a cumulative hierarchy for the three middle categories, Comprehension, Application, and Analysis, but empirical support was weak for ordering the last two (see Chapter 16[2]).

As required in a cumulative hierarchy, the original categories were presumed not to overlap. Indeed, some of the boundaries of the original six categories were designed to make distinct categories by arbitrary stipulation. An important characteristic of the revised Taxonomy, however, is that in order to conform to the language that teachers use, the six categories are allowed to overlap on a scale of judged complexity. Therefore, the revision places much greater importance on teacher usage than on developing a strict hierarchy.

This change is clearly illustrated in the case of the category *Understand*. Looking at the ways *Understand* is used, these are clearly broader than the definition given to its predecessor, Comprehend. Therefore, the subcategories that define the limits of the *Understand* category are allowed to overlap *Apply*. For example, *Understand* is one step less complex than *Apply* in the six-category hierarchy. Therefore, *explaining*, which is a cognitive process listed within *Understand*, would also be expected to be a step down in complexity from the simplest process in *Apply*. This is not the case. Instead, this is one instance where the process (in this case *explaining*) equals or exceeds the judged complexity of the next category up in the hierarchy (in this case *Apply*).

If we were to prevent categories from overlapping, we would have had to place *explaining* in *Apply, Analyze, Evaluate,* or *Create*. But, explaining isn't a kind of applying, or analyzing, evaluating, or creating. It exemplifies a kind of understanding, and so that is where we categorized it, even though it is certainly a more complex process than most simple instances of application.

Does that mean that we don't have a kind of hierarchy? We don't think so. Conceptually, if we marked off the judged range of each category on the cognitive process dimension along a continuum from simple to complex, the center of each category going from *Remember* to *Create* would be successively greater in complexity. Furthermore, although we have changed the definitions slightly,

---

[2] Chapter 16 appears only in the hardcover edition of this book.

we do not believe we have altered them sufficiently that the empirical evidence found for the original categories is invalidated for the revision. This evidence supports the hierarchical order for the least complex categories (described in Chapter 16).

12. THE ORDER OF SYNTHESIS/CREATE AND EVALUATION/EVALUATE WAS INTERCHANGED

We interchanged the order of the top two cognitive process categories, placing *Create* as the most complex category instead of *Evaluate*. A rationale for this reordering is given in Chapter 16.

Figure A.1 summarizes the structural relationship of the six original categories and the revised structure.

FIGURE A.1   Summary of the Structural Changes from the Original Framework to the Revision

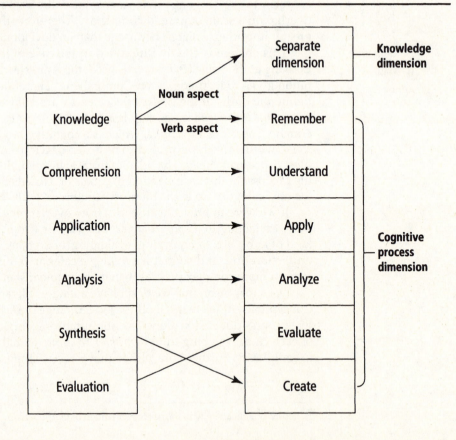

THE INCLUSION OF UNDERSTANDING AND THE OMISSION OF PROBLEM SOLVING AND CRITICAL THINKING

Two of the many questions that could be raised about the revision are:

- In the changes, why did "comprehension" become "understand"?

- Why weren't important processes like problem solving and critical thinking included?

These two questions are important and we spent considerable time discussing them as well as several others. (In fact, several times David Krathwohl reminded us that the original group spent considerable time on these questions as well. This was his way of telling us to "move on.")

With respect to understanding, the authors of the *Handbook* were concerned that, insofar as possible, the categories did not overlap. But that is difficult when a term takes on a wide range of different meanings. Consider the many possibilities of meanings when teachers want their students to "*understand* Ohm's law." They could include *applying* the law, *analyzing* a problem to determine whether the law is applicable, *evaluating* the use of Ohm's law in a problem, or even combining the law with others to solve a problem (a *creative* process).

Another example of the wide range of possibilities in "understand" is suggested by Wiggins and McTighe (1998, pp. 44–62). They argue that when we truly understand, we can explain, can interpret, can apply, will have perspective, can empathize, and will have self-knowledge—a wide range of meanings that include aspects normally considered affective (e.g., empathize) instead of cognitive. To many, this may be stretching the common connotation of the term, but, because of this possible fuzziness, the original group avoided the term "understanding" and used "comprehension."

Discussion of the *Handbook* in the years since its development has made clear that teachers miss having a place where the term "*Understand*" can "fit." The result is that, in determining how best to construct our framework, we considered a different criterion—namely, that the framework should embrace the terms that teachers frequently use in talking about education. We replaced "Comprehension" with "*Understand*" simply because the group working on this volume gave more weight to the universal usage of the term in selecting names for the categories.

Two other terms, "problem solving" and "critical thinking," seem to have characteristics similar to "understand." They are widely used and likewise tend to become touchstones of curriculum emphasis. Both generally include a variety of activities that might be classified in disparate cells of the Taxonomy Table. That is, in any given instance, objectives that involve problem solving and critical thinking most likely call for cognitive processes in several categories on the process dimension. For example, to think critically about an issue probably involves some *Conceptual knowledge* to *Analyze* the issue. Then, one can *Evaluate* different perspectives in terms of the criteria and, perhaps, *Create* a novel, yet defensible perspective on the issue.

In contrast with understanding, then, critical thinking and problem solving tend to cut across rows, columns, and cells of the Taxonomy Table. With respect to problem solving, for example, the particular rows, columns, and cells selected, and the order in which specific cognitive processes and knowledge subtypes would be expected to be used, would depend to a great extent on the particular type of problem being solved and/or the subject matter within which the problem was posed. Thus, unlike understanding, critical thinking and problem solving did not seem to be prime substitutes for any single category in the framework. Therefore, despite our interest in employing the terms teachers use, we did not see a way to effectively include problem solving or critical thinking as major headings in our revision.

Condensed Version of the Original Taxonomy of Educational Objectives: *Cognitive Domain*[1]

KNOWLEDGE

1.00 KNOWLEDGE

Knowledge, as defined here, involves the recall of specifics and universals, the recall of methods and processes, or the recall of a pattern, structure, or setting. For measurement purposes, the recall situation involves little more than bringing to mind the appropriate material. Although some alteration of the material may be required, this is a relatively minor part of the task. The knowledge objectives emphasize most the psychological processes of remembering. The process of relating is also involved in that a knowledge test situation requires the organization and reorganization of a problem such that it will furnish the appropriate signals and cues for the information and knowledge the individual possesses. To use an analogy, if one thinks of the mind as a file, the problem in a knowledge test situation is that of finding in the problem or task the appropriate signals, cues, and clues which will most effectively bring out whatever knowledge is filed or stored.

1.10 KNOWLEDGE OF SPECIFICS

The recall of specific and isolable bits of information. The emphasis is on symbols with concrete referents. This material, which is at a very low level of abstraction, may be thought of as the elements from which more complex and abstract forms of knowledge are built.

---

[1]*Handbook*, pp. 201–207.

1.11 KNOWLEDGE OF TERMINOLOGY

Knowledge of the referents for specific symbols (verbal and non-verbal). This may include knowledge of the most generally accepted symbol referent, knowledge of the variety of symbols which may be used for a single referent, or knowledge of the referent most appropriate to a given use of a symbol.

- To define technical terms by giving their attributes, properties, or relations.*
- Familiarity with a large number of words in their common range of meanings.

1.12 KNOWLEDGE OF SPECIFIC FACTS

Knowledge of dates, events, persons, places, etc. This may include very precise and specific information such as the specific date or exact magnitude of a phenomenon. It may also include approximate or relative information such as an approximate time period or the general order of magnitude of a phenomenon.

- The recall of major facts about particular cultures.
- The possession of a minimum knowledge about the organisms studied in the laboratory.

1.20 KNOWLEDGE OF WAYS AND MEANS OF DEALING WITH SPECIFICS

Knowledge of the ways of organizing, studying, judging, and criticizing. This includes the methods of inquiry, the chronological sequences, and the standards of judgment within a field as well as the patterns of organization through which the areas of the fields themselves are determined and internally organized. This knowledge is at an intermediate level of abstraction between specific knowledge on the one hand and knowledge of universals on the other. It does not so much demand the activity of the student in using the materials as it does a more passive awareness of their nature.

1.21 KNOWLEDGE OF CONVENTIONS

Knowledge of characteristic ways of treating and presenting ideas and phenomena. For purposes of communication and consistency, workers in a field employ usages, styles, practices, and forms which best suit their purposes and/or which appear to suit best the phenomena with which they deal. It should be recognized that although these forms and conventions are likely to be set up on arbitrary, accidental, or authoritative bases, they are retained because of the general agreement or concurrence of individuals concerned with the subject, phenomena, or problem.

- Familiarity with the forms and conventions of the major types of works, e.g., verse, plays, scientific papers, etc.
- To make pupils conscious of correct form and usage in speech and writing.

---

*Illustrative educational objectives selected from the literature.

1.22   KNOWLEDGE OF TRENDS AND SEQUENCES

Knowledge of the processes, directions, and movements of phenomena with respect to time.

- Understanding of the continuity and development of American culture as exemplified in American life.
- Knowledge of the basic trends underlying the development of public assistance programs.

1.23   KNOWLEDGE OF CLASSIFICATIONS AND CATEGORIES

Knowledge of the classes, sets, divisions, and arrangements which are regarded as fundamental for a given subject field, purpose, argument, or problem.

- To recognize the area encompassed by various kinds of problems or materials.
- Becoming familiar with a range of types of literature.

1.24   KNOWLEDGE OF CRITERIA

Knowledge of the criteria by which facts, principles, opinions, and conduct are tested or judged.

- Familiarity with criteria for judgment appropriate to the type of work and the purpose for which it is read.
- Knowledge of criteria for the evaluation of recreational activities.

1.25   KNOWLEDGE OF METHODOLOGY

Knowledge of the methods of inquiry, techniques, and procedures employed in a particular subject field as well as those employed in investigating particular problems and phenomena. The emphasis here is on the individual's knowledge of the method rather than his ability to use the method.

- Knowledge of scientific methods for evaluating health concepts.
- The students shall know the methods of attack relevant to the kinds of problems of concern to the social sciences.

1.30   KNOWLEDGE OF THE UNIVERSALS AND ABSTRACTIONS IN A FIELD

Knowledge of the major schemes and patterns by which phenomena and ideas are organized. These are the large structures, theories, and generalizations which dominate a subject field or which are quite generally used in studying phenomena or solving problems. These are at the highest levels of abstraction and complexity.

1.31 KNOWLEDGE OF PRINCIPLES AND GENERALIZATIONS

Knowledge of particular abstractions which summarize observations of phenomena. These are the abstractions which are of value in explaining, describing, predicting, or in determining the most appropriate and relevant action or direction to be taken.

- Knowledge of the important principles by which our experience with biological phenomena is summarized.
- The recall of major generalizations about particular cultures.

1.32 KNOWLEDGE OF THEORIES AND STRUCTURES

Knowledge of the *body* of principles and generalizations together with their interrelations which present a clear, rounded, and systematic view of a complex phenomenon, problem, or field. These are the most abstract formulations, and they can be used to show the interrelation and organization of a great range of specifics.

- The recall of major theories about particular cultures.
- Knowledge of a relatively complete formulation of the theory of evolution.

INTELLECTUAL ABILITIES AND SKILLS

Abilities and skills refer to organized modes of operation and generalized techniques for dealing with materials and problems. The materials and problems may be of such a nature that little or no specialized and technical information is required. Such information as is required can be assumed to be part of the individual's general fund of knowledge. Other problems may require specialized and technical information at a rather high level such that specific knowledge and skill in dealing with the problem and the materials are required. The abilities and skills objectives emphasize the mental processes of organizing and reorganizing material to achieve a particular purpose. The materials may be given or remembered.

2.00 COMPREHENSION

This represents the lowest level of understanding. It refers to a type of understanding or apprehension such that the individual knows what is being communicated and can make use of the material or idea being communicated without necessarily relating it to other material or seeing its fullest implications.

2.10 TRANSLATION

Comprehension as evidenced by the care and accuracy with which the communication is paraphrased or rendered from one language or form of communication to another. Translation is judged on the basis of faithfulness and accuracy, that is, on the extent to which the material in the original communication is preserved although the form of the communication has been altered.

- The ability to understand non-literal statements (metaphor, symbolism, irony, exaggeration).
- Skill in translating mathematical verbal material into symbolic statements and vice versa.

2.20 INTERPRETATION

The explanation or summarization of a communication. Whereas translation involves an objective part-for-part rendering of a communication, interpretation involves a reordering, rearrangement, or a new view of the material.

- The ability to grasp the thought of the work as a whole at any desired level of generality.
- The ability to interpret various types of social data.

2.30 EXTRAPOLATION

The extension of trends or tendencies beyond the given data to determine implications, consequences, corollaries, effects, etc., which are in accordance with the conditions described in the original communication.

- The ability to deal with the conclusions of a work in terms of the immediate inference made from the explicit statements.
- Skill in predicting continuation of trends.

3.00 APPLICATION

The use of abstractions in particular and concrete situations. The abstractions may be in the form of general ideas, rules of procedures, or generalized methods. The abstractions may also be technical principles, ideas, and theories which must be remembered and applied.

- Application to the phenomena discussed in one paper of the scientific terms or concepts used in other papers.
- The ability to predict the probable effect of a change in a factor on a biological situation previously at equilibrium.

4.00 ANALYSIS

The breakdown of a communication into its constituent elements or parts such that the relative hierarchy of ideas is made clear and/or the relations between the ideas expressed are made explicit. Such analyses are intended to clarify the communication, to indicate how the communication is organized, and the way in which it manages to convey its effects, as well as its basis and arrangement.

4.10   ANALYSIS OF ELEMENTS

Identification of the elements included in a communication.

- The ability to recognize unstated assumptions.
- Skill in distinguishing facts from hypotheses.

4.20   ANALYSES OF RELATIONSHIPS

The connections and interactions between elements and parts of a communication.

- Ability to check the consistency of hypotheses with given information and assumptions.
- Skill in comprehending the interrelationships among the ideas in a passage.

4.30   ANALYSIS OF ORGANIZATIONAL PRINCIPLES

The organization, systematic arrangement, and structure which hold the communication together. This includes the "explicit" as well as the "implicit" structure. It includes the bases, necessary arrangement, and the mechanics which make the communication a unit.

- The ability to recognize form and pattern in literary or artistic works as a means of understanding their meaning.
- Ability to recognize the general techniques used in persuasive materials, such as advertising, propaganda, etc.

5.00   SYNTHESIS

The putting together of elements and parts so as to form a whole. This involves the process of working with pieces, parts, elements, etc., and arranging and combining them in such a way as to constitute a pattern or structure not clearly there before.

5.10   PRODUCTION OF A UNIQUE COMMUNICATION

The development of a communication in which the writer or speaker attempts to convey ideas, feelings, and/or experiences to others.

- Skill in writing, using an excellent organization of ideas and statements.
- Ability to tell a personal experience effectively.

5.20   PRODUCTION OF A PLAN, OR PROPOSED SET OF OPERATIONS

The development of a plan of work or the proposal of a plan of operations. The plan should satisfy requirements of the task which may be given to the student or which he may develop for himself.

- Ability to propose ways of testing hypotheses.
- Ability to plan a unit of instruction for a particular teaching situation.

5.30   DERIVATION OF A SET OF ABSTRACT RELATIONS

The development of a set of abstract relations either to classify or explain particular data or phenomena, or the deduction of propositions and relations from a set of basic propositions or symbolic representations.

- Ability to formulate appropriate hypotheses based upon an analysis of factors involved, and to modify such hypotheses in the light of new factors and considerations.
- Ability to make mathematical discoveries and generalizations.

6.00   EVALUATION

Judgments about the value of material and methods for given purposes. Quantitative and qualitative judgments about the extent to which material and methods satisfy criteria. Use of a standard of appraisal. The criteria may be those determined by the student or those which are given to him.

6.10   JUDGMENTS IN TERMS OF INTERNAL EVIDENCE

Evaluation of the accuracy of a communication from such evidence as logical accuracy, consistency and other internal criteria.

- Judging by internal standards, the ability to assess general probability of accuracy in reporting facts from the care given to exactness of statement, documentation, proof, etc.
- The ability to indicate logical fallacies in arguments.

6.20   JUDGMENTS IN TERMS OF EXTERNAL CRITERIA

Evaluation of material with reference to selected or remembered criteria.

- The comparison of major theories, generalizations, and facts about particular cultures.
- Judging by external standards, the ability to compare a work with the highest known standards in its field—especially with other works of recognized excellence.

References

Airasian, P. W. (1994). Impact on testing and evaluation. In L. W. Anderson & L. A. Sosniak (Eds.), *Bloom's taxonomy: A forty-year retrospective*, Ninety-third Yearbook of the National Society for the Study of Education (pp. 82–102). Chicago: University of Chicago Press.

Alexander, P., Schallert, D., & Hare, V. (1991). Coming to terms: How researchers in learning and literacy talk about knowledge. *Review of Educational Research, 61*, 315–343.

American Association for the Advancement of Science. (1993). *Benchmarks for science literacy.* New York: Oxford University Press.

American Heritage Dictionary of the English Language (3rd ed.). (1992). Boston: Houghton Mifflin.

Anderson, J. R. (1983). *The architecture of cognition.* Cambridge, MA: Harvard University Press.

Anderson, L. W. (1995). *International encyclopedia of teaching and teacher education*, 2nd ed. Oxford, UK: Pergamon Press.

Anderson, L. W. (Ed.), & Sosniak, L. A. (Eds.). (1994). *Bloom's taxonomy: A forty-year retrospective.* Ninety-third Yearbook of the National Society for the Study of Education. Chicago: University of Chicago Press.

Armstrong, D. G. (1989). *Developing and documenting the curriculum.* Boston: Allyn & Bacon.

Baker, E. L., O'Neil, H. F., & Linn, R. L. (1993). Policy validity prospects for performance-based assessment. *American Psychologist, 48*, 1210–1218.

Baron, J. (1994). *Thinking and deciding.* Cambridge, UK: Cambridge University Press.

Baxter, G. P., Elder, A. D., & Glaser, R. (1996). Knowledge-based cognition and performance assessment in the science classroom. *Educational Psychologist, 31*, 133–140.

Bereiter, C., & Scardamalia, M. (1998). Beyond Bloom's Taxonomy: Rethinking knowledge for the knowledge age. In A. Hargreaves, A. Lieberman, M. Fullan & D. Hopkins (Eds.), *International handbook of educational change* (pp. 675–692). London: Kluwer Academic Publishers.

Bloom, B. S. (1949). *A taxonomy of educational objectives.* Opening remarks of B. S. Bloom for the meeting of examiners at Monticello, Illinois, November 27, 1949. Unpublished manuscript.

Bloom, B. S. (circa 1971). *Some suggestions for chapters III, IV, V.* Unpublished and undated manuscript.

Bloom, B. S. (Ed.), Engelhart, M. D., Furst, E. J., Hill, W. H., & Krathwohl, D. R. (1956). *Taxonomy of educational objectives: Handbook I: Cognitive domain.* New York: David McKay.

Bloom, B. S., Hastings, J. T., & Madaus, G. F. (1971). *Handbook on formative and summative evaluation of student learning.* New York: McGraw-Hill.

Bobbitt, F. (1918). *The curriculum.* Boston: Houghton Mifflin.

Boekaerts, M., Pintrich, P. R., & Zeidner, M. (2000). *Handbook of self-regulation.* San Diego: Academic Press.

Bransford, J. D., Brown, A. L., & Cocking, R. R. (1999). *How people learn: Brain, mind, experience and school.* Washington, DC: National Academy Press.

Broudy, H. S. (1970). Can research escape the dogma of educational objectives? *School Review, 79,* 43–56.

Brown, A., Bransford, J., Ferrara, R., & Campione, J. (1983). Learning, remembering, and understanding. In P. H. Mussen (Series Ed.), J. Flavell & E. Markman (Vol. Eds.), *Handbook of child psychology: Vol. 3. Cognitive development,* 4th ed. (pp. 77–166). New York: Wiley.

Bruer, J. T. (1993). *Schools for thought: A science of learning in the classroom.* Cambridge, MA: MIT Press.

Case, R. (1998). The development of conceptual structures. In W. Damon (Series Ed.), D. Kuhn & R. Siegler (Vol. Eds.), *Handbook of child psychology: Vol. 2. Cognition, perception, and language* 5th ed. (pp. 745–800). New York: Wiley.

Chi, M. (1992). Conceptual change within and across ontological categories: Implications for learning and discovery in sciences. In R. Giere (Ed.), *Cognitive models of science.* Minnesota Studies in the Philosophy of Science, Vol. 15 (pp. 129–186). Minneapolis, MN: University of Minnesota Press.

Chi, M., Feltovich, P., & Glaser, R. (1981). Categorization and representation of physics problems by experts and novices. *Cognitive Science, 5,* 121–152.

Chi, M., Slotta, J., & deLeeuw, N. (1994). From things to processes: A theory of conceptual change for learning science concepts. *Learning and Instruction, 4,* 27–43.

Chung, B. M. (1994). The taxonomy in the Republic of Korea. In L. W. Anderson & L. A. Sosniak (Eds.), *Bloom's taxonomy: A forty-year retrospective,* Ninety-third Yearbook of the National Society for the Study of Education (pp. 164–173). Chicago: University of Chicago Press.

Clandinin, D. J., & Connelly, F. M. (1992). Teacher as curriculum maker. In P. W. Jackson (Ed.), *Handbook of research on curriculum* (pp. 363–401). New York: Macmillan.

deJong, T., & Ferguson-Hessler, M. (1996). Types and qualities of knowledge. *Educational Psychologist, 31,* 105–113.

DeLandsheere, V. (1977). On defining educational objectives. *Evaluation in Education: International Review Series, 1,* 73–190.

Detterman, D. K., & Sternberg, R. J. (1993). *Transfer on trial: Intelligence, cognition, and instruction.* Norwood, NJ: ABLEX.

Dewey, J. (1916). *Democracy and education.* New York: Free Press.

Dochy, F., & Alexander, P. (1995). Mapping prior knowledge: A framework of discussion among researchers. *European Journal of Psychology in Education, 10,* 224–242.

Doyle, W. (1992). Curriculum and pedagogy. In P. W. Jackson (Ed.), *Handbook of research on curriculum* (pp. 486–516). New York: Macmillan.

Dreeben, R. (1968). *On what is learned in schools.* Chicago: University of Chicago Press.

Duncker, K. (1945). On problem solving. *Psychological Monographs, 58*(5), Whole No. 270.

Dunne, J. (1988). Teaching and the limits of technique: An analysis of the behavioural-objectives model. *The Irish Journal of Education, 22,* 2, 66–90.

Eisner, E. W. (1979). *The educational imagination.* New York: Macmillan.

Ellis, J. A. (1999). Letter to the Editor. *Newsweek,* September 27, p. 15.

Flavell, J. (1979). Metacognition and cognitive monitoring: A new area of cognitive-developmental inquiry. *American Psychologist, 34,* 906–911.

Frymier, J. (1996). *Accountability in education: Still an evolving concept.* Bloomington, IN: Phi Delta Kappa Educational Foundation.

Furst, E. J. (1981). Bloom's taxonomy of educational objectives for the cognitive domain: Philosophical and educational issues. *Review of Educational Research, 51,* 441–453.

Gandal, M. (1996). *Making standards matter.* Washington, DC: American Federation of Teachers.

Gick, M. L., & Holyoak, K. J. (1980). Analogical problem solving. *Cognitive Psychology, 12,* 306–355.

Gick, M. L., & Holyoak, K. J. (1983). Schema induction and analogical transfer. *Cognitive Psychology, 15,* 1–38.

Ginther, J. R. (1972). *A radical look at behavioral objectives.* Paper presented at the annual meeting of the American Educational Research Association, Chicago, April, 1972.

Glatthorn, A. A. (1998). *Performance assessment and standards-based curricula: The achievement cycle.* Larchmont, NY: Eye on Education.

Haladyna, T. M. (1997) *Writing test items to evaluate higher order thinking.* Boston: Allyn & Bacon.

Halley, J. M. (1999). Letter to the Editor. *Newsweek,* September 27, p. 15.

Hambleton, R. K. (1996). Advances in assessment models, methods, and practices. In D. C. Berliner & R. C. Calfee (Eds.), *Handbook of educational psychology* (pp. 899–925). New York: Macmillan.

Hannah, L. S., & Michaelis, J. U. (1977). *A comprehensive framework for instructional objectives: A guide to systematic planning and evaluation.* Reading, MA: Addison-Wesley.

Harrow, A. (1972). *A taxonomy of the psychomotor domain: A guide for developing behavioral objectives.* New York: David McKay.

Hauenstein, A. D. (1998). *A conceptual framework for educational objectives: A holistic approach to traditional taxonomies.* Lanham, MD: University Press of America.

Hirst, P. H. (1974). *Knowledge and the curriculum: A collection of philosophical papers.* London: Routledge & Kegan Paul.

Jackson, P. W. (1968). *Life in classrooms.* New York: Holt, Rinehart and Winston.

Joyce, B., and Weil, M. (1996). *Models of teaching* (5th ed.). Englewood Cliffs, NJ: Prentice-Hall.

Kappel, F. R. (1960). *Vitality in a business enterprise.* New York: McGraw-Hill.

Keil, F. (1998). Cognitive science and the origins of thought and knowledge. In W. Damon (Series Ed.) & R. Lerner (Vol. Ed.), *Handbook of child psychology: Vol. 1. Theoretical models of human development* 5th ed. (pp. 341–413). New York: Wiley.

Kelly, A. V. (1989). *The curriculum: Theory and practice* (3rd ed.). London: Paul Chapman Publishers.

Kendall, J. S., & Marzano, R. J. (1996). *Content knowledge.* Aurora, CO: Mid-Continent Regional Educational Laboratory.

Klopfer, L. E. (1971). Evaluation of learning in science. In B. S. Bloom, J. T. Hastings & G. F. Madaus (Eds.), *Handbook on formative and summative evaluation of student learning* (pp. 561–641). New York: McGraw-Hill.

Krathwohl, D. R. (1964). The taxonomy of educational objectives: Its use in curriculum building. In C. M. Lindvall (Ed.), *Defining educational objectives* (pp. 19–36). Pittsburgh: University of Pittsburgh Press.

Krathwohl, D. R. (1994). Reflections on the taxonomy: Its past, present, and future. In L. W. Anderson & L. A. Sosniak (Eds.), *Bloom's taxonomy: A forty-year retrospective,* Ninety-third Yearbook of the National Society for the Study of Education (pp. 181–202). Chicago: University of Chicago Press.

Krathwohl, D. R., Bloom, B. S., & Masia, B. B. (1964). *Taxonomy of educational objectives, the Classification of Educational Goals; Handbook II: The affective domain.* New York: David McKay.

Krathwohl, D. R., & Payne, D. A. (1971). Defining and assessing educational objectives. In R. L. Thorndike (Ed.), *Educational measurement* (pp. 17–45). Washington, DC: American Council on Education.

Lambert, N. M., & McCombs, B. L. (Eds.). (1998). *How students learn: Reforming schools through learner-based education.* Washington, DC: American Psychological Association.

Levy, C. M., & Ransdell, S. (Eds.). (1996). *The science of writing.* Mahwah, NJ: Erlbaum.

Lewy, A., & Bathory, Z. (1994). The taxonomy of educational objectives in continental Europe, the Mediterranean, and the Middle East. In L.W. Anderson & L. A. Sosniak (Eds.), *Bloom's taxonomy: A forty-year retrospective,* Ninety-third Yearbook of the National Society for the Study of Education (pp. 146–163). Chicago: University of Chicago Press.

Mager, R. F. (1962). *Preparing instructional objectives.* Palo Alto, CA: Fearon Press.

Mandler, J. (1998). Representation. In W. Damon (Series Ed.), D. Kuhn & R. Siegler (Vol. Eds.), *Handbook of child psychology: Vol. 2. Cognition, perception, and language* 5th ed. (pp. 255–308). New York: Wiley.

Manzo, K. K. (1999). The state of curriculum. *Education Week,* May 19, 21–26, 28.

Marsh, C. (1992). *Key concepts in understanding curriculum.* London: The Falmer Press.

Marshall, H. H. (Ed.). (1996). Recent and emerging theoretical frameworks for research on classroom learning: Contributions and limitations. *Educational Psychologist, 31*(3 & 4), 147–240.

Mayer, R. E. (1992). *Thinking, problem solving, and cognition* (2nd ed.). New York: Freeman.

Mayer, R. E. (1995). Teaching and testing for problem solving. In L. W. Anderson (Ed.), *International encyclopedia of teaching and teacher education,* 2nd ed. (pp. 4728–4731). Oxford, UK: Pergamon.

Mayer, R. E. (1999). *The promise of educational psychology: Learning in the content areas.* Upper Saddle River, NJ: Prentice-Hall.

Mayer, R. E., & Wittrock, M. C. (1996). Problem-solving transfer. In D. C. Berliner & R. C. Calfee (Eds.), *Handbook of educational psychology* (pp. 47–62). New York: Macmillan.

McGuire, C. (1963). A process approach to the construction and analysis of medical examinations. *Journal of Medical Education, 38,* 556–563.

McKeough, A., Lupart, J., & Marini, A. (Eds.). (1995). *Teaching for transfer.* Mahwah, NJ: Erlbaum.

Metfessel, N. S., Michael, W. G., & Kirsner, D. A. (1969). Instrumentation of Bloom's and Krathwohl's taxonomies for the writing of educational objectives. *Psychology in the Schools, 6,* 227–231.

Moore, W. R., & Kennedy, L. D. (1971). Evaluation of learning in the language arts. In B. S. Bloom, J. T. Hastings & G. F. Madaus (Eds.), *Handbook on formative and summative evaluation of student learning* (pp. 399–446). New York: McGraw-Hill.

Mosenthal, P. B. (1998). Defining prose task characteristics for use in computer-adaptive testing and instruction. *American Educational Research Journal, 35,* 269–307.

National Council for the Social Studies. (1994). *Curriculum standards for social studies: Expectations of excellence.* Washington, DC: Author.

National Council of Teachers of English and International Reading Association. (1996). *Standards for the English language arts.* Urbana, IL: Author.

National Council of Teachers of Mathematics. (1989). *Curriculum and evaluation standards for teaching mathematics.* Reston, VA: Author.

National Research Council. (1996). *National science education standards.* Washington, DC: National Academy Press.

Nickerson, R., Perkins, D., & Smith, E. (1985). *The teaching of thinking.* Hillsdale, NJ: Erlbaum.

Orlandi, L. R. (1971). Evaluation of learning in secondary school social studies. In B. S. Bloom, J. T. Hastings & G. F. Madaus (Eds.), *Handbook on formative and summative evaluation of student learning* (pp. 449–498). New York: McGraw-Hill.

Paris, S., Lipson, M., & Wixson, K. (1983). Becoming a strategic reader. *Contemporary Educational Psychology, 8,* 293–316.

Paris, S., & Winograd, P. (1990). How metacognition can promote academic learning and instruction. In B. F. Jones & L. Idol (Eds.), *Dimensions of thinking and cognitive instruction* (pp. 15–51). Hillsdale, NJ: Erlbaum.

Paul, R., & Nosich, G. M. (1992). *A model for the national assessment of higher order thinking.* Santa Rosa, CA: Foundation for Critical Thinking. (ERIC Document Reproduction Service No. ED 353 296)

Phye, G. D. (Ed.). (1997). *Handbook of classroom assessment.* San Diego, CA: Academic Press.

Pintrich, P. R., & Schrauben, B. (1992). Students' motivational beliefs and their cognitive engagement in classroom tasks. In D. Schunk & J. Meece (Eds.), *Student perceptions in the classroom: Causes and consequences* (pp. 149–183). Hillsdale, NJ: Erlbaum.

Pintrich, P. R., & Schunk, D. H. (1996). *Motivation in education: Theory, research, and applications.* Englewood Cliffs, NJ: Merrill Prentice-Hall.

Pintrich, P. R., Wolters, C., & Baxter, G. (in press). Assessing metacognition and self-regulated learning. In G. Schraw (Ed.), *Metacognitive assessment.* Lincoln, NE: University of Nebraska Press.

Popham, W. J. (1969). Objectives and instruction. In W. J. Popham, E. W. Eisner, H. J. Sullivan & L. L. Tyler, *Instructional objectives* (pp. 32–52). American Educational Research Association Monograph Series on Curriculum Evaluation, No. 3. Chicago: Rand McNally.

Postlethwaite, T. N. (1994). Validity vs. utility: Personal experiences with the taxonomy. In L. W. Anderson & L. A. Sosniak (Eds.), *Bloom's taxonomy: A forty-year retrospective,* Ninety-third Yearbook of the National Society for the Study of Education (pp. 174–180). Chicago: University of Chicago Press.

Pressley, M., & Van Meter, P. (1995). Memory: Teaching and assessing. In L. W. Anderson (Ed.), *International encyclopedia of teaching and teacher education* (pp. 439–444). Oxford, UK: Pergamon Press.

Pressley, M., & Woloshyn, V. (1995). *Cognitive strategy instruction that really improves children's academic performance.* Cambridge, MA: Brookline Books.

Rebarber, T. (1991). *Accountability in education.* Paper presented at the National Conference of State Legislatures, Washington, DC.

Rohwer, W. D. Jr., & Sloane, K. (1994). Psychological perspectives. In L. W. Anderson & L. A. Sosniak (Eds.), *Bloom's taxonomy: A forty-year retrospective,* Ninety-third Yearbook of the National Society for the Study of Education (pp. 41–63). Chicago: University of Chicago Press.

Royer, J. M., Ciscero, C. A., & Carlo, M. S. (1993). Techniques and procedures for assessing cognitive skills. *Review of Educational Research, 63,* 201–243.

Rugg, H. (1926a). Curriculum-making and the scientific study of education since 1910. In H. Rugg (Ed.), *Twenty-sixth yearbook of the National Society for the Study of Education, Part I.* Bloomington, IL: Public Schools Publishing Company.

Rugg, H., et al. (1926b). The foundations of curriculum-making. In H. Rugg (Ed.), *Twenty-sixth yearbook of the National Society for the Study of Education, Part II.* Bloomington, IL: Public Schools Publishing Company.

Ryle, G. (1949). *The concept of mind.* London: Hutchinson.

Schneider, W., & Pressley, M. (1997). *Memory development between two and twenty.* Mahwah, NJ: Erlbaum.

Scriven, M. (1967). The methodology of evaluation. In R. E. Stake et al. (Eds.) *Perspectives on curriculum evaluation. AERA Monograph Series on Curriculum Evaluation, No. 1.* Chicago: Rand McNally.

Seddon, G. M. (1978). The properties of Bloom's taxonomy of educational objectives for the cognitive domain. *Review of Educational Research, 48,* 303–323.

Shane, H. G. (1981). Significant writings that have influenced the curriculum: 1906–81. *Phi Delta Kappan, 63,* 311–314.

Shulman, L. (1987). Knowledge and teaching: Foundations of the new reform. *Harvard Educational Review, 57,* 1–22.

Simpson, B. J. (1966). The classification of educational objectives: Psychomotor domain. *Illinois Journal of Home Economics, 10* (4), 110–144.

Slotta, J., Chi, M., & Joram, E. (1995). Assessing students' misclassifications of physics concepts: An ontological basis for conceptual change. *Cognition and Instruction, 13,* 373–400.

Smith, E. R., & Tyler, R. W. (1942). *Appraising and recording student progress.* New York: Harper.

Smith, M. U. (Ed.). (1991). *Toward a unified theory of problem solving: Views from the content domains.* Hillsdale, NJ: Erlbaum.

Snow, R., Corno, L., & Jackson, D. (1996). Individual differences in affective and cognitive functions. In D. Berliner & R. Calfee (Eds.), *Handbook of educational psychology* (pp. 243–310). New York: Macmillan.

Sosniak, L. A. (1994). The Taxonomy, curriculum and their relations. In L. W. Anderson & L. A. Sosniak (Eds.), *Bloom's taxonomy: A forty-year retrospective,* Ninety-third Yearbook of the National Society for the Study of Education (pp. 103–125). Chicago: University of Chicago Press.

Steffe, L. P., & Gale, J. (Eds.). (1995). *Constructivism in education.* Mahwah, NJ: Erlbaum.

Stenhouse, L. A. (1970–1971). Some limitations of the use of objectives in curriculum research and planning. *Pedagogia Europaea.*

Sternberg, R. (1985). *Beyond IQ: A triarchic theory of human intelligence.* New York: Cambridge University Press.

Sternberg, R. J. (1997). Intelligence and lifelong learning: What's new and how can we use it? *American Psychologist, 52,* 1134–1139.

Sternberg, R. J. (1998). Principles of teaching for successful intelligence. *Educational Psychologist, 33,* 65–72.

Tennyson, R. D. (1995). Concept learning: Teaching and assessing. In L. W. Anderson (Ed.), *International encyclopedia of teaching and teacher education* 2d ed. (pp. 457–463). Oxford, UK: Pergamon Press.

Thorndike, R. M., Cunningham, G. K., Thorndike, R. L., & Hagen, E. P. (1991). *Measurement and evaluation in psychology and education* (5th ed.). New York: Macmillan.

Tyler, R. W. (1949). *Basic principles of curriculum and instruction.* Chicago: University of Chicago Press.

U.S. Department of Education. (1994). *Goals 2000: A world class education for every child.* Washington, DC: Author.

Vosniadou, S., & Ortony, A. (Eds.). (1989). *Similarity and analogical reasoning.* Cambridge, UK: Cambridge University Press.

Weinstein, C. E., & Mayer, R. (1986). The teaching of learning strategies. In M. Wittrock (Ed.), *Handbook of research on teaching* 3rd ed. (pp. 315–327). New York: Macmillan.

Wellman, H., & Gelman, S. (1998). Knowledge acquisition in foundational domains. In W. Damon (Series Ed.), D. Kuhn & R. Siegler (Vol. Eds.), *Handbook of child psychology: Vol. 2. Cognition, perception & language* 5th ed. (pp. 523–573). New York: Wiley.

Wiggins, G., & McTighe, J. (1998). *Understanding by design.* Alexandria, VA: Association for Supervision and Curriculum Development.

Wilson, B. G. (1971). Evaluation of learning in art education. In B. S. Bloom, J. T. Hastings & G. F. Madaus (Eds.), *Handbook of formative and summative evaluation of student learning* (pp. 499–598). New York: McGraw-Hill.

Wilson, J. W. (1971). Evaluation of learning in secondary school mathematics. In B. S. Bloom, J. T. Hastings & G. F. Madaus (Eds.), *Handbook of formative and summative evaluation of student learning* (pp. 643–696). New York: McGraw-Hill.

Zimmerman, B. J., & Schunk, D. H. (Eds.) (1997). *Self-regulated learning: From teaching to self-reflective practice.* New York: Guilford Press.

Credits

Chapter 8, **Attachment A** From *Nutrition Mission, A Nutrition Education Unit for Grades* 1–3 by Linda Lynch and Sheila Kelley, 1993. Reprinted by permission of Current, Inc.

Chapter 13, **Attachment A** "Brandywine School District Intermediate Writing Criteria." Brandywine School District, New Castle County, Delaware. Reprinted with permission. **Attachment B** From *Macmillan/Mcgraw-Hill Performance Assessment Handbook*, Levels 8–9, p. 45. **Attachment C** "Revision and Editing Checklist" from Delaware Department of Education. Copyright © Delaware Department of Education. Reprinted with permission. **Attachment D** "Primary Trait Scoring Report Writing" by Christine Evans, Brandywine School District, Delaware. Reprinted by permission of the author.

Index

A

Abstract knowledge, 5, 51, 272, 275
Abstractions (knowledge of), 273
Accountability programs, 19, 248
Activities. *See* Instructional activities
"Activity-driven" planning, 113
Addition Facts vignette, 111, 116, 158–170
   assessment in, 116, 165–167, 248
   instructional activities in, 159–165, 242, 255
   links to Taxonomy Table, 238–239, 242
   misalignment in, 169, 250
Affective, 258, 259, 269
Alignment, 206
   in Addition Facts vignette, 169
   of assessments with objectives, 249–252
   final check on, 254–255
   generalizations related to, 249–255
   of instructional activities with assessments, 252–254
   of instructional activities with objectives, 254–255
   in *Macbeth* vignette, 148–149
   mis- (*See* Misalignment)
   in Nutrition vignette, 130–131
   in Parliamentary Acts vignette, 184
   in Report Writing vignette, 225–226
   in Taxonomy Table, 10, 117, 255, 256
   in Volcanoes? Here? vignette, 205–206
Analyzing/analysis, 5, 30, 31, 79–83, 263, 267, 275–276
   applying *vs.*, 34
   critical thinking and, 269
   distinguishing differences as part of, 7, 8, 10

   in *Macbeth* vignette, 141, 143, 145, 147, 148
   in Nutrition vignette, 123, 125, 126, 130, 131
   of others' work by teachers, 96–97
   in Parliamentary Acts vignette, 177, 234
   prior learning and, 106
   in Report Writing vignette, 211, 215, 216, 217, 218, 222, 224, 225, 226
   time demands of, 257
   understanding *vs.*, 123
   in Volcanoes? Here? vignette, 193, 234
Applying/application, 5, 30, 31, 77–79, 233, 263, 267, 275
   in Addition Facts vignette, 159, 163, 164, 168, 169, 170
   analyzing *vs.*, 34
   contextualized cognitive process and, 91
   in Parliamentary Acts vignette, 172, 174, 176, 181, 184
   in Report Writing vignette, 211, 215–219, 222, 224, 225, 226
   understanding and, 269
   in Volcanoes? Here? vignette, 197–207, 239
Assessment, 89. *See also* Performance assessment
   in Addition Facts vignette, 116, 165–167
   authentic, 88
   and constructivist learning, 65
   contextualized cognitive process and, 91
   educational objectives and, 15, 19–20
   external, 233, 247–249, 253
   focused *vs.* distributed, 101

Assessment *(continued)*
  formal *vs.* informal, 130, 169, 203, 222, 225, 226, 245
  formative *vs.* summative, 101–102 (*See also* Formative assessment; Summative assessment)
  global objectives and, 19–20
  "high stakes," 248
  instructional activities aligned with, 128, 132, 233, 242–244, 252–254
  in *Macbeth* vignette, 143–148, 253
  of metacognitive knowledge objectives, 60–62
  in Nutrition vignette, 115, 127–130, 252–253
  objectives aligned with, 10, 233, 249–251
  in Parliamentary Acts vignette, 116, 179–184, 248, 252
  in Report Writing vignette, 221–225, 248
  validity of, 96, 247, 249, 251
  in Volcanoes? Here? vignette, 194, 201–205, 206, 247, 255
"Assessment conversation," 198, 200, 205, 206, 207, 246
Assessment tasks
  instructional activities and, 252–253
  mathematics example of, 22
  prototypical, 247
Attributing, 14, 31, 74, 79, 82–83, 96
  classifying *vs.*, 131
  interpreting *vs.*, 82
  in *Macbeth* vignette, 141, 143
  in Nutrition vignette, 123, 131
  organizing and, 81
  remembering *vs.*, 34

B

Behavior
  behaviorism *vs.*, 13–14
  cognitive process *vs.*, 12, 13–14
  educational objectives and, 16
  verbs associated with undesirable, 107
Behaviorist view, 40, 43

C

Categorizing (knowledge of categories), 7, 8, 10, 27, 29, 48, 49–50, 72–73
  in Addition Facts vignette, 116
  classifying and, 14
  factual knowledge *vs.*, 49
  knowledge of terminology *vs.*, 194
  in Nutrition vignette, 114, 236
  of objectives, 34–36
  in original version of taxonomy, 273
  principles and generalizations in, 51
  in Report Writing vignette, 216, 218, 226–227
  in Volcanoes? Here? vignette, 194
Cause-and-effect models, 14, 75–76, 172, 191, 194
Checking, 31, 36, 83–84
  in Nutrition vignette, 119, 120
Classifying (knowledge of classifications), 7, 8, 10, 14, 27, 29, 30, 31, 48, 49–50, 72–73
  attributing *vs.*, 131
  factual knowledge *vs.*, 49
  generating and, 86
  mis-, 49–50, 104
  in Nutrition vignette, 116, 120, 122, 123, 130, 131
  of objectives, 22, 34–36, 105–107, 105–109, 114
  in original version of taxonomy, 273
  principles and generalizations in, 51
  in Volcanoes? Here? vignette, 195, 197
Cognition
  knowledge about, 27, 29, 43, 44, 55 (*See also* Metacognitive knowledge)
  meta- (*See* Metacognitive knowledge)
  motivation and, 59
Cognitive complexity, 5, 234–235
  in Addition Facts vignette, 170
  conceptual knowledge and, 27
  evaluation and, 234–235
  instructional activities and, 239
  in *Macbeth* vignette, 148, 149
  metacognitive knowledge and, 235, 239
  in Parliamentary Acts vignette, 234
  prior learning and, 106
  problem solving and, 235
  in Report Writing vignette, 226
  transfer and, 232, 235
  and types of knowledge, 238
  in Volcanoes? Here? vignette, 234
Cognitive process, 5, 23, 38, 39, 43, 44, 63–92, 267–268
  behavior *vs.*, 12, 13–14

knowledge and, 35, 107–108, 232, 233, 238–241, 256
in original *Handbook*, 265–266
remembering as (*See* Remembering)
retention *vs.* transfer in, 63–64
subject matter and, 88
Taxonomy Table and, 116, 118
Cognitive psychology, 14, 27, 40, 41
declarative knowledge in, 41–42
metacognitive knowledge and, 44
models in, 48, 258
Cognitive science, 14, 40
Cognitive tasks, knowledge about, 44, 56, 57–59, 61
Comparing, 30, 31, 75
in Addition Facts vignette, 161, 162
differentiating *vs.*, 80
generating and, 86
in *Macbeth* vignette, 137, 140, 151
in Volcanoes? Here? vignette, 190, 206, 235
Comprehension, 263, 266, 267, 269, 274
Conceptual knowledge, 5, 27, 29, 34, 41, 48–52, 233
in Addition Facts vignette, 161, 162, 163, 164, 168, 169, 170, 237
analyzing, 9, 10
contextualized cognitive process and, 89, 90, 91
critical thinking and, 269
factual *vs.*, 41–42, 45, 170
in *Macbeth* vignette, 40, 137, 139, 140, 141, 143, 145, 147, 149, 237, 239
in Nutrition vignette, 114, 115, 120, 122, 123, 126, 128, 130, 131
in Parliamentary Acts vignette, 116, 172, 174, 176, 177, 178, 179, 181, 183, 184, 185, 234, 237
procedural *vs.*, 52–53
in Report Writing vignette, 211, 213–217, 219–227, 237
subtypes of, 49–52
and transfer of learning, 42
understanding, 239 (*See also* Understanding)
understanding of, 35, 42, 50, 77

in Volcanoes? Here? vignette, 190, 191, 194, 195, 196–205, 207, 234, 237
"Conceptual restructuring," 190, 234, 250
Constructivist perspective, 38, 41, 43, 65
Content
defined, 12
educational objectives and, 16
instructional objectives and, 16
knowledge *vs.*, 12–13, 39–40
objectives and, 12
"packaging" of, 13
subject matter, 12, 13
Content knowledge, 12, 19, 27, 41
Content standards, 19
Content validity, 252
Contextual knowledge, 27, 29, 41, 57–59
Contextualized cognitive process, 88–89
Creating, 5, 30, 31, 84–88
cognitive complexity and, 235
contextualized cognitive process and, 91
critical thinking and, 270
implementing and, 78
in *Macbeth* vignette, 141, 142, 145, 147, 148, 149
metacognitive knowledge and, 60
in Nutrition vignette, 119, 120, 126, 128, 130
in Parliamentary Acts vignette, 172, 178, 181, 184, 234
in Report Writing vignette, 213, 214, 219, 221, 222, 225, 226
synthesis *vs.*, 263, 266–268
in Volcanoes? Here? vignette, 203, 205, 234
Criteria (knowledge of), 27, 29, 52
evaluating based on, 83, 96
in *Macbeth* vignette, 143, 145, 151, 235
in original version of taxonomy, 273, 277
procedural knowledge and, 54–55
Critical thinking, 269–270, 270
Critiquing, 31, 36, 83, 84
Cultural knowledge, 44, 58, 59
Curriculum
"latent," 240
standards-based, 19
state standards for, 247–248 (*See also* State standards/testing)

Curriculum *(continued)*
  teachers as makers *vs.* implementers of, 10–11
  textbook-based, 7
Curriculum developers, global objectives for, 15
Curriculum units, 111–112
  instructional units and, 112
  integrative, 112
  interdisciplinary, 112
  vignettes and, 112
Currriculum units, vignettes and. *See* Vignettes

D
Differentiating, 31, 79, 80–81
  contextualized cognitive process and, 90
Domain knowledge, 41
Domain specificity, 41

E
Educational objectives, 1–3, 15–16, 23, 39. *See also*
    Objectives
  assessment instruments and, 19–20
  cognitive processes and, 18
  community endorsement of, 22
  content standards and, 19
  curriculum units and, 111–112
  debate about, 20–21
  example of context in, 89–91
  examples of content standards as, 19
  examples of specificity in, 16
  expressive outcomes and, 21
  and factual *vs.* conceptual knowledge, 42
  instructional objectives *vs.*, 19
  knowledge and, 18, 265
  in original version of taxonomy, 271–277
  specificity of, 105, 242
  in standards-based curriculum, 19
  state standards and, 18
  transfer and, 63
Evaluating/evaluation, 5, 30, 31, 83–84, 263, 267,
    268
  analyzing and, 80
  cognitive complexity and, 234–235
  contextualized cognitive process and, 91
  critical thinking and, 270
  in *Macbeth* vignette, 142, 147

  in Nutrition vignette, 119, 120, 125–126,
    127, 128, 130
  in Parliamentary Acts vignette, 116, 172,
    174, 179, 183, 184, 185, 186, 234
  in Report Writing vignette, 216, 219, 225,
    226
  in Volcanoes? Here? vignette, 234
  vs. evaluation in original version of taxonomy,
    263, 268
  of knowledge of techniques, 53
  of metacognitive knowledge, 237
  in Nutrition vignette, 114, 122
Executing, 30, 31, 36, 77–78
  contextualized cognitive process and, 90
  implementing *vs.*, 99, 101, 102
  prior learning and, 106
Exemplifying, 30, 31, 71–72
  generating and, 86
  identifying and, 107
  in *Macbeth* vignette, 139, 140, 141
  in Nutrition vignette, 114, 122, 130
  in Parliamentary Acts vignette, 178
Expertise, 41, 42, 49–50, 58
Experts, 30, 42
  classifications/categories and, 49
  factual knowledge and, 47
  generalizations and, 51
  procedural knowledge of, 52, 54
Explaining, 14, 30, 31, 36, 75–76, 267
  contextualized cognitive process and, 90
  different meanings of, 96
  generating and, 86
  in *Macbeth* vignette, 143
  in Parliamentary Acts vignette, 172
  remembering *vs.*, 249
  understanding and, 269
  in Volcanoes? Here? vignette, 190, 194
Expressive outcomes, 21, 23
External assessments, 233, 247–249, 253

F
Factual knowledge, 5, 8, 27, 29, 34, 41, 45–48, 233
  in Addition Facts vignette, 117, 159, 161, 165,
    168, 239
  assessment of, 247

conceptual *vs.*, 41–42, 45, 170
contextualized cognitive process and, 89, 90, 91
in *Macbeth* vignette, 39–40, 137, 141, 142, 145, 148
metacognitive knowledge and, 61
in Nutrition vignette, 122, 123, 125, 131
in Parliamentary Acts vignette, 116, 172, 174, 175, 177, 178, 181, 184, 185
procedural *vs.*, 52–53
remembering, 8, 9, 239 (*See also* Remembering)
in Report Writing vignette, 213, 214, 219, 221, 222, 225, 226
types of, 45–48
in Volcanoes? Here? vignette, 194, 196–207, 247
vs. knowledge of classifications and categories, 49
Formal assessment, 169, 203
misalignment and, 250
in Report Writing vignette, 130, 222, 225, 226
summative assessment as, 245
Formative assessment, 101–102, 184, 233, 245–249
in Nutrition vignette, 130
in Volcanoes? Here? vignette, 205, 246 (*See also* "Assessment conversation")

G
Generalizations (knowledge of), 27, 29, 51, 52, 73, 273
in Addition Facts vignette, 159
in original version of taxonomy, 274
Generating, 31, 36, 85, 86–87
contextualized cognitive process and, 91
in *Macbeth* vignette, 139
in Volcanoes? Here? vignette, 203
Global objectives (Goals), 12, 15, 20
assessment instruments and, 19–20
community endorsement of, 22
expressive outcomes and, 21
instructional objectives *vs.*, 16, 17
mathematics example of, 18
specific *vs.*, 16, 17, 19
state standards and, 18, 19
Goals 2000, 15, 37

H
Handbook, 15–16, 20, 23, 35, 257
criticism of, 258
evaluating discussed in, 234–235
metacognitive knowledge and, 44, 45
multiple-choice format in, 258
"templates" in, 35

I
Implementing, 30, 31, 36, 74, 77. *See also* Using
checking and, 83
comparing and, 75
creating and, 78
executing *vs.*, 77, 99, 101, 102
in Nutrition vignette, 130
prior learning and, 106
procedural knowledge and, 78–79
understanding and, 78
"Indicators," 18–19
Inferring, 30, 31, 36, 73–75
assessment and, 74–75, 96
comparing and, 75
generating and, 86
in *Macbeth* vignette, 140, 142
in Parliamentary Acts vignette, 177
strategies for, 57
in Volcanoes? Here? vignette, 197, 198
Informal assessment, 169, 203
formative assessment as, 245
in Report Writing vignette, 130, 222, 225, 226
Information, specialized and technical, 274–277
Information processing models, 55
Instantiating, 72
Instruction, 30
addressing long-standing problems in, 232–259
for different *vs.* similar objectives, 8
Taxonomy Table and, 7–8, 11, 110
time and (*See* Classroom/instructional time)
Instructional activities
in Addition Facts vignette, 159–165, 242, 255
assessment and, 233, 242–244, 253–254
cognitive complexity and, 239
curriculum units and, 112–114
for different *vs.* similar objectives, 8
educational objectives and, 15

Instructional activities (*continued*)
  learning and, 244
  in *Macbeth* vignette, 137, 139, 148, 242, 243, 253, 255
  in Nutrition vignette, 120–127, 128, 242, 252, 255
  objectives aligned with, 233, 252
  objectives inferred from, 245
  objectives linked with, 242, 244, 257
  objectives *vs.*, 17, 18, 96, 106–107, 132, 206–207, 233, 241–245
  in Parliamentary Acts vignette, 174–179, 242, 252
  performing *vs.* learning from, 233
  purpose and, 21, 233
  in Report Writing vignette, 213–221, 242
  Taxonomy Table and, 7–8, 11, 96, 99–101, 103, 104, 117, 118
  in Volcanoes? Here? vignette, 191–201, 207, 242
Instructional materials, 13, 112, 113
Instructional objectives, 15, 16
  community endorsement of, 22
  curriculum units and, 112
  debate about, 20–21
  expressive outcomes and, 21
  standards-based curriculums and, 19
  state standards and, 18
  vs. global objectives, 16, 17
Instructional units. *See also* Curriculum units
  contextualized cognitive process and, 91
  cross-disciplinary, 184–185
  curriculum units and, 112
  educational objectives and, 19
  integrated, 184
  objectives for lessons *vs.*, 19
  and objectives *vs.* completion of activities, 206–207
  planning, 277
  Taxonomy Table and, 105
  vignettes for (*See* Vignettes)
Instructional validity, 247, 252, 253
Integrating, 81
Intellectual abilities/skills, 274–277
Intent, 107
  attributing, 14, 96
  objectives and, 23

  standards and, 18
  teaching and, 3
Interpreting, 30, 31, 70–71
  attributing *vs.*, 82
  contextualized cognitive process and, 89, 90
  in *Macbeth* vignette, 139, 145
  in original version of taxonomy, 275
  understanding and, 269
  in Volcanoes? Here? vignette, 190

K
Knowledge, 5, 23, 38–62
  about cognition (*See* Metacognitive knowledge)
  about cognitive tasks, 44, 56, 57–59, 61
  abstract *vs.* concrete, 5 (*See also* Abstract knowledge)
  of algorithms, 27, 29, 52, 53, 77
  of categories (*See* Categorizing)
  choosing varieties of, 236–238
  of classifications (*See* Classifying)
  cognitive process and, 35, 232, 233, 238–241
  cognitive processes and, 35, 232, 233, 238–241
  conceptual (*See* Conceptual knowledge)
  concrete *vs.* abstract, 5 (*See also* Abstract knowledge; Concrete knowledge)
  conditional, 27, 29, 41, 44, 57–59
  content *vs.*, 12–13, 39–40 (*See also* Content knowledge)
  contextual, 27, 29, 57–59, 88–89
  of criteria (*See* Criteria [knowledge of])
  cultural, 44, 58, 59
  declarative, 41
  defined, 13
  disciplinary, 41, 42, 48, 53
  discourse, 41
  domain, 41
  educational objectives and, 18, 265
  episodic, 41
  of epistemologies, 52
  explicit, 41
  factual (*See* Factual knowledge)
  of generalizations, 27, 29, 51, 52
  "historically shared," 13
  "inert," 42
  instructional objectives and, 19
  "making sense" of, 38, 63, 90–91

metacognitive (*See* Metacognitive knowledge)
methods (*See* Methods [knowledge of])
of models (*See* Models [knowledge of])
in original *Handbook*, 265, 271–277
of paradigms, 52
of principles (*See* Principles [knowledge of])
procedural (*See* Procedural knowledge)
process related to type of, 107–108, 256
relevant (*See* Relevant knowledge)
of schemas, 42
scientific (*See* Science; Scientific knowledge)
self-, 27, 29, 43, 59–60
semantic, 41
situational, 41, 44, 58
skills, 27, 29, 52, 53
sociocultural, 41
of specific elements (*See* Factual knowledge;
    Specific elements/details [knowledge of])
strategic, 27, 29, 41, 44, 56–67, 135, 138
of strategies (*See* Strategies [knowledge of])
of structures, 27, 29, 51–52
subject matter content *vs.*, 39–40
tacit, 41
of techniques (*See* Techniques [knowledge of])
of terminology, 27, 29, 45, 47
of theories (*See* Theories [knowledge of])
types of, 27–30, 40–62, 236–241
Knowledge acquisition, 65

L
Learning, 89
active *vs.* passive view of, 38
activities and, 244
alignment and, 256
assessment and, 233
common *vs.* idiosyncratic, 21
constructivist, 65
context and, 88
"doing" *vs.*, 244
from expressive outcome activities, 21
global objectives for, 15
grades and, 251
"how to learn," 35
incidental, 23 (*See also* Outcomes, intended *vs.*
    unintended)
meaningful (*See* Meaningful learning)

motivation and, 59
objectives in, 1–11, 21–22
prior, 105–106
process-knowledge relationships and, 240
retention of (*See* Retention)
rote, 64, 65
situational, 55
strategies for, 43, 56
Taxonomy Table and, 97–99, 249
theory of, 258
transfer of (*See* Transfer)
Lessons
curriculum units and, 112
instructional units and, 112
Lessons (*continued*)
objectives for units *vs.*, 19
Taxonomy Table and, 105
Logical fallacies, 277

M
Macbeth vignette, 39–40, 111, 116, 136–157
activities *vs.* objectives in, 243
assessment in, 143–147, 253
grading in, 251
instructional activities in, 137, 139, 148, 242, 253,
    255
links in Taxonomy Table for, 238–239
misalignment in, 149, 250, 251, 253
summative assessment in, 246
types of knowledge in other vignettes *vs.*, 236,
    237
"Making sense," 38, 63, 90–91
Mathematics, 6, 277
adapting Taxonomy Table for, 259
algorithms in, 53
analyzing in, 7
conceptual knowledge and, 7
contextualized cognitive process and, 88, 89
objectives and, 5, 7, 9, 18–19, 22
procedural knowledge and, 54
standards and, 18
Mathematics examples, 18–19, 22, 88–89
Meaningful learning, 38, 63, 64–65, 250
contextualized cognitive process and, 89
in Volcanoes? Here? vignette, 190, 234
Memory, 30, 232

Metacognitive knowledge, 5, 27, 29, 35, 41,
  258–259
  in Addition Facts vignette, 159, 164, 168, 169,
    170, 237, 239
  analyzing and, 239 (*See also* Analyzing/
    analysis)
  assessing objectives involving, 60–62
  cognitive complexity and, 235, 239
  contextualized cognitive process and, 89, 90, 91
  creating and, 239 (*See also* Creating)
  evaluating and, 239 (*See also* Evaluating/
    evaluation)
  in *Macbeth* vignette, 40, 239
  metacognitive control *vs.*, 43
  in Nutrition vignette, 120, 125, 130, 237,
    39
  in Parliamentary Acts vignette, 237, 239
  procedural knowledge *vs.*, 53
  rationale for, 43–44
  in Report Writing vignette, 215, 217
  subtypes of, 55–56, 61–62
  teaching, 238
  in Volcanoes? Here? vignette, 237, 239
Methods (evaluation of), 277
Methods (knowledge of), 27, 29, 52
  in original version of taxonomy, 273, 275
  subject-specific, 54
Misalignment, 10, 104, 233
  in Addition Facts vignette, 169, 250
  causes of, 250–251
  in *Macbeth* vignette, 149, 250, 251, 253
  in Parliamentary Acts vignette, 184, 250,
    251, 252
  in Report Writing vignette, 226, 254
  in Volcanoes? Here? vignette, 250, 253
Models
  assessment, 247
  cause-and-effect, 14, 75–76, 172, 191, 194
  cognitive, 43, 48, 55, 59, 258
  cultural, 55
  explaining and, 76
  information processing, 55
  knowledge of, 27, 29, 33–34, 42, 51–52
  for measuring higher-level thinking, 258
  mental, 48

  of multiple-choice item formats, 258,
    264
  neo-Piagetian, 55
  Piagetian, 41
  situational learning, 55
  social cognitive, 59
  social constructivist, 43
  Tyler, 12, 13–14, 16
  in Volcanoes? Here? vignette, 203
  Vygotskian, 55
Monitoring, 43, 55–56, 83, 239
Motivation, 43, 59–60
  in Volcanoes? Here? vignette, 196
Multiple-choice item formats, 258, 264

N
Nutrition vignette, 111, 119–135
  assessment in, 115, 127–128, 129, 252–253
  criteria in, 120, 126, 128, 130, 253
  instructional activities in, 120–127, 128, 242, 252,
    255
  misalignment in, 250
  types of knowledge in other vignettes *vs.*, 236,
    237

O
Objectives, 1–11
  abstract *vs.* concrete, 250
  in accountability programs, 19
  in Addition Facts vignette, 158–159, 250
  alignment of instruction, assessment, and, 10,
    35–36 (*See also* Alignment)
  assessment aligned with, 10, 233, 249–251 (*See
    also* Alignment)
  assessment for different *vs.* similar, 8–9
  assessment instruments and, 19–20
  assessment *vs.*, 17, 18
  classifying, 22, 34–36, 105–109, 114
  comparing levels of, 16–17
  completion of activities *vs.* achievement of,
    206–207
  complex, 148, 224 (*See also* Cognitive
    complexity)
  concrete, 244, 250
  consistency among, 35–36

and content *vs.* knowledge, 12–13
continuum of, 4, 15, 16–17
debate about, 12, 20
difficulty in stating, 22–23
educational (*vs.* global or instructional), 15,
    16–17 (*See also* Educational objectives)
explicit *vs.* implicit, 3, 12, 17
expressive, 21
external assessment linked with, 249, 251
function of, 16, 17
global (*vs.* instructional or educational), 16, 17
    (*See also* Global objectives)
inferred from instructional activities, 245
instructional, 112
instructional activities aligned with, 233 (*See
    also* Alignment; "Alignment question")
instructional activities linked with, 242, 244, 257
instructional activities *vs.*, 17, 18, 96, 106–107,
    132, 206–207, 233, 241–245
instructional approaches for different *vs.*
    similar, 8
instructional (*vs.* global or educational), 16, 17
    (*See also* Instructional objectives)
as intentions, 23
in *Macbeth* vignette, 137, 243, 250
in Nutrition vignette, 119–120, 251
in Parliamentary Acts vignette, 171–174, 250
precise *vs.* vague, 4, 244
as prerequisites or facilitators, 224
problems with/criticisms of, 12, 20–23
in Report Writing vignette, 210–213
restricted use of, 22–23
specific *vs.* global, 12, 15, 19
specificity of, 12, 15–17, 20–21, 105 (*See also*
    Specificity)
in standards-based curriculums, 19
stating, 22–23
structure of, 12–14
subject matter standards as, 19
Taxonomy Table and, 5, 6–7, 27, 30–36, 103, 104,
    117, 118
tests and, 17, 19
Tyler model of, 12, 13–14, 16
for units *vs.* lessons, 19
vignettes and, 112–113, 115 (*See also* Vignettes)

vocabulary regarding, 18–20
in Volcanoes? Here? vignette, 190–191, 207,
    250
Organizing, 6, 36, 79, 81–82
    attributing and, 81
    cognitive process and, 31
    contextualized cognitive process and, 89
    differentiating and, 81
    experts and, 42
    in original version of taxonomy, 272
    in Report Writing vignette, 216, 226
Outcomes, 216–217
    assessable, 23
    cognitive vs. other, 23
    explicit, 23
    expressive, 21, 23
    global objectives and, 15
    intended vs. unintended, 21 (*See also* Learning,
        incidental)
    learning-based, 23
    objectives and, 17, 20–21
    standards for, 18
    student-oriented, 23

P
Parliamentary Acts vignette, 111, 116,
    171–189
    assessment in, 116, 179–183, 248, 252
    cognitive complexity in, 234
    external assessment in, 248
    instructional activities in, 174–179, 242,
        252
    links in Taxonomy Table for, 238–239
    misalignment in, 184, 250, 251, 252
    summative assessment in, 184, 245
    types of knowledge in other vignettes *vs.*, 236,
        237
Performance assessment, 247–248. *See also*
    Assessment
    alignment and, 253, 257
    educational objectives and, 15
    multiple-choice item formats and, 258
    objectives and, 21–22, 243
    Taxonomy Table and, 105
Perspective, 269, 270

Planning, 31, 86, 87, 113
   checking and, 83
   of cognition, 56
   contextualized cognitive process and, 89
   models and, 33–34
   in Nutrition vignette, 126, 130
   in original version of taxonomy, 276–277
   in Report Writing vignette, 225
   in Volcanoes? Here? vignette, 207
Precise information, 272
Predicting, 74, 142
Principles (knowledge of), 27, 29, 51, 52, 237
   in Addition Facts vignette, 161, 162
   in Nutrition vignette, 119, 120
   in original version of taxonomy, 274, 275, 276
Problem solving, 41, 44
   cognitive complexity and, 235
   disciplinary knowledge vs. general, 53
   and knowledge of specific details, 49
   and meaningful learning, 65
   recalling vs., 249
   strategies for, 56, 57, 59
   Taxonomy Table and, 104, 269–270
   understanding vs., 269–270
Procedural knowledge, 5, 27, 29, 34, 41, 52–55, 77, 233
   in Addition Facts vignette, 159, 163, 164, 168, 169, 170, 237
   applying, 77, 239 (See also Applying/ application)
   contextualized cognitive process and, 89, 90, 91
   executing and, 77–78
   factual and conceptual vs., 52–53
   implementing and, 78–79
   Macbeth example of, 40
   metacognitive vs., 53
   in Nutrition vignette, 120, 128, 130, 237
   in Parliamentary Acts vignette, 174, 176, 179, 181, 184, 185, 234, 237
   in Report Writing vignette, 211, 215–219, 222, 224, 225, 226
   in Volcanoes? Here? vignette, 196–207, 237, 239
Procedures (knowledge of), 273, 275. See also Procedural Knowledge
Producing, 31, 86, 87–88
   contextualized cognitive process and, 89
   in Macbeth vignette, 145
   in original version of taxonomy, 276–277
   in Parliamentary Acts vignette, 178
   in Report Writing vignette, 213, 214, 219
Proposed set of operations, 276–277
Psychomotor domain, 258, 259

R
Recalling, 30, 31, 57, 61, 68, 69–70
   in Addition Facts vignette, 158, 242
   contextualized cognitive process and, 89, 90, 91
   in Nutrition vignette, 123
   in original version of taxonomy, 272
   prior learning and, 106
   problem solving vs., 249
   recognizing vs., 194
   in Volcanoes? Here? vignette, 194
Recognizing, 30, 31, 57, 61, 68, 69
   contextualized cognitive process and, 90, 91
   identifying as, 107
   labeling vs., 143
   in Macbeth vignette, 143
   in original version of taxonomy, 276
   recalling vs., 194
   in Volcanoes? Here? vignette, 194
Reduce-reuse-recycle example of, 33
Regulation, 43, 55–56
   self-, 43, 44, 238
Rehearsal, 56–57, 59, 130, 238
Relations, abstract, 277
Relationships (analysis of), 276
Relevant knowledge, 30, 43, 44, 64–65, 68
   constructivist learning and, 65
   generalizations and, 51
   in Report Writing vignette, 211, 222, 226
   transfer of, 65
   in Volcanoes? Here? vignette, 193, 198
Remembering, 5, 30, 31, 65–70, 233, 266, 267
   in Addition Facts vignette, 116, 117, 159, 161, 165, 168, 239
   alignment and, 253
   attributing vs., 34
   contextualized cognitive process and, 90, 91
   explaining vs., 249
   of factual knowledge, 8, 9
   identifying and, 107

interpreting *vs.*, 71
in *Macbeth* vignette, 137, 145, 148
metacognitive knowledge and, 61
in Nutrition vignette, 114, 115, 120, 123, 130, 131
in Parliamentary Acts vignette, 116, 171, 172, 175, 177, 181, 183, 184
prior learning and, 106
process-knowledge relationship in, 107, 239
recall and (*See* Recalling)
in Report Writing vignette, 214
retention and, 241 (*See also* Retention)
transfer and, 63, 241 (*See also* Transfer)
understanding and, 170
in Volcanoes? Here? vignette, 194, 196–207, 247
Report Writing vignette, 111, 210–231
assessment in, 221–224, 248
external assessment in, 248
instructional activities in, 213–221, 242
misalignment in, 226, 254
types of knowledge in other vignettes *vs.*, 236, 237
Retention, 63–64, 65, 232
contextualized cognitive process and, 90, 91
Taxonomy Table and, 241
Rote learning, 64, 65

S
Scientific knowledge, 38, 47, 54
Scoring guide, 233
district, 247–248
example of alignment involving, 254
in Nutrition vignette, 135, 235
in Report Writing vignette, 222, 229, 231
Scoring rubrics
alignment and, 253
example of alignment involving, 254
"kid-friendly," 213, 219, 228
in Nutrition vignette, 126, 131–132, 135
in Parliamentary Acts vignette, 185
in Report Writing vignette, 213–214, 219, 225, 226, 229, 231
in Volcanoes? Here? vignette, 201–203, 206, 209, 210, 235
Selecting, 80, 210, 211, 216, 222

Self-analysis, by teachers, 95–96
Self-awareness, 55, 59–60
Self-knowledge, 27, 29, 43, 59–60, 61, 269
Self-reflection, 55
Self-regulation, 43, 44, 238, 239
Sequences (knowledge of), 273
Situational knowledge, 41, 44, 58
Situational learning models, 55
Skills/abilities, 27, 29, 52, 53, 274–277
Sociocultural knowledge, 41
Specific facts (knowledge of), 271–272
Specificity, 12, 15–17, 20–21
assessment and, 21–22
cognitive complexity and, 22
domain, 41
of educational objectives, 105, 242
of instructional objectives, 16
Taxonomy Table and, 105
unit-level *vs.* lesson-level, 19
Standards, 3–4
cognitive process and, 30
content (*See* Content standards)
differences in interpretation of, 249
evaluating based on, 83
original version of taxonomy and, 277
publicly stated, 19
state-level, 6, 18, 247–248
in Tyler's model, 14
Standards-based curriculum, 19. *See also* Content standards
State standards/testing, 6, 18, 247–249
Stimulus-response associations, 14
Strategic knowledge, 27, 29, 41, 44, 56–67, 135, 138, 235, 238
Strategies (knowledge of), 43, 56–57, 235
for memorizing, 8, 56, 59, 158–170, 239, 242, 250
metacognitive knowledge and, 239
for problem solving, 56, 57, 59
self-knowledge and, 59–60
Structure
cognitive process and, 30
implicit *vs.* explicit, 276
of objectives, 12–14
Structures (knowledge of), 27, 29, 51–52
in original version of taxonomy, 273, 274, 276

Students, 89
  choices of, 149–150
  point of view of, 34–35
Subject matter
  cognitive process and, 88
  as content domain, 12–13
  expressive outcomes activities and, 21
  generalizations and, 51
  global objectives about, 15
  "packaged," 13
  principles and, 51
  procedural knowledge and specific, 53–55
  and stating objectives, 22
Subject matter content, knowledge vs., 39–40
Subject matter standards, objectives as, 19
Summarizing, 30, 31, 56, 59, 73
  generating and, 86
  in Nutrition vignette, 126
Summative assessment, 101–102, 233,
    245–249
  in Macbeth vignette, 246
  in Nutrition vignette, 130
  in Parliamentary Acts vignette, 184
  in Volcanoes? Here? vignette, 246
Synthesis, 263, 266, 268, 276

T
Taxonomy of Objectives
  adaptation of, 259
  alignment in, 10, 103–104, 117, 251–252, 255,
    256 (See also Alignment)
  alternative frameworks for, 259 (See also
    Framework)
  assessment and, 8–9, 11, 101–102, 102–105,
    117, 118, 247, 249, 254
  cognitive complexity and, 235–236
  cognitive process dimension of, 63–92, 265–266,
    267–268
  condensed original version of, 271–277
  contextualized cognitive process and, 91
  curriculum and, 11, 241
  domains of, 258–259
  hierarchy of, 267–268
  inclusion of metacognitive knowledge in, 43,
    44, 258
  instructional activities and, 7–8, 11, 99–101, 117,
    118
  knowledge dimension of, 38–62, 265
  learning and, 97–99, 249
  motivation in, 59–60
  need for, 3–5
  nouns in, 108–109, 114, 117, 266
  objectives linked with external assessment in,
    249
  process-knowledge relationships and, 238
  for teachers' analysis of others, 96–97
  teachers and, 11, 238–239, 264
  for teachers' self-analysis, 95–96
  teaching philosophy and, 239
  terminology in, 41, 265–266, 269–270
  unsolved problems with, 257
  using, 95–109, 263–264
  verb-noun combination in using, 107, 265
  verbs in, 107, 114, 117, 244–245, 266
  vignettes to illustrate use of, 110–118 (See also
    Vignettes)
Teacher roles, for different vs. similar objectives, 8
Teachers, 89, 243
  authority of, 240
  communication among, 11
  as curriculum makers vs. implementers, 10–11
  English, 258
  and external assessments, 248
  as facilitators, 240
  global objectives for, 15
  ingenuity of, 242
  judgment and empowerment of, 20
  major concerns of, 117
  Taxonomy Table and, 11, 238–239, 264
  vignettes written by, 110–118 (See also Vignettes)
Teaching, 89
  analyzing one's own, 95–96
  of different types of knowledge, 238, 240
  "missed opportunities" in, 238–239
  by modeling, 214, 215, 224
  objectives and, 3–4
  organizing questions in, 6
  philosophy in, 40, 241
  process-knowledge relationships and, 240
  reasoned and intentional aspects of, 3

standards and, 3–4
"to the test," 20, 249
Techniques (knowledge of), 27, 29, 52, 273
  examples of, 53
  for memorizing, 8
  in original version of taxonomy, 276
  subject-specific, 54
Terminology
  education, 36–37
  knowledge of, 27, 29, 45, 47, 194
  for knowledge types, 41, 265
  "popular" or "folk," 47
  in Taxonomy Table, 41, 265–266, 269–270
Testing
  alignment and, 253
  for complex behaviors, 258
  for higher-level thinking, 258
  of hypotheses, 277
  metacognitive knowledge and, 44, 59, 83
  statewide, 233, 247–248, 249
Tests
  fill-in-the-blank, 258
  litigation and, 19
  in *Macbeth* vignette, 155–157
  multiple-choice, 258, 264
  objectives and, 17, 19
  sample items on, 258
Theories (knowledge of), 27, 29, 42, 48, 51–52, 237
  implicit, 50
  in original version of taxonomy, 273, 274, 275
  in Volcanoes? Here? vignette, 191
Thinking
  context and, 88
  critical, 269–270
  higher-level, 258
  inductive *vs.* deductive, 57
  in Nutrition vignette, 123, 125, 130
  strategies for, 56, 57
"Thinking aloud," 214, 215
Time
  analysis and, 257
  classroom/instructional (*See* Classroom/
    instructional time)

knowledge of trends and sequences with respect to, 273
objectives and, 16, 17
Transfer, 42, 63–64, 65, 232
  contextualized cognitive process and, 90, 91
  and meaningful learning, 65
  Taxonomy Table and, 241
Translation, 86, 274–275
Trends (knowledge of), 273, 275

U
Understanding, 5, 30, 31, 70–76, 233
  in Addition Facts vignette, 158–164, 168, 169,
    170
  alignment and, 253
  analyzing and, 80, 123
  applying and, 77
  attributing *vs.*, 82
  comprehension *vs.*, 263, 266, 267, 269, 274
  of conceptual knowledge, 35, 42, 50, 77
  contextualized cognitive process and, 91
  creating and, 78
  critical thinking *vs.*, 269–270, 270
  differentiating *vs.*, 80
  experts and, 42
  generating and, 86
  identifying and, 107
  implementing and, 78
  in *Macbeth* vignette, 116, 137, 139–143, 145, 147,
    148, 149, 239
  in Nutrition vignette, 114, 115, 119, 120, 122,
    123, 125, 130, 131
  of objectives, 4, 5, 6–10
  in Parliamentary Acts vignette, 116, 172, 174,
    176, 177, 178, 181, 183, 184, 234
  problem solving *vs.*, 269–270, 270
  process-knowledge relationship in, 107, 239
  remembering and, 170
  in Report Writing vignette, 214
  in Volcanoes? Here? vignette, 190, 191, 194, 195,
    196–205, 207, 234, 247
Units. *See* Curriculum units; Instructional units
Using, 38, 63, 90–91. *See also* Implementing
  objectives, 16, 17, 22–23
  in Report Writing vignette, 216

Using (*continued*)
    Taxonomy Table, 95–109
    transfer and, 63

V

Validity
    of assessment, 96, 251
    content, 252
    of external assessments, 249
    instructional, 247, 252, 253
    of logical statements, 57
Values, 59
    attributing, 14
    and stating objectives, 22
    Taxonomy Table and, 241
Vignettes. *See also* Addition Facts vignette;
    Macbeth vignette; Nutrition vignette;
    Parliamentary Acts vignette; Report Writing
    vignette; Volcanoes? Here? vignette
    analyzing, 114–117
    assessment and, 112–113, 115

central components of, 112–114
characterization of, 110–112
commentaries on, 118
instructional activities and, 112–114, 115
objectives and, 112–113, 115
organization and structure of, 117–118
purpose of, 110, 118
Volcanoes? Here? vignette, 110, 111, 190–209
    assessment in, 194, 201–204, 206, 247, 255
        (*See also* "Assessment conversation")
    cognitive complexity in, 234
    formative assessment in, 205, 247 (*See also*
        "Assessment conversation")
    instructional activities in, 191–201, 207,
        242
    links in Taxonomy Table for, 238–239
    misalignment in, 250, 253
    summative assessment in, 246, 247
    types of knowledge in other vignettes *vs.*,
        236, 237

5.1 THE COGNITIVE PROCESS DIMENSION

CATEGORIES & COGNITIVE PROCESSES	ALTERNATIVE NAMES	DEFINITIONS AND EXAMPLES
1. REMEMBER—Retrieve relevant knowledge from long-term memory		
1.1 RECOGNIZING	Identifying	Locating knowledge in long-term memory that is consistent with presented material (e.g., Recognize the dates of important events in U.S. history)
1.2 RECALLING	Retrieving	Retrieving relevant knowledge from long-term memory (e.g., Recall the dates of important events in U.S. history)
2. UNDERSTAND—Construct meaning from instructional messages, including oral, written, and graphic communication		
2.1 INTERPRETING	Clarifying, paraphrasing, representing, translating	Changing from one form of representation (e.g., numerical) to another (e.g., verbal) (e.g., Paraphrase important speeches and documents)
2.2 EXEMPLIFYING	Illustrating, instantiating	Finding a specific example or illustration of a concept or principle (e.g., Give examples of various artistic painting styles)
2.3 CLASSIFYING	Categorizing, subsuming	Determining that something belongs to a category (e.g., Classify observed or described cases of mental disorders)
2.4 SUMMARIZING	Abstracting, generalizing	Abstracting a general theme or major point(s) (e.g. Write a short summary of the event portrayed on a videotape)
2.5 INFERRING	Concluding, extrapolating, interpolating, predicting	Drawing a logical conclusion from presented information (e.g., In learning a foreign language, infer grammatical principles from examples)
2.6 COMPARING	Contrasting, mapping, matching	Detecting correspondences between two ideas, objects, and the like (e.g., Compare historical events to contemporary situations)
2.7 EXPLAINING	Constructing models	Constructing a cause-and-effect model of a system(e.g., explain the causes of important 18th Century events in France)
3. APPLY—Carry out or use a procedure in a given situation		
3.1 EXECUTING	Carrying out	Applying a procedure to a familiar task (e.g., Divide one whole number by another whole number, both with multiple digits)
3.2 IMPLEMENTING	Using	Applying a procedure to an unfamiliar task (e.g., Use Newton's Second Law in situations in which it is appropriate)